Henry and [...] [...]nine children in 1892, with, far [...] [...] and Eugénie who drowned in 1900, and, seated far right, Gyles Brandreth's grandfather, Benjamin Brandreth.

Odd Boy Out

Gyles Brandreth is a writer, broadcaster, veteran of *Just A Minute*, *QI* and *The One Show*, former MP and Government Whip, now Chancellor of the University of Chester and founder of the 'Poetry Together' project bringing schoolchildren and older people together to learn poetry by heart. His many books include the best-selling poetry anthology, *Dancing by the Light of the Moon*, and the international best-seller about spelling and punctuation, *Have You Eaten Grandma?* With Susie Dent, the lexicographer from *Countdown*, he co-hosts the award-winning podcast, *Something Rhymes With Purple*. With Dame Sheila Hancock he presents *Great Canal Journeys* on Channel 4. With Dame Maureen Lipman he is a regular on *Celebrity Gogglebox*.

Gyles Brandreth's forebears include Jeremiah Brandreth, the last person to be beheaded for treason in England, George R Sims, who wrote the ballad *Christmas Day in the Workhouse*, and Eugénie, wife of Napoleon III and the last Empress of France. Gyles is married to writer and publisher Michèle Brown and has three children, seven grandchildren, and lives in London with his wife, his jumpers, and Nala, the neighbour's cat.

www.gylesbrandreth.net
Twitter: @GylesB1

Odd Boy Out

GYLES BRANDRETH

MICHAEL JOSEPH

MICHAEL JOSEPH

UK | USA | Canada | Ireland | Australia
India | New Zealand | South Africa

Michael Joseph is part of the Penguin Random House group of companies
whose addresses can be found at global.penguinrandomhouse.com.

First published 2021
001

Copyright © Gyles Brandreth, 2021

The moral right of the author has been asserted

Set in 13.5/15.5pt Garamond MT Std
Typeset by Jouve (UK), Milton Keynes
Printed and bound in Great Britain by Clays Ltd, Elcograf S.p.A.

The authorized representative in the EEA is Penguin Random House Ireland,
Morrison Chambers, 32 Nassau Street, Dublin D02 YH68

A CIP catalogue record for this book is available from the British Library

HARDBACK ISBN: 978–0–241–48371–8
TRADE PAPERBACK ISBN: 978–0–241–48372–5

www.greenpenguin.co.uk

The things a man has heard and seen are threads of
life, and if he pull them carefully from the confused
distaff of memory, any who will can weave them into
whatever garments of belief please them best.

W. B. Yeats

Best trust the happy moments. What they gave
Makes man less fearful of the certain grave,
And gives his work compassion and new eyes.
The days that make us happy make us wise.

John Masefield, 'Biography'

It is curious to look back over life, over all the varying
incidents and scenes – such a multitude of odds and
ends. Out of them all what has mattered? What lies
behind the selection the memory has made? What
makes us choose the things that we have remembered?
It is as though one went to a great trunk full of junk in
an attic and plunged one's hands into it and said, 'I will
have this – and this – and this.'

Agatha Christie, *An Autobiography*

Contents

Prologue: Permission to speak

'What are you up to?'

My wife popped her head around my study door. She never knocks. She likes to keep me on my toes.

'I'm writing a book,' I said.

'A book?' Her face fell. (She's reached the age when quite often she looks more severe than I think she means to – like the Queen who, when she isn't actively smiling, can look positively grumpy.) 'A book? Another one?'

'Yes.'

'Oh, Gyles, does the world really need another book by you?'

'Well, er –'

She had come into the room now. She was looking down at me bent over my laptop. 'Sit up,' she said automatically. 'Come on, straight back.'

I lifted my head.

She sighed. 'I don't know why I bother. I've been saying it for fifty years. You don't take a blind bit of notice. Look at you, you bent old thing. It's like being married to Methuselah.' She picked up the cold mug of tea from my desk. (I make about ten cups of tea a day, but I only drink about an inch out of any of them.) 'Why on earth do you want to write another book?'

I had an answer to that. 'We need the money,' I said. 'We have three children and seven grandchildren and haven't we discovered over the years that money is the one thing keeping us in touch with them?'

She gave a wan smile. 'And what's this book going to be about, then?'

'Me,' I said.

'Oh no,' she cried, 'not again. Me, me, me, that's the story of your life.'

'Perhaps that should be the title?' I countered brightly.

'No one's interested in you, Gyles – they really aren't. We know you've got an ego the size of the planet and, bless, you think everything revolves around you, but it doesn't, it really doesn't. Nobody's interested. Nobody cares. They don't even know who you are.'

'A few people do,' I bleated.

'Not that many,' she said crisply. 'Often they don't even get your name right. "Charles Branston – was he the jumper man? *Countdown*? *Gogglebox*? Teddy bears? Wasn't he an MP for a while?" They've sort of heard of you, but they're not sure why.' She was warming to her theme now. 'Come on, Gyles, why would *anyone* want to read *your* memoirs?'

'Not memoirs,' I said quickly. 'More . . . memories. Growing up, leaving home, that sort of thing. We all have memories, don't we? And never mind whether they know me or not, some of my memories might chime with theirs. That might interest them.'

She paused. She put the mug of cold tea back on my desk. 'Mm, memories.' She looked at me, not unkindly. 'And what's your very first memory, then?'

Her question startled me. I don't believe she had ever asked me that before – and we have known one another a very long time. We met at 3.00 p.m. on Thursday, 6 June 1968. I wanted her in that very moment, at that instant. I pursued her from that afternoon onwards, relentlessly. She is still here because she is immensely tolerant. I'm still here because I haven't caught her yet.

'My first memory?' I said. I hesitated. 'The coronation, I suppose. June, 1953. I sort of remember being on my father's shoulders, in the streets, in a crowd, waving a flag. It was raining. And I remember our television. We got it specially for the coronation – hired from Radio Rentals. I remember standing close to the television set, right up against the screen, pointing my finger at the Queen – and my sisters telling me to get out of the way.'

'Oh,' said my wife, chuckling, 'we're going to get the Queen on page one, are we? You and the Queen together, in fact.'

'People are fascinated by the Queen. Who was at Buckingham Palace on coronation day to do the Queen's make-up?'

'Remind me. You have told me. More than once.'

'Oscar Wilde's daughter-in-law.'

'Of course.'

'People are fascinated by the Queen. A lot of people dream about the Queen. At least I've met her.'

'Don't overdo the name-dropping, Gyles. It's irritating. And don't go too heavy on the Oscar Wilde stuff. We all know how you love the 1880s, but we're in the 2020s now – you could do with a few readers under eighty.' She sighed and picked up the mug again. 'How long's it going to take?'

'A hundred and twenty days – at a thousand words a day.'

'If you must, you must. But try not to bang on too much. Remember: less is more.'

'I'll do my best.'*

'And avoid being too predictable. You always fall back on the same old things, Gyles – Winnie-the-Pooh and woolly jumpers, how you love words and poetry. If you're going to do this, surprise yourself. Dig a bit deeper than usual.'

'Really? Should I write about you, then?'

'For God's sake, no. Keep me out of it. This is about you. Who are you? An egomaniac who can't stop talking. We know that – but why? That's the question.' She smiled. 'Good luck.'

As she left the room, I looked down to the screen, this

---

* I have tried, but not succeeded entirely. This runs to 140,000 words, about half the length of my last book and a quarter the length of the one before that. Count your blessings.

screen – the screen that was blank until ten minutes ago. A moment later, her head reappeared briefly around the door. 'You could begin with your favourite story about the Queen, I suppose. It's quite funny.'

In the run-up to one of her jubilees, I found myself in the Royal Box with the Queen – and the Duke of Edinburgh – at the Royal Variety Performance. I was writing a book about them, and because, for a few years, I had been the chairman of one of Prince Philip's pet charities – the National Playing Fields Association (he was president, the Queen was patron) – I managed to get privileged access to the royal couple. For several months I was allowed to walk with them, to talk with them, as they went about their official duties.

Sitting next to Prince Philip at the Royal Variety Performance and listening to his banter was rather like being caught in the commentary box at the Eurovision Song Contest with Graham Norton on speed. You got two hours of non-stop caustic quipping. Most of it was Greek to me, but I got the gist. In this particular year the show's finale featured an excerpt from *The Full Monty*, the stage musical based on the movie about a group of unemployed steelworkers from Sheffield who form a male striptease group, like the Chippendales. The musical comes to a climax with the lads doing a full striptease – *everything* comes off. But as they complete the strip, as their gold lamé thongs finally hit the stage floor, there's a blinding lighting effect: bright lights are shone from the stage straight into the audience's eyes to dazzle them and spare their blushes. Bizarrely, this male striptease show was what the organisers of the Royal Variety Performance reckoned the elderly sovereign and her consort (then in their eighties) would really enjoy.

Prince Philip glanced down at his programme and saw the word 'Finale'. His spirits soared. Below the word 'Finale' he read the title of the final item: 'The Full Monty'. He turned to the Queen and said, 'Look, cabbage, we've reached the finale and do you see what they're doing? "The Full Monty". I think we're going to enjoy the finale, for a change. "The Full Monty" – I imagine it's going to be a tribute to Field Marshal Montgomery and the battle of El Alamein.'

His Royal Highness and Her Majesty were quickly, sorely and rudely disabused, as on to the stage strutted eighteen strapping lads, waxed, tanned, oiled, and wearing nothing but a shimmying codpiece and a couple of golden tassels apiece. They marched centre stage and performed a ludicrous dance to ghastly music, culminating in the full strip-off.

Suddenly they were all stark bollock naked.

Fortunately, on cue, as their thongs bit the dust, there was the blinding lighting effect – so you could not see a thing . . . if you were seated in the Stalls.

However, if you were seated immediately adjacent to the stage, in the Royal Box, you could see it all – and, as we know, the problem with naked dancing is that not everything stops when the music stops.

The Queen did not flinch. Elizabeth II gazed steadily at the hideous jingling-jangling sight, without a flicker of an eyelid or a furrowing of the brow.

I sat in the corner of the Royal Box, ashen-faced and aghast.

The Duke of Edinburgh leant towards me and murmured reassuringly, 'You needn't worry. She's been to Papua New Guinea, she's seen it all before.'

PART ONE
Growing Up

When you were just a little boy somebody
ought to have said 'hush', just once.

Mrs Patrick Campbell

1. What's in a name?

They say everyone has a secret. What's yours? We will come to mine in due course. My hero, Oscar Wilde, had several. He reckoned the secret of his success lay in his name. Oscar Wilde had a thing about names. He believed that to live in the imagination and memory of the public you needed to have a name of just five letters – like Jesus or Plato. Or Oscar. Or Gyles.

Or Jumbo.

P. T. Barnum, the great American showman (and friend of my great-great-grandfather), bought Jumbo the Circus Elephant from London Zoo in 1881. In 1882, Oscar Wilde was in New York on one of his lecture tours and was introduced to Jumbo at Barnum and Bailey's Circus. 'His name will live for a hundred years,' said the flamboyant Irish playwright of the mighty African elephant. Oscar was right. He was right, too, when he noted that the five-letter people the public have a soft spot for are usually known by their first names (like Elvis or Cilla – or Boris, even) while those the public don't, aren't (like Trump).

'A century from now,' predicted Oscar, 'my friends will call me Oscar and my enemies will call me Wilde.'

As you read this, I hope you will think of me as Gyles.

In Ancient Rome the predictive power of a person's name was summed up in the Latin tag *'nomen est omen'*, meaning 'the name is a sign'. I am as I am, in part, because of what I'm called. Gyles isn't a bad name (I quite like it), but why is mine spelled with a 'y'? It's the most ridiculous affectation. What were my parents thinking? (Of course, it could have been worse. At school there was a girl in my class whose surname was Balls. Her first name was Ophelia. I kid you not.)

My full name is Gyles Daubeney Brandreth because my father claimed family kinship with Sir Gyles Daubeney (1451–1508), first Baron Daubeney, Knight of the Garter, soldier, diplomat, courtier, politician. This Gyles (whose tomb you can visit in Westminster Abbey) knew Edward IV. He attended the coronation of Richard III. He was Master of the Mint and Lord Chamberlain to Henry VII. His son, Henry Daubeney, was present at the Field of the Cloth of Gold, the celebrated summit that took place in 1520 between King Henry VIII of England and King François I of France. In 1538, Henry Daubeney became first Earl of Bridgewater, but despite having two top-drawer wives (one, Elizabeth Neville, kinswoman to Edward IV; the other, Katherine Howard, daughter of Thomas Howard, 2nd Duke of Norfolk), he failed to have any children. His titles died with him.

My father, Charles Daubeney Brandreth (1910–81), never produced proof of this illustrious connection, but he reckoned there must be something in it because his acknowledged forebears (and therefore mine) included, over many generations, a good number of people named either Gyles or Henry Daubeney. In my late pre-adolescence (around the time I was also devoting many happy hours to perfecting a rather stylish autograph) I spent a good deal of time at the local library poring over copies of *Burke's Dormant and Extinct Peerages*, working out how I might establish my right to reclaim the family titles.

When he was about the same age, the young Alexander Boris de Pfeffel Johnson was asked what he hoped to be when he grew up, and replied, 'King of the World.' My aspirations were less exalted. I simply felt I should be Gyles, 3rd Baron Daubeney, 2nd Earl of Bridgewater.

I had other childhood fantasies, of course. At six or seven, I had a Peter Pan fixation. My parents played along with it: at some expense my father hired an authentic Captain Hook costume from Berman's, the theatrical costumiers. (You can see us dressed to kill on the back cover.) In 1958, when I was ten, Pope Pius XII died, and I decided my destiny was one day to succeed St Peter as Bishop of Rome. When my father pointed out that we were Anglicans not Catholics, I settled for being Archbishop of Canterbury. With an eiderdown for a chasuble, one of my father's ties as a stole, and a woollen tea cosy (knitted by Auntie Ida) as my mitre, I conducted regular church services in my bedroom, using the liturgy as set out in the Book of Common Prayer, with my large collection of string and glove puppets serving as my congregation. I realise now that when I married my Sooty to my Sweep, it was probably the Church of England's first gay wedding.

A little later, when I was eleven or twelve, I spent many afternoons on my own, trolling up and down the side streets of Marylebone – the part of London that was then home to the wholesale rag trade. There, a tad furtively, I studied the mannequins in the shop windows, thinking how good I'd look as a well-shaped woman, imagining the gorgeous figure I'd cut on the catwalk. This was at the end of the 1950s, when the French model and actress Brigitte Bardot was reckoned to be the most beautiful girl in the world. I reckoned I would look exactly like her.

By the time I was fourteen I had moved on in my fantasies, to lead a make-believe double life: working by day as a tail-coated waiter in a grand hotel in the south of France and, by night, as an effortlessly charming, and deadly efficient, confidence trickster. A few hearts were broken, but other than that, no physical harm was done as I pursued my secret life of crime.

In real life, there have been a number of lawyers in the Brandreth family (my father and grandfather were both barristers and solicitors in their time; my son, Benet, is a QC and part-time judge) but, so far as I know, no convicted criminals. In 1817 Jeremiah Brandreth was the last man to be beheaded in England, but that was for treason.

Jeremiah was an unemployed stocking-maker and political activist from Sutton-in-Ashfield in Nottinghamshire. He was

a Luddite, opposed to the mechanisation of the textile industry, and bent on revolution. He was nothing if not ambitious.
On 9 June 1817 he led a small band of men from The White
Horse pub in Pentrich along the road to Nottingham. The
plan was first to take Nottingham Castle and then to move on
to London to join 50,000 more men, capture the Tower of
London, overthrow the government, cancel the national debt
and 'end poverty for ever'. Unfortunately for the 'Nottingham
Captain', as he was known, the Pentrich rebels counted a spy
among their number. They were barely three miles down the
road when they were surprised by twenty mounted troops
from the 15th Regiment of Light Dragoons. The rebellion
was routed and Brandreth and his co-conspirators were sent
for trial at the Old Bailey.

With two others, Jeremiah was convicted of High Treason
and sentenced to be hanged, drawn and quartered. The
quartering – which involved the dissecting of the condemned
individual while they were still alive – was commuted by a mer-
ciful Prince Regent. Jeremiah was hanged outside Derby Gaol
on 7 November 1817; then his head was cut off with an axe.

Two hundred years after Jeremiah's death, I travelled to
Pentrich and retraced his footsteps. I handled the block on
which he was beheaded. I even found what is believed to be
his unmarked grave. I keep a portrait of him on the wall at
home, a print of a picture painted at the time of his arrest:
'Jeremiah Brandreth, the Nottingham Captain, a correct like-
ness'. He is wearing white trousers, a blue tunic and a black
stovepipe hat; he has wistful brown eyes, a full dark beard, and
a clay pipe in his mouth; his hands and feet are manacled. He
was known as 'the hopeless radical'. I feel he had a good heart.

Jeremiah was a working man. The original Gyles Daubeney
was an aristocrat. I am middle class, as most of my family have
been for the past two hundred years. Not upper middle class
(none of my sisters were debutantes), not lower middle class
(we never called a napkin a serviette), just bang-in-the-middle

middle class. I have a detailed family tree going back to 1767 and, on my father's side, the branches hang heavy with professional men (solicitors, doctors, accountants, stockbrokers, bank managers, civil servants) and their wives – all housewives, of course.

My only granddaughter, Isolde, born in 2007, finds this difficult to believe, but up until the early 1960s to be a housewife and mother was the accepted lot of the middle-class woman. Even in the mid-1980s, when Isolde's mother (my daughter Aphra, destined to be an environmental economist and politician) was a little girl, there were mothers who brought their offspring to nursery school having already cooked and served their husbands a full English breakfast. I remember one of these young mums always had a glass of dry sherry ready poured, alongside a dish of home-made cheese straws, waiting on the hall side table for her husband when he came home from his hard day at the office. When we went to dinner parties with these people, the men were expected to wear black tie and, after pudding, the ladies would withdraw to chat in the hostess's bedroom or the drawing room, while their menfolk stayed at table, enjoying their port, brandy and cigars. Amazingly, that was less than forty years ago.

Not every female in the family tree was a housewife. Eugénie de Montijo (1826–1920, née Kirkpatrick, my father's grandfather's second cousin) was the last Empress of France, as the wife of Napoléon III. She ended her days in exile, in Farnborough. As a little boy, just after the First World War, my father was taken to see her there. (By appointment, you can visit her tomb in the crypt of St Michael's Abbey, Farnborough. It's magnificent. I'm hoping for something along the same lines myself.)

Dame Louisa Brandreth Aldrich-Blake (1865–1925) was one of the first British women to enter the world of medicine and the very first to obtain the degree of Master of Surgery. You will find a bust of her in a corner of Tavistock Square, not far from the London hospital where she spent most of her working life.

My father's first cousin, Beryl Dean (1911–2001), was an artist, costume designer and ecclesiastical embroiderer. Some-time head of the Royal School of Needlework, you can find her remarkable creations (part Modernist, part Byzantine) in churches (St George's Chapel, Windsor), museums (the V&A) – and our kitchen. She had a round face like a pale full moon, which she covered with a heavy dusting of white powder. She was resolutely minded but softly spoken, and a bit of a genius – possibly the only member of the family whose work will stand the test of time.

Sometimes I imagine my life as a movie from the 1950s, with Cousin Beryl played by Margaret Rutherford. Beryl's best friend in real life was Auntie Hope, my father's sister – to be played by Peggy Mount. Auntie Hope's husband, Uncle Wilfrid, was an actuary (whatever that is), and for him I'd cast either Raymond Huntley or Richard Wattis. My father (because I loved him) has to be played by John Le Mesurier with a touch of Terry-Thomas. My mother (I loved her, too) can be Hattie Jacques.

In the 1970s when Auntie Hope was dying of cancer (this is for real now), she did not know it. In those days, because the outcome for cancer patients was so poor, they were often not told their diagnosis. At home, the disease, if mentioned at all, was referred to, in hushed tones, as 'you-know-what' or 'the big C'. Auntie Hope was growing thinner and weaker by the day. My father (who to the end of his days said his nightly prayers kneeling by his bedside) prayed for a miracle. The local vicar suggested my parents take matters into their own hands by joining him on the parish pilgrimage to Lourdes. My parents spent money they hadn't got, and went. And there, in the little market town in the foothills of the Pyrenees, where in the 1850s the Virgin Mary was said to have appeared to the young St Bernadette, they found the shrine, pushed past the other pilgrims, many on crutches and in wheelchairs, and successfully collected a phial of holy water from the grotto's spring and brought it back home in triumph.

Many miracles have been credited to Bernadette, and my parents returned to Auntie Hope's bedside full of hope. Their plan was to administer the holy water to the dying woman and await the miracle. Their challenge was that they couldn't tell Auntie Hope what they were doing, or why. Their solution was to give her a cup of coffee made with the Lourdes water.

When Auntie Hope died a few hours later, my father took up the matter with the vicar.

'How did you get her to drink the holy water?' asked the vicar.

'We boiled it and mixed it with her Nescafé.'

'You *boiled* it?' wailed the clergyman. '*You boiled it!* You boiled away its efficacy, you fool. Of course, the poor lady died.'

Not long after Auntie Hope's death, her widowed husband, Uncle Wilfrid, proposed to Beryl, his late wife's first cousin and also her lifelong best friend. Cousin Beryl accepted. At the wedding reception my father – Hope's brother, Wilfrid's brother-in-law, Beryl's cousin – was invited to propose a toast to the happy couple.

He did so, with a flourish, inviting the assembled guests to raise their glasses: 'To Wilfrid and Beryl – and the triumph of experience over Hope!'

My father's little jokes didn't always quite come off. If Uncle Wilfrid didn't appreciate this one, he did not show it. Wilfrid had a dry sense of humour, but did not give much away. As well as having a second wife called Beryl, he had a younger sister called Beryl, too. She had been a dancer and was married to the actor Arnold Peters, who starred in the TV ads for Werther's Original Toffees and played Jack Woolley in *The Archers* for thirty-one years. They were a lovely couple – and totally straightforward. Uncle Wilfrid was straightforward, too, and sensible, and solvent. I think that's why my father may have resented him. My father was straightforward (decent and honest), but he wasn't always sensible, and I now realise that he was never solvent.

His life was ruined by money worries.

It's a mistake to think that the middle classes are always well off. They aren't. My father, a good man and a successful solicitor, died when he did – in 1981, aged seventy-one – because he had run out of funds. There were other reasons (that we will come to) but, essentially, he died when he did because he had reached the end of his rope and couldn't hang on.

I got my first glimmer of his money worries when I was about eight. My mother's mother had just died and my father took me with him to the undertakers to make the arrangements for her funeral.

'We're going to Kenyon's,' he announced, almost gleefully. 'They did Queen Victoria's funeral. They're the biggest and the best – and they're family.'

And they were. My father's grandfather's first cousin had married Etta Kenyon, granddaughter of the founder of the firm.

'We'll get a special price,' said my father.

And we did. I remember the experience because it was both amusing and embarrassing at the same time.

The first thing my father said to the undertaker was, 'We're family, don't you know? We get the family rate.'

The undertaker was baffled, but obliging.

My father then told one of his favourite jokes – the one about the preacher at the funeral who promised the congregation that on the Day of Judgement there would be a fearful reckoning, leading to much 'weeping and gnashing of teeth'. From the back of the church, one of the congregation called out, 'What about them that's got no teeth?' The preacher thundered back, 'Teeth will be provided!'

My father had false teeth. He belonged to the generation that did. One summer holiday, I remember, he lost them swimming off the beach in Dinard. They were washed out of his mouth by a wave. Two German girls, holidaymakers, joined us in the search for them and, miraculously, after an hour of frantic paddling and diving, one of them found them. My father was overjoyed. 'The *Fräulein*'s found my fangs!' he cried, jubilantly waving them in the air for all to see. He was an odd mixture of stoic stiff-upper-lip and eccentric exuberance.

The undertaker at Kenyon's chuckled at the jokes as he and my father leafed through the catalogue of coffins on offer, my dad joshing cheerily that – 'at no extra cost, please – we're family' – we'd need one that was extra-large and possibly reinforced – because his mother-in-law had been 'a big girl and heavy with it' – and then, after much humming and hawing, like an awkward young man with a wine list, choosing the second-cheapest casket on the menu.

When my father died and I organised his funeral, I went to Kenyon's, of course. I wanted to ask for the family rate, but I was young at the time and hadn't the nerve. Now I'd be bolder. Now, too, I reckon I'd get a discount without flaunting my family connections.

These days, I earn much of my living on the public-speaking circuit, giving motivational talks and hosting awards ceremonies. For three years running, I am proud to say that I have hosted the British Funeral Directors Awards. It's a surprisingly jolly event, usually held at the Royal Lancaster Hotel, off Lancaster Gate. It's a little different from other awards ceremonies, because at the BFDA, when you come up to the stage to collect your prize you don't then return to your seat with it. No. When you have been handed your trophy, you are expected to shuffle backwards to the rear of the stage, where the curtains part briefly and you disappear behind them. The organisers know what they're doing. There are two big prizes at the end of the evening. One is for the Crematorium of the

Year, known as the *Crème de la Crem*. The other is the Lifetime Achievement Award – for thinking outside the box.

My father only ever asserted his kinship with the Kenyons when death was in the air. At other times, he was much prouder of another, more prominent if less useful, member of the family: his grandmother's nephew, George R. Sims. You have probably never heard of him, but only a century ago his was a household name.

George R. Sims (1847–1922) was a celebrated journalist (the thinking man's Piers Morgan), a popular poet (the Pam Ayres of his day), a successful playwright (as prolific as Alan Ayckbourn – at one time he had four shows running in the West End simultaneously), a novelist (he wrote best-selling detective stories), a breeder of bulldogs, a lover of boxing, a devotee of the turf, a *bon vivant* and a gambler. He made a fortune (earning £150,000 in royalties and fees in a good year – the equivalent of several million in today's money) and lost much of it on the gaming tables and at the racing track. He also lived in high style (a mansion in Regent's Park; his own coach and six horses) and gave away a great deal of cash to charity.

He was a good man. He wrote extensively about the plight of the London poor and came up with practical projects to help improve hygiene and housing in the East End. His campaign to secure the pardon and release of a Norwegian, Alfred Beck, who had twice been imprisoned because of mistaken identity, led to the establishment, in 1907, of the Court of Criminal Appeal.

For forty-five years, without missing a single Sunday, he wrote his weekly newspaper column, called 'Mustard and Cress'. According to the *Times* obituarist:

> ... so attractive and original was the personality revealed in his abundant output—for he was a wonderfully hard worker—that no other journalist has ever occupied quite the

same place in the affections not only of the great public but also of people of more discriminating taste.

In London, Paris and New York, the great public flocked to the theatre to see his melodramas, comedies and romances. He wrote Christmas pantomimes for Drury Lane, and his dramatic and sentimental ballads were performed in music halls and domestic parlours across the Empire. His most famous was the one that begins:

> It is Christmas Day in the Workhouse,
> And the cold bare walls are bright
> With garlands of green and holly,
> And the place is a pleasant sight . . .

If you have heard of him at all it is probably because of that one line: 'It is Christmas Day in the Workhouse'. It was because of the poem's success that he was nominated to succeed Alfred, Lord Tennyson as Poet Laureate in 1892.

Fame is fickle. Today, almost nobody knows George R. Sims. When my father was a boy, *everybody* knew George R. Sims. And George R. Sims knew everybody – from the Prince of Wales to London's most notorious criminals (he had a fascination bordering on obsession with the identity of Jack the Ripper), from Gilbert and Sullivan to Oscar Wilde. He was especially happy to have a friendship with the American writer Ambrose Bierce. GRS collected several of Bierce's 'diabolical' definitions before they appeared in print.

Acquaintance (n.) A person whom we know well enough to borrow from, but not well enough to lend to.

Bore (n.) A person who talks when you wish him to listen.

Love (n.) A temporary insanity curable by marriage.

Sims collected witty people. He also collected actresses. He was married three times and widowed twice. He was twenty-eight when he married Sarah Collis; she was twenty-six. He was forty-one when he married Annie Harris; she was twenty-eight. He was fifty-four when he married Florence Wykes; she was twenty-seven. GRS met Birmingham-born Florrie ('this charming young brunette', a 'dashing little damsel', according to *The Sketch* of 23 October 1901) when she was playing the principal soubrette in a Sims musical, *El Capitan*, 'around the suburbs'. Their marriage lasted until his death in 1922.

Between marriages, GRS had an affair with another of his leading ladies, one of the most celebrated actresses of the age: Mrs Patrick Campbell – the original Eliza Doolittle in Bernard Shaw's *Pygmalion* and the lady who described marriage as 'the deep, deep peace of the double bed after the hurly-burly of the chaise longue'. Mrs Pat (as she was known – her real name was Stella) had a way with words. Famously, when GRS introduced her to some of his homosexual friends, she remarked, 'My dear, I don't care what they do, so long as they don't do it in the street and frighten the horses.'

My father delighted in telling me tales of our celebrated cousin – his life, his loves, his many triumphs, and the occasional disaster. Sims invented a hair tonic he claimed could cure baldness. He called it Tatcho (an anagram of Chatto – the name of his publisher) and marketed it big time.

Mr Geo R. Sims' TATCHO for the hair and lack of hair

Tatcho is a brilliant, spiritous tonic, the colour
of whisky, free from all grease

In bottles, 1/-, 2/9d, and 4/6d, at Chemists
and Stores around the world

Around the world, alas, despite endorsements from the likes of Lady Collins, Lady Sykes, and the US Consul General in Tangiers, the public did not respond as hoped, and Sims and his business partners lost a lot of money on the venture.

To mark my sixty-fifth birthday, in 2013, at considerable cost, my darling wife managed to procure me a vintage shilling bottle of Tatcho, 'Mr George R. Sims' miracle hair restorer'.

If you know what I look like, you will know it doesn't work.

2. The Pill Man

George R. Sims – the man you've never heard of – has coloured my whole life. In some ways, I think my life has ended up being a paler version of his.

The man who coloured my father's whole life is someone you've never heard of either – but he, too, was once a household name. Better than that, he was one of the richest men in the world.

Benjamin Daubeney was born on 23 June 1809 in the English village of Newtown in Derbyshire, just down the road from the home of the soon-to-be-beheaded Jeremiah Brandreth in Sutton-in-Ashfield. Benjamin was the son of William Daubeney and Ann Brandreth. According to family legend, the Catholic Daubeneys did not approve of the union between their William and a daughter of the renegade Protestant Quaker Brandreth family and refused to recognise it. As a consequence, William Daubeney quickly disappeared from the scene. Ann Brandreth found a new partner, by the humbler name of Holmes; and young Benjamin came to be brought up between the Holmes household in the Midlands and his maternal grandparents' home in the North-West.

Benjamin's maternal grandfather was one Dr William Brandreth, a physician from Liverpool with a large practice in the poorer parts of the city and a reputation as something of a miracle-working medicine man. Since the 1770s this Dr Brandreth had been mixing his own special preparation of herbs and vegetable substances that produced remarkable results when taken for severe cases of constipation, biliousness, and almost every other ailment known to man, woman or child. These were Brandreth's Pills – containing aloes, gamboge, colocynth and sarsaparilla, apparently 'among the most powerful cathartic cannon in the botanical armoury' – and the foundation of the family fortune.

From the age of nine, young Benjamin was assisting his old grandfather in the mixing of the potent medicine. At thirteen, Benjamin was out and about selling Dr Brandreth's pills to local apothecaries and grocery stores. At sixteen, he was as good as running the family business. At eighteen, on Christmas Eve 1827 (I mention the date because I think it will make an affecting snow-filled scene when the film comes to be made), he married his first wife, Harriet Smallpage. At nineteen, in 1828, he abandoned his stepfather's name of Holmes, put his Daubeney name on the back burner, and became 'Benjamin Brandreth' and, by agreement with the rest of the family, the sole proprietor of all rights in Dr Brandreth's pills.

He was a young man in a hurry and on a mission. He established offices in London and Liverpool and began to market his medicine throughout the British Isles and, by mail order, across the British Empire. By the time he was twenty-five, he was ready to take on the New World. On Thursday, 26 March 1835, Benjamin Brandreth, accompanied by his wife Harriet, their four small children and one servant, set sail from Liverpool for New York on the good ship *President*. The crossing took a fortnight. They arrived at Ellis Island on 9 April. Just twelve weeks later, on Wednesday, 1 July 1835, the following advertisement appeared on the front page of the New York *Sun*.

Notice. Dr Brandreth, MD VPL VS, shortly arrived from London, respectfully announces that he may be consulted on Mondays, Wednesdays and Saturdays from 9 in the morning until 8 in the evening, at his office 187 Hudson Street, New York by all persons requiring medical aid particularly those suffering from Dyspepsia or Indigestion, nervous complaints, gout or rheumatism . . . consumption and all affections from the lungs, asthma . . . dropsy, loss of appetite, languor, tremor, headache, costiveness, worms of all kinds, hysteric diseases, restlessness and frightful dreams and all complaints to which females are subject. The sufferers of these diseases may, on application to Dr Brandreth, be certain of speedy relief and in most cases an effectual cure.

Isn't that wonderful? Where were Dr Brandreth's pills when the coronavirus struck? The pills were a virtual cure-all and, more than that, as Dr Brandreth explained on the side of the box they came in: 'The great advantage of using Brandreth's Pills in sickness is that they *never make any mistakes*, often prolonging, never shortening life.' That was the point: they were harmless and they might be helpful – especially when it came to dealing with worms. By way of proof, in a large bottle on display in his office, Brandreth kept a fourteen-inch worm that had been evacuated by a grateful patient.

Admittedly, when he arrived in America, Benjamin was not actually a doctor entitled to the initials listed after his name, but he soon put matters right. In December 1835, the Reformed Medical Society of New York granted him a diploma based on his prior experience. In January 1836, the New York Eclectic Medical College made him a Doctor of Medicine on the same basis.

The first year in America was not easy. Benjamin was making the pills himself, mixing the ingredients in his rooms in Hudson Street, with Harriet pasting the labels on to the boxes, while their eldest, George, not yet nine, counted out the pills. Soon after their arrival in New York, their baby, Jane, died of the croup – a respiratory infection usually caused by a virus. And on 23 May 1836, Harriet died in childbirth. She was not yet thirty.

Despite these tragedies – perhaps spurred on by them – Benjamin kept growing his business. In his second year of trading he sold 400,000 boxes of his pills at 25 cents a box – around $10 in today's money. He had outgrown his premises in Hudson Street and looked to move to somewhere where he could grow the herbs and vegetable ingredients he needed and harness water power to grind them into compounds for pill production. He settled on the village of Sing Sing, thirty miles north of New York City, and built a factory on the banks of the River Hudson, not far from the Sing Sing penitentiary. (In the 1960s, during my gap year, I visited both. The prison survives. Despite being listed on the National Register of Historical Places in 1980, the factory, alas, has not. Developers. Bastards.)

Sixteen months after Harriet's death, in September 1837, the young entrepreneur married his second wife, Susan Frances Leeds of New York. We know little about the union other than the fact it was not a success. The couple were together for no more than a fortnight, and the marriage ended in an acrimonious divorce. In February 1840, Benjamin found his third wife, a girl from Sing Sing, Virginia Graham, destined to be my great-great-grandmother. Benjamin was thirty. Virginia was half his age. According to family legend she was actually fourteen. That's what Auntie Carlie told my mother many years later when they were sharing family secrets. Benjamin, apparently, would return from a hard day in the pill factory to find his child bride playing with her dolls. Later records state that she was born in 1822, which would make her rising eighteen at the time of the marriage. (We'll stick with that version when we make the movie. You can't be too careful nowadays.)

Over the years, Virginia bore Benjamin twelve children, ten of whom survived to adulthood. As his family grew, so did his business. Soon he was producing more than a million boxes of pills a year – and diversifying. He bought Allcock's Porous Plasters, medicated adhesives 'for muscular aches and pains', 'used and preferred by all'. He founded a bank. And then another. He became a New York State Senator. He ran for Congress.

He was a figure to reckon with and his pills were *everywhere*.

Herman Melville featured them in *Moby Dick*. Edgar Allan Poe wrote a story in which the characters pondered what the pills' ingredients might be. Phineas Taylor Barnum, the circus king, took Dr Brandreth's pills, he said, 'morning, noon and night' and valued them so much that he sought out their progenitor to salute him in person. 'Dr Brandreth is a liberal man,' Barnum later wrote, 'and a pleasant, entertaining and edifying companion. He deserves all the success he has ever received. Long may he wave!'

Barnum began taking the pills in 1836, in his early days as a showman, travelling through the states of Alabama, Mississippi and Louisiana. He had not been feeling well. 'I became convinced by reading Dr Brandreth's advertisements that I needed his pills.' He bought some. 'The effect was miraculous!' He went on taking them his whole life long, even after he discovered from Dr Brandreth that the pills he first bought on that tour of the Deep South may not have been the genuine article, but counterfeit pills produced by profiteering bootleggers. That didn't matter to Barnum. As far as he was concerned, so long as Dr Brandreth's name was on the box, the pills would work their magic. It was the Brandreth brand that did the trick.

At universities where they teach the history of marketing, Dr Brandreth is credited as the inventor of 'brand' management. (He is also credited as the inventor of the advertising hoarding. The giant signs promoting Brandreth's pills that he put up across New York were the first of their kind.) Notwithstanding Barnum devoting a chapter of his book *Humbugs of the World* to him, I don't think Brandreth was a huckster. He believed in his medicine, and he believed in the power of advertising. He taught Barnum his philosophy:

> Advertising is like learning – a little is a dangerous thing. The reader of a newspaper does not see the first insertion of an ordinary advertisement; the second insertion he sees, but

does not read; the third insertion he reads; the fourth insertion he looks at the price; the fifth insertion, he speaks of it to his wife; the sixth insertion he is ready to purchase; and the seventh insertion he purchases.

The insertions for Brandreth's pills appeared not once, but tens of thousands of times. Brandreth spent more, far more, on newspaper advertising than anyone had ever done before. He reaped the rewards. In 1848, he built himself a mansion that boasted thirty rooms and ten bathrooms. In 1851, he bought 24,000 acres of forest in the Adirondacks and founded Brandreth Park – to this day the largest private park in America. In 1857, he built the Brandreth Hotel, near Canal and Broadway in New York City – the Trump Tower of its day. When he died – in 1880, aged seventy-one – he was reckoned to be one of the richest men on earth.

What happened to the money? None of it ever trickled down to me.

Of course, when he died he had a dozen surviving children and, some more, some less, they all got a slice. The daughters married well: they came with a handsome inheritance. The sons did their best to carry on the family business. The sixth son, Henry Daubeney Brandreth (1845–1915), my great-grandfather, was sent back to England to run the European end of the business empire. He does not appear to have done so very well. Henry was interested in family, faith, philanthropy, animals and practical jokes, but not, it seems, in business.

Henry had a wife, Adelaide, and nine children, the eldest being my grandfather, Benjamin Daubeney Brandreth, born in 1872 and named in honour of both his illustrious grandfather, the Pill Man, and his Daubeney forebears, the friends of Henry VII.

The European pill business was headquartered in Birkenhead, on the Wirral peninsula, along the west bank of the River

Mersey, opposite the city of Liverpool. Henry's family settled into a handsome three-storeyed house looking out over the golf links at Hoylake nearby. They lived well, with plenty of servants (outdoor, indoor, gardeners, coachmen, ladies' maids, kitchen maids, one valet, one laundress, one cook, one butler, one waitress, one page boy); a wing for the younger children (who had nursemaids, a tutor and governesses, both a French *mademoiselle* and a German *Fräulein*); stables for the horses (to pull the four-wheel landau and the governesses' carriage) and the fat pony (who pulled the two-wheel dog cart); and a small menagerie (dogs, cats, and an enclosed veranda that served as an aviary for Adelaide's many canaries). The smaller children spent much of their lives in the nursery. The older ones were sent away to boarding schools.

The family went up to London occasionally – the London offices for the pill business were in the Strand, so they had ringside seats to view the parades for Queen Victoria's jubilees, for her funeral, and for the coronation of Edward VII – and they set off to Wales for three months every summer. For several years, they rented an old stone farmhouse at Betwys-y-Coed and then, in 1897, Henry acquired a 99-year lease from Lord Penrhyn on a 9,000-acre shooting estate at Pont-y-Pant, five miles up the Lledr Valley from Betws-y-Coed. Around the main house were formal gardens (including a large rose garden, bordered by beds of pansies of all colours) and tier upon tier of planted terraces rising up the hillside. Beyond were two lakes teeming with brown and speckled trout, a five-mile salmon river, streams, woods, moors covered with purple heather, peat moss, ferns and bracken, and towering over it all, snow-capped Snowdon in the distance and Moel Siabod nearby, whose 2,500-ft summit marked the estate's boundary line.

Henry acquired the estate for the shooting and the fishing but, according to Annie, his youngest, his chief delights were the glass-covered hothouses that produced huge grapes, and his self-styled 'Animalarium' that housed the dogs and the cats, the guinea pigs and the rabbits, the white rats and the Japanese mice, the white pig, the canaries, the doves and the parrot – as well as the odd stray lamb in springtime.

Looking at formal photographs taken of Henry in the 1890s, he has the appearance of a stern Victorian paterfamilias. According to little Annie, he was nothing of the sort: 'Father was short, inclined to be stout, and very jolly. He would come to the nursery and play bear, getting down on all fours while we children climbed on his back.' Henry's wife, Adelaide, always known as Addie, was the solemn one: 'Mother had a reserved nature; she was stately, dignified, very fastidious.' In later life, apparently, Addie greatly admired, and somewhat resembled, Queen Mary.

Her lot was not easy. Her husband had acquired the estate to hold shooting parties and to entertain – which he did, in some style. Night after night – sometimes six nights a week – thirty people would sit down to a formal seven-course dinner. The gentlemen were in white tie, the ladies were in evening gowns, the guests included the local aristocracy, political and military figures, and notables from the world of commerce – but Henry, intriguingly, did not stand on ceremony.

Henry liked to tell a story and had an 'an endless supply of Scottish and Irish tales' with which he regaled his guests. They were funny. According to Annie, James, the butler, standing erect and motionless behind her father's chair, would regularly be obliged to clap his white-gloved hand over his mouth and make a rush for the door so as not to be seen laughing out loud. 'Father loved a practical joke – especially if a particularly celebrated guest was present. At such times Mother showed distinct signs of uneasiness, but Father was irrepressible.'

His favourite party piece involved a length of rubber tubing, with a small round rubber bulb at one end and a small round rubber disc at the other. Henry would hide the disc under the guest of honour's plate and then, at intervals, squeeze the bulb hidden in his hand beneath the table, causing the guest's plate to tilt ever so slightly. Some guests were disconcerted, some were annoyed, others were amused; Adelaide was always embarrassed.

What infuriated her most was that Henry was happy to have the dogs in the dining room, even at the grandest dinners. Mostly the animals lay quietly under the table at their master's feet, but occasionally the mischievous Scottish terrier would pick a fight with the Airedale and the red setter would decide to join the fray. Once jaws were locked, the master's commands were of no avail. Henry would resort to the soda syphon on the sideboard and douse the fighting dogs with sharp jets of water.

Henry found all this vastly entertaining. Poor Addie did not. She was also aware, painfully so, that the grand guests at her table were there because of the shooting and the fishing and her husband's wealth, not because they were proper friends. Addie moved in the best society but she knew that the best society did not regard her as 'one of us'. The Brandreth fortune came from Brandreth's Pills. The Brandreths were 'in trade'. And they were American.

With fellow Americans, of course, they were people of some standing. They were friends, for example, of Andrew Carnegie, one of the richest men (and greatest philanthropists) in history. He had them over to stay at Skibo Castle, his Scottish home. He introduced them to Woodrow Wilson, the future US President. But *knowing* the right people is not the same as *being* the right people. Henry's heritage might have included the first Earl of Bridgewater, but that was a long time ago. Addie was a small-town American of Irish and Dutch descent. As Henry explained to his daughter, Annie, 'You, my child, are a thoroughbred little mongrel.'

That, of course, is why, when Annie fell in love with Wilfred – the son of General Sir Hugh Gough and grandson of Viscount Gough – and the handsome young man held the eighteen-year-old girl in his arms, kissing her forehead, kissing her eyes, and whispering, 'You are all the world and more than all the world to me,' both of them knew that marriage was impossible.

Many years later, an interviewer famously asked the romantic novelist Dame Barbara Cartland whether she thought class barriers had disappeared and was told that of course they had – otherwise, why on earth did she find herself sitting there being interviewed by him? The barriers may have disappeared, but class consciousness is still part and parcel of British life – hence the success of *Downtown Abbey*, the popularity of *Keeping Up Appearances*, and our ongoing fascination with every aspect of royalty.

None of this troubled my great-grandfather, Henry Brandreth – and for a reason. He had found God. Around the year 1882, Henry had a wonderful dream in which the Lord showed him the futility of worldly things. In this dream, Henry and the Almighty found themselves alone together in a huge amphitheatre watching the most magnificent firework display. It was extraordinarily beautiful, according to Henry, but no sooner had the fireworks flared up into the sky than they burned bright and disappeared. In the darkness that followed, the Lord took Henry by the hand and repeated I John 2: 17, 'And the world passeth away, and the lust thereof: but he that doeth the will of God abideth for ever.'

When he woke from his dream, Henry was a changed man. His father's pill business and his wife's social aspirations now meant nothing to him. 'Ye cannot serve God and Mammon,' he declared, with feeling. While continuing to maintain his estate in his customary style, he gave away money to missionaries, built chapels where he could, and spread the word of the Lord with zeal and humility. The household gathered every morning in the hallway for prayer, and every Sunday, fifty or sixty people (the family, the guests, the servants, the gamekeepers and their wives) were expected in the dining room for an hour or more of Henry's heartfelt home-spun evangelism.

31

Poor Addie put up with this. She did not like it – she tended not to emerge from her bedroom until lunchtime, letting her daughter Annie approve the day's menus with Cook – but she accepted her lot and lived out her life, as women did (and do), with forbearance and fortitude. And she loved the part of North Wales in which she and her family lived – a part of the world, so her gregarious and God-loving husband told her, that had been described in Deuteronomy 11: 11–12: 'But the land . . . is a land of hills and valleys, and drinketh water of the rain of heaven: a land which the Lord thy God careth for: the eyes of the Lord thy God are always upon it, from the beginning of the year even unto the end of the year.'

Henry was a happy man, neglectful of business, but busy with the work of the Lord – while still finding time for fishing and shooting, for walking the dogs and playing practical jokes. And then a new century dawned and his world changed.

On Wednesday, 15 August 1900, three days into the grouse-shooting season, Henry and his guests and their guns set off early for their shoot. Addie and all the children who were still living at home – Adeline, Eugénie, Virgie, Carlotta and the youngest two, Harry and Annie – decided it was so warm it was a perfect day for a swim, or at least a paddle. The River Lledr – no more than a wide stream – ran through the estate, no further than a hundred feet from the main house. The sun was high and hot: the fast-running water in the river proved to be very cold. The river bed was shallow on one side, but deepened rapidly on the other. While the others sat on the bank, Virgie and Eugénie, the only two who could swim, dived in. Suddenly, from the far side of water, there was a scream – Eugénie had cramp. Virgie went to help her and both girls disappeared in a moment, drowned in the running water.

The rest of the party stood helpless on the riverbank, shrieking.

Harry, sixteen but no swimmer, began to wade into the river.

His mother ran to pull him back. 'No, no,' she wailed. 'I can't lose more of my children – no, Harry, don't go.'

Harry pulled back and stood with his mother and sisters watching the dreadful scene.

All the men of the house were on the moors shooting. Eventually, Huws, an old man who worked on the estate, heard the cries and came to help. He brought an extension ladder, stretched it out across the neck of the pool, and with a gaff managed somehow to pull both girls' bodies to the shore.

When Henry and his guests finally arrived on the scene, there lay Eugénie and Virgie on the riverbank, side by side, lifeless. Eugénie was twenty-four, Virgie twenty-two.

Fifty years later, Annie wrote:

Never, never so long as I live will I forget that scene. Even at this present moment I can hear Mother sobbing and Father repeating in a firm unfaltering voice, though rung through with anguish, 'The Lord gave and the Lord hath taken away – blessed be the name of the Lord.'

According to Annie, Henry's faith was wonderful. 'He never for an instant doubted the goodness and love of God. I never heard him ask "Why?" For him it was enough that his Heavenly Father had permitted this to happen.'

Though all this occurred more than a hundred and twenty years ago, I think of those poor drowned girls every day. On the table in front of me now is the small memorial card, printed in silver on cream, and sent to those who could not attend their burial in the little cemetery on the steep hillside in the shadow of Moel Siabod in North Wales. In the room next door to where I am writing this, I have large, framed formal photographs of each of them hanging on the wall. I see them every day and see in their eyes a look of my own daughters.

I can imagine no greater horror than losing a child before their time. It happens, of course. It has happened to at least five of my school and university contemporaries – Libby Purves and Michael Rosen among them. With time and fortitude, and because, if you have other children, you have no choice, they have battled on with courage, grace and good humour. One does. You do. But seeing the portraits of Virgie and Eugénie on the wall every day, I feel for them. And, irrational though it is, whenever the doorbell rings unexpectedly, my heart jumps and I look through the spyhole, fearful that there will be police officers waiting there with terrible news.

These days, everyone feels they have the right to be happy. It was different in my great-grandparents' day. They read the Book of Psalms and were taught that life is 'a vale of tears': happiness is not for this world, but for the next.

In time of travail, faith helps, I am sure. Towards the end of his life, Carl Jung, the Swiss psychiatrist and founder of analytical psychology, looked back on the case histories of his many patients and concluded that those with a faith had been happier than those without.

I come from a family of religious zealots (on both my father's and my mother's sides) and I like going to church. Church-going was central to my childhood and I still attend Holy Communion at 8.00 a.m. most Sunday mornings at my local church. I go because it's a habit and it's comforting, and because it's an old church where people have been worshipping for a thousand years and I like to feel part of that continuity; I go because I love the language of the Book of Common Prayer; I go, too, because we are blessed with a group of intelligent and good-humoured clergy whose preaching is worth listening to. I am not sure how much I believe, but I enjoy the discipline and the experience – and it seems sensible to keep your options open.

Faith helps, but it's not essential. I have a lot of actor friends for whom the Bible means little, but Shakespeare means everything. From childhood onwards, I was lucky enough to

34

know the actor Donald Sinden. Remembered for his fruity voice and for starring in sitcoms like *Never the Twain* and *Two's Company*, he was also a great classical actor.

Donald had two sons and, in 1996, the elder of them, Jeremy, died of lung cancer, aged forty-five. A year or two later, visiting Donald in his dressing room one afternoon between performances, we talked about death and it became clear to me that Shakespeare was as important to him as the Bible had been to my great-grandfather.

I asked Donald if he brooded much about Jeremy.

'No, no, not at all,' he replied, scooping the ash from his cigarette off the dressing table. He looked at me with shining eyes and quoted *Hamlet*: 'If it be now, 'tis not to come; if it be not to come, it will be now; if it be not now, yet it will come: the readiness is all.'

Since I have mentioned him, I must just tell you what fun Donald Sinden was. Do forgive the occasional aside. I'll try not to overdo it, but since this is an autobiography I feel I should tell you about my heroes and role models as well as my forebears.

I first saw Donald Sinden onstage on 2 January 1964 in a very funny Royal Shakespeare Company production of *The Comedy of Errors*. (I can be precise about the date because I keep a diary. I kept the programme, too. And the ticket, 10*s*. 6*d*. in the Stalls.) I first met him on 9 May 1965. He was thinking of sending his sons to my school and I was charged with showing the family around. I felt I knew him anyway because the father of my best friend at school was a theatrical agent and Donald Sinden was his star client. From then until he died in September 2014, aged ninety, I spent many of my happiest hours in Sir Donald's company. He always made me laugh – even at his funeral, when he arrived in a coffin painted in wide stripes of salmon pink and cucumber green, the colours of the Garrick Club tie.

He was at his happiest at the Garrick, the Covent Garden club for actors, artists, writers, lawyers and the like. Founded in 1831, its early members included Charles Kean, Henry Irving and Herbert Beerbohm Tree.

'You know, W. S. Gilbert, another Garrick man, described Tree's Hamlet as "funny without being vulgar". Isn't that wonderful?' Donald gossiped about these men as though they had been personal friends.

He loved the heritage of the theatre and he taught me to love it – and respect it, too. When Sir John Gielgud died, Donald inherited much of the great man's personal wardrobe and, knowing I had known Gielgud and had written his biography, Donald kindly came over to our house with one of Gielgud's dress shirts as a present for me.

'Did I ever tell you about the television programme I did, years ago, with Edith Evans and John Gielgud?' he asked conspiratorially, lips puckering, twinkling eyes narrowing. 'We were shown film clips of the great players of yesteryear and invited to give our reactions. During the bit of Ellen Terry, Edith nodded off – *nodded off* during Ellen Terry! And when they showed a bit of Olivier's Othello and asked Gielgud what he made of it, John didn't know what to do: "Oh, no, no, no, no, no, no." That was all he could say.' Donald wheezed with delight at the recollection.

I once asked him how his love of theatrical stories began.

'My first job,' he told me, 'in the early 1940s, when I was still in my teens, was entertaining the troops with an outfit called MESA [Mobile Entertainments, Southern Area] run by a fellow named Charles F. Smith, one of the unsung heroes of the British stage. He'd started going to the theatre in the days of Henry Irving, the great Victorian actor-manager, and he knew everybody. During the war, most of the London theatres were closed, so actors were continuously on tour and they'd all come through Brighton, where we were. Every Sunday, Charles would have a party in his flat and we young ones were invited to meet these astonishing luminaries of an earlier era. John Martin-Harvey, Marie Tempest, Irene Vanbrugh – I sat at their feet and heard them talk about the people *they* had seen. I fell under their spell. And I learnt so much.'

'Who taught you the most?'

'The first master comedian I learnt from was Lawrence O'Madden – forgotten now, but, oh, his timing!' Sir Donald's bright eyes filled with tears. 'He'd be beside me onstage and under his breath he'd say, "Wait for it, w-a-i-t for it, wait – for – it . . . *Now!*" A laugh is like the roof of a house. It starts under the eaves and works its way to the top and then rolls down the other side. You wait till it's halfway down the far side before you move on. I am fascinated by the craft, by how it works. It was Ralph [Richardson] who told me, "You've got to have a least five consonants in a tag line. You can't get a laugh on a vowel."

'I once asked John Gielgud, "What are the most essential things about acting?" With hardly a pause he replied, "Feeling and timing," and then, head erect, his eyes twinkled to the side, as he added, "I understand it is the same in many walks of life."'

When I was quite young, I asked Donald to define the difference between actors and the rest of the world – the people the actors call 'civilians'.

'Oh,' he chuckled, drawing even more deeply than usual on his cigarette. 'Actors are more open, freer, more accepting of one another, more immediately intimate. We share our vulnerability. In what other business are you invited to kiss a perfect stranger full on the lips?' He stubbed out his cigarette and smacked his lips. 'You know the story of the young actor who was set to play Hamlet for the first time and, wanting to understand the full psychology of the part, asked an older actor in the company if he thought that Hamlet had actually slept with Ophelia? The old actor pondered for a moment. "I don't know about the West End, laddie," he said, "but we always did on tour."'

It was said of Laurence Olivier that he was only himself onstage. I do not think that was true of Donald Sinden. He may have been most alive, most intensely happy, when he was onstage, but he was not acting when he was off it. He was stagey, fruity, over the top, but not as a pose or a mask or as a cop-out. That's how he was. Just because he loved an anecdote, and lived and breathed the theatre, that does not make him shallow. He was theatrical, but profoundly so. The way to his heart was through his stories.

'Stop me if I've told you this one before,' he'd say.

'I want to hear it again,' I'd reply – and I always meant it.

'You like my stories?'

'I *love* your stories. I think I like the inkwell story best.'

'Ah, ah, yes, yes . . . A young actor in weekly rep hated his leading man – loathed and despised him. The young actor kept a diary and in it he confided the details of his obsession. "Tonight, *he* killed my exit." "Tonight, *he* ruined my finest scene."

'Then came, "Monday, 6.15 p.m. Dear Diary, tonight I believe I am going to get the better of *him*. We open a new play and I have a speech ten minutes long. Downstage. In the light. Facing out front. And *he* is upstage, seated at a desk, with his back to the audience. I think I must win . . ."

'Later, a slightly drunken hand added, "11.45 p.m. HE DRANK THE INK!"'

3. My father's stories

Where were we?

Oh, yes . . . on a hillside in North Wales in the summer of 1900, with my great-grandparents, burying two of their daughters.

The deaths of Virgie and Eugénie changed everything. Henry and Addie, with Annie and her governess, went away for the winter, travelling through Belgium and France, horse-riding in the *bois* outside Brussels, taking long walks along the banks of the Seine, where, in those days, the peasant women still congregated to wash their linen. When the family returned to North Wales, life went on, but it was not the same. Apart from the shadow of the tragedy, Henry now had money worries. In Britain and across the Continent the Brandreth Pills business was falling off (Henry had paid it scant attention), and his elder brothers running the still-successful American end of the empire back in New York were wearying of providing him with ever-greater subsidies. Even as his responsibilities lessened when his children began to leave home, he still found himself unable to make ends meet.

As Annie put it, many years later, 'Poor Father never could live within his income, no matter how large; a trait handed down to his daughter, I regret to say.'

And to his grandson, as we shall see.

Henry and Addie's eldest son, Benjamin, my grandfather, had – as soon as he was able – got out of trade and into a profession. His parents were unashamedly American, but Ben had been brought up in England and chose to become a British citizen and an English barrister. Because he was the eldest child, and a lawyer, and seen by all the family as 'the sensible one', he was charged by his father with the task of securing more funds to keep his parents in the style to which they were accustomed.

In the box in which I found the memorial card for Virgie and Eugénie, I also came across this letter, sent by my grandfather, then twenty-nine, to his father, then fifty-six.

20 Exchange Street, Liverpool
21st January, 1902

My Dear Father,
I have nothing to report with reference to negotiations for a loan, but I think that if in the meantime you will consider the following figures you will see that your estimate of £2,400 a year for living expenses is very liberal . . .

It was, indeed – at a time when £50 per annum was for many a working wage.

In 1905, my great-grandparents gave up the unequal struggle and returned to America. Tragedy went with them. In 1909, their youngest son, Harry, always the most adventurous of the family, died in an accident on a ranch in Tampico in Old Mexico, aged twenty-five. 'Safe, safe at last,' sobbed Addie when she heard the news.

Henry died in 1915, aged seventy, secure in the love of God. Addie went stoically on to her eighty-fourth year and, in 1929, was laid to rest beneath a fine monument in the graveyard at Ossining, alongside her husband (who spent the family fortune) and his father (who made it).

I don't know if my father ever met his grandparents. He referred to his father's letter about the loan now and again, and, when he did, he liked to say his father had only been encouraging his own father to 'manage with nine servants – much as Lord Curzon's accountant had advised him to do in similar circumstances'.

The circumstances were not that similar. The first Marquess Curzon of Keddleston had nine staff in the kitchen alone.

'Does your lordship really require a *second* pastry chef?' asked the accountant, as gently as he could.

'So,' sighed Lord Curzon, 'it has come to this – a fellow's not even to be allowed a biscuit with his sherry. Bah!'

George Nathaniel Curzon was a Tory grandee of the old school, Viceroy of India, Foreign Secretary, and very possibly, had he not been in the House of Lords, Prime Minister instead of Stanley Baldwin in 1923. My father had a whole repertoire of 'Curzon stories' and usually introduced them with a verse designed to show how grand the great man was:

> My name is George Nathaniel Curzon,
> I am a most superior person.
> My cheeks are pink, my hair is sleek,
> I dine at Blenheim twice a week.

For a number of years Curzon was Chancellor of Oxford University and when, in 1921, Queen Mary was to be entertained at Curzon's old college, Balliol, he was asked to approve the proposed menu in advance. He returned it to the Bursar with the single comment: 'Gentlemen do not take soup at luncheon.'

One evening, according to my father, a little before the outbreak of the 1914–18 War, Curzon and a friend were strolling down London's Regent Street when they came upon the window of Garrard's, the jewellers. They paused to take in the range of gold and silverware on display, and Curzon's eye was caught by a small silver cylindrical object nestling on a tiny blue velvet cushion at the rear of the window.

'What's that?' Curzon enquired of his companion.

'What?'

'That, up there,' said Curzon, pointing to the piece of silver.

'Why, Curzon,' said his friend, 'that is a napkin ring.'

41

'What on earth is a "napkin ring"?' asked Curzon.

'Surely you've come across a napkin ring before now, Curzon?'

'No, truly, never. Pray, what is it for?'

'Well,' explained his companion, 'there are some people who cannot afford fresh linen at every meal, so that after breakfast they will take their napkin and fold it not once, but twice, and then roll it into a tube and insert the napkin into that silver ring to keep the same napkin to use again at luncheon.'

Curzon shook his head in disbelief. 'Can there be such poverty?'

My father measured out his life in anecdotes. He told me any number of stories about the celebrated figures of his boyhood – the politicians and statesmen like Lord Curzon and Lloyd George, the writers and artists like Max Beerbohm and Augustus John, particularly the great advocates like F. E. Smith and Sir Edward Marshall Hall – but he did not talk about his family very much. He mentioned the Pill Man now and again; his grandparents only rarely; and his parents not at all.

I know my grandfather – my father's father, Benjamin Daubeney Brandreth – started out as a barrister in Liverpool and I know he ended up as a solicitor in Bournemouth, but how and why and when he moved from one end of the country and one side of the legal profession to the other, I have no idea. My father never told me. Perhaps I never asked.

Or perhaps my father did not talk about his parents because he didn't want to. If he had pictures of them, I never saw them. I seem to recollect a small snapshot of me and my grandparents in their garden in Poole, in Dorset, when I was just a toddler, but I must have got that wrong. I discovered (only just now, this morning, rummaging through a box of old papers) that my grandfather died in 1947, before I was born.

On his father's and his mother's sides, my father had twelve uncles and aunts in all. Three died young, as we have seen, and four went back to live in America, but of the rest the only one I can remember him mentioning was Auntie Carlie.

Auntie Carlie hadn't returned to America with her parents in 1905. She had stayed in North Wales and married an Irishman called Herbert McComas – like Oscar Wilde, a Gold Medal winner at Trinity College, Dublin, and described by my father as 'leprechaun-like and very amusing'. I know that my parents once went to visit Auntie Carlie in Dolwyddelan and returned with Mr McComas's diminutive evening dress suit which they gave to me for my dressing-up box. The tailcoat had the most wonderful midnight-blue lining and pure silk facing to the lapels. I wore it regularly when I was about eleven and going through my Fred Astaire phase.

My father had a brother and two sisters. The brother, another Benjamin, born in 1904, was six years older than my father, and brighter, and better looking. He was a bacteriologist, teaching at Queen's College, Cambridge, when he was killed in a blackout accident in the first year of the Second World War. I don't think I ever heard my father speak of him.

My father did talk about his sisters. Auntie Hope you already know. We visited her and her family quite often when I was a boy. They lived in Mill Hill in North London, comfortably, solvently, in a handsome suburban villa that my father would gently mock as we drove up to it – though I think he envied Auntie Hope's garden. Her pergola was her pride and joy – and the time she asked Franklin Engelmann a question on *Gardeners' Question Time* her finest hour. I liked her.

I liked Auntie Helen, too. She was the elder daughter who never married, but stayed at home to look after her parents, and received her reward when she inherited their house. She was my godmother and I remember, as a young teenager, going on my own to visit her in Poole. She took me to the tea room at Bobby's, the old department store in Bournemouth, and we had toasted teacakes and Victoria sponge. I remember that she smoked non-stop and kept a tortoise in the garden. The tortoise reputedly had been around since Victoria was Queen. Small, thin, with iron-grey hair and spectacles, quiet but with a twinkle, Auntie Helen devoted herself to her parents during their lifetime and afterwards to the RSPCA. She was the treasurer of the Poole branch, I think. As George Eliot has it at the end of *Middlemarch*: 'the growing good of the world is partly dependent on unhistoric acts.' Auntie Helen and Auntie Hope were good people: 'and that things are not so ill with you and me as they might have been, is half owing to the number who lived faithfully a hidden life, and rest in unvisited tombs.'

Like Auntie Hope, Auntie Helen died of cancer. She was sixty-six and had become so thin that a gust of wind simply blew her off her feet in the street one day. That was the beginning of her end. When she died, in 1972, she left me £700 in her will. It is the only legacy I have ever received. Michèle and I were buying our first flat at the time. I do hope there's a heaven. I'd love Auntie Helen to have known how grateful we were.

When Auntie Helen died, the house in Poole was sold quite quickly. My father will have needed his share of the proceeds. His money worries never went away and they were acute just then. My parents were 'between flats': the lease on the last one (a Victorian mansion flat off Baker Street, large but dark) had come to an end and they hadn't yet found another they could afford. My parents were living in a single room in a faded hotel in Bayswater. My younger brother, yet another Ben, was fourteen and, during school holidays, he shared the room, sleeping on a put-you-up bed in the corner, curtained off by an arrangement of blankets my father had strung up between the wardrobe and the door. The room was let as a double room, which meant my parents had to pretend Ben wasn't there. At breakfast my father would pocket an extra boiled egg and discreetly wrap toast and butter in his handkerchief to take upstairs for Ben. In the evening, he would loiter in the lobby and say, to no one in particular, 'I've just been seeing our boy off – he's staying with an aunt, you know.' The deception was not necessary. Nobody noticed or cared. But I think my father (always one for amateur theatricals) rather liked the excitement of the subterfuge.

At the time Auntie Helen died, I was twenty-four and Pa was sixty-two. (We always called him Pa. 'Dear sweet lovable Pa' – my brother, my sisters and I, we all called him that.) He went down to Poole on the train to look over the family house one last time before the house clearers moved in. I volunteered to keep him company. It was an oddly crowded train, I remember – I think we had to stand for most of the journey. We chatted happily all the way there and just as happily all the way back (the Brandreths are always talking). My father scarcely mentioned his family.

When we got to the house, which Auntie Helen had kept much as it was when her mother had died almost twenty years before, my sisters and cousins had already been and taken whatever they wanted – linen and crockery, mostly, and some family portraits. As we wandered from room to room, I asked my father what he was thinking of taking.

'Nothing,' he said lightly.

'What about this?' I asked.

We were looking at a large, framed certificate given to 'Miss Jessie Beatrice Dean in recognition of Patriotic Services rendered to the Borough of Bromley during the Great War'. Jessie Dean was one of my father's aunts – his mother's unmarried sister. She had volunteered in her local hospital's Supply Department throughout the 1914–18 War.

'We can't let this go,' I said.

'You have it,' said my father.

I have it still. I looked at it every day during the coronavirus crisis and thought of the hundreds of thousands working and volunteering for the good of their fellow citizens in our time, just as my great-aunt had done at another time of international crisis a hundred years before.

My father encouraged me to take whatever family bits and pieces I wanted. There would be no room for any of it in the hotel in Bayswater. As well as my great-aunt's framed certificate, this is what I chose:

- a miniature portrait of the original Dr Brandreth, the man who first created Brandreth's Pills in 1770
- a large oil portrait of the Pill Man himself, painted (not very well) around 1870
- the carriage clock the Pill Man gave to his son when Henry married Addie
- a wonderful painting of Prince, my great-grandfather's favourite dog, a huge white-and-black Newfoundland, described by Annie in her memoir as 'the guardian of all us children'
- the framed photographs of Virgie and Eugénie
- my great-grandparents' dining-room table – yes, the one at which they entertained their thirty guests at those seven-course dinners in the 1880s and 1890s.

We almost missed the dining table. It was in the front room at Poole, made comparatively small and square and covered with a green baize cloth. In a cupboard under the stairs we found the eight leaves that had to be added to the table to extend it to its full length. Two of the leaves were missing. My father recalled that his father had used them to make a handsome wooden case for a wireless in the 1920s when sound broadcasting was introduced and the BBC first took to the air. My father remembered the table well. He recalled being made to dance on it when he was a little boy.

I am writing this at that table. As I write, the Pill Man is looking down at me. The house I live in was built in 1881. I post my letters in a small red postbox built into the wall not twenty yards from my front door. It has been there since before Queen Victoria's Golden Jubilee. For much of my time, in my head I live in that Victorian world.

Though you don't think of me as a novelist, I have published nine novels and a lot of children's fiction. The novels sell especially well in France. (My wife says, 'You must have a particularly good translator.' I do. In France they take me seriously. Once, on French TV, I was interviewed at length by a critic who was under the misapprehension that I was Julian Barnes. When I told the real Julian Barnes about the mistake, the award-winning author of *Flaubert's Parrot* seemed distinctly unamused.)

The first of my novels is called *Who Is Nick Saint?* It features Clement Clarke Moore who wrote perhaps the most famous Christmas verse ever written – the one that begins: ' "Twas the night before Christmas, when all through the house / Not a creature was stirring, not even a mouse . . .' Moore's son was the Pill Man's next-door neighbour in Ossining.

My most recent novel is about Jack the Ripper and features George R. Sims who, you'll recall, as well as being a Ripper obsessive, wrote 'Christmas Day in the Workhouse'. All but one of the six novels in between are set in the late nineteenth century, in London or New York. My favourite children's story, *Max, The Boy Who Made a Million*, opens in the house that my great-great-grandfather once owned on Fifth Avenue.

In the 1870s, to promote his pills, Dr Brandreth published entertaining puzzle books, diaries and calendars. In the 1970s, I earned the bulk of my living writing and publishing puzzle books, diaries and calendars. My wife has often pleaded with me to forget my forebears and create something that's set in the here and now and doesn't depend for its inspiration on these family ghosts.

I find it difficult. I like the ghosts. I think of them as friends as well as relations.

Sometimes we take out the leaves from their hiding place

behind the curtains in our front room and extend the table. At a pinch, and borrowing the kitchen chairs, we can seat twenty-four – and when we do, for Christmas or a family birthday, I sit at the head of the table, where he sat, and think of my great-grandfather sitting there a hundred and fifty years ago squeezing a rubber bulb in his hand in the hope of lifting the guest of honour's soup bowl.

I am not a great one for practical jokes, but I like playing dinner party games and the one night in the year when we do try to use the table is on 23 April, when we mark Shakespeare's birthday with a dinner and a Shakespeare quiz. I try to do my great-grandfather proud and invite some of the great Shakespeareans of our day to join us. We don't have a day's good shooting to offer them, but we do have a Shakespeare quiz. What were the names of King Lear's dogs? (Tray, Blanch and Sweetheart.) Who was the first Black actor to play Othello in London? (Ira Aldridge, in 1825.) What are Hamlet's last words? ('The rest is silence.')

My father did enjoy practical jokes. He was especially fond of what he called his 'dribble glass'. It was a crystal wine glass with a built-in invisible crack around the rim. If one of my sisters had a boyfriend come to call, Pa would offer him a drink in the dribble glass and wait eagerly for the wine to spill on to the unfortunate young man's shirt and tie. It was an odd thing to do, partly because it was unkind (and Pa was a kind man), but chiefly because Pa always affected to be desperate to get his daughters married and off his hands.

His sense of humour was puckish. His party piece involved putting an empty cup upside down on a saucer and then flicking the cup into the air so that it landed the right way up, right in the middle of the saucer. One night, after supper in the kitchen, he showed me how to do the trick. He flicked up the cup and, as it landed, it broke the saucer clean in two. He did it again with a fresh saucer. Again the cup broke the saucer. By the time we got to bed, Pa had succeeded in smashing four cups and sixteen saucers – all the saucers we owned at the time, as I recall.

When we left the house in Poole, on the pavement outside, he took a deep breath, as though taking in a draught of fresh air, and said, 'End of an era – that's that.'

I didn't dare ask what had happened to the tortoise. They can live to be a hundred and fifty, so he may be hiding in his corner of the garden still.

I did not ask my father about his life. What I know of it is simply what he chose to tell me.

He told me how much he hated his boarding school: St Lawrence College, a minor public school on the East Kent coast, at Ramsgate. He made it sound like Hogwarts, without the girls or the magic. He seems particularly to have despised a boy called Perfect. I think my father may have had to be Perfect's fag, cleaning his boots and toasting and buttering his crumpets to order. Or perhaps Perfect, as head boy, may have been licensed to beat him. Every public school in the land allowed beatings in those days. I think Perfect was the only person I ever heard my father speak ill of. Needless to say, Perfect lived up to his name. He went on to become a Church of England clergyman and eventually returned to the school, this time as headmaster. In 2018, they opened the Canon Perfect Centre at the school in his honour. My father will have been spinning and spitting in his grave.

Pa hated school, but loved university. At Exeter College, Oxford, he had the time of his life. He read law (not too assiduously: he got a third-class degree) and discovered freedom, women, golf and theatre. As I write I am looking at the framed group photograph of the cast and company of the production of Milton's poetic drama *Samson Agonistes*, presented in the Fellows' Garden at Exeter College, in May 1930. My father played the part of Old Manoah, Samson's father. He was nineteen at the time, but in full make-up, with a flowing white wig and beard, he looks a convincing eighty. His performance was wonderful. I can vouch for that. He spoke the great speeches from the play at the least prompting for the rest of his life. If ever anything went wrong at home, Pa would immediately spread his arms wide and cry: 'Come, come; no time for lamentation now, / Nor much more cause.'

His performance was acclaimed – by the Poet Laureate among others. John Masefield came to the show, along with other literary luminaries of the day. The producer was a young English don, Nevill Coghill, a friend of C. S. Lewis and J. R. R. Tolkien, whose students had recently included the poet W. H. Auden and would one day include the actor Richard Burton. Coghill befriended my father and, later, me. I'm not sure the rest of my father's life ever lived up to those heady Oxford days.

University done, he had to settle on a career. There was still a bit of Brandreth Pill money trickling down to the founder's great-grandchildren, but it was no longer enough to live on and, within a few years, for the English end of the family, it dried up altogether. Pa wanted to be an actor – he had a histrionic gift. In his teens and twenties he learnt reams of prose and poetry by heart – the death of Bill Sikes from *Oliver Twist*, ballads by W. S. Gilbert and George R. Sims – and performed them successfully to family and friends. In the early days of cinema, before the talkies really got going, it wasn't unusual to have live performers appear onstage in front of the screen to entertain the audience between films. Pa persuaded the manager of his local Gaumont to let him have a go. It was not a success. Even if he looked a little like Harold Lloyd, a gangly young Englishman in glasses was no competition for Clark Gable and Gary Cooper.

If he couldn't be an actor, he would have liked to be a barrister and a politician, just like his great hero, F. E. Smith. Pa was born in Hoylake and brought up on the Wirral, where the most famous 'local boy made good' was Frederick Edwin Smith, always known as 'FE'. Smith started life as an estate agent's son; he ended up as the youngest Lord Chancellor since Judge Jeffreys and the first Earl of Birkenhead. Pa had all FE's celebrated courtroom exchanges at the tip of his tongue.

Judge: I have read your case, Mr Smith, and I am no wiser now than I was when I started.
FE: Possibly not, My Lord, but far better informed.

Judge: What do you suppose I am on the bench for, Mr Smith?
FE: It is not for me, My Lord, to attempt to fathom the inscrutable workings of Providence.

FE: At the time of the alleged assault, the accused admits that he was as drunk as a judge.
Judge: I think you will find, Mr Smith, that the expression is 'drunk as a lord'.
FE: As Your Lordship pleases . . .

My father wanted very much to be a barrister, but his father (an exact contemporary of FE) had been one and knew from experience how precarious life at the criminal bar could be. Pa was persuaded to take the safer, less exciting course. He became a solicitor.

The early 1930s were his 'salad days' when he was 'green in judgement' (he had any number of lines from Shakespeare at the tip of his tongue, too) and, judging from letters and diaries I have recently found, sometimes exuberantly happy, sometimes profoundly sad. After Oxford, when he went on holiday to Germany, it was the Germany of Sally Bowles and Marlene Dietrich. He met more than one *schönes Mädchen* and drank more than one Bavarian beer. Those were the highs. Then he returned to England and faced the humdrum reality of living alone in digs and being articled to a medium-sized firm of London solicitors specialising in road traffic offences. Those were the lows.

His digs were in a lodging house in Gower Street, in Bloomsbury, and it was from there, one Saturday morning in the run-up to Christmas 1936, that he took a thirty-minute walk that changed his life – and made mine what it is. He had read in the newspaper that at Selfridge's Department Store in Oxford Street they were selling a new board game that had taken America by storm. My father arrived at the shop as it opened and bought the first set of Monopoly sold in Britain.

He took it back to his digs in triumph and, before taking it home to his family in Poole for Christmas, thought he would like to try out the game himself. His landlady wasn't interested in board games, but she told him that a Canadian law student and her mother had recently moved into a room on the ground floor. Perhaps they'd be happy to play Monopoly with him one evening?

They were. And that's how my father met my mother. They played Monopoly and they fell in love.

Ten weeks later, they eloped.

4. My mother's secrets

My mother, Alice Addison, was born in India on 10 April 1914. She never left. India was her north, her south, her east, her west. India was her everything. Even as she lay dying, ninety-six years later, in an NHS hospital in Isleworth, West London, in her mind's eye she was surrounded by the babul and wild olive trees of her Indian childhood. She did not hear the rumbling of the traffic on the Brentford High Street. She was listening out for the familiar screech of the Indian pea-fowl and the caw of the Himalayan snowcock. Her last treat was one of her favourites: bread and butter spread with guava jelly. (She would have preferred ghee to butter, of course, but what can you expect in Isleworth? She didn't think the mangoes from the local Sainsbury's were up to much, either.) Three days before she died, I walked alongside her bed as two hospital porters trundled her from her ward to the side-room where they moved the patients who were nearing their end. The porter wearing a turban was holding my mother's hand. She looked up at him with the sweetest smile on her crinkled face and tears in her half-closed red-rimmed eyes and whispered, '*Dhanwaad Ji!*' – 'Thank you' in Punjabi.

When my mother died, in the early spring of 2010, her India had been long gone. It was Pakistan now. My mother was born in Rawalpindi (she always called it Pindi), the city conquered by the British Raj in 1849, Pakistan's fourth-largest city today. From 1851, it was the largest garrison town for the British Indian Army. In 1914, on the eve of the First World War, the Indian Army was one of the two largest volunteer armies in the world, with a strength of 240,000 men. The British Army at home only had a strength of 247,000 men.

My mother's father, Lance Addison, started out as a boy soldier in the Indian Army. He retired as Lieutenant Colonel Addison MBE in 1947, at the time of partition, when Pakistan was carved out of India and both were granted their independence.

I have a large, framed group photograph taken of him and his men before they set off for a mountain trek sometime in the 1920s. My grandfather is sitting, smiling, his hands on his bare knees, in the middle of the front row – a lone white face surrounded by thirty brown ones. The Indian army was his family and his life. His ladder, too. His forebears were shepherds and farm labourers from Lancashire.

My mother's mother, Mary Leach, was a missionary and a woman of near-fanatical Christian fervour. Behind her back (and to the undertaker at Kenyon's), my father made little jokes about Granny and the missionary position, but he would never have dared do so in her presence. She was not someone you'd trifle with. I have letters that she sent to Pa telling him that she could see the Devil sitting on his shoulder and that if he failed to 'smite Satan with all the strength at his command' the poor man would be condemned to an eternity in the burning fires of Hell. She meant it. And he knew it.

When I knew her, as a little boy in the 1950s, she was an old lady, white-haired, large and shapeless, dressed from neck to ankle in black like a rhinoceros beetle. Because of her bulk and trouble with her knees, she used to pull herself along the street holding on to the railings – complaining that there were no longer as many railings as there should be because they had been taken down to be used in the making of munitions during the war. She was formidable and forbidding, but I liked her. She taught me a card game called Fish, and when she died she left me £10 to buy a small drum kit.

Mary Leach was forbidding, but not grand. She came from humble stock and made no attempt to hide it. Her family hailed from Dumfries in Scotland, but she was born and brought up in Bradford in West Yorkshire. Her father worked in the Poor House there, initially as a warder supervising the poor and destitute as they queued for their porridge each morning and evening, and their bread and broth and beer at lunchtime. In time, John Leach worked his way up the workhouse ladder and was appointed Keeper of the Poor House and had his portrait painted by a local artist, John Hunter Thompson – who, incidentally, in his youth had been a friend of Branwell Brontë and painted the fine portrait of Charlotte Brontë that now hangs in the Brontë Parsonage at Haworth.

There is a touch of the Brontë, if not the Dickens, about my grandmother's story. Both her parents died in the last great pandemic of the nineteenth century and Mary, not yet a teenager, was sent from Bradford back to her grandparents in Dumfries. She was too much for them. They couldn't cope and did what many did in similar circumstances at the time: they packed the young girl off to Canada.

Between the late 1860s and the late 1930s, more than 100,000 'juvenile migrants' were despatched to Canada from the British Isles. The 'child emigration movement', as it was known, was well intentioned and well organised. Churches and charities sent boatloads of orphaned, abandoned and pauper children to start new – and better – lives in Britain's oldest Dominion. They arrived by ship and were sent, first, to 'receiving and distributing homes' for assessment, and then on to the families ready to welcome them either for adoption or, more often, as a source of cheap labour and domestic help. Inevitably, some were appallingly treated and abused, while others found new lives that were infinitely better than those they had left behind in British workhouses and slums.

Mary Leach was luckier than many, though she did not think so. She was adopted by a Toronto lawyer, William Bishop, and his wife, Margaret, good people by all accounts, who were looking for a daughter, a sister for their sons, someone they could dress up like a doll and, at the same time, expect to earn her keep by helping with chores around the house. Mary was a strong-willed child. She wanted to be neither a doll nor a housemaid. More than that, she did not want to have younger brothers foisted on her. And, most of all, she did not wish to change her name from Mary Leach to Mamie Bishop. The Bishops were insistent: she was their daughter now and they had always wanted a girl called Mamie. Mary rebelled. Her real parents might be dead, but she remembered them and she was adamant – as perhaps only a young teenage girl can be – that she would abandon neither her family name nor the Christian name she had been given at her baptism. Hurt and disappointed, the Bishops returned Mary Leach to the receiving and distributing home for reallocation.

Mary despised the name Bishop for the rest of her life, even when (or perhaps particularly when) it became the most celebrated name in Canada. Her might-have-been younger brother was Billy Bishop, destined to become Billy Bishop VC, CB, DSO & Bar, the most famous, the most decorated, the most daring Canadian and British flying ace of the First World War. In the fullness of time he became an Air Marshal. Toronto City Airport is named after him now.

I cannot tell you the name of the next family that took in my grandmother. All I know is that the head of the household was a kindly clergyman who allowed her to keep her name and to be herself. He also encouraged her to let her faith flower and to give her life over to the service of the Lord. Alleluia! She was up for that. They sent her to the Toronto Bible College whose mission was to train laypeople as 'Sunday School teachers, Pastors' Assistants, and as City, Home and Foreign Missionaries'. That is how she found herself, in her early twenties, in northern India, on a donkey, with a Bible, spreading the word of the Lord.

According to my mother, Mary was good at what she did – and fearless. She travelled hundreds of miles on her donkey, always unaccompanied, and succeeded in making converts to

Christianity in every village she visited. According to my father, the villagers took the religious tracts, the sweets and the bars of chocolate she brought with her, did their best to learn the Lord's Prayer to be obliging, and then, the moment she was back on her donkey and riding away, reverted immediately to their heathen – or rather, their Hindu or Islamic – ways.

On Sundays, missionary Mary went to matins in the Indian Army garrison church in Pindi. It was there that she spotted my grandfather, young Lance Addison, singing in the choir. She was thirty by then and ready to have children. He was ten years her junior, fair-haired, fresh-faced, British and, apparently, pliable. He agreed to marry her. They had two children in short order, my mother and my Uncle John, but the marriage was not a success.

In 1914, soon after my mother was born, the First World War broke out. ('Not as a direct consequence,' Pa liked to say.) By August 1914, the Indian army was sending men to fight in Europe, my grandfather among them. In all, more than a million Indian troops served overseas during the war and more than 74,000 Indian soldiers lost their lives in the service of the Empire. Lance Corporal Addison was one of the lucky survivors. It turns out he was one of the lads as well. He was away from India for seven long years and when not on active service he was based at Woolwich Arsenal. There he met a girl who worked in one of the munitions factories. They fell in love. They had an affair.

They wanted to marry. In a letter that cannot have been easy to write or to receive, my grandfather confessed all this to his wife back in Pindi. Understandably, she did not take it well. She might forgive, she would not forget, nor would she for a moment countenance the possibility of a divorce. A Christian marriage was indissoluble. 'We shall be man and wife,' she told him, 'until death do us part.' And so it was.

My grandmother knew her Bible. Galatians 6: 7 was one of her favourite texts: 'Be not deceived; God is not mocked: for whatsoever a man soweth, that shall he also reap.' When my grandfather's mistress died in the Spanish flu pandemic of 1919, my grandmother was not surprised.

My grandfather returned to Pindi. When my mother, aged eight, sitting on the veranda sipping lemonade and playing cards with her ayah, saw a young man in military uniform come up the steps and ask if her mother was at home, she looked at him and had no idea who he was. Her father had come home. As Robert Frost explained in a poem published at the beginning of that war: 'Home is the place where, when you have to go there, / They have to take you in.'

My grandfather lived with my grandmother while she remained in India. When she left with her children to go to Canada so that they could go to university there, he stayed on in India. They did not meet again. When she moved from Toronto to London with my mother in 1936, before they settled into their digs in Gower Street, my grandmother went to Woolwich Arsenal and, in the local churchyard, found where my grandfather's wartime mistress was buried – and danced on her grave.

She kept a photograph of the moment. I saw it once, years ago. My mother must have shown it to me. But who took the photograph? My mother, perhaps. I don't know. All I know is that Granny considered herself a married woman until her dying day and in her will bequeathed just one possession to her husband: her wedding ring.

In 1947, when partition and independence came to India and Pakistan, Grandpa Addison finally returned to England. He went to live in Accrington, in Lancashire, with his unmarried sister, Edith, the headmistress of the local primary school. I went to visit him quite often in the 1960s and 1970s. He was a sweet old man, with pink cheeks and white downy hair, who enjoyed a pipe and a game of cards. When he died, my father and I went up to Accrington for his funeral. My mother stayed in London.

I remember the funeral well. There were only a handful of mourners, all at the front of the church – and three elderly women right at the back. I noticed the women because I was surprised to see them there. In those days, forty years ago, women did not go to funerals in the North. My grandfather's sister wasn't there. Great-Aunt Edith was back at the house preparing the ham sandwiches and the fish-paste rolls for the wake. My father, joshing, suggested that the three elderly ladies might have been 'Grandpa's girlfriends'. The undertaker (from Kenyon's, of course – 'they're family'), overhearing my father, chipped in to explain that the elderly trio were simply 'regulars'. Apparently, at almost every funeral you will find at least two or three mourners who are just there for the outing and a change of scene.

The unhappiness of my grandparents' marriage notwithstanding, my mother had a blissful childhood. She spent much of it at boarding school. My father went to St Lawrence College, at Ramsgate on the Isle of Thanet, and hated it. My mother went to Lawrence College, at Ghora Gali in the Murree Hills, the foothills of the Himalayas, and loved every moment. It's where she wanted her ashes scattered. Lawrence College was a school for the children of Indian Army officers. It's still there, now as a school administered by the Pakistan army, but with the same motto: 'Never give in.' I spoke the school song at my mother's funeral.

> To set the cause above renown,
> To love the game beyond the prize.
> To honour, while you strike him down,
> The foe that comes with fearless eyes.

> To count the life of battle good
> And dear the land that gave you birth.
> And dearer yet the brotherhood
> That binds the brave of all the earth.

Today and here the fight's begun,
Of the great fellowship you're free.
Henceforth the school and you are one
And what you are, the race shall be.

My mother and the school were one, always. Without exaggeration, Lawrence College cropped up in every conversation I can remember having with her. She was only in India for the first eighteen years of her life, but the experience was seemingly so rich and rewarding, nothing else ever quite came up to it. Her best friends back in England were three girls she had known at school. Two had married clergymen and come to regret it. One came to regret it on her honeymoon. On the boat home from India, her husband said his prayers on his knees by his bunk and then, according to my mother, remained on his knees 'making the most horrible demands on his young wife'. They were innocent girls at Ghora Gali.

One of Ma's friends, Peggy Lynch, was hard of hearing and never married. She and her mother used to come to our home in the 1950s for Sunday lunch, and when my father was carving the chicken – a Sunday lunch treat in those days – he'd tease poor Peggy by asking if she'd like some breast, before correcting himself and saying, 'White meat! White meat! I do apologise. I didn't mean to use the "B" word.' But he did, of course. It was those little moments of naughtiness that kept him going.

My mother's only lifelong friends were schoolfriends. My mother's favourite meals were Indian. Karahi, haleem, halwa puri, lamb curry with saag on the side – these were a few of her favourite things. If you wanted to give her a present, you made your way to Drummond Street, by Euston Station, and bought her a box of absurdly syrupy Indian sweets.

At home she did not like to cook, and while my father had a few signature dishes – haddock simmered in milk was my favourite – he wasn't up to preparing Indian cuisine. Besides, he didn't like it. I didn't like it much, either. Pa and I infinitely preferred Chinese food, but Pa was in the business of keeping Ma mellow, so whenever we went out it was almost invariably for an Indian meal – and one at which she ordered her curry 'extra, extra hot' to underline her Indian credentials and, perhaps, I now see, to express her distress at not being still in Ghora Gali where she really belonged.

When she left India in the 1930s to go to university, her plan was to study Indian law and then return to the country of her birth – where she would practise law and marry the Maharajah of Jaipur. The Maharajah was just two years her senior and, according to my mother, quite taken with her. He was quite taken quite often. He was married three times, and his three wives lived in the same household together. In later life his girlfriends included a number of English ladies. Ma was not among them.

Ma had many romantic and dramatic tales of her Indian childhood. How close she was to the Maharajah I don't really know. I do know that returning to school one year, travelling on the train from Pindi to the Murree Hills, the brother of one of her friends foolishly put his head out of the train window and had it knocked off by a train coming in the opposite direction. His headless body fell back into the carriage.

In India, English girls had standing. Out of India, from the age of twenty, my mother spent a lifetime feeling insecure. She knew how India worked. She was never comfortable with the English way of doing things. She knew from the British newspapers and magazines she read in Pindi as a girl what the best of British was supposed to be – shopping at Harrods, dining at The Savoy, sending your children to Cheltenham Ladies' College and to Eton – but beyond that she was out of her depth.

As a little boy growing up in London, I loved going to Harrods. My mother must have taken me there once a week. I remember best the wonderful smells of cheeses and fresh flowers as we walked through the Food Hall, and the mysterious misshapen men in green uniforms who worked the lifts. I realise now that they were disabled war veterans. I thought then that they were green goblins taking me up to the enchanted kingdom on the third floor, home of the toy department, the children's hairdresser and the pet zoo. Until I was fourteen I only had my hair cut at Harrods. And after the haircut, and before tea in the Soda Fountain, we always walked around the pet zoo. I wanted my own monkey (they always had a selection for sale), and my mother wanted one, too (she had had one as a child in Pindi), but we had to agree with Pa that it wouldn't be fair to keep a monkey in a fifth-floor flat off the Earl's Court Road, so we settled instead on an Indian parrot called Mitou.

Mitou had green feathers, with flashes of yellow and pink, sharp black talons and a formidable scarlet-coloured beak. He would squawk loudly, but he wouldn't talk at all. Pa tried to teach him to say 'To be or not to be', to no avail. Because the Brandreths have always been animal lovers, Mitou was let out of his cage every day and allowed to fly around the sitting room. He would sometimes perch on Pa's head, which was fun. He would regularly poo all over the sofa, which was not. Mitou also liked to chip away at wood. He left little beak marks on the backs of our prized Ercol armchairs; he ate much of the gold-painted frame around the convex mirror that hung over the fireplace; and, most distressingly to Pa, he chewed away the spines of Pa's precious leather-bound six-volume 1745 edition of *The Complete Works of William Shakespeare*. (I loved those books. I loved the texture and smell of the yellowing pages. I particularly loved the old-fashioned typeface because the letter S looked like the letter F. 'Where the bee sucks, there suck I . . .')

Harrods told us Mitou could live for twenty-five years or longer. He lived with us for three. One morning Ma went into the sitting room and cried out in alarm, 'Where's Mitou? Where's he gone?'

The bird's cage was open. The sitting room window was open, too. Pa never admitted to the crime, but we all knew he was the guilty party. And years later, he tacitly acknowledged it when he began boasting that all the wild parakeets in West London were descended from Mitou.

My mother was at home at Harrods. My father was, too – despite the horrific bill that came in once a month. I can see him now, sitting at the kitchen table, drawing deeply on his cigarette, shaking his head and sighing, 'Oh God, the Harrods bill!' He'd tear it open and go through it line by line. 'How on earth can a child's haircut cost fifteen shillings?' he'd wail. 'It's criminal.' That said, he never missed the Harrods new year sale. He always took me along with him on the final Saturday, when he would buy himself a new bowler. The uniform of all professional men in London in the 1950s included a furled umbrella and a bowler hat. Whether he needed a new one or not, he always bought one at the January sale and allowed me to keep his old ones in my dressing-up box.

Because they met over the Monopoly board my father had bought there in 1936, my parents had a soft spot for Selfridge's, too. At Christmas, I was usually taken to see Father Christmas at both stores. In those days, you got to sit on Santa's lap. The gift you were given by Santa at Harrods was more expensive and came gift-wrapped, but I preferred the Selfridge's experience because there Santa had a sidekick called 'Uncle Holly' – a jolly Pickwickian figure, who wore an emerald-coloured tailcoat and sported a sprig of holly in his green top hat. For a while, I thought I might quite like to be Uncle Holly when I grew up.

My mother did not like to venture too far from home, but once or twice she took me to Gamage's, the huge department store at Holborn Circus, opened in the 1870s and famous for the size of its toy department and the fantastic model railway that ran the length of it. I was more into magic, dressing-up and puppetry than toy trains and racing cars, so Gamage's was a bit wasted on me. Not so Daniel Neal of Portman Square, the children's clothes shop where I went with my mother to get my school uniform. As an adult, I've always hated buying clothes, but as a child I was very happy being fussed over by the assistants at Daniel Neal. I particularly liked the X-ray machine in the shoe department. You tried on the new shoes and then, to check their fit, put your feet into the machine where 'thanks to the genius of fluoroscope' you could see your toes wriggling inside the shoes. Eventually, in the 1960s, the machines were banned because they exposed children, their parents and the shop assistants to unhealthy doses of radiation. 'Nothing lasts really,' as Celia Johnson said in *Brief Encounter* (one of my mother's favourite films), 'neither happiness nor despair. Not even life lasts very long.'

My mother was comfortable with the British brand names she was familiar with from childhood, so my Sunday best came from Harrods, my school uniform came from Daniel Neal and the name tapes had to be Cash's. Other, less expensive name tapes were to be had, but only Cash's would do. My mother spent hours sewing name tapes into all our clothes – and for her, I think, it was more than a labour of love. J. & J. Cash had been supplying woven name tapes to the children of the Empire since 1846. My mother felt secure following in the established tradition. In the 1990s, when I was an MP and I told her that one of my colleagues was Bill Cash MP, a direct descendant of one of the founders of Cash's, she was so happy: it felt like a validation of all the hours she had spent with her needle and thread sewing my name into my vests and underpants.

The colour of the embroidered lettering on my name tapes was always brown. On my sisters' name tapes it was always green – the colour of the uniform worn by the girls at Cheltenham Ladies' College, where all three of my sisters were sent to school. Long after they had left the school, their green serge knickers were still being used around our house as

64

dusters. The girls were sent to Col (as it was always known), because that was the boarding school to which English middle-class girls had been sent for a hundred years. It was a good school but, from first term to last, paying the school fees was a nightmare for my father and I am not sure that my mother will ever have felt entirely at ease around the other, more assuredly pukka parents. I didn't think about it then, but I realise now that the Col parents my own parents were most friendly with were a couple who could afford to send their daughters to the school because they had won a fortune on the football pools.

My mother knew about English society – she enjoyed P. G. Wodehouse, she read the *Daily Mail*, she subscribed to *The Lady* and *Nursery World* – and, though far from shy as a person, she was timid when it came to venturing into territory with which she was not wholly familiar. The society she did enjoy was the Anglo-Pakistan Society. She was happy going to their jamborees – meeting fellow sons and daughters of the Indian Empire and being entertained by the Pakistani High Commissioner or, more usually, his cultural attaché. Members of the Bhutto family had been to Lawrence College, so when I told Ma that I had come across Benazir Bhutto at Oxford and again, later, when I was an MP, she felt that was as it should be.

She was excited, too, to hear from me about the reception I attended at Buckingham Palace when I was chairman of the National Playing Fields Association. The Duke of Edinburgh, as president of the association, was hosting the party. Wheeling me around the State Dining Room, he said to me, 'Do you know the President of Pakistan? You can talk to him. Here he is.'

The Duke left me to it, and I did my best – treading carefully, uncertain of the current political climate in Pakistan, and so taking the safe option of talking about Lawrence College and my mother and the Maharajah of Jaipur . . . but I quickly sensed I wasn't getting very far. The small talk soon dried up and Prince Philip, seeing me flailing, came to the rescue and pulled me away.

I said apologetically, 'He wasn't an easy ride, and he didn't look quite how he looks in the photographs.'

'Who do mean?' asked the Prince.

'General Zia,' I said, 'the President of Pakistan.'

'He's the president of the Pakistan Playing Fields Association, you blithering idiot.'

My mother avoided social gaffes by avoiding society. Come to think of it, she avoided anything that took her out of her comfort zone. I remember us going to visit Auntie Hope in Mill Hill and my mother remaining in the car at the roadside while my father and I went inside for tea. Auntie Hope would come out with a cup of tea and a slice of cake and hand it to Ma through the car window. That was an odd way to behave – or so it seems now. Then I just took it for granted.

5. 'Balance on the wrong side'

Perhaps my mother was odder than I realised. Or perhaps she was just unhappy. She spent a lot of time in bed, and I know people with depression do that. In my teens and twenties, when she was in her forties and fifties, whenever anything cropped up that she wanted to avoid, she simply retreated to bed – demanding hot-water bottles be brought to her, along with nursery food: slices of bread and butter cut up into little squares, with guava jelly spread on top, and a glass of lemon barley water on the side.

Properly understanding someone else isn't easy, as I have discovered through more than half a century living with my wife, as I am discovering writing this book now – trying to work out what my parents were really like so I can share with you at least my version of them. How well did you, do you, know your mother?

'All that I am, or ever hope to be,' Abraham Lincoln famously said, 'I owe to my angel mother.'

Is that true of you and yours? I think all that I am I got from both of my parents, from my wife, from my children, from my sense of my own heritage, and from the fantasy worlds I grew up in and from which I have never quite escaped.

As a small boy, my favourite author was Enid Blyton – then (and still) the best-selling children's author in the history of publishing. As an adult, I got to know Enid Blyton's daughters and I asked them what Enid Blyton was like as a mother.

'She was a wonderful mother,' Gillian told me.

'Enid Blyton?' said Imogen. 'She wasn't a mother at all.'

My sisters' portraits of our mother would each be very different from mine – and more critical, perhaps.

Ma had five children: my three sisters, born in 1938, '39 and '42; then me, born in 1948; then another boy who miscarried to be replaced a few years later by an adopted son, my brother Ben. When Ben was adopted as a baby in 1958, my oldest sister, Jennifer, was twenty – and dead against it. She could see that my father, then forty-eight, didn't have the energy for another child – nor the money to feed, clothe and educate it. But Pa gave Ma anything she wanted.

Ma was wonderful with children once they were out of nappies – and until they were about ten. Then she wanted them packed off to boarding school. I was ten when Ben arrived. His natural mother was a girl from around the King's Cross area, I think. His father was a Cypriot. I remember being taken to see him when he was still a baby in hospital, suffering from jaundice. Ben is dead now, but he was a good guy. My parents gave him a good education and a happy childhood. He ended up in America, where he did a lot of first division amateur acting (his English accent helped), and earned his living as a carpenter. That's what killed him. He died of asbestosis.

Having Ben gave my mother several contented years. Having Ben also shortened my father's life. Of course, the smoking didn't help. Nor did the fortune teller who read Pa's palm at Dreamland in Margate when he was still a teenager and told him he would die aged seventy-one. She was very precise about it and he carried the prophecy with him, like a death sentence, all his life.

Like many of his generation, Pa was an inveterate smoker from his schooldays onwards. Over the years, the brands he favoured might vary – always rather classy brands: through the 1950s and 60s he moved from Craven 'A', to Olivier, to du Maurier – but 'Lady Nicotine' (as he called her) was the mistress who was with him, morning, noon and night. The sheets and blankets on his side of my parents' bed were always pockmarked with cigarette burns. Pa regularly fell asleep with a lit cigarette in his mouth.

My bedroom was between our kitchen and my parents' room. Late into the evening, night after night, before bed, my father sat at the kitchen table, with a cup of tea and a cigarette, sorting through the bills again and again, totting up the figures relentlessly in a vain attempt to make ends meet. I'd hear him sighing and muttering and then from her bed I'd hear my mother calling out, 'Cooee, ducky, is it time for cocoa? I'd love a cocoa. And maybe a fresh hot-water bottle?'

'Coming, hon,' my father would call back. ('Hon' was pronounced 'hun', as a diminutive of 'honey'.)

I would then listen as he performed the cocoa-making ritual: two spoons of cocoa powder, two spoons of demerara sugar, a splash of cold water, mix into a smooth paste. Add milk, warmed, not brought to the boil. He would take it through to her and then go back to the kitchen to top up her hot-water bottles. I waited for the noise of the whistle on the kettle. The noise of that whistle as the water came to the boil is one of my favourite sounds of childhood. He returned to her with her bottles and then collected the bucket she kept by the bedside to pee in and emptied it into the loo.

On the way back to the kitchen he always paused and looked at the pair of framed prints that hung on the corridor wall just outside my bedroom. Both prints featured a drawing of an early-Victorian gentleman in his nightcap and dressing gown, sitting in his counting house, spectacles on nose, quill pen in hand, account books lying open on the table in front of him. In one picture, he looks as merry as a grig. In the other, he is utterly downcast. Below the pictures the legends read: 'Balance on the right side – happiness', 'Balance on the wrong side – misery'.

That was the story of my father's life and it's told in the scraps of paper on the table in front of me now – pages torn from notebooks covered in figures. That he kept so many of them shows how the calculations weighed on him. They wore him down. Eventually, they wore him away.

I've picked up one at random. I'm not sure of the year – the late 1950s, I'd guess.

JULY position
OWING

1. To Bank – overdraft £200
2. To Bank – agreed quarterly repayment £75
3. Surtax – put off from Jan by consent £153
4. Rent – due 30 June £100
5. Cost of wash basin – £25
6. Car deposit – £176
7. Insurance – £18
8. School fees – £97
9. Wallace Greig – balance of charges £60
10. Enton Hall – £57
11. Gapps – £30
12. Harrods – £24
? Italy holiday?
? Gyles to France?

I am sure I went to France that year. I went to France every year. And my parents and Ben may have gone to Italy, too. Ma insisted on holidays – regardless of the cost.

So that July my father was committed to £1,015 of expenditure against an income, according to his notes, of £908 before tax. And that expenditure did not include day-to-day expenses, nor the bills that would fall due at the end of the quarter: the service charge on the flat, the TV rental, the electricity and the telephone. My sisters were teenagers then and making a lot of telephone calls. Whenever they were on the line, Pa hovered close to the phone, muttering, 'Every call costs money, every minute costs money. If he's that interested, let him call you!'

Pa never got on top of his finances. As a senior partner in a medium-sized firm of London solicitors, he was earning good money, but he always spent more than he earned and as a consequence was never free from anxiety. He had a humorous, engaging and persuasive manner and he used it to the full – negotiating with the bank to extend the overdraft, negotiating with the tax man to delay the tax, negotiating with his partners to free up some cash by buying some of his shares, negotiating with one of his father's schoolfriends, a rich old gentleman called Shirley Jones, for 'another small subvention' to help tide him over while he was waiting, hoping, Micawber-like, for something to turn up.

Something did turn up now and again. Relations died and left legacies – some quite substantial, but none ever quite enough. As the years went by, Pa took to selling family bits and pieces, but nothing fetched as much as he hoped. He sold his mother's wedding dress and her Victorian porcelain dolls for a reasonable amount, but his grandfather's prize salmon (preserved in a case of formaldehyde) and the boxes of cigarette cards he had collected as a boy – 'Heroes of the Great War', 'Sportsmen of our Time', 'Film Stars of the 1920s' – did not bring in very much.

Neither of my parents was personally extravagant. Outside the Harrods sale, they did not buy expensive clothes. My mother had her hair done once a week at a salon in Chelsea called Josephine's, but she did not hanker after perfume or jewellery. She did like cut flowers. I remember the year my father forgot her birthday, and got me out of bed at four in the morning so I could keep him company as we sneaked out of the house and drove to Covent Garden market. No one would sell him a simple bunch of flowers, so Pa bought a whole bucket of gladioli and we managed to get them home and on to the breakfast table before Ma woke up. Every Saturday morning I kept him company, too, as he drove her to her ten o'clock hair appointment at Josephine's. We would then wait for her in the ABC tea room nearby, where Pa always had a Bath bun with his tea and I always had two rounds of buttered toast with strawberry jam. He usually popped a small handful of sugar lumps into his coat pocket while no one was looking. He was always good at the small economies.

Pa smoked, but cigarettes were much less expensive then and, though my parents enjoyed the odd glass of wine, it was never vintage stuff. They belonged to the generation that enjoyed Mateus Rosé and Chianti in a bottle wrapped in straw. Outside of the Indian and Chinese meals, they weren't fancy eaters. Gapps, the local grocers, delivered the food and it was standard stuff: fruit, veg, pressed meats and sardines in tins; fish for Friday; sliced cold ham and cutlets or a chicken for the weekend. Meat rationing did not end until 1954. We did treat ourselves to Gold Top milk, and Pa and I took it in turns to have the cream from the top on our breakfast cereal – Shredded Wheat for him, Weetabix for me.

Wallace Greig, the Harley Street dentist, was an extravagance, too, I suppose, but Sir Michael Redgrave, the actor, and his family went to him. Wallace Greig was very good, and my father's teeth were very bad, so it must have seemed worth it at the time. I did not trust the dentist. On my first visit to him, aged six, he forced a large black rubber mask over my nose and mouth and pumped me full of gas. That's the way anaesthesia was administered at the dentist in those days. Pa noted derisively that Wallace Greig insisted on giving each of us – two adults and five children – a comprehensive check-up at the start of every September in the hope of being paid by the end of December so that he could afford to take his annual trip to the West Indies in mid-January.

The London mansion flats we lived in were always spacious, but never grand. The furniture was serviceable. There was fitted carpet in the sitting room, Indian rugs in the bedrooms, linoleum in the kitchen and the corridor. If you can remember the television series *Rumpole of the Bailey*, and can picture the flat the Rumpoles lived in, you will know exactly what my parents' flat was like. I don't think we had a cleaning lady. We had a carpet sweeper, I recall, that distributed more fluff than it collected, and a squeegee mop with a broken handle held together with one of Pa's old pyjama cords. We didn't have a washing machine. My sisters and I took the laundry to the launderette once a week (curiously, I enjoyed watching the washing go round and round: I studied my reflection in the porthole and pretended I was looking into a film camera and adjusting my features for my close-up) and Ma sent the sheets and Pa's shirts to the London Laundry Company. They were collected from the flat every Wednesday in a handsome grey box held together with leather straps, and returned the following week, with each item beautifully wrapped in white tissue paper. My mother wasn't interested in domestic chores. My father always did the washing-up. I can picture him standing at the sink, his cigarette ash falling into the soapy water. It's why at home, to this day, at the end of the evening I always clear up in the kitchen. I like to wipe the surfaces exactly as my father did.

From the time I was born until she was a relatively old lady, my mother was always, more or less, overweight. I am not sure why. I suppose she ate too much – or too much of the wrong things. She did love those Indian sweets. Perhaps she ate too much because she was unhappy – or angry? I don't know. I do know that it was a constant issue, a running sore. She bought all her clothes from a shop called Evans Outsize and was permanently on one kind of diet or another. Once or twice a year, she went for a week or ten days to Enton Hall, or Edstone Hall, or Tunstall Hall, 'health hydros', where, according to Pa, 'For a mere twenty-five guineas, you spend a week living off lemon juice and lettuce leaves and being beaten with birch twigs.'

Pa always drove Ma to the fat farm (as he called it) and

I sometimes went with him. She always planned to lose a stone, but never did. This could have been because Pa would visit her in her room in the evening and at weekends, on the sly, climbing in through her window with secret supplies – bacon sandwiches and bags of Indian sweets – hidden in the pockets of his raincoat. I remember the time we went to collect her from her favourite health hydro in Warwickshire. She had already checked out, but Pa said, 'Don't worry. I know where she'll be.'

We found her at a corner table, upstairs in the Cobweb Tea Rooms in Stratford-upon-Avon, polishing off a buck rarebit.

'I know it's naughty, ducky,' she giggled nervously, 'but I do like a little treat.'

'I know,' said Pa, with a happy smile. 'Who's bought his hon a little box of jalebis?'

Eventually, twenty years after my father died, the weight problem disappeared. My mother met a doctor in California who told her only to eat as much food as she could fit into the palm of her hand. She did as she was told. She was a child in so many ways – albeit a very bright one. At school in India she sat in the middle of the front row in lessons and invariably came top of the class. She got into the University of Toronto, the University of London and Oxford University at a time when 90 per cent of university students were men. Later in life, she became a pioneering teacher, working with children with dyslexia, and was viewed by the parents of those children as nothing less than a miracle worker. In a nutshell, she was happiest and at her best with people from India and Pakistan, and with children aged between five and eleven years of age.

Why am I telling you all this about my parents?

Because this is an autobiography, and Wordsworth was right: 'The Child is father of the Man.' I am what Ma and Pa made me. My wife has managed to make a few improvements along the way, but, fundamentally, I am my parents' creature – still

74

locked inside my own childhood, still living with my childhood dreams and fears.

Michèle says to me quite often (and often a little despairingly), 'Gyles, you're almost seventy-five and you're still trying to please your parents, aren't you?'

I suppose I am. I owe them everything. It is the least I can do.

6. I am born

My parents were married on Monday, 15 March 1937. I was born on Monday, 8 March 1948. A good deal happened in between, including the Second World War, the deaths of my uncle and my grandfather, and the births of my three sisters.

My parents married in secret because they knew none of their parents would give the marriage their blessing. They were of a marriageable age (Pa was twenty-six, Ma was twenty-two), but they were both young for their years and quite naïve. My father booked the wedding at Marylebone Register Office. He turned up on the right day at the right time with his bride-to-be and a wedding ring – and a little joke for the registrar about the ides of March.

'Where are your guests?' asked the registrar.

'It's just us,' said Pa.

'Where are your witnesses?' asked the registrar.

'What witnesses?' said Pa. 'It's just us.'

'There must be two witnesses to the marriage,' explained the registrar. He kindly offered the services of his clerk as one of them.

Pa ran out into the Marylebone Road and persuaded a flower seller outside Marylebone Station to abandon his stall for fifteen minutes to serve as the other.

Married, excited, anxious, the happy couple returned to their digs in Gower Street and broke the news to the bride's mother. Mrs Addison (Missionary Mary) was appalled. She raged, she railed, she ranted, she wept. She invoked the wrath of God. She wept some more.

The chastened newly-weds set off on their honeymoon. Pa

had booked a caravan somewhere near the coast in Dorset. They arrived after dark and in the rain. The caravan was small and cold and not kitted out for romance. The single bunk beds were narrow and uncomfortable. Beware the ides of March!

Undaunted, the young lovers returned to London. They moved to rooms in London Street, behind Paddington Station. They bought themselves a double bed. They bought themselves a car, a Morris Cowley. My father kept the bill:

Price of car	£8. 0. 0.
Insurance	£4. 10. 0.
Tax	£1. 13. 0.
	£14. 3. 0.
Deposit	£6. 0. 0.
	£8. 3. 0.
HP Charges	£1. 10. 0.
	£9. 13. 0.

He agreed to pay off the balance at the rate of £1 a month and, with a little help from his parents, he managed it.

His parents did not approve of him marrying (he was too young; it was too soon), but they liked my mother when they met her. They could see she was a good Christian girl. She was studious and wore spectacles: she wasn't flash or flighty. They were sorry, of course, that her parents were separated. They were sorrier still that her mother, Mrs Addison, was having to live so modestly, getting by on whatever her husband sent over from Rawalpindi. Charlie (as they called my father) was only just starting out as a solicitor. Funds would be tight. The Brandreth business in America had diversified and was still profitable – now run by one of the founder's grandsons and manufacturing porous plasters, nail polish, liners for ammunition boxes and 'Havahart' traps (for catching wild animals humanely), as well as the original little vegetable pills – but the British Brandreths weren't getting a penny of any of it.

That didn't bother my parents. Who needs money when you've got each other and a new double bed? (In Italy they call bed 'the poor man's opera'.) Charlie and Alice were married in March 1937. Jennifer Hope arrived in May 1938. Virginia Helen arrived in June 1939.

And then, in September 1939, war broke out.

The arrival of baby daughters meant my mother had to abandon her university studies before taking her degree – to her (and especially her mother's) eternal regret.

The arrival of the Second World War meant my father had to join up.

Pa started out a lance corporal in Field Security, stationed in Deptford, Bermondsey and Rotherhithe.

He ended up, six years later, a major at the British Military Government HQ in the North Rhine-Westphalia region, stationed in Düsseldorf, Cologne and Aachen. In between, he found himself, mainly on a motorbike, with the Intelligence Corps in Algiers, Miliana, Tunis, Bari, Bruges and Bonn. In the spring of 1944, he took part in the capture of Monte Cassino (a campaign that resulted in 55,000 Allied casualties) and in April 1945, he was in Caserta with Field Marshal Alexander at the signing of the agreement that formalised the surrender of German forces in Italy, ending the Italian campaign.

None of this did he ever talk about. As I recall, there were only three wartime episodes in his repertoire of anecdotes. The first involved him going to an Arab dentist in Algiers. The dentist looked into Pa's mouth and told him, in Arabic but with sufficient gestures to make his meaning understood, that he had a rotten tooth that had to come out. Pa nodded. The dentist nodded – and smiled. The smile alarmed my father because it revealed a mouth containing a black tooth, a yellow tooth and a gold tooth all in a row, as well as gaps where at least two other teeth should have been. Continuing to chatter away merrily in Arabic, from his trouser pocket the dentist now produced a long, thin piece of string and, brooking no argument, proceeded to tie one end of the string tightly around Pa's rotten tooth. He then tied the other end of the string around the handle of his open surgery door.

'*Hza saeidaan!*' whooped the dentist as, with tremendous force, he slammed the door shut and Pa's tooth shot from his mouth like a bullet from a Luger.

Pa always claimed the Arab dentist was considerably more efficient, and *very* considerably cheaper, than Mr Wallace Greig of Harley Street.

Pa also liked to talk about the theatre productions he staged during the Italian campaign. His leading actor gloried in the name of Captain Clutterbuck and, according to my father, Clutterbuck's finest hour was ruined by an unexpected German raid. I don't remember the detail of the story, only the punchline: 'And the Kraut – what a critic!'

The story Pa told with most relish dated from 1940, England's darkest hour. He was about to be posted overseas, he knew not where. Overhead, the Battle of Britain – what the Germans called '*die Luftschlacht um England*' ('the Air Battle for England') – was being fought. Its outcome was uncertain. The Blitz over London, where my parents and two baby sisters were living, lasted eight months, from 7 September 1940 to 11 May 1941. My mother had come to England from Canada, and her brother was still living there. British women and children were being evacuated to Canada. Pa decided his wife and babies should be among them. He arranged a passage, booking the best berth on offer from the Ellerman Lines, and took my mother and the girls up to Liverpool.

When they reached the dockside, they found there was a problem. Two steamships had been due to sail. The second had been cancelled and its passengers transferred to the first.

In consequence, Mrs Brandreth and her family were being moved from their promised berth on the first deck to another – just as good, apparently – on the fourth deck. My father kissed his wife and baby girls goodbye at the Customs shed and took the train back to London.

At two in the morning, stretched out across the double bed, sleeping the sleep of a man who has solved a problem and done the right thing by his wife and bairns, Pa was woken by a desperate rat-tat-tatting on the front door. He ignored it at first, but eventually, of course, he answered. And there they were: his wife, Alice, in tears, with his young daughters in her arms, and their cases all around them.

When Ma had boarded the ship she hadn't been shown to a berth on the fourth deck. She was taken to a small cabin on the eighth deck, at the very bottom of the ship. She had to get to it by ladder. With two babies, it was impossible. She disembarked in considerable distress and made her way back to London.

Three days after the ship left Liverpool on its way to Quebec, the SS *City of Benares* was torpedoed by a German submarine, 253 miles west-south-west of Rockall. The ship sank within 30 minutes, with heavy loss of life, including the deaths of 77 evacuee children.

Intriguingly, one of the survivors was a fifteen-year-old boy named Anthony Quinton. I say 'intriguingly' for a reason. Since I first read them in my twenties, I have loved the twelve novels that make up *A Dance to the Music of Time*, Anthony Powell's fictionalised portrait of English society in the mid-twentieth century. Once highly acclaimed, the novels have rather fallen from favour now, but I loved everything about them, most particularly the way the same characters danced unexpectedly into and out of the narrator's life at different stages of it. So it was for me with Anthony Quinton, who grew up to become one of the foremost academic philosophers of his day and a Fellow of New College, Oxford. That's where I first met him, in December 1966, when he interviewed me after I applied for a place there.

I last met him in December 1999, by which time he had become Lord Quinton, President of Trinity College, Oxford, Chairman of the British Library, star of *Round Britain Quiz*. The occasion was what promised to be a memorable evening at the Garrick Club in London.

My friend Iain Sproat (former MP, former Arts Minister) had called me. 'We are having a dinner in honour of Anthony Powell on his ninety-fourth birthday – a select group, Tony Quinton in the chair, should be quite special. Would you and Michèle like to come?'

We said we'd love to. Delighted to be asked ourselves, we thought about it and realised it was the kind of event that our friend, the actress Joanna Lumley, would love too. I called Sproatie back. 'We have a friend who is a huge fan of Anthony Powell's. I know she'd be excited to come to the dinner. Would there be room?'

'All the places have gone,' said Sproatie, with a heavy sigh. 'Everyone wants to be there. Sorry.'

'It's Joanna Lumley.'

'Oh,' chirruped Sproatie, suddenly changing his tune. 'I'm just looking at the seating plan. I think we can manage something. She'll have to squeeze in next to me, I'm afraid.'

The great night came. We all gathered at the Garrick at 7.30 p.m., in a private room as planned. Some guests had brought first editions to be autographed; others had come with gifts for the great man. Joanna arrived bearing a present, a home-made birthday card and a special hand-picked posy of country flowers for Mr Powell. We stood around, clutching our gifts, having drinks, making small talk, feeling oddly nervous and excited, waiting for 'the arrival'.

At eight o'clock, Sproatie turned to the room and announced, 'Lord Quinton, ladies, gentlemen, dinner is served. Take your places, if you please.'

A hush fell.

'It's only just eight,' said Joanna. 'Shouldn't we wait for the guest of honour?'

Sproatie laughed. 'Anthony Powell's not coming,' he said. 'He's ninety-four.'

'We know he's ninety-four,' I said, blanching, 'that's why we're all here.'

'You didn't think he was coming, did you?'

Well, yes, we did, rather . . . We sat down, not knowing what to say.

Lord Quinton looked around the table, beaming. 'Worse things happen at sea,' he said, genially – which is when I remembered he was one of the survivors of the sinking of the SS *City of Benares*. After dinner, he went on to lead an interesting discussion on *A Dance to the Music of Time*.

Meanwhile, during dinner, my friend Sproatie spent a lot of time talking about the edition of *The Complete Works of Pushkin* that he was publishing – apparently under the auspices of Mrs Gorbachev. He was selling the complete set for a mere £1,200! Alarmingly, across the table, I heard Joanna agreeing to buy one. I watched, appalled, as she took out her chequebook and handed Sproatie the money. The books sit, unopened, on the top shelf of her bookcase to this day.

Where were we? Oh, yes, September 1940. The sinking of the SS *City of Benares*.

I followed through the thread of Anthony Quinton because I am realising as I write this that my life – like yours – is made up of a motley collection of threads and I see now – for the first time because I have not thought about it before – that the threads of my life stretch back to a time before I was born. For example, a page or so ago I mentioned the gloriously named Captain Clutterbuck, who served in Italy with my father in 1944 and could have been a character in *A Dance to the Music of Time*. Well, Captain Clutterbuck turned up in my life thirty years later, in the mid-1970s, when he was running a company creating cartoon and stop-motion animation programmes for television – shows like *The Herbs* and *The Wombles*. He brought Paddington Bear to the small screen for the first time and then, because of his fondness for my father, gave me the little Paddington used for the TV series, along with Paddington's furniture (his bed, his armchair, his kitchen stove), for the teddy bear museum my wife and I founded in Stratford-upon-Avon in the 1980s. That little Paddington now lives in the Brandreth Bear House at Newby Hall in North Yorkshire.

It was Graham Clutterbuck who introduced me to Michael Bond, creator of Paddington Bear. Michael told me that Paddington's personality was inspired by his own father. According to Michael, Bond Senior was unfailingly courteous. On the family's summer holidays on the Isle of Wight he always wore his hat when swimming in the sea, in case he needed to raise it to anyone. I already knew that Paddington was based on a bear that Michael had bought for his wife in the toy department at Selfridge's – the place, you will recall, where my father bought the game of Monopoly that led to him meeting my mother.

So there they were in 1940, my mother and father, expecting to be apart for the rest of the war, but thrown together again. If they hadn't been, who knows what would have happened? I might never have been born. Certainly, my third sister, Hester, would not have been conceived in 1941.

In the event, and judging from the scores of affectionate letters they exchanged when my father was at the front in North Africa and Germany, both my parents had what people rather curiously call 'a good war'. I once asked an eminent psychiatrist why it is that people of my parents' generation so often spoke about the Second World War as being, in some ways, the happiest time of their lives. My mother lived in London through the Blitz. The house she lived in was bombed.

My sister Jennifer was blown out of her pram by an explosion in the next street. My father's brother was killed in the blackout. In North Africa and Italy, my father was involved in campaigns that claimed more than 100,000 Allied lives. How on earth could anyone talk of any of that being part of the happiest time of their life?

'It's easy to explain,' said the psychiatrist. 'Yes, bombs were falling in London during the Second World War, but consequently there was a sense of community in London, a sense of shared purpose and common values, a feeling that "we're all in this together" – and that makes people very happy indeed. And, yes, your father was at the front, on and off, for six years. The soldiers, the sailors, the airmen who fought in the Second World War were risking their lives on a daily basis – but, on a daily basis, they were also being *tested*. All the research shows that being tested, being challenged, is a key element to finding happiness. You very rarely find people who are sitting around, not doing very much, who are happy.'

My father was tested by the war, and not found wanting.

I have seen photographs taken of him on leave. He began the war looking like Harold Lloyd. He ended it looking like Jack Hawkins. And with VE Day in May 1945 came a personal liberation. He was still serving in the army, but he was looking to the future. I think because his elder brother had died – the brilliant brother who was the golden boy, the brother whose name I never heard my father mention – Pa emerged from the family shadows and found the confidence – and the courage – to do what he had always wanted to do. He ceased to be a solicitor. He applied to the Inner Temple and qualified to be a barrister.

The dream did not last, but it was sweet while it did.

Demobilised in December 1946, Pa was called to the Bar in 1947 and went immediately to Germany to serve in the legal division of the Allied Control Commission. After the war, each of the main allies – the British, Americans, Russians and French – gave themselves a chunk of defeated Germany and set up a civil and military authority to administer their own occupied zone. They needed British barristers to show the Germans how justice should be done. Pa was the man for the job.

As a boy, alongside the great F. E. Smith, Pa's hero had been Sir Edward Marshall Hall KC, known as 'The Great Defender', the barrister reckoned to have saved more people from the hangman's noose than any other. Thanks to Pa's stories, I could tell you far more about Marshall Hall and his great cases ('The Camden Town Murder', 'The Green Bicycle Case', 'The Brides in the Bath'), his unhappy marriage, his spell in parliament, than I can about Pa's own family.

Marshall Hall was a noted wit, and Pa had all his best courtroom quips ever at the ready. His favourite, as I remember, had occurred during the trial of an Irish labourer. At one point the presiding judge turned to Marshall Hall and remarked, 'Is your client not familiar with the maxim *res ipsa loquitor*?'

To which Marshall Hall had immediately responded, 'My Lord, on the remote hillside in County Donegal where my client hails from, they talk of little else.'

Pa did score one notable success in the British military courts in Germany. A journalist was charged with treason – a capital offence – for allegedly giving succour (and a revolver) to Arthur Kannenberg, Hitler's butler at Berchtesgaden, the Führer's holiday home in Bavaria. The journalist had met the butler in a barber's shop in Berchtesgaden in 1945, not long after Hitler's suicide and the German surrender, and believed him when he claimed he was being threatened by former SS men and gangs of 'Werewolves' – members of the Nazi resistance movement set up in 1944. The journalist befriended the butler (and gave him the revolver) to get a story. It was a complicated case, involving seven charges, missing witnesses, and arguments about international law. But the good news is: Brandreth got him off.

'You saved my life,' the journalist wrote to my father, in a letter Pa proudly pasted into his scrapbook. '*You saved my life* – I don't believe a lesser counsel could have done it.'

I have got the scrapbook on the table as I write this. As well as all the cuttings featuring 'The Case of Hitler's Butler', there are accounts of Pa's other courtroom triumphs, both as an advocate and, later, still in Germany, as a magistrate. *Picture Post* magazine featured him across three pages, showing their readers how: 'Charles Brandreth presides over a trial of Austrian child traffickers and demonstrates to the Germans how British justice is done.'

As part of the Allied Control Commission in Germany for six years after the Second World War, my father *was* somebody. And my mother, living in Germany with him, almost felt at home again. The British zone in occupied Germany was like British India before independence – the British were the benevolent white imperialists and the defeated Germans were the natives. In India, my mother (descended from Lancashire shepherds and the Keeper of the Poor House in Bradford) had been brought up surrounded by ayahs and house servants, punkah wallahs and houseboys. In Germany, she lived in style again, with a butler, a cook, a girl to help around the house, and a nanny to look after the children.

These were good years for Alice and Charles Brandreth, and the best thing about these good years is that I was born.

I was born late on a Monday night in the British Forces Hospital in North Rhine-Westphalia, in Wuppertal, a city that had been one of the most bombed in Germany (40 per cent of all its buildings had been destroyed during the war) and is now the greenest in the country, famous for its woods and parks. This note from my father to my mother was written a few hours before my arrival.

Düsseldorf
8 Mar 48

My beloved,
Miss Prince has been making enquiries for me at the hospital and they
say I ought not to come up tonight. But I'll be with you in the morning,
or as soon as they'll let me see you.

    Dearest sweetheart, I am at your side now in spirit helping you bear
up in your pain. Neither of us will get much sleep tonight!

    I have just seen that Ki has had a baby girl (Patricia Rosemary), so
you'll be in the fashion with a daughter.

    I care more for you, my darling, than for anyone else and my only
prayer is that you are soon safe and well again. God bless you, my
dearest ducky.

    Your C

Gould is waiting to take this note. I am hoping he may bring some
small message from you. My only one to you is I LOVE YOU!

As I type this, my father's note – written on a small visiting
card in his clear, elegant hand – sits propped up against my
computer screen. I have it – and the envelope in which it was
delivered to my mother – because my father kept all his papers.
To the side of my desk sit three of my father's metal deed
boxes, stuffed to overflowing. There are several more in the
basement. The ones on the floor here are marked (in my
father's hand): 'Gyles – memorabilia'.

Every aspect of my life has been recorded. From the
moment of my birth onwards, my father kept everything:
notes, cards, correspondence, medical records, school reports,
photographs, press cuttings, *everything*.

I arrived in the world feeling special because to my parents,
I know, I was special. Apart from anything else, I was a boy!

That mattered to my father. He had had three girls – and he
loved them – but he was ready for a son. He would have made
the best of having a fourth daughter – of course, he would.

He was reconciled to the prospect. As he mentioned to Ma in his note, their good friends Ki and Ronnie Price had just had a girl. In fact, had I been a girl my mother had already agreed I should be called Mercedes because she knew that, next to a boy, that's what my father most wanted: a Mercedes.

He never got the car (and I felt bad in the 1970s when I bought my first Mercedes because it should have been his, not mine), but he did get the boy: Gyles Daubeney, named after my illustrious fifteenth-century forebear, and baptised by the Anglican vicar of Wuppertal with three godparents whose names I had quite forgotten until I came across my baptismal certificate just now. I can't pretend they proved to be very useful, or even attentive, as godparents, but I am not complaining because I am a godfather four times over and I have done next to nothing for my godchildren. I can just about remember their names: I certainly don't remember their birthdays. I should have done what Noël Coward did with his many godchildren and sent them each a card on *my* birthday.

Speaking of godparents, the Duke of Edinburgh told me when I was writing his biography that a German newspaper had reported that His Royal Highness had twenty-four illegitimate children and that this had been confirmed by Buckingham Palace. It transpired that the newspaper had misinterpreted 'godchildren' for 'love children'.

That I was the long-longed-for son certainly made a difference to how I was treated within the family. I was the miracle child, the golden wonder. My wife says that my father was still 'banging on about it' when she first met him, twenty years after I was born. I remind her that the Emperor Napoléon Bonaparte famously said that if you want to understand a man you should look at what the world was like in the year that man turned twenty-one. It was in 1931 that my father turned twenty-one, only three years after women in Britain won universal suffrage on the same terms as men. (It was 1944 before French women were given the vote.) My father reflected

The tomb of Sir Gyles Daubeney at Westminster Abbey

Jeremiah Brandreth, executed 1817

Cousin Eugénie de Montijo, wife of Napoleon III and last Empress of France

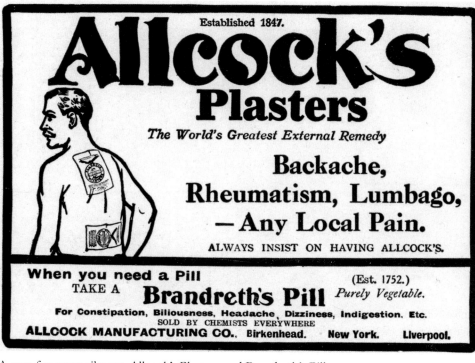

A cure for every ailment: Allcock's Plasters and Brandreth's Pills

The founder of the family fortune:
Benjamin Brandreth, 1809-1880

Tatcho – the George R Sims' hair restorer

GB's grandfather, Major Lance Addison, third from right, with fellow Indian Army officers

GB's mother, Alice, with her older brother, John, and their mother, Mary Addison, in Rawalpindi in 1915

Charles Brandreth as Old Manoah in Milton's *Samson Agonistes*, Oxford, 1930, second from left

GB's father, far left, with his older brother, Benjamin, and his two sisters, Helen and Hope, at the outbreak of the First World War, 1914

Three generations of Brandreth barristers: Benjamin Brandreth, Charles Brandreth, Benet Brandreth – with young GB in 1961 trying on his father's wig and young Cornelius Brandreth trying on his father's QC's wig in 2019

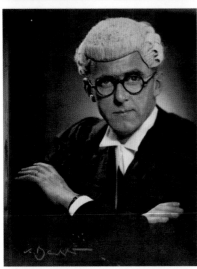

With Julian Fellowes, 1953

With Jane Sarah Dorothea Hoos, riding Muffin the Mule, Broadstairs, 1953

[*left*] GB, ready to travel, 1954
[*right*] GB on the balcony at Kensington Mansions, 1956

GB and Pa, 1954

GB and Ma, Broadstairs, 1956

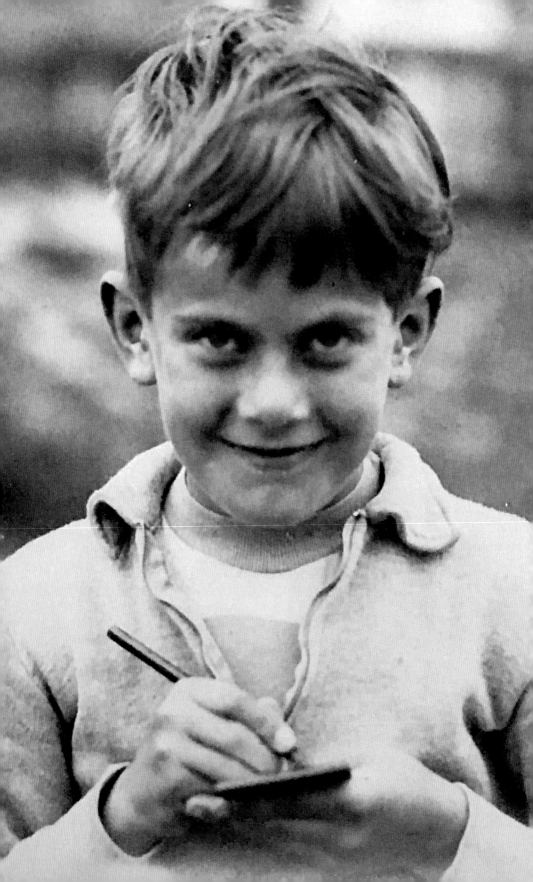

GB, trying to look angelic, in the choir at Holy Trinity Brompton, London, 1957

GB giving his all on stage at the Pavilion on the Sands, Broadstairs, 1958, with Cecil Barker

Betteshanger School choir, summer 1959: GB front row centre; standing left, Major Douch and Mr Stocks; standing right, Mr Gargiulo and Mr Glading

GB at Betteshanger, the first summer, 1959, photographed by Mr Glading

GB with Ma, Pa and Ben on holiday in France, 1961

In Mr Glading's room at Betteshanger, summer 1961

the views and values of his generation. When he was at Oxford, aged twenty-one, there were virtually no women undergraduates and, up until the mid-1930s, the females who appeared in college and university stage productions (like Pa's fondly remembered *Samson Agonistes*) were either professional actresses hired for the role or the wives or daughters of dons.

My wife judged my father harshly on this issue. I understand why. When I met her, she was studying history at St Anne's College, Oxford, but my father insisted on calling the place 'The Society of Home Students' because that's what it had been known as in his day, forty years earlier. My sister, Hester – my third sister and only five years older than my wife – was more tolerant of Pa's old-school misogyny, though even she wondered in later life if her struggles with mental health were because when she had been born my father had so wanted a boy.

Hester became the family's 'problem child' within a year or two of my birth. From before the age of ten, she was rebellious and temperamental; she had highs and lows; made scenes, was rude, caused rows. My parents did not know what to do, so they sent her to the Tavistock Clinic, founded in 1920 as the Tavistock Institute of Medical Psychology. I don't think they knew what to do, either. Before and throughout her teens, she endured years of treatments and therapies – from hours of Freudian psychoanalysis to bucketloads of drugs (these were the pioneering years of lithium and benzodiazepines), to what used to be called 'electroshock therapy', in which seizures were electrically induced in the poor girl's brain in the hope of providing relief from her perceived mental disorders.

I remember, as quite a small boy, going to visit Hes in one of the several institutions in which she found herself. I went with Pa to keep him company.

'Where are we off to?'

'The loony bin.'

'Tooting?'

'Yes.'

'To see Hes?'

'Yes.'

'How's she doing?'

'Not good. If she's in the straitjacket again, don't tell Ma.'

'Oh dear. Is it that bad?'

'Yes, they're going to give her the Dr Frankenstein treatment today.'

We found her with electrodes attached to her skull, about to have 120 volts of electricity shot through her brain. My father made a joke of it to help him cope, and because that was his way. He loved her dearly, but he teased her, too. She wore thick gig-lamps and had a conspicuous nose – just like Pa's. Eventually, she got contact lenses, had a nose job on the NHS, and found light at the end of her tunnel of trauma. I don't know that any of the 'treatments' ever helped her. It was time, and her strength of character and powerful sense of humour, that did the trick. Throughout it all, she loved Pa unconditionally, but was he the author of her problems? Or, unwittingly, was I?

How did being a boy affect me?

When I was writing my biography of the Duke of Edinburgh, I came across a fascinating figure: Marie Bonaparte, Prince Philip's aunt (married to his uncle, Prince George of Greece), a great-grandniece of Napoléon I, and consequently an in-law of sorts of my kinswoman, the Empress Eugénie, wife of Napoléon III.

Marie Bonaparte (1882–1962) was intelligent, restless, remarkable. Her lovers included Aristide Briand, eleven times Prime Minister of France. Her enthusiasms included sex, her pet chows and Dr Sigmund Freud. In 1925 she entered analysis with Freud in Vienna and trained as a psychoanalyst. She went on to become a pivotal figure in the French Psychoanalytical Society and the international psychoanalytical community. She experimented with early forms of genital surgery and under-went an unusual procedure to alter the position of her clitoris. She was sympathetic to the view of Freud's mentor, Jean-Martin Charcot, that when looking for the root cause of nervous disorders, '*C'est toujours la chose génitale, toujours, toujours.*' It was to her that Freud posed his celebrated question, 'What does a woman want?'

'A good question,' the Duke of Edinburgh said to me, laughing. 'And one to which I think we still don't have the answer.' (Pa would have endorsed that.)

Marie Bonaparte became one of Freud's closest friends. She lavished gifts on him. In the aftermath of the Nazi Anschluss, she used her connections and her considerable financial resources to help secure his – and his family's – safe passage from Vienna to London, in 1938. She became a close friend, too, of Freud's daughter, Anna Freud, the pioneer of child psychoanalysis, and one of the many consulted by my parents in their search for a cure for their third daughter's maladies.

When I was writing my biography of Prince Philip, I travelled to 20 Maresfield Gardens, in Hampstead – the Freud family's London home, now the home of the Freud Museum – to meet Brett Kahr, noted Freudian psychologist and a student of the life and work of Marie Bonaparte, to discover what it does to you if you happen to be a boy born into a family of older sisters – like Prince Philip, or, indeed, like me.

'Philip was the only boy, literally a beautiful blue-eyed boy, born into a household of devoted, doting women,' said Brett, smiling genially, perched on Dr Freud's own couch. 'And you were a beautiful blue-eyed boy, too, Gyles, weren't you? He was the fifth child, you were the fourth, but you were both the longed-for son. So, after all those girls, here is a boy – and what do boys have that girls do not have? A penis. Into this world of women – in your case, a mother, three daughters, a nanny, a maid, with grandmothers not far away – comes this perfect boy. It is very exciting. There is within the household – in the phrase of Phyllis Greenacre, a Freudian from the 1950s – "penis awe". It is unspoken, but it is there. And the admiration and devotion of these women, especially the older sisters, will have given you, as you grew up, what might be termed a certain "phallic swagger", a sense of self-assurance and self-confidence, a certain cockiness.'

I think that might explain everything, don't you?

7. A London childhood

I don't remember anything about my life in Germany. Judging from the photographs in the album that is lying open on the table as I write this – tiny black-and-white photographs with narrow white borders and crenulated edges, pasted on to the page with brief captions underneath, all in my father's elegant, sloping hand – I was a beautiful baby: blond, blue-eyed, bonny. And a happy one, too. In every one of several dozen pictures I seem to be laughing: on the rug (with no clothes on); on the beach at Nordeney (with no clothes on); in the pram (waving); in the high chair (blowing bubbles with my food); getting a present from St Nicholas at a Christmas party at Tegernsee; feeding a fawn at Hanover Zoo; dressed in little lederhosen blowing out the candles on my third birthday.

Of course, I am laughing. What did I have to complain about? The pictures show my three adoring sisters gazing down at me and, again and again, my father holding me proudly in his arms. I remember my mother telling me how much I was doted on by a German couple who helped look after me: Bertha and Hans. He had been a circus clown before the war, and before I was three he taught me to stand on my head and walk a tightrope. Seventy years on, I can still stand on my head, and my personal trainer marvels at my balancing ability, but I have no recollection of Bertha or Hans, grateful as I am to them for their devotion.

What's true of me is true of you. Most of us recall very little of our earliest years because our hippocampus – the part of the brain that stores memories – develops gradually. But even if we cannot recall specific events from when we were very young, what happened to us as babies and toddlers nevertheless leaves a lasting impression. As my Freudian analyst friend Brett Kahr puts it: 'The first few years of life are, paradoxically, both forgettable and yet powerful in shaping the adults that we become.' I don't remember it, but as a small child I was the centre of attention, adored and indulged.

In the summer of 1951, my parents' German idyll came to an end. The Allied Control Commission was winding down. Pa had done his bit administering British justice to the defeated enemy, and it was time to come home. Time to try his luck at the English criminal bar. It was what he had wanted to do for as long as he could remember.

He didn't do badly. In fact, judging from the press cuttings in his scrapbook, he did rather well: defending a minor mobster, getting a radio personality who'd been charged with speeding off the hook, securing an Italian *contessa* her divorce – the sort of stuff that merited a few paragraphs on page 5 of the London *Evening News*. Barristers, then and now, are self-employed: they get paid for the work they do and the more work they do and the better they do it the more work they get and the more they get paid for it. It can be a slow business at the beginning, and that was the challenge for Pa. Most barristers start their careers in their mid-twenties, when they are single and without responsibilities. Pa was forty-one, with four children and a wife who, understandably, had expectations of a comfortable 1950s English middle-class lifestyle.

Pa secured himself a seat in a good set of chambers in King's Bench Walk, between Fleet Street and the Thames Embankment. He got work because the clerks there recommended him to solicitors, who recommended him to their clients. He also got work undertaking what were known as 'dock briefs' – cases where the brief for the defence was given directly to a barrister chosen by the prisoner in the dock. Years later, Sir John Mortimer QC, playwright and novelist, also an Inner Temple man – who was in the same chambers as my father, starting out at the same time as Pa, though several years his junior – explained to me how the 'dock brief' system worked.

'Imagine a Paris bordello,' said Sir John, licking his lips and blinking at me from behind thick pebble-glass spectacles. 'The *madame* shows you into the anteroom where the girls on offer are lounging about on red velvet sofas in varying states of alluring *déshabillé*.' His spectacles seemed to be misting up as he warmed to his theme. 'You survey the scene as calmly as your growing excitement allows and then you pick the *poule de luxe* whose charms most take your fancy.' He produced a crumpled handkerchief and vigorously blew his nose. 'It was the same in court. We sat there on the wooden benches in the well of the court, wigged and robed, doing our best to look willing and able. The accused in the dock would give us the once-over and take his pick.'

Sir John remembered Pa with affection. 'Your father had a distinct advantage. He was fifteen years older than the rest of us. He didn't look like a callow youth. He had grey hair, as I recall. And he didn't have a shiny new wig like the rest of us. He had his father's old wig, so he looked as if he'd been around for a few years. Clever trick. My father was a barrister, too. I should have tried it.'

In 1951, Pa had grey hair, high hopes and an allowance from his father's boyhood friend, Shirley Jones. It was the allowance that enabled my father to survive and to pay the school fees. The girls were all set for Cheltenham Ladies' College. Where was the golden boy to go?

I arrived in London in 1951, aged three, speaking English and (thanks to Bertha and Hans) speaking German, too. Clearly, I had, if not quite the gift of tongues, at least a gift for languages. My parents couldn't find a German school in London, so they sent me to the French Lycée in South Kensington instead. I began in the *jardin d'enfants* – the day nursery – which was in a small building away from the main school, somewhere off The Boltons. The only memory I have of it is a good one.

After lunch we always had a rest. Each of us was given a thick brown blanket and we had to roll ourselves up tight inside it – like the filling of a sausage roll – and lie on the polished wooden floor, all in rows, all facing the same direction, with our eyes shut. I remember how hard the floor seemed and how comforting the blanket was. I can see its colour now: dark chocolate. I can smell it: musty, but nice, like the smell of apples in a storeroom. Most of all, I can feel the texture of the blanket. When I was about fifteen and read Rupert Brooke's poem 'The Great Lover', I came across the line where he describes 'the rough male kiss of blankets' and I thought, suddenly, excitedly, 'Yes, that's it – that's the feel of the blanket we rolled up in for our afternoon rest at the *jardin d'enfants*.'

Now, seventy years later, when I am lying awake at night, I pretend I am rolled up in that all-encompassing, heavy, itchy, smelly brown blanket again. I was safe there. And happy. I seem to recall that the *mademoiselle* who was in charge of our class sat on an upright chair in front of us, knitting quietly while we slept. I can hear the rhythmical click-click of her needles.

But perhaps I have imagined that.

We lived in and around South Kensington throughout the 1950s, mostly in flats taken on short leases, once in a house, and for a month or two in a respectable but faded hotel, just opposite Gloucester Road tube station. My mother liked hotel life. So did I. As a little boy, I pictured myself as a bellhop, immaculately dressed in a sky-blue uniform with brass buttons down the front and a matching pillbox hat, running around the hotel delivering telegrams to the residents. Later, I went through my waiter-as-seducer-and-confidence-trickster phase. Later still, a friend introduced me to the 'secret floor' at the Randolph Hotel in Oxford. It's the floor the guests don't know exists, above the official top floor. It's where the staff live – and anything goes.

I have since discovered that almost every grand hotel has

one. In the mid-1950s, the American actress and singer Kay Thompson published a series of humorous story books about a naughty little girl called Eloise who, like Miss Thompson, lived at the Plaza Hotel in New York. My mother and I loved those books. They depicted one of our shared fantasy worlds. A long time later, Liza Minnelli told me that she was Kay Thompson's goddaughter and that she, Liza, was the model for Eloise. I wish my mother had known that. My mother adored Judy Garland. Every Easter, while my father was hiding the Easter eggs, she would sing her favourite songs from *Easter Parade*.

Back in 1951, our first London address was 42 Lower Sloane Street, a tall, handsome, red-brick house on the road that runs south from Sloane Square. I think we had the ground-floor flat that opened out on to communal gardens at the back. I don't remember the inside of the flat at all, but I have a faint recollection of running up and down the garden making *woo-woo* whooping noises wearing a 'Red Indian' feather headdress, and a distinct memory of riding my tricycle along the pavement, unaccompanied, all the way from the Good As New second-hand clothes shop at one end of the street to the colourful flower barrow on the corner of Sloane Square at the other. I loved pedalling up and down that street. I could go faster than either the milkman or the rag-and-bone men on their horse-drawn carts. I always saluted them as I raced past. They always saluted back. It seems they, too, knew I was somebody special.

I have only two friends from that time whose names I can still recall. One was a girl called Jane Sarah Dorothea Hoos. Ma and Pa both always said her name in full, as if it came in inverted commas, as though she might be a character in a verse by A. A. Milne: 'Yes, Gyles, "Jane Sarah Dorothea Hoos" is coming over to play. Won't that be fun?'

I think it must have been, because we spent a lot of time together. We played hopscotch in the street and she always won. Girls are invariably better at hopscotch than boys. I was more successful when we played lines and squares – that's the game where, going along the pavement, you've got to move from square to square, from paving stone to paving stone, never putting a foot on any of the lines in between.

> Whenever I walk in a London street,
> I'm ever so careful to watch my feet;
> And I keep in the squares,
> And the masses of bears,
> Who wait at the corners all ready to eat
> The sillies who tread on the lines of the street,
> Go back to their lairs,
> And I say to them, 'Bears,
> Just look how I'm walking in all the squares!'

Ma loved the verses of A. A. Milne and knew most of them by heart. Curiously, looking at the pictures of me and Jane Sarah Dorothea Hoos, we seem often to be dressed more like children from the 1920s world of Christopher Robin than the post-war world of 1950s austerity. Jane Sarah Dorothea Hoos has quite a wardrobe of pretty flower-covered frocks and I look quite dandy in my cream-coloured soft felt bowler hat. Judging from the photographs, she was six to my four, assured, self-contained and (I now see) extraordinarily attractive. I am often in costume (dressed as a policeman or a clown, or wearing a kilt), larking about; she is always demure. I think the best picture is the pair of us riding a life-size Muffin the Mule on the seafront at Broadstairs. She has allowed me to sit in the front, I notice.

The other friend from that era whose name I still know is Julian Fellowes. You will know him, too. He became an actor, then an Oscar-winning screenwriter, and then the creator of *Downton Abbey*. Indeed, Julian is the only Oscar winner with whom I have shared a bath. I was five and he was four at the time. (The Oscar winners with whom I've shared a shower is another gether altothing, as Princess Margaret used to say.)

In 1953, either just before or just after the coronation, I know we moved from Lower Sloane Street, SW1, to live in the basement of the Fellowes' house in Wetherby Place, SW7. I am not sure how that came about, or why. Hoping he might, I emailed Julian with some fun pictures of us together in the playground and the paddling pool at Normand Park, in Fulham. He has just emailed back.

Dear Gyles,

What marvellous photographs, complete with that strange, slanting fringe that little boys were given then. It looked okay for one minute after brushing, and then it looked bonkers for the rest of the day.

My father [a diplomat stationed in Ethiopia] developed TB towards the end of the war and my mother, ever intrepid, had to go to Africa to bring him back. This she did, and got him into the military hospital (King Edward's?) at Midhurst in Sussex. My brother Rory and I were not yet born, so she had two sons, the younger one a baby, and somehow she had to sort out a place for them to live, all on her own. She found 2 Wetherby Place which had suffered damage from the building directly opposite being blown up (it was still a bomb site in 1953), so all the windows had been broken, etc., and she managed to negotiate a long lease, on the proviso that she would renovate it. However, in 1944/45, it was fairly impossible to find any casual labour so she had to do most of it herself. At first there was no running water, and she would take the bus, in Gloucester Road, up to the cinema in High Street Kensington, and wash there at the end of every day, before going back to her parents' house.

Eventually, she got the place sorted out, just in time for my father's return from hospital. She had already let the basement flat for a bit of income, and so they lived in the rest of the house. There was a break in about 1948 when they went to Cairo for two or three years, when Pa was posted to the Embassy there as Second Secretary or something. He worked with Donald Maclean, whom he disliked, but my mother was great pals with Melinda Maclean. They were both pretty shocked by what happened later, especially as Pa had worked closely with Guy Burgess in London, whom he liked enormously. He had worked with Kim Philby too, but they were not close. Even so, he must have been investigated. Anyway, in 1951 (I think), we came home (I had been born in Cairo in 1949), and returned to 2 Wetherby. The arrival of all of you was not long after that. I cannot remember how our parents knew each other, but I do recall that they were friendly, more friendly than just tenants, so I imagine it must have been because of an introduction by a mutual friend. Your parents (but you will know this better than I) were looking for a house and then I seem to remember they had a very welcome inheritance while they were there, which they all celebrated together. At any rate, that was part of the legend they left behind. My mother would sometimes look after you, and your mother would sometimes look after me, hence the famous bath and our day at Normand Park in Fulham.

I hope some of this is useful.
Love,
Julian

It's more than useful, I'd say. Ethiopia, Egypt, virtually the complete Cambridge spy ring, the bomb site across the street, the boys in the bath . . . It's a complete mini-series in three paragraphs.

Julian in his seventies (and now Baron Fellowes of West Stafford) looks exactly as he did aged four. He is still good company and endearingly unpretentious about his hugely successful work. 'What you have to understand about period drama is that it's "history light."' He is both witty and wise. Not long ago, I did a Q&A with him as a fund-raiser for the British Film Institute. He rather shocked the young actors in the audience. 'Be grateful to be typecast,' he told them. 'If you are a type they're looking for, how lucky you are. Stick with it.'

Pa's mother (the lady who links us to the Empress Eugénie, Kenyon's the Undertakers, and George R. Sims) died in 1953, so that must have been the source of the inheritance we celebrated with the Fellowes family. In any event, that's when we moved to 27 Oakley Street, SW3, another handsome, Victorian terraced house, on a street that runs from the King's Road down to Cheyne Walk and the River Thames.

It used to be said that everyone lives in Oakley Street at some point in their lives. Oscar Wilde and his mother lived there for a while. Scott of the Antarctic lived there with his mother. Bob Marley and David Bowie lived there around the same time, but at different numbers. When I met him, the footballer George Best was living at No. 87, the same number as Oscar and Lady Wilde. Donald Maclean, Cambridge spy friend of the Fellowes, had lived at No. 29, in the house next door to ours.

I remember nothing of our house except the stairwell. It was always dark. And hanging on the first landing was a large oil painting. It was the portrait of a man. He was bearded and wore a black suit. I don't know who he was, but he frightened me. Indeed, that painting introduced me to fear. I can remember running past it down the stairs as fast as I could. It filled me with dread.

Because of the painting, I have avoided opportunities to revisit Oakley Street. According to my diary, I was last there on Saturday, 6 October 1973. I went to 15 Oakley Street that day to have lunch with Richard Goolden, an old actor whose claim to fame was playing the part of Mole in the original stage adaptation of *The Wind in the Willows*, in 1929. He went on playing the part almost until he died, in 1981, aged eighty-six. Richard

Goolden *was* Mole: small, bent, gnome-like, and completely delightful. Over lunch he chattered away merrily about Kenneth Grahame (who wrote the book) and A. A. Milne (who wrote the play) – he knew both of them – and about life in the trenches during the First World War when he was in charge of the latrines. He scurried about the house – it was his family house, left to him by his mother – and, when I told him how much I liked our chicken soup, ran off to the kitchen and returned triumphantly waving the empty Swiss Knorr soup packet at me. After lunch he took me into the kitchen and showed me his collection of empty Swiss Knorr soup packets – hundreds of them. He did not throw anything away. He took me upstairs to the top room in the house – bare floorboards with old suitcases and cardboard boxes all over the place – and showed me the shelves where he had kept every bank statement and chequebook stub that he had had since he first opened a bank account, in 1914.

The worlds created by Kenneth Grahame and A. A. Milne were two of my mother's favourite worlds. She introduced me to them and we were both very happy there. The worlds my father introduced me to were less cosy, more dangerous. He was a *Treasure Island* and a *Robinson Crusoe* man. And, at bedtime, while Ma was reading me nursery rhymes about Christopher Robin, Pa was performing dramatic monologues at my bedside – complete with melodramatic gestures. By the time I was six, I knew some impressive chunks of Milton's *Samson Agonistes*. I am sure it is those bedtime stories and poems that gave me my lifelong love of language. If I was going to write a verse about my parents it would begin a little differently from Philip Larkin's: 'They tuck you up, your mum and dad . . .'

In the 1950s my mother was what most middle-class British women were: a stay-at-home housewife. She hankered after something more, and eventually she found it, but while I was small I had no idea she was anything other than completely contented with her domestic lot. I don't think she was very interested in housework or cooking, but she got on with both. I remember helping her shell peas. I loved popping the pod and being allowed to eat every tenth pea raw. I remember, too, helping her with her knitting. I had to sit on a footstool facing her with my wrists held out while she unravelled her wool, slowly looping it around them. I felt I sat there like that, with my hands stuck out, for hours on end. I realise now it was probably only a matter of minutes.

We had happy times together – '*chiggy*' she would have called them: it's a Hindi word. Pa was at work, the girls were away at school, Griggs the cat was asleep on the sofa, Mitou the parrot hadn't yet arrived: it was just Ma and me – and tea. Tea was always the same: Marmite and tomato sandwiches, with the white bread sliced thin and the crusts cut off. Ma drank Indian tea, poured from a small metal teapot into her favourite bone-china cup, and I had a glass of cold chocolate-flavoured Nesquik. On high days, I also had a lemon or chocolate Lyons' cupcake. Meticulously, I peeled the silver tinfoil off the side of the cake without damaging any of the crenulations on the icing. Then I ate it, slowly, deliberately, in a state of near ecstasy, eyes closed, nibbling my way round the edge.

From June 1953, when we got our Radio Rentals television for the coronation, Ma and I always watched *Watch with Mother* together, too. *Andy Pandy* was on Tuesdays, and Ma's favourite. I thought Andy was a bit of a drip, but I liked Teddy and I had a soft spot for Looby Loo. My favourite was *The Flowerpot Men*, on Wednesdays: Bill and Ben with Little Weed and a tortoise called Slowcoach. These were black-and-white puppet shows: in every shot you could see the strings attached to the puppets.

These characters also appeared in the children's weekly, the *TV Comic*, that I bought with my pocket money every Thursday. Muffin the Mule, Sooty and Noddy were the star attractions.

I had my own Muffin string puppet, of course, and my own glove puppets of Sooty and Sweep. My Noddy was a doll made of rubber, with a real bell attached to the top of his blue cap. He came to bed with me every night and slept under the pillow. Growler, my teddy bear, watched over us from the foot of the bed.

In time I moved on to *The Dandy* (where I preferred Korky the Cat to Desperate Dan), *The Beano* (naturally, I adored Lord Snooty and his Pals) and *The Beezer*, but while I tried the hugely popular *Eagle* for a while, the adventures of Dan Dare and the green Mekon never caught my imagination. I did not want to travel into outer space.

Neither of my parents was interested in science or sport, so neither was I. My father loved golf (though he rarely played it) and we had to watch the Oxford vs Cambridge University Boat Race every year, but beyond that my sporting life as a child consisted of the occasional round of crazy golf with my mother, and listening to the football results on TV on Saturday afternoons. There was something hypnotic – almost poetic – about the way the announcer intoned them.

Stirling Albion, nil:	Ayr United, one
Queen of the South, two:	Dundee United, three
Hamilton Academical, one:	Albion Rovers, two
Arbroath, nil:	Forfar Athletic, nil

I have only watched one football match in my life: the World Cup Final in 1966. (We won. When I watch, we win. Clearly, I need to watch more often.) I cultivated George Best when I met him in 1970 because he was famous. It was at a party in Dublin, where I made the mistake of introducing George to Sinéad Cusack. (She bunked off with him instead of me.) In 1990, I hosted a dinner for Sir Stanley Matthews on his seventy-fifth birthday because I knew he was a legend – and I do love a legend. He was also extraordinary: he told me how he was earning £5 a week at the height of his fame, and happy to be. Later, when we showed some film footage of highlights from his career, he sat next to me looking down at his knees. (As Shakespeare has Henry V put it: 'There's nothing so becomes a man as modest stillness and humility.')

As an adult I have encountered some of the great sporting figures of our time – and their families. In Jamaica, not long ago, Usain Bolt's auntie told me she could run just as fast as her nephew: 'I had to chase him when he was a little boy and I always caught him – always!' But as a child the world of sport passed me by.

I didn't want action. I wanted laughs. While other small boys were reading about Roy of the Rovers, I was reading about Billy Bunter.

William George Bunter of Greyfriars School was as famous in his day as Harry Potter of Hogwarts is now. Truly. Of course, there was a difference. The *Harry Potter* books are all about magic. Billy Bunter was all about obesity. And corporal punishment. Billy Bunter was a fat boy: that was the joke. It was his corpulence that made him comical – along with his gig-lamps, his greediness, laziness, deceitfulness and incorrigible conceit. Known as 'The Fat Owl of the Remove', he was a schoolboy Falstaff and, like Falstaff, blind to his own faults. He saw himself as heroic, handsome, full of guile, and he dismissed the boys who ragged him and the masters who caned him as 'unutterable beasts'.

Bunter was huge in every sense. Created by Charles Hamilton (1876–1961), under the pen name Frank Richards, he featured in the best-selling weekly boys' story paper, *The Magnet*, from 1908 to 1940. I discovered him in strip-cartoon form in the *TV Comic* and on television, where he was watched by millions between 1952 and 1961. In the TV series (there were 52 half-hour episodes in all), the actor Gerald Campion played 'the fat ass' – to perfection. The other schoolboys were played by boy actors (the young Michael Crawford among them), but

Campion was a man in his thirties – forty, in fact, by the time the series ended. I got to know Campion in the 1970s, when he was running Gerry's Bar, a private members' drinking club for theatre people in the West End, and by one of those *Dance to the Music of Time* quirks, I can claim a link with him even today. He turns out to have been my personal trainer Tamsyn's husband's aunt's husband. (Oh yes, I've known them all.)

In the 1970s, I wrote a biography of Bunter's creator, Charles Hamilton. I admired him because he had created a character of near-mythic proportions (and it's not given to many to do that) and because, operating as Frank Richards and with at least twenty-five other pen names, he features in the *Guinness Book of Records* as the world's most prolific author.

Given Bunter's huge popularity in the 1950s, I thought we should revive Bunter on TV in the 1980s. With my then agent, Laurie Mansfield (agent to the stars, and the man who brings us the Royal Variety Performance every year), and Greg Smith (producer of the *Confessions of . . .* films), I thought we should revive Bunter on TV. We acquired the rights. I wrote a pilot script. We secured the acting talents of the young Christopher Biggins to play Bunter and the old Sir John Gielgud to play Dr Locke, the headmaster of Greyfriars. With high hopes for a Sunday teatime classic serial slot, we set off to make our pitch to the BBC Commissioner and . . . wait for it . . . found ourselves face to face with one of the largest ladies I have ever met. Billy Bunter had a stout sister, Bessie Bunter. Our BBC Commissioner was a dead-ringer for Bessie.

'What's so funny about a boy being fat?' she asked, reasonably enough. 'And just because you've got Sir John Gielgud wielding the cane, I don't think it makes child beating any more acceptable, do you?'

Every summer throughout the 1950s we went for a family holiday to Broadstairs, the little seaside town on the Isle of Thanet in East Kent. We went by car – a cream-coloured

Volkswagen Beetle. I loved our Beetle because it looked a bit like Noddy's car and because it appeared to work by magic. The engine was in the boot, so when you opened the bonnet there was nothing there. It was a compact two-door car, intended for four people. My three sisters squeezed into the back and squabbled. Ma sat in the front passenger's seat, reading the map and squawking. She never learnt to drive, had no feel for the road, and consequently squeaked and squealed and yelped at every turning, sharp bend and set of changing lights along the eighty miles from South Kensington to the door of our guesthouse in Viking Bay. I sat happily on my father's lap, between his knees, hands on the wheel, helping him steer (and steering entirely whenever he was lighting one of his cigarettes), working the indicators (they popped out from the right and left of the body of the car) and, very occasionally, being allowed to honk the horn. Pa was a good driver. He had never taken a test (he was driving before tests were introduced in 1934) and never had an accident. He rose above the squealing and squawking and drove with commendable composure, in a haze of white cigarette smoke, while leading us all in non-stop games of 'I spy', 'The parson's cat' and 'I packed my bag'.

We went to Broadstairs in the 1950s because it's where middle-class families had been going for their 'summer hols' for a hundred years. Pa's parents and grandparents used to go to Broadstairs. As a boy he went to school in Ramsgate, nearby. Pa knew Broadstairs like the back of his hand.

The town lies above a small, historic harbour with cliffs on either side. It boasts seven bays of golden sand. I can still name them, in the correct order, from south to north: Dumpton Gap, Louisa Bay, Viking Bay, Stone Bay, Joss Bay, Kingsgate Bay and Botany Bay. Pa and I would leave Ma in a deckchair by a windbreak on the beach in Viking Bay, with a pot of tea on a tin tray, her knitting and her copy of *The Lady*, while we went exploring.

Year in, year out, there was a ritual to our exploring. We *always* went to Stone Bay to revisit the rock on which my father and grandfather had carved their initials in 1918 as the tide rose around them and they feared they faced a certain death by drowning – until they discovered a hidden flight of steps built into the chalk cliff, which lead them from the rising water up through the cliff to the monastery at the summit. (Their initials and the stone steps, now locked behind an iron gate, are still there.) We *always* went to the Cliff Promenade to find the house with the thirty-nine steps that gave John Buchan the title of his famous novel.

We *always* went to several of the places where Charles Dickens used to stay on his many visits to Broadstairs, between 1837 and 1859. He wrote *David Copperfield* while staying at Bleak House. That book, Pa explained to me, was Dickens's own story. We never failed to visit Betsey Trotwood's house – it had been the home of a real lady whom Dickens had known: a Miss Mary Pearson Strong – and when we got there, Pa would immediately cry out 'Donkeys! Get those donkeys off my green!' echoing the character in the novel. He had assorted quotations from *David Copperfield* in his repertoire and he would adapt them to suit the moment. After I had run around the green chasing away the imaginary donkeys, he would paraphrase Miss Trotwood: 'Never be mean in anything; never be false; never be cruel. Avoid those three vices, Gyles, and I can always be hopeful of you.'

It was on one of those sunny, windy, thrilling exploring days that Pa and I found ourselves in Kingsgate, on the cliff top, walking back towards Broadstairs. Suddenly, Pa stopped and put his hand on my shoulder.

'That's him,' he said.

'Who?'

'Frank Richards,' he said, 'the man who writes Billy Bunter – that's him, over there.'

I looked across the road and there he was, the world's most

prolific author, standing alone in his small front garden, smoking a pipe and inspecting his roses. He was wearing a fawn-coloured cardigan and a skullcap. He looked elderly (he was nearly eighty), but not old, and very, very nice. That was the moment when I thought: one day, I might be a writer, too.

Later, when researching his biography, I learnt a lot about Frank Richards – about the lost love of his life (the American girl who got away), about his shyness (and the absurd toupée he used to wear before he acquired his skullcap), about his financial troubles (he had to sell the rights in Bunter to pay his gambling debts: he had a weakness for the casinos of Monte Carlo), about how he got the better of George Orwell when they debated the merits of his schoolboy stories in the 1940s – and today, in a box in the basement, I have a mass of his private papers and manuscripts, given to me by his agent, all typed on the same 1905 Remington that he used throughout his working life – but back then, all I knew was that I had seen him with my own eyes and it was, as I said to Pa, 'one of the greatest moments in my life so far'.

Looking at the family photo albums of the period, it's clear that my sisters came to Broadstairs, too. I remember them being in the car but, curiously, I don't have any recollection of them on the holiday with us when we got there. It's evident from the photographs that I wasn't alone watching the Punch and Judy show on the front, or riding the donkeys along the beach, or going shrimping in Louisa Bay, but in my memory it's always just me on my own – with Pa or Ma in the background somewhere, nearby but not in focus.

Pa, I know, was not always there. He drove us down and drove us back, but in between he would return to London to work. I had fun when he wasn't there, too. Ma and I were good companions. We both liked having treats and planned our days around them. Every day included a morning visit to Morelli's ice-cream parlour on Victoria Parade and an afternoon expedition to buy me a present.

Yes, every day of the holiday, I got a present – and they were wonderful presents, too. Which ones do I remember? The Pelham puppets, of course (string puppets – my favourite was Mr Turnip, another TV character), and the glove puppets (I had the complete cast of *Cinderella* in glove puppets), and the magic tricks (especially the wine glass that was filled with wine you couldn't spill, and the rubber egg in which you could hide a red silk scarf the size of a tea towel).

But most of all, best of all, the fancy-dress costumes. I loved dressing up.

8. Dressing up

I know Grayson Perry a little and I like him a lot. He is a wonderful artist and a great communicator, but I have to admit that I find his penchant for dressing up in women's clothes a tad disconcerting – which is odd, since I've been doing it myself, off and on, all my life. Why? I wonder.

My Freudian friend Brett Kahr says it's simply me being playful, 'And that's a good thing, Gyles.'

Grayson Perry says of himself, 'I just love dressing up in everything a man is supposed not to be, in all that vulnerability, sweetness, preciousness and impracticality.'

Grayson, of course, is a committed transvestite, and has been since he was a boy.

'I've got a lot of baggage,' he told me once, 'more than you, perhaps.'

More than me, certainly. Grayson was four when his father left home after discovering that his mother was having an affair with a milkman, whom she later married and whose 'tyranny' Grayson came to fear. For Grayson in his teens, creating for himself a female alter ego called Claire was about sexuality, escape and excitement.

'To put on a dress was to don a suit of lights,' he says, 'the "forbidden other" shocking my skin at every contact point,' adding (he is very funny), 'of course, it could have been static, as I'm talking about the early 1970s when crimplene was everywhere.'

I have never been in the Grayson Perry league. I don't have his baggage – or his courage or his imagination. I just put on a frock now and again for fun, to feel different, to show off in disguise. I legitimise it by doing it in a show. I've never been a secret cross-dresser.

When I became an MP in 1992, my closest friend at Westminster was Stephen Milligan MP, reckoned the high-flyer of our intake. He was the first to be promoted, and everyone assumed he would be Foreign Secretary within ten years. Instead, he was dead within twenty-two months – apparently asphyxiated playing a sex game in his house in Hammersmith.

He had supper with me and my wife on Saturday night, played a round of golf on Sunday morning, and went home alone for a quiet night in. When he failed to appear at the House of Commons on Monday, his secretary decided to go over to his place to investigate.

There was no reply when she rang the doorbell, so she let herself in and there she found him, dead, lying on the floor in the kitchen, naked apart from a pair of stockings and a suspender belt, with an electrical flex tied round his neck, an orange in his mouth and a black plastic bin liner over his head. The bag was over his head and the flex around his neck to restrict the amount of oxygen getting to his brain and so increase the sexual thrill. It seems autoerotic asphyxiation kills thousands every year.

John Major, the Prime Minister, was asked about Stephen on the radio and reflected that he felt the poor fellow 'must have been pretty unhappy, pretty miserable'. I don't think so. I think Stephen was just having fun and it went horribly, tragically wrong.

Michèle and I went to his funeral, near his family home in the country. Stephen's father was hard of hearing so we had to bellow our words of condolence to him and he boomed back. He insisted that we thank God for Stephen's happy life and considerable achievements. We were moved by his Christian fortitude. As I have said before, I can think of nothing worse than losing your child in your own lifetime.

After the funeral in the village church, we had to troop out into the graveyard for the interment. We were only thirty or forty feet from the hedge surrounding the churchyard, and right along the lane, standing on stepladders, were the press photographers – by the dozen. Stephen was laid to rest to the sound of clicking cameras. They were only there because of the stockings and suspenders.

I knew Stephen well. I had known him since we were at Oxford together. I knew his girlfriend. She had no idea about his fetish for women's underwear. I had no idea, either. I am not like that. At least, I don't believe I am – though, now I come to think about it, when I was in a show called *Zipp!* in the early (and possibly aptly named) noughties, I spent several months wearing stockings and suspenders, and rather enjoyed it.

Zipp! was a celebration of musical theatre. We promised the audience one hundred musicals in one hundred minutes – 'or your money back'. With a cast of five, at breakneck speed we zipped through a century of theatrical hits, from *Chu Chin Chow* to the latest offering from Andrew Lloyd Webber. In the course of the show I gave you my Ginger Rogers in *Mame*, my Barbra Streisand in *Hello, Dolly!* and, for the finale, my Judy Garland as Dorothy singing 'Over the Rainbow' from *The Wizard of Oz*. I was very happy waiting in the wings to come on as Dorothy. I loved the cut of my dress and the feel of my figure. As Grayson Perry explained to me, 'The little girl look is the crack cocaine of femininity.'

The bit the audience seemed to like most was the sequence from *The Rocky Horror Show* where suddenly I appeared centre stage wearing little more than fishnet stockings, a black suspender belt and a huge golden codpiece (it was stuffed, I remember, with a scrunched-up copy of the *Daily Mail*). Whether it was the erotic power of my performance or the absurdity of seeing someone who had recently been a Conservative MP dressed to kill in a kinky rig-out, I don't know, but at every performance it drove the punters wild.

The show opened at the Assembly Rooms in Edinburgh as part of the Festival Fringe, in August 2002. The backstage facilities were limited, so I took to putting on my codpiece, suspenders and stockings before going over to the theatre, in the flat that I was renting. One day, as I was changing, I glanced out of my bedroom window and across the way, in the flat facing mine, I saw a woman at her window watching me. She was there every day at the same time. With binoculars.

Zipp! was a huge hit in Edinburgh. We won the award for the most popular show, and played to capacity. There was even a modest black market in tickets. That year, ours was the show you had to see. I remember, after one performance, having a drink outside a bar in George Street, when the great Sir Ian McKellen, whom I barely knew, stopped to say hello to me.

He smiled, leant towards me conspiratorially, and asked, 'Are you still wearing your stockings and suspenders, Gyles?'

'Yes,' I said. 'How did you know?'

He grinned. 'Because I'm still wearing mine.'

Performers like dressing up, and I like performers who dress up in style. Today I am a friend of the gloriously named Baga Chipz, the young drag queen best known for competing in the first British series of *RuPaul's Drag Race*. Baga's real name is Leo Loren, and he took to me the moment he discovered that I had worked with three of the most memorable female impersonators of our time: Daniel Patrick Carroll, George Logan and Patrick Fyffe – better known as Mr Danny La Rue, Dr Evadne Hinge and Dame Hilda Bracket.

Dan in his prime (I first saw him in the 1960s) was beyond belief gorgeous – an utterly convincing girl until he opened his mouth and drawled, 'Watcha, cock!' When he was young he looked like Brigitte Bardot; when he was old he looked like Barbara Cartland.

Hinge & Bracket were a drag act with a difference. They offered character and comedy instead of glamour and sex appeal. They played a pair of elderly lady musicians, one acerbic (Dr Hinge), one flamboyant (Dame Hilda), and entertained with reminiscences from their imagined musical careers interspersed with comical renditions of favourites from the light operatic repertoire. I met them first in the 1970s when they took part in a charity gala I staged at the Oxford Playhouse. Also on the bill that night were two of Britain's most distinguished theatrical dames, Peggy Ashcroft and Flora Robson, neither of whom had heard of Hinge & Bracket. In consequence, they took them at face value. At the drinks party after the show, I overheard Dame Peggy telling Dame Flora that she believed Dame Hilda was an Australian opera singer, adding, *sotto voce*, 'I think Dr Hinge is her companion as well as her accompanist.'

In the 1980s, I scripted two series of the Hinge & Bracket TV sitcom *Dear Ladies*, for BBC2, and got to know and love them. As a double act, they were a delicious combination. As individuals, they were very different. For George Logan, Dr Hinge was a part. For Patrick Fyffe, Dame Hilda was a way of life. George introduced me to aspects of the gay scene I had not come across before: a club where the waiters wore roller skates, silk boxer shorts and nothing else; friends who liked nothing more than to be stripped naked, tied to a tree and sprayed with shaving foam. Patrick was more circumspect. He and his mother came to spend Christmas with us one year and it was like having the cast of *Arsenic and Old Lace* at the lunch table.

Patrick occasionally found a young straight man over whom he could pine hopelessly, but the real focus of his world was Dame Hilda and her life at home in Stackton Tressel, the fantasy village in Suffolk that he had created for her to live in. When he dressed as Dame Hilda, he became Dame Hilda. When he came across the reality of men secretly dressing up as women, he was less comfortable. He bought a house in Wimbledon and up in the attic, hidden inside the roof, he found a stash of female clothes – dresses, underwear, false breasts and hips – all Edwardian. He realised that one of the previous occupants of his house must have been a man who had liked dressing up as a woman behind closed doors. Patrick couldn't bear it. He sold the house and moved to Bath.

*

I have appeared professionally in panto onstage, but have only played a dame on TV. I love panto: it is Britain's only unique contribution to world culture. (Discuss. Everyone has opera, ballet, tragedy and farce: only we have panto as we know it.) I have written two histories of British pantomime and a biography of the great Victorian music hall and panto star, the original Mother Goose, Dan Leno, celebrated as 'the funniest man on earth' and, in his day, after the Prince of Wales, probably the most famous man in the land. I have known several of the great dames of our time – Arthur Askey, Stanley Baxter, Cyril Fletcher, Terry Scott, Christopher Biggins – and I can tell you that playing a dame is skilled, specialist work. It is not female impersonation. A panto dame is a bloke in a frock.

As a rule, when I dress up as a woman, I want to be the real thing. I don't do it secretly, ever. I do it for public consumption, just once in a while. In my sixties, I played Lady Bracknell in *The Importance of Being Earnest*. (I modelled my look on the Queen's grandmother, Queen Mary. I managed that Becher's Brook of a line about 'a handbag' by laughing my way through it.) Aged twelve, I played Rosalind in *As You Like It*. Aged seven, I played Christopher Robin's nursemaid, Alice, in a stage rendering of A. A. Milne's poem 'Buckingham Palace'. That's when it began, in 1955, this thing with dressing up as a girl.

We had moved house yet again. Pa was doing quite well at the Bar, but not well enough. He was earning £2,000 a year when he needed £3,000. His father's boyhood friend, Shirley Jones, wrote from Gleneagles, Perthshire (or the Imperial, Torquay, or whichever other grand hotel and hydro he was living in at the time) to say that, alas, with supertax and the state of the stock market and his increasing age and this and that, the subsidies to the house of Brandreth had to stop. Poor Pa hung up his wig and gown, folded away his dreams, and reverted to the more humdrum but more secure life as a London solicitor, specialising in motoring law.

We moved from 27 Oakley Street, Chelsea, SW3, to 42

Kensington Mansions, Earl's Court, SW 5. It was not a move up in the world. At the former address, we had been surrounded by artists and bohemians. Now we were surrounded by Australian dentists.

I didn't mind. I was glad to see the last of that sinister painting on the landing. I liked our new address. It was convenient for my growing portfolio of out-of-home commitments. I had joined the local Cubs, who met at a church two streets away, and I felt I was making my mark. At Easter, Akela, our pack leader, was especially impressed by my plasticine-and-moss model of Jesus in the Garden of Gethsemane. At Christmas, Briss, the Scoutmaster, recruited me for the Kensington Scouts' Gang Show. A kindly, tall and balding man, with hairy legs and knobbly knees, Briss was surprised to learn that I had a full nurse's outfit in my dressing-up box at home – complete with navy skirt, blue blouse, white apron and nurse's cap – but since I had, and I seemed keen to wear it, the part of Alice was mine. 'Dyb, dyb, dyb. Dob, dob, dob.' I did my best and I seem to remember (though it was sixty-five years ago) it went down rather well.

The downside of 42 Kensington Mansions is that we lived on the very top floor of the red-brick Victorian block. There was no lift – and eighty-four stairs to climb. The upside was that the flat was large and light – and I had the biggest and best room, the one on the corner, the one overlooking the Earl's Court Exhibition Centre, as my playroom. Yes, I had a small bedroom as well, but next to it this huge playroom all to myself. I have had several treasured spaces in my life – the floor of the *jardin d'enfants* where I was wrapped up in the brown blanket, the branches of the ilex tree that was my secret hideaway in the grounds of my prep school, the grand office (with William Morris wallpaper) that was mine for one term when I was President of the Oxford Union, the Quiet Room in the Library at the House of Commons, the room at home in south-west London where I am writing this now – but none of them can rival my playroom at No. 42. It was my magic kingdom, my Prospero's cell, and my window on the world. Looking down to the left, I could see the platforms of Earl's Court tube station and to the right, across Warwick Road, the sprawling Exhibition Centre, as ugly as an aircraft hangar, as inviting as a funfair.

Pulled down in 2014, the Exhibition Centre was a cavernous multi-purpose space that had opened in 1887 with an American-themed exhibition, featuring a full-scale rodeo show starring Buffalo Bill Cody (Queen Victoria had been and been amused), and, over the next 125 years, had gone on to host every kind of exhibition and entertainment, from the Boat Show, the Caravan Show and the Motor Show, to concerts with David Bowie and Led Zeppelin.

Pa went to the Motor Show most years, hankering after the latest Mercedes, while settling for a second-hand Ford Consul to replace the old Volkswagen. Pa and Ma went to at least two of the American evangelist Billy Graham's revivalist rallies there in the mid-1950s. Pa was intrigued, Ma was moved, but neither went forward when the great preacher called on them to come towards the stage to be saved. Ma always took me with her to the Ideal Home Exhibition. I loved coming home with a shopping bag full of free samples: sachets of soap flakes, tiny tubs of powdered cake mix and – my favourite, always – a miniature loaf of Hovis brown bread the size of a Dinky car box. (Thirty years later, those little loaves were my inspiration when I came up with the idea of opening a Museum of the Miniature in Stratford-upon-Avon. My wife vetoed the idea and we opened our Teddy Bear Museum instead.)

I was taken every year to the Royal Tournament, the first, oldest and biggest military tattoo in the world. All three of the armed services took part and the hundreds of troops involved were billeted on site. After the show, you could visit the horses in their stables and inspect the military vehicles at close range. My sister Hester loved the horses (Hes was horse mad, like the Queen, and, also like the Queen, instead of dolls she had her own model horses with real horse-hair manes and tails she could brush and groom) and I enjoyed saluting the military personnel and being saluted in return.

In 1956, the Moscow State Circus came to Earl's Court for the first time and, after the show, we toured the menagerie, petting the dogs, patting the horses, visiting the lions and tigers in their cages (with much tut-tutting from Pa, who did not approve of wild animals in circuses) and then . . . wait for it . . . meeting, in person, the circus's star attraction, Popov the Clown.

In my life I have been blessed: I have met princes, presidents, Oscar winners, Nobel laureates, men who have walked on the moon, but I don't think any of those encounters, exciting as they were, can rival the moment I shook hands with Popov, then (and perhaps still) the most famous clown in the world. I was eight; he was twenty-six. I was just a boy living in Earl's Court, but I could walk the tight-rope and I could dream; he was an international star, a mime artist, a juggler, a tightrope-walker (like me), a red-nosed, orange-haired, check-capped clown. He was my dream – and there he was, standing in the sawdust, no more than a hundred yards from my front door, shaking my hand.

I don't think we were frightened of clowns in the 1950s. That fad came later – along with the word 'coulrophobia', coined in the 1970s, to mean 'a morbid fear of clowns'. Coco the Clown (born in Latvia in 1900, died in Northampton in 1974) was England's Popov when I was a boy – as famous then as Mr Bean or Peppa Pig are now – but not, to me, as special because he was local. Popov was *global* and he had shaken my hand. I was thrilled but, curiously, I also took it in my stride. I knew I was special. I took it as my due.

Coco the Clown featured in *TV Comic* throughout the 1950s, and in 1956 I became hooked on a new American TV series, *Circus Boy*. Naturally, I had a clown costume. In fact, I think I had two. Cowboy, pirate, policeman, spaceman – you name it, I had the outfit. I could dress up as everybody, from

Robin Hood to Davy Crockett. In 1956, of course, we all had Davy Crockett racoon-tail hats. We all went to see the Walt Disney *Davy Crockett* film. There is no one of my generation who does not know the tune to these words:

> Born on a mountain top in Tennessee
> Greenest state in the land of the free
> Raised in the woods so's he knew ev'ry tree
> Kill'd him a b'ar when he was only three
> Davy, Davy Crockett, king of the wild frontier!

As well as a Davy Crockett hat, I had a Lone Ranger mask. I loved that TV series, too. It starred Clayton Moore as the masked cowboy hero, with Jay Silverheels, in real life an Indigenous actor from Canada, grandson of a Mohawk chief, as his sidekick, Tonto. Famously, the TV series' theme tune was the overture to a Rossini opera, and gave rise to the popular definition of an 'intellectual' as someone who can listen to the *William Tell* overture without thinking of the Lone Ranger. 'Hi-ho, Silver! Away!'

I realise now how completely my father had abandoned his ambitions for the Bar, because he gave me his barrister's wig and gown for my dressing-up box. I liked dressing up as a lawyer – almost as much as I liked dressing up as a priest.

You will recall that in 1958, when I was ten and John XXIII was elected Bishop of Rome, in London SW5 I had planned to hold my own pontifical Mass and crown myself Pope, until Pa explained to me that we were Anglicans, not Catholics, and I had to settle for being Archbishop of Canterbury. I conducted my own church services in my playroom overlooking the Earl's Court Exhibition Centre – matins mainly, but occasionally Holy Communion (with Ritz crackers as the wafers, Ribena as the wine, and my array of glove puppets as the communicants), and once, with my teddy bear Growler standing in for the deceased, the Burial of the Dead.

9. Flying solo

I went to church a lot as a little boy – usually on my own. People find this hard to believe nowadays, but I travelled quite freely around London as a child. Children did.

Unaccompanied, I rode my tricycle around the block from the age of four; from the age of five, I went to the corner shop on my own, often taking money and a note from my father asking the tobacconist to kindly let me have 20 Craven 'A' for him, as well as a packet of Spangles for me; from the age of six, I used to travel to school every day by underground all by myself.

Well, I thought I was all by myself. I discovered from my mother (fifty years later) that while I was sitting happily on my own in one carriage, she was standing secretly in the next carriage keeping an eye on me. She only did that for a while. It wasn't far from home at Earl's Court to school at South Kensington (two stops on the District Line and a five-minute walk at either end) and my parents very much believed in encouraging independence at an early age.

Just after my seventh birthday, in April 1955, I went on my first solo holiday abroad. My parents (actually, I think it was just Pa and one of my sisters) dropped me off at the British European Airways terminal in Cromwell Road and, somehow, eight hours later, in my school cap and coat, with my ticket, passport and name tag in a plastic bag tied around my neck, carrying a small leather suitcase, I found myself seven hundred miles away, at the Kinderheim Freudenberg, somewhere near Thun in the middle of Switzerland. The challenge wasn't catching the plane at Heathrow: nice BEA stewardesses were on hand to hold my hand all the way. The challenge was arriving in Zürich and catching the train to Thun. My parents had not thought it through. And nor had I. At seven, I spoke perfect French, but I had landed in the German-speaking part of Switzerland.

I don't remember the detail of that day, but I do recall the trauma. I still have dreams about the nightmare of getting from the air terminal in Zürich to the railway station and the right track for the train to the destination I needed – in a language I had once spoken but no longer understood. But, of course, I made it, safely, and all in one piece, and that's the point. 'In at the deep end' is not a bad rule in life.

That said, I don't think the holiday was altogether a success. I look chirpy enough in the photographs, but the other boys and girls in the pictures (Austrian, German and Swiss) look decidedly sullen. I think the bosomy white-aproned house-mother, *Schwester* Hopteller, was a kindly soul, but beyond the delicious smell of the piping-hot semolina she served at supper, with a dollop of cold black cherries in syrup on top (one of the great aroma memories of my life), my only lasting recollection of the holiday is of the walk we took up the mountainside one afternoon. There were seven or eight of us children, all about the same age judging from the photographs, and as we climbed up the path we straddled across it, all holding hands. And then one of us, the girl on the end – a Swiss girl called Jeanne, I think – grabbed hold of the wire fence that ran along the edge of a field of cows. It was an electric fence and the shock shot through us all like a bolt of lightning.

At the age of three, I had spoken German as well as English. By the time I was seven, all my German had disappeared. Now I spoke French, and French that was good enough for me to be taken for a French boy. At the age of five, I had moved on from the *jardin d'enfants* near Gloucester Road to the main *Lycée Français de Londres* at South Kensington. My memories of the school are mostly happy ones – apart from the lunches on Wednesday.

At the Lycée, though half the children were British, or at least 'international', we were taught entirely in French. To this day I have a Frenchman's handwriting and a confusion of cultural references. You think of King Alfred, I think of Charlemagne; you know 'The Owl and the Pussy-cat', I know *'Maître Corbeau, sur un arbre perché'*; you revere Florence Nightingale, I've got a thing about Jeanne d'Arc. In the school's vast playground (a tarmacked-over bomb site opposite the Natural History Museum) we played French playground games. In the refectory we ate French food – including fish on Fridays (we were assumed to be Catholics), horse meat on Thursdays (quite tasty actually), and on Wednesdays, for pudding, as a midweek treat, dried dates.

The dates, small, sticky, dark reddish brown, looking like large legless beetles, were stringy in texture and revolting to taste. Even at a distance of sixty-five years, the thought of them makes my gorge rise. They were uneatable, but there was always a teacher – a *monsieur* or a *ma'm'selle* – at the table to make sure we ate them. I came to dread Wednesdays because of those dates. They came from French Algeria and, though the dates themselves were disgusting, the box they arrived in was attractive. I collected the labels from the box lids because when you had enough of them you could send off to an address in France for a French Foreign Legionnaire's plastic *képi*.

Beyond the dates, the only bad memories I have of my Lycée years involve three boys: two of them bullies, one of them a friend. I have found a photo of one of the bullies at a birthday party of mine: he looks malevolent, a seven-year-old version of a thin-faced floppy-haired spiv from a post-war British film noir. I am sure both boys went on to lead blameless lives in international high finance, but at school they would ambush me at the entrance to South Ken tube station, demanding that I hand over the twopence I'd been given to buy my after-school sweets. I was a coward and I gave in to them.

I have always been a physical coward – it's my one great regret in life. My father wasn't, my son isn't. They both served in the British Army and have done deeds of derring-do: Pa careering across North Africa on his motorbike, disappearing on secret missions behind enemy lines; Benet abseiling off cliff tops, competing on the Cresta Run. I have done nothing like that. Riding a camel in Dubai, I squawked all the way – and 'all the way' was about ten metres. Sitting on top of an elephant in India, I didn't dare look down. The moment the pilot switches on the 'Fasten your seat belts' sign, I start to whimper. It's pathetic, I know. Shaming. When, early in our married life, a burglar tried to get into our flat through a basement window, my wife chased him off while I cowered behind the sofa.

I get it from my mother, I'm sure, but that's no excuse. Anaïs Nin said, 'Life shrinks or expands in proportion to one's courage.' She was right, and my lack of courage has made me miss much and achieve less than I might have done. I once had a long conversation with Nicholas Soames about his grandfather, Winston Churchill. Nicholas said Churchill's greatest attribute was physical courage; he maintained great leadership is impossible without it. (This was a few years ago, when Nicholas was quite a size. He has since lost a lot of weight, which is commendable, though I rather miss the bear of a man he once was. I loved the answer given by one of his former girlfriends when asked what it was like being made love to by 'Fatty' Soames. 'It's like having a wardrobe fall on top of you with the key sticking out,' she said.)

Piotr was a Polish boy in my class and my friend, sort of, though all I can remember of him now is the time when, downstairs at the ABC tea room opposite South Ken tube station, he asked me to shut my eyes and open my mouth. I did as he asked . . . and he put a spoonful of mustard into my mouth. I felt humiliated and betrayed. It was just a boyish prank, of course, but why do we remember these childish childhood hurts? (I have not thought about Piotr in sixty years, but just now, to check the spelling, I googled his name and there he was, 'pioneering the application of dynamic risk management to multi-manager and global equity portfolios' – one of them, it seems, 'a Cayman-domiciled fund'. I might have guessed that Piotr would cut the mustard.)

I had proper friends, as well, at the Lycée. Susan was one. She had blonde hair, kept in a ponytail, and glasses. I seem to remember that her parents owned a pub somewhere near World's End. (World's End is at the end of the King's Road in Chelsea. When I first went there, I was about five and believed it really was the place where the world ended.) Upstairs at the pub there was a large function room hired out for private parties. Susan and I played hide and seek in there, until the afternoon when, running along the shiny bar counter, I slipped and fell off the bar on to a marble-topped side table and gashed my lip. I didn't take it like a man.

The point about Susan is that I was happy to share my sweets with her. We had similar tastes. We both liked Aeros and Rolos. We both loved aniseed balls and gobstoppers. For a penny you could buy a huge gobstopper that gradually changed colour as you sucked it. Susan and I took it in turns to inspect each other's tongues and swap gobstoppers every time the colour changed. We shared the liquorice straw, too, when we pooled our resources to buy a sherbet fountain.

My friends – both the ones I liked and the ones I didn't – came to my parties (always a party for my birthday in March; often another for Hallowe'en in October; usually fancy dress) and I went to theirs. I must have gone on playdates as well, but beyond that traumatic day at World's End I don't remember many. I don't see my childhood in terms of my family and friends. I see it mostly in terms of *me* – me alone, and me busy.

So busy.

What on earth was I doing?

*

I was living in my own world in my vast playroom. Walking the streets of west London as though I owned them. Sometimes, after school, I took myself off to the museums. There is a long pedestrian subway that runs from South Kensington station beneath the length of Exhibition Road. It was opened in 1885 to provide sheltered access to the newly built museums of Albertopolis above. When I started using it, in 1955, I don't think it had changed much since Victorian times. It was dank and dark, even at the height of summer. It had a distinctive, sour smell and an eerie echo. Usually I ran along it, looking neither to left nor right, simply aiming to reach my destination as quickly as possible.

To the right, into the Victoria and Albert museum, where I made a beeline either for the costume gallery or the Great Bed of Ware. (The bed was always a slight disappointment: it was never as big as I expected it to be. It still isn't. I often find myself at the V&A nowadays, usually at night, speaking at charity dinners or hosting awards ceremonies. I always make a point of visiting the Great Bed before I leave, for old times' sake.)

To the left, up the steps into the Natural History Museum, through the central hall, under the mighty 100-foot-long replica of the dinosaur *Diplodocus carnegii* (given to the museum by my great-grandfather's chum, Andrew Carnegie – oh yes!), up the wide stone stairway to the gallery on the first floor on the right where, for hours on end, I would study drawer upon drawer of birds' eggs – and then take out my sketching book and attempt (not at all well) to do line drawings of the many species of owl on display.

Nothing is wasted in this life. I now live in Barnes in southwest London, an old village with a lovely heritage. Stephen Langton, Archbishop of Canterbury, preached in our local church on his way back from the signing of Magna Carta in 1215. In the 1700s, Henry Fielding, one of my favourite authors, lived by the village pond. In 1712, when he first came to England, Handel lived in a house that stood where my house stands now, overlooking Barn Elms, a stretch of ground that runs along the south bank of the Thames. Pepys writes about visiting Barn Elms in his diary. He enjoyed meeting the girls who plied their trade there. ('Music and woman I cannot but give way to, whatever my business is.')

Anyway . . . in 1989, as chairman of the Barn Elms Protection Association, I travelled from south-west London to Slimbridge, in Gloucestershire, to visit the famous ornithologist Sir Peter Scott, artist, conservationist and only son of Robert Falcon Scott, the Antarctic explorer who lost his life on the ill-fated expedition to the South Pole in 1912. Sir Peter was barely two years old when his father died and had no recollection of him, but he told me that Robert Scott, in a last letter to his wife, advised her to 'make the boy interested in natural history if you can; it is better than games'.

In 1948, the year I was born, Peter Scott founded what became the Slimbridge Wildfowl and Wetlands Trust and I went to see him, to persuade him to help create something similar in London on the site of the redundant Thames Water Reservoirs at Barn Elms. We had tea in his sitting room, the walls covered with his celebrated paintings of birds in flight. Sir Peter was very sweet, gentle and softly spoken. I boomed rather, that day. I feel bad about it now. He was frail – and a great man. I was pleased to meet him – honoured. We talked about the Duke of Edinburgh and J. M. Barrie (Sir Peter's godfather – he was amused I knew) and then I told him how, as a child, I had studied the birds' eggs at the Natural History Museum.

He said, 'My father brought back some of those.'

We bonded over the eggs and shook hands. I told him I was the chairman of the Barn Elms Protection Association, and said, 'Let's save Barn Elms and create a Wildfowl and Wetlands Trust for London.'

He agreed. 'It can be a memorial to us both.'

He died four months later. Happily, the Wildfowl and Wetlands Trust at Barn Elms is thriving still. I am looking out over it as I write this.

One of the other myriad ways I kept myself busy as a small boy in London was by going to church. Up to the age of ten, I was a choirboy at Holy Trinity, Brompton Road, a choirboy at St Mary Abbots, Kensington High Street, and a server at St Stephen's, Gloucester Road – all at the same time. Did my parents want me out of the house? When not going to Cubs, my weekday evenings were given over to a round of choir practices and evensongs, my Saturdays were devoted to weddings, and Sundays I spent ricocheting around Kensington, plunging in and out of cassocks and surplices, from first communion to last compline.

I regarded it as work – and it was paid. At Holy Trinity, Brompton, we got two shillings for a wedding and half a crown for a funeral. At matins on a Sunday morning, while singing the anthem, we pint-sized trebles would scan the congregation, pew by pew, carefully assessing the frailty of the worshippers, and then, when back on our knees in the choir stall, we would beseech God to gather up the most vulnerable at His earliest convenience and put another Sung Mass for the Dead our way. Week in, week out, I am happy to report, the Almighty answered our prayers. (He does. On every aeroplane flight I ever take, during take-off and landing, with my hands clutching the arms of my seat, my back tensed and my eyes tight shut, I recite the Lord's Prayer over and over again. I have never been on a plane that fell out of the sky.)

At Holy Trinity, Brompton, and at St Mary Abbots, the money was a bonus. It wasn't the chief attraction. I sang in the choir mainly because I enjoyed the performing and, even more, I enjoyed the processing. I liked the outfit, too, particularly the feel of the starched white ruff around my neck. I don't think I was very good at the singing: I have never had a feel for music. At St Stephen's, Gloucester Road, no singing was required. I went there for love – and the smell of the incense. Built in the 1860s, St Stephen's was (and is) a traditional Anglo-Catholic church: all smells and bells. I was the server and boat boy, the sole child about the place. My role was to be the attendant page to the priest who carried the thurible – the censer bearing the burning incense whose smoke was wafted this way and that at key moments during our rituals. I walked alongside the priest, carrying a boat-shaped silver vessel containing extra supplies of dry incense should they be required. My job was to keep half a pace behind him, always on his left, to follow him everywhere, to do exactly as he did – genuflecting when he did, kneeling when he did, abasing myself with hands and face to the floor at the ringing of the sanctus bell. The stone tiles in the sanctuary were hard to kneel on and sometimes, I confess, at the most sacred moments of the Mass, when I was certain all others' eyes were closed, I lifted my head an inch or two off the floor and took a sneaky peek around me. For me, the service was a theatrical rather than a spiritual experience . . .

. . . which reminds me – if you'll forgive a quick aside – of the story the theatre director Peter Hall told me, which the actor Dinsdale Landen had told him about his days as an assistant stage manager at Worthing in the early 1950s. Young Dinsdale was simply a 'walk-on' when the great Sir Donald Wolfit visited the theatre as the guest star to play the part of Othello. At the dress rehearsal, Wolfit approached Dinsdale and said he thought it would be a good idea for Othello to have a page who followed him everywhere. He handed Dinsdale a loin cloth, told him to black up, and said he'd got the part. Dinsdale did not know the play but, following Wolfit's instruction, just went wherever Wolfit went, ever the dutiful page, one step behind him, always in attendance.

But at one point during the first performance Dinsdale found himself in a scene in which he felt oddly ill at ease. 'He had an instinct about it,' said Peter.

Suddenly, Dinsdale heard the great actor's voice hissing, 'Not in Desdemona's closet, you cunt.'

I loved being the boat boy at St Stephen's. I think my role there encapsulated what would become my place in life: onstage, somewhere special, at the centre, where the action is, part of the show, but without ultimate responsibility. I loved it, too, because the building was beautiful and the priests treated me as both an equal and a friend. My favourite among them was Father Howard, a small, round and bespectacled man (he looked a bit like Billy Bunter in a cassock) who took me under his wing and, now and then, when no one was looking, let me try on his biretta.

After the last service on a Sunday I would escort Father Howard around the church, holding the candle snuffer for him. At each of the church's many side altars we would genuflect, I would pass him the snuffer, he would extinguish the candles, return the snuffer to me, we would genuflect again and move on. One Sunday we departed from our usual route and he led me across the vestry, through a narrow wooden door into a tiny chapel beyond. On a trestle in the middle of the room was a bare coffin with large orange candles standing at each corner. We knelt by the coffin; Father Howard said a prayer; we snuffed out the candles and came out.

As I pulled off my surplice, I asked Father Howard, 'Was that person dead?'

'No,' said Father Howard, smiling, 'he is very much alive, and he will live for ever. That's the joy of death.'

I was happy being part of the St Stephen's family and honoured when, at Christmas – in the year I turned ten, I think – I was invited to give a reading in the Service of Nine Lessons and Carols. Alarmingly, it was the first reading, the one from the Book of Genesis where God tells sinful Adam that he has lost the life of Paradise and that his seed will bruise the serpent's head. I hadn't the first idea what any of it meant, and, worse, the final sentence of the lesson read: 'it shall bruise thy head, and thou shalt bruise his heel'. At that stage in my life, I really couldn't roll my 'r's. I said: 'it shall bwoose thy head, and thou shalt bwoose his heel'.

The way I spoke the line still haunts me (it features in my bad dreams), but I don't know why, because the reading – to a packed congregation (my biggest audience to date) – was judged a success. At the end of the service, another of the readers, an elderly gentleman, tall and thin, wearing rimless spectacles and with a tentative, tortoise-like smile, found me in the vestry and congratulated me.

'Do you know who this is, Gyles, who's shaking your hand?' asked Father Howard.

'No,' I said.

'This,' said Father Howard, 'is the great poet Mr T. S. Eliot. Mr Eliot is one of our churchwardens.'

I had not heard of T. S. Eliot, but I liked the look of him and, because I was a well-brought-up child, I asked him about his poetry. Not surprisingly, he did not mention *The Waste Land* or the *Four Quartets*. He told me about the poems he had written for his godchildren – *Old Possum's Book of Practical Cats* – and wondered if I might like to learn one of them for him. He suggested 'Macavity: the Mystery Cat'.

I went away and I learnt it in a week. I can remember it still. That's the joy of learning poetry as a child. It's always in there somewhere: it never goes away.

10. Name dropping

I suppose it was at about this time that I became interested in 'collecting' famous people. One day Pa was driving us along Knightsbridge when suddenly his cigarette twitched and ash cascaded down his front. 'Look!' he cried. 'Going into the Hyde Park Hotel – it's Randolph!'

'What? Randolph the red-nosed reindeer?' I answered, peering out of the car window, trying to be amusing.

'Randolph Churchill,' said Pa, impatiently, 'Winston's son.'

I knew who Winston Churchill was and Pa explained that Randolph was his only son, a journalist, 'a bit of a bad hat', famously married to the notorious Pamela Harriman. Pa and Randolph had been at Oxford at the same time. 'Not easy being the son of a great man,' said Pa. 'Doesn't look too well, does he? Drinks too much.'

Randolph was only forty-seven at the time but, heavy, hunched and stooped, he looked very old to me as he slowly made his way up the hotel's front steps.

Years later, I climbed those hotel steps quite often. It was at the Hyde Park Hotel that I made one of my attempts on the record for the longest-ever after-dinner speech. (Eleven hours on that occasion.)

It was at the Hyde Park Hotel, too, that I once had lunch with another of the Churchill offspring: Mary Soames, Randolph's youngest sister and her father's favourite child. She spoke sadly of her brother – 'He always had to have an argument with everybody' – and of her father with unqualified affection. 'Even when he was a very old man and his mind was wandering, I loved to sit and listen to him talk.' Churchill hated having to go to bed. After dinner, he would linger at the dining-room table late into the evening, lighting another cigar, demanding another brandy and telling another story from his long and incredible life. Mary would sit, enraptured.

Her mother, Clementine, would look reprovingly at the clock and say, 'Winston, it's gone midnight.'

Churchill would then eye the clock himself and rumble, 'Command the moment to remain.'

Mary told me that her mother had owned a marble cast of her father's hand, made after his death. His hand was quite small and delicate – surprisingly so. She said that her mother cherished the cast. 'It meant that she could go on holding his hand even after he had gone.'

A few years later still, at Mary's London house, she said to me, 'I've heard you say you've shaken every British Prime Minister's hand since Churchill.'

'Starting with Harold Macmillan,' I said, proudly, 'all the Prime Ministers since him.'

'Well,' she said, smiling, holding out the marble cast of her father's hand. 'Now you can add Winston Churchill to your list.'

Randolph died in 1968, aged fifty-seven. Pamela, his first wife, was seventy-seven when she died, in 1997 – having run through a multitude of lovers and husbands over the years, and ending up as American ambassador to Paris.

By then, I knew their son, another Winston. We were neighbouring MPs, up in the North-West, and I was his whip. I liked him, though he wasn't an easy MP to manage. As a Churchill, he felt he could vote as he pleased (not easy, when the government of the day has next to no majority) and come and go as it suited him. Once, he turned up for a ten o'clock vote with only seconds to spare. I looked at him reprovingly.

'I'm here!' he cried.

'I'm grateful,' I said. 'We'll overlook the casual attire.'

'Yes,' he laughed, 'it's maddening. I've been running late since lunch. The service at the Cipriani was dreadfully slow today.'

He had been to Venice for the day. Oh yes, it's a different world, the world of the Churchills.

I recall Mary's son, Nicholas Soames, putting his head around the door of the whips' office to explain why he might have to miss the odd vote. His second wife had just had a baby.

'I like it to be handed to me like a machine gun, lightly oiled,' he boomed. 'There's a crisis back at base, though, 'cawse Nanny Caroline's gawn and the new gal doesn't arrive till Thursday. Cue for me to decamp on manoeuvres – four nights at the Dorchester, eh? Eh?'

Politics meant nothing to me before I was ten. The premiership of Sir Anthony Eden and the Suez Crisis of 1957 entirely passed me by. Sport meant nothing to me, either, though I registered the death of the 'Busby Babes', the eight Manchester United footballers killed in the Munich Air Disaster of February 1958. A month later, another death, in another aeroplane accident, made a greater impact on me.

I had seen – and loved – the film *Around the World in 80 Days*. Based on the Jules Verne story, it starred David Niven and an international cast including, among many, Noël Coward (my mother's favourite) and Fernandel, a French actor (with a face like a horse) who, as I was a Francophile Lycée boy, was one of my childhood heroes. The film was produced by Mike Todd, a household name in his capacity as the third of Elizabeth Taylor's seven husbands – and the only one she did not divorce. On 22 March 1958, Todd's private plane, *The Liz*, crashed in New Mexico. The following morning, Sunday 23 March, I left our flat early to go off to church for the first service of the day. On the doormat, outside our front door, were the Sunday newspapers, just delivered. I saw the headline, pushed open the letter box and, to share the news, shouted the headline through the door: MIKE TODD DEAD.

Immediately, I felt ashamed. I knew, even as I turned away from the front door and ran down the eighty-four steps to the street below, that I had done a bad thing, shouting about someone's death through the letter box. That moment of embarrassment has stayed with me all my life. Strange as it may seem to you (and strange as it seems to me now), it remains one of the most humiliating recollections of my childhood.

As a rule, I didn't get my news from the newspapers (Ma read the *Daily Mail*, Pa read *The Times*), I got it from the radio. I had my own wireless from an early age – I had *everything* from an early age. It was a small crystal set, which I kept under my pillow and listened to in bed every night. On the Home Service, the most famous newsreader was called Alvar Lidell. I felt he was a friend of the family because, though I never met him, Pa talked about him a lot. He and Pa had been at Exeter College, Oxford, at the same time. (Actually, most people seemed to have been at Oxford at the same time as Pa.)

I loved Alvar Lidell's voice. I loved its clarity and authority. He was Swedish by birth, but brought up in Britain, and had what used to be called an 'Oxford accent'. (It became known as a 'BBC accent', in part because of Lidell.) Pa had it, too. He handed it on to me, and my son, poor sod, has it now – although in a much milder form than the fruity Alvar Lidell original. It's a bit of an embarrassment, these days, but once upon a time it was the accent to which people aspired. You could go to evening classes to learn how to 'speak the Queen's English and sound like Alvar Lidell'.

Mr Lidell gave me the news on the BBC Home Service, while over on the Light Programme, a comedy show called *Take It From Here* was giving me my laughs. The show was scripted by Frank Muir and Denis Norden – and, when I was just eight, I met them! They came to open the Scouts' Summer Fair at Holy Trinity, Brompton: I remember they were both impeccably dressed, enormously tall, thin, gangly and affable. They were in their late thirties, though when you are eight everyone who isn't a child seems to be the same sort of age – unless they are obviously old, in which case they seem simply ancient. Messrs Muir and Norden talked over each other and appeared to find everything either one of them said frightfully amusing. One had a moustache and a lisp and wore a light-coloured suit. The other had black hair, horn-rimmed spectacles and wore a dark suit. At that time, I didn't know which was which, though thirteen years later I certainly did. When I was twenty-one, Frank Muir changed my life.

I can't recall any of their banter from 1956, but I do recollect the ripple of warmth their presence generated. They came past the Cubs' stall I was helping to man (hitting the rat as it came down the drainpipe) and I realise now that it was my first encounter with what today I think of as 'sunshine people' – people who, like Morecambe and Wise, really do bring you sunshine in their smile and make the world a happier and a better place. They brought a lady with them called Nancy Spain. I hadn't heard of her, but she was famous, too – according to Pa, more famous than Muir and Norden. She was a novelist, a newspaper columnist, a great-niece of Mrs Beeton (of *Household Management* fame), and what used to be called 'a radio personality'. She was also, according to Pa, rumoured to be 'of a sapphic tendency'. That meant nothing to me, but I knew it was intended to be something naughty, because Pa always put on a silly grin whenever he said something he knew he shouldn't – which he liked to do when Ma wasn't nearby but a shockable vicar might be.

Take It From Here ran on the radio from 1948 to 1960 and starred a rumbustious, heavily moustachioed ex-RAF officer and comedian called Jimmy Edwards. In 1953 (when I started listening to the show) a young June Whitfield joined the cast. She played the irascible Jimmy Edwards's good-hearted daughter, Eth, in the weekly sketch about the Glum family, which was the highlight of the show. When I was seven or eight, my uncannily accurate impression of June Whitfield as Eth in 'The Glums' was my favourite party piece. I also did passable impressions of some of my other radio favourites from the 1950s, notably

Tony Hancock and Frankie Howerd. I loved the voice (and style) of Kenneth Williams in *Hancock's Half Hour* and *Beyond Our Ken*, but try as I might I couldn't impersonate him. My Spike Milligan and Harry Secombe weren't too bad – which is odd, because I didn't like *The Goons* at all.

There were a couple of old stagers I adored listening to on my crystal set, but unless you are of my vintage (or even older) you won't have heard of either of them, I fear. Jack Hulbert was an actor, writer and director, married to Cicely Court-neidge, an Australian actress and comedienne. Both had been born in the early 1890s. Even as a little boy (not knowing what they looked like, only hearing their voices on the wireless), I could tell there was something old-fashioned about them – but I loved that. Curled up in bed, my crystal set held against my ear, listening to them under the pillow on a Saturday night at eight o'clock, I felt I was being taken back to the world of Edwardian music hall . . . even though I hadn't the first idea what Edwardian music hall had been like. Their Saturday-night show featured miniature dramas, as well as monologues and music. One of the playlets I heard them performing (just the once, in 1957) made such an impression on me that I used a plot device from it in my first murder mystery, *Oscar Wilde and the Candlelight Murders*, half a century later, in 2007.

One of the quaint songs Cicely Courtneidge sang became a personal anthem. In its way, it has guided my life. Originally written (by Ivor Novello and Alan Melville – another of Pa's exact contemporaries) for a show called *Gay's the Word* in 1959, the song was called 'Vitality'.

> Vitality!
> It matters more than personality, originality or topicality,
> For it's vitality that made all those topliners top!
> They each had individuality but in reality their speciality
>   was a vitality
> Enough to make hits out of flops!

Dame Cicely (as she became in 1972) had vitality in spades. Energy, I have discovered over the years, is the dynamic that drives everything. With sustained energy you can achieve almost anything. Without it, forget it.

I once asked Sir John Gielgud, 'What makes a "star" performer?'

He told me, 'Energy, an athletic voice, a well-graced manner, certainty of execution, some unusually fascinating originality of temperament. Vitality, certainly, and an ability to convey an impression of beauty or ugliness as the part demands, as well as authority and a sense of style.'

Cicely Courtneidge had all that. So did Sir John. So did Laurence Olivier. So did Danny Kaye.

In 1956, when my mother took me to the cinema to see Danny Kaye in *The Court Jester*, I was bowled over by his vitality. Instantly, he became my favourite star and it became my favourite film. (Possibly, it still is, along with *Ruggles of Red Gap* and *Paddington 2*.) If you've not seen it, you must. It's a ridiculous medieval musical romp, with Kaye as the hapless hero and Basil Rathbone as the villain. It's hilarious. And sixty-five years on, I am still quoting lines from it on a regular basis . . . 'The pellet with the poison's in the vessel with the pestle; the chalice from the palace has the brew that is true!' (Get it? Got it? Good. If you know the film, you're with me. If you don't, move on.)

My mother loved the Hollywood movies of her teenage years and she introduced them to me when they were shown at either the Classic Cinema in the King's Road or the Classic, Baker Street. When it was just the pair of us, we sat on the right-hand side of the cinema. When Pa came too, we sat on the left-hand side where smoking was allowed. I saw all of the great Fred Astaire and Ginger Rogers films through a haze of pale grey smoke.

Ma's favourite film was probably the 1940 Hollywood version of *Pride and Prejudice*, starring Greer Garson and Laurence

Olivier. We went to it every time it was revived and sat there, as you could in those days, to watch it twice through. The Americanisms in it grated on me, but I was mesmerised by Olivier as Mr Darcy. I saw him next as Max de Winter in *Rebecca* – and then I discovered his *Henry V*. Olivier's rendering of the Saint Crispin's Day speech on the eve of the Battle of Agincourt was the most thrilling and moving thing I had ever heard:

> And Crispin Crispian shall ne'er go by,
> From this day to the ending of the world,
> But we in it shall be remember'd;
> We few, we happy few, we band of brothers . . .

Saint Crispin's Day falls on 25 October and is the feast day of the Christian saints Crispin and Crispinian, twins who were martyred around the year 286. The Battle of Agincourt took place on St Crispin's Day in 1415, when the English achieved a famous victory despite being greatly outnumbered by the French. In the 1990s, when I was an MP and parliamentary private secretary at the Department of National Heritage, and the government was looking to introduce an October bank holiday, I suggested St Crispin's Day – to no avail.

Olivier's three Shakespeare films – *Henry V* in 1944, the black-and-white *Hamlet* in 1948, *Richard III* in 1955 – introduced me to Shakespeare. I was a pre-teen Olivier groupie. I bought books about him; I cut out photographs of him from newspapers and magazines; I made my own Olivier scrapbook. I had an LP record of his *Hamlet* and recited all the great speeches in unison with him. I had my own gramophone player (of course) and I still have that *Hamlet* and all the other records I got in the late 1950s.

Everyone else was listening to Little Richard ('Tutti Frutti'), Bill Hayley and the Comets ('Rock Around the Clock'), Elvis Presley ('All Shook Up') and their English counterparts, Tommy Steele, Cliff Richard and Adam Faith. I barely knew their names. I only owned one pop record: 'He's Got the Whole World in His Hands', sung by Laurie London. It was a No. 1 hit in 1958 and I asked for it as a tenth birthday present. I liked the look of Bethnal-born Laurie, who was only fourteen. I thought I could do what he was doing, but I realise now that I totally misread the song: it's a spiritual, and God is the one with the whole world in his hands. When I sang it in my playroom at 42 Kensington Mansions, I thought it was Gyles who had the whole world in his hands!

A few of the records in my collection (like the Olivier *Hamlet*, like the D'Oyly Carte Company recordings of *The Mikado* and *The Pirates of Penzance*, and a selection of French cabaret songs performed by the likes of Edith Piaf and Charles Trenet) were LPs (long players that revolved at 33⅓ rpm); most were EPs (extended players that went round at 45 rpm) and featured golden moments from the stage shows I had been to see.

I saw a lot of Christmas shows as a little boy – *Noddy in Toyland*, *Toad of Toad Hall*, *Cinderella* and, almost every year, either *Where the Rainbow Ends* or *Peter Pan*, at the Scala Theatre in Goodge Street, behind Tottenham Court Road – but the first show I *remember* going to see was *Alice Through the Looking-Glass* at the Palace Theatre in the King's Road, Chelsea, at Christmas 1955. (It was built as a variety theatre in 1903 and demolished to make way for Heal's department store in the 1960s.) The married couple Michael Denison and Dulcie Gray played the White Knight and the Red Queen. They were very amusing. (I got to know them, years later; they were delightful, and devoted to one another. Not necessarily very exciting as performers – in the profession Dulcie Gray was nicknamed 'Gracie Dull' – but dependable. And decent. And charmingly old school. Dulcie told me that when Michael heard that his cancer was terminal, he dressed himself in his very best suit to break the news to her.) But the reason I remember the production wasn't the Denisons: it was Alice, played by a fourteen-year-old Juliet Mills. The moment I saw her, I felt a thrill I had never known before. She was so beautiful, so care-free, so playful, so intelligent, so curious, so *alive*. It was love at first sight and though I wasn't yet eight, believe me, it was the real thing.

I am very grateful to my parents. They took me to see so much in the 1950s. When I went to a matinée with my mother, we usually queued for gallery seats, arriving at the theatre in the morning and hiring a folding stool from the box office to sit on in the street while waiting for the day tickets to come on sale three-quarters of an hour before curtain up. It was a long haul climbing up the stone steps to 'the gods' (as the top bal-cony was known), but this was before Ma got as chubby as she became – and we were used to it, with our eighty-four stairs to climb at home. Sometimes, for a treat, we had seats in the Stalls and Ma would order tea for the interval. It was served – in a proper teapot, with a side plate of biscuits – and passed along the row by an usherette. I loved the rituals of going to the theatre: the expectant hush as the house lights dimmed and the red-plush front curtains quivered before they rose; the iron Safety Curtain coming down and going up during the interval; standing to attention for the National Anthem, which was played at every performance.

Pa always came with us when we went to see a Gilbert and Sullivan opera at the Savoy Theatre in the Strand. Until 1961, fifty years after Gilbert's death, the D'Oyly Carte Company had a monopoly on the operas and presented them exactly as they had been produced originally: same sets, same costumes, same orchestrations, same moves, same encores. When I saw John Reed playing Ko-Ko in *The Mikado*, in 1959, he was doing it precisely as George Grossmith had done it in the original production, in 1885. I loved knowing that. I loved sitting in the Stalls of this beautiful Victorian theatre (the first public build-ing in the world to be lit entirely by electricity) seeing a show that hadn't changed in seventy-five years. It was as good as being a Victorian! And better than that, as Pa reminded us every time we went, our kinsman George R. Sims had been a personal friend of Richard D'Oyly Carte, the original producer, and of W. S. Gilbert, who wrote the words, *and* of George Grossmith, the star. (Incidentally, with his brother Weedon, George Grossmith wrote *The Diary of a Nobody*, which was one of Pa's favourite books and is now one of mine. It is very funny and very touching. If you have not yet read it, you have a treat in store.)

There were more vintage delights for me when my parents started taking me to the Players' Theatre, underneath the arches beneath Charing Cross Station. On offer at the Players' was a faithful recreation of Victorian music hall, and when I first went there, at the end of the 1950s, some of the performers *were* Victorians. It was at the Players' that I saw the celebrated male impersonator Hetty King. She was nearly eighty, but dressed in her sailor suit, giving us 'All the Nice Girls Love a Sailor', she still had the swagger and the vitality, and that curious, androgynous sex appeal. It was at the Players', too, that Pa introduced me to his friend 'Wee' Georgie Wood, a top-of-the-bill music-hall star, who first trod the boards in 1900, when Victoria was Queen. Georgie was only 4 foot 9 inches tall, and well into middle-age he still appeared onstage dressed as a child, billed as the 'Boy Phenomenon', until the day a theatre advertised him as the 'Boy Euphonium'. His diminutive size helped make him his fortune, but he regretted it always. As an old man, with tears trickling slowly down his wizened face, he told me that he had to give up the girl of his dreams when her mother said to him, unforgivably, 'Let's face it, Georgie, you're a midget.'

As well as music hall, the Players' presented musicals – the most famous and successful of which was *The Boy Friend*, a 1920s pastiche by Sandy Wilson that transferred to the West End and ran for years. I loved the show when I saw it in the late 1950s, and thirty years later, in the late 1980s, when for

two seasons I played Baron Hardup in *Cinderella*, I sang a song
from it with the Ugly Sisters: 'It's Never Too Late to Fall in
Love'. (You couldn't sing that song now: it's about old men
patting and pinching pretty young things. You'd be arrested.)
In the early 1970s, when I was in my early twenties, I became
a friend of Sandy Wilson and used to visit him and his partner, Chak Yui, at their flat off the Gloucester Road. Bizarrely,
the flat overlooked the vestry of St Stephen's Church and they
claimed to remember seeing me in my server's cassock and
surplice when I was a little boy.

'We rather fancied you,' said Sandy, 'didn't we, Chak?'

(Now *they'd* be arrested!)

Chak grinned and said something incomprehensible in
Chinese or Malay.

'We still do,' added Sandy, courteously.

Even more bizarrely, although they lived together in happy
acrimony for more than fifty years, neither Sandy nor Chak
ever appeared to understand a word the other said.

Salad Days was my other musical childhood favourite. The
show – written by Julian Slade and Dorothy Reynolds –
opened at the Theatre Royal, Bristol, in June 1954, and
transferred to the Vaudeville Theatre, in London, on 5 August
1954, where it ran for 2,283 performances and became the
longest-running show in musical theatre history, until it was
overtaken by *My Fair Lady* in America (in 1956) and *Oliver!* in
the UK (in 1960). I had an EP of *Salad Days*, of course, and
knew all the songs by heart.

Years later, after Dorothy Reynolds had died, I wrote a
musical with Julian Slade. He was a lovely man, diffident but
delightful. By the time I knew him, he was in his fifties and
drinking too much. We would meet to work in his flat (the basement of his mother's house off the Fulham Road) and he would
sit there, with his cardigan buttoned up all wrong, smiling a ser-
aphic smile, and murmuring, 'I just want to look at you.'

'We've work to do, Julian!' I'd say, robustly.

'Have we? Must we?' he'd ask, getting to his feet somewhat gingerly and pottering off to fetch another glass of wine.

'Yes,' I'd say firmly, producing my script from my briefcase.

'I've got a little tune for you,' he'd say, coming back to the piano.

'Is it new? Is it for the show?'

'Oh, yes!' He would then play something quite charming that he had written thirty years before.

I don't think any of us realised how serious his problem was until we had a cast picnic just before our show opened at the Arts Theatre, Cambridge. Sitting on rugs on the grass, simultaneously we found ourselves all looking at Julian who was holding a large bowl of blancmange in his lap and solemnly spreading great handfuls of it all over his face.

Our show was a musical about the life and work of A. A. Milne. I had the idea for it because, in several respects, Milne was the man I would like to have been: he wrote quite beautifully – humorous pieces for *Punch*, hugely successful West End plays, novels and detective stories – and he created the world of Christopher Robin and Winnie-the-Pooh. But I am not sure he was a very nice man, and he and his wife had an unhappy marriage.

Through Julian I met the real Christopher Robin, A. A. Milne's only son, who kindly gave our show his blessing and, even better, became a friend. When I first met him, Christopher had just turned sixty. He seemed older. He was a little bent, with owlish glasses and a mischievous twinkle in his eye. I had been warned that I would find him painfully shy, diffident about his parents, reluctant to talk about Pooh. In fact, he was consciously charming, courteous, gentle but forthcoming. 'Of course, we must talk about Pooh,' he said at once. 'It's been something of a love–hate relationship down the years, but it's all right now.'

Our Milne musical opened in July 1986, in the week Prince Andrew married Sarah Ferguson (hope was in the air!), and played to capacity. The boy soprano Aled Jones, fresh from his chart-topping triumph with 'Walking in the Air', played Christopher Robin. Julian, understandably, fell totally in love with him and whenever he saw Aled simply burst into tears. He wasn't alone. In the show, when Aled sang 'Christopher Robin Is Saying His Prayers', kneeling at the foot of his bed, there wasn't a dry eye in the house.

Thanks to Aled we were all set for a West End run, but our golden boy was fifteen, unfortunately, and his voice was on the edge of breaking. My wife volunteered to go round to his dressing room with rubber bands before each perform-ance – and Aled was ready to play ball, so to speak – but it wasn't to be, and after a two-week triumph in Cambridge the show folded. (These days, Aled and his family live two streets away from us in Barnes. He married a trapeze artiste from a circus family – I call her Claire Zippo, though she is really Claire Fossett. They have a reinforced chandelier in their sit-ting room, so when the mood takes her she can swing from it.) Everyone loved Aled on our show – and they loved his parents, too, who were always in attendance as chaperones. Peter Bayliss, then in his sixties, a fruity, gurgling, grumbling, muttering, mumbling, character actor of the old school (who had also sung that naughty song from *The Boy Friend* – and definitively) played the part of A. A. Milne's father and took a particular shine to Aled. During rehearsals Peter invariably asked to have Aled sit on his lap at lunchtime. Now *he'd* be arrested!

Julian and Sandy, the Polari-speaking thespians on the radio show *Round the Horne*, were named in honour of Julian Slade and Sandy Wilson. Both composers were great fun in different ways (Julian was sweet; Sandy was waspish) and considerable achievers, but they wrote bijou musicals for smallish theatres. They weren't in the major league. The mega-hit musical of my childhood was undoubtedly *My Fair Lady*. I had the EP of *Salad Days*. But I had the LP of *My Fair Lady*. Who didn't?

The musical, based on Bernard Shaw's 1913 play *Pygmalion*, with book and lyrics by Alan Jay Lerner and music by Frederick Loewe, opened at the Theatre Royal, Drury Lane, in April 1958, with Julie Andrews (who had starred in *The Boy Friend* on Broadway) as Eliza Doolittle, and the great Rex Harrison as her mentor (and tormentor), the professor of phonetics, Henry Higgins.

Harrison was another of my boyhood heroes. By the time I was eleven, as well as being able to give you all of Hamlet's soliloquies, and most of the great Gilbert and Sullivan patter songs, I could do every one of Professor Higgins's numbers from *My Fair Lady*, with the precise Harrison timing. I like to think I still can. 'Damn, damn, damn, damn – I've grown accustomed to her face . . .'

Six times married, 'sexy Rexy' was always admired but not always loved within his profession. He carried on working until three weeks before he died, aged eighty-two, in 1990. He had pancreatic cancer, but preferred to be onstage than at home. He used to say, 'Nobody is as interesting to spend an evening with as a really good part.' Towards the end, he was almost blind and occasionally walked off the edge of the stage because he couldn't see where he was going. He was still touring his Higgins in his seventies. 'Damn, damn, damn – fuck!' he'd cry as he disappeared into the orchestra pit.

I met him towards the end of his life – because of his poor eyesight. He was coming out of the Ritz Hotel, in London, wearing his trademark trilby – looking every inch as you'd hope he would – and bumped into me at the foot of the steps. He was on his way to Le Caprice restaurant nearby, where I was going, too, so we walked there together.

When we arrived and I was helping him off with his coat, he enquired, 'Why have you brought me here, young man?'

I explained to him that I hadn't, but he seemed happy to talk to me all the same.

He told me that at his first ever appearance onstage, at the

Liverpool Playhouse, he had only one line. He had to run on and say excitedly, 'It's a baby – fetch a doctor.' Unfortunately, he ran on and said, 'It's a doctor – fetch a baby.'

As a screen actor he was flawless. As a husband, he was impossible. One of his wives, Elizabeth Rees-Williams (once married to the actor Richard Harris, now married to my friend, the former MP, Jonathan Aitken), told me, 'Rex was so grand it was intolerable.' She said, 'When it was just the two of us at home and I wanted us to have supper in the kitchen, he simply wouldn't. He pretended not to know where the kitchen was. He would sit upstairs, alone in the dining room, in his dinner jacket and black tie, waiting for me to join him. He changed for dinner every night. Ridiculous. Eventually, I couldn't stand it.'

Many of his colleagues couldn't stand him. Famously, one evening when he was appearing in *My Fair Lady* on Broadway, in 1955, Rex and Stanley Holloway (who played Pa Doolittle in the show) came out of the stage door together after the performance. As usual, there was a long line of fans waiting to greet Harrison and ask for his autograph. But Rex wasn't in the mood. His limousine was waiting and he stalked past the fans and got straight into his car. As he walked by them, one of the fans tried to attract his attention by tapping him on the sleeve with his autograph book.

Holloway observed the scene and remarked, 'That must be the first time in recorded history that we have witnessed a case of the fan hitting the shit.'

I have been lucky enough to know a lot of lyricists. My friend Tim Rice (triple Oscar winner and the guy who provided the words to all the best of Andrew Lloyd Webber's musicals) told me that the reason *My Fair Lady* has to be counted as one of the greatest-ever musicals is that it contains at least eight hit songs. 'Most musicals these days get put on if they've got just one hit song – two if you're lucky. *My Fair Lady* has eight – *eight!*'

Tim has written sixteen stage musicals, most of them huge hits. I have had a go at a couple. Once, at a party (hosted by the newspaper tycoon Conrad Black, before he fell from grace), Andrew Lloyd Webber came up to me, grabbed me by both hands and, eyes shining, said, 'Here you are. We must write a musical together – a funny one. We must. We *must!*'

I was flattered and excited until Tim told me, 'I doubt he even knows who you are. He says that to every writer he ever meets.'

I see Tim quite often (he's one of the sunshine people) and we have invented a game we like to play called 'Unlikely Encounters'. The idea is that you have to describe a meeting that has taken place – *really* taken place – between two unlikely people. Whoever comes up with the unlikeliest pairing wins the game. Not long ago, I thought I was going to score when I told Tim how, at a drinks party I had recently hosted, I had introduced the literary novelist Margaret Drabble to the near-the-knuckle comedian Jim Davidson, and the pair had got on like a house on fire – because neither knew who the other was.

Tim said, 'Not bad,' and then told me how, at the Paris première of *Jesus Christ Superstar*, in 1971, he had introduced Salvador Dali to Frankie Howerd. Beat that.

You can't. Or can you?

Another of my composer-lyricist friends is the double Oscar winner Leslie Bricusse. He wrote *Dr Dolittle* for Rex Harrison, 'Goldfinger' for Shirley Bassey and any number of mega-hits, including 'What Kind of Fool Am I?' for the show he created with Anthony Newley, *Stop the World – I Want to Get Off.* I bought the LP of that for my collection in 1961. Anyway, back to the 'Unlikely Encounters' game. In 1958, Leslie had recently met his gorgeous wife-to-be, Yvonne Romain. He went to her parents' home in St John's Wood to collect her for a hoped-for date, but was disconcerted when her mother opened the front door: firstly to see a photograph on the hall table of Yvonne in the arms of Elvis Presley, and then to find

Yvonne rushing past him, down the front steps and into a waiting car, in which was sitting . . . wait for it . . . Boris Karloff. How about that for an unlikely double? The explanation is that Yvonne was a young starlet who had recently filmed a musical with Elvis and was about to make a horror film with Boris.

I love Leslie and Evie (as we call Yvonne). They know *everybody*, and are generous about everybody, including Rex Harrison, who hated the animals on *Dr Dolittle* – really, *really* hated them – but was such a pro that, look at the film, you'd think he adored them. Having said Leslie is generous about everybody, he does make an exception for Ron Moody (Fagin in *Oliver!* in 1960 – I bought the LP of that, too) . . . but that's another story.

That's the trouble with stories, they lead on to other stories. When we last saw the Bricusses we took them to the Ritz. We chose the Ritz because it still has the prettiest dining room in London and the floor is carpeted. Leslie, at ninety, is a little hard of hearing and the clattering wooden floors of most restaurants are consequently not to his liking. Imagine our alarm when we arrived at our table to find Leslie already there and asking the manager to tell the pianist to 'stop making that dreadful din'. Leslie couldn't hear himself think. The pianist, needless to say, had been playing a medley of Leslie's greatest hits.

Where were we? Oh, yes, with lyricists I have known. I knew Alan Jay Lerner, who wrote *My Fair Lady*. Small, wiry, razor-sharp, he had three Oscars and eight wives. One of them claimed, 'Marriage is Alan's way of saying goodbye.' He also wrote my other favourite musical of my childhood, *Gigi*. Set in Paris at the turn of the twentieth century and based on a short story by Colette, *Gigi* tells the tale of an innocent young girl who is being prepared for life as a rich man's mistress.

I see now that it's a dreadful, shaming story about grooming – but as a boy I adored it, and I remember that my daughter

Aphra, when she was a young teenager and saw it onstage, adored it, too. In the movie, Leslie Caron is the delectable Gigi, but the star turn for my money is, and always was, Maurice Chevalier, as Honoré, an old roué who encourages his nephew (played by Louis Jourdan) to claim the young Gigi as his own. Chevalier, seventy at the time the film was made, became another of my boyhood heroes. When he came to London to appear in his one-man show at the Savoy Theatre, my parents took me and we all cheered as he introduced what became his most famous song: 'Thank Heaven for Little Girls'.

Now *he'd* be arrested.

We should have known better, but we didn't.

Having loved Billy Bunter, I went on to love another 1950s schoolboy comedy on TV – this one written by Frank Muir and Denis Norden and starring their *Take It From Here* star, Jimmy Edwards. *Whack-O!* was so called because it was set in a comically dreadful public school where the headmaster's chief delight was whacking the boys with his ever-present, ever-swishing cane. Now he'd *definitely* be arrested! (In fact, the assistant headmaster *was* arrested. Arthur Howard, younger brother of the film star Leslie Howard, father of the Shakespearean actor Alan Howard, and another of Pa's exact contemporaries, played Jimmy Edwards's somewhat simple-minded deputy in *Whack-O!* In 1961, he was arrested for importuning and sentenced to a week's imprisonment.)

As a boy, I loved going to musicals, and if there was a musical I especially loved – like *My Fair Lady* or *Oliver!* or *Follow That Girl* – I would make sure I was given the LP or the EP of the show and, shut up alone in my playroom, I would play it again and again, hour after hour.

I was very happy on my own.

11. The Pavilion on the Sands

I am picturing myself, aged nine, in my playroom in our top-floor Earl's Court flat, surrounded by all my precious possessions: my notebooks, my scrapbooks; the paraphernalia for my magic shows; my puppets and my puppet theatres (I had three in all: a Punch and Judy tent, a full stage with proscenium arch for my marionettes, and a traditional Pollock's toy theatre bought from their shop in Scala Street); my array of costumes and hats (kept in two large skips because my original dressing-up box had become too small); my make-up tin (with sticks of Leichner's 5 and 9 – the smell of the greasepaint: another of the great aroma memories of childhood) and the old Romeo y Julieta cigar box where I kept my beards and moustaches; my LPs, my EPs and my assorted 78 rpms – including three records of BBC sound effects, from 'dawn chorus' to 'door slammed in anger', and Sir Malcolm Sargent conducting the National Anthem. (I needed to have a recording of the National Anthem to play before my performances. I needed the Malcolm Sargent recording because I knew he had been knighted on the same day as Laurence Olivier, in 1947. I had a photograph of them both in my Olivier scrapbook. Olivier has blond hair, having dyed it for filming his *Hamlet*.)

And then, of course, there was Growler, my teddy bear, as well as Sooty and Sweep, Mr Turnip, Muffin the Mule and Nozo, a four-foot-tall, air-filled clown-like plastic doll with a red nose: you could knock him over but he always bounced back. (There was a lesson in life there: I knew that.) And then there was my bookcase (I've got it still) for my copies of A. A. Milne and Enid Blyton, my *Rupert* and *Beano* annuals, my *Tintin* and my *Babar* books, and my *Complete Works of William*

Shakespeare. I could quite contentedly spend a day in my room alone. Like Shakespeare's Prospero, my library 'was dukedom large enough' for me.

I did have friends, but I don't think they meant much to me. I liked Ekarath Panya, who was in my class at the Lycée. He was a Prince of Laos (I think his father was the Laotian ambassador; I think his grandfather was king.) I had mastered a couple of Yul Brynner's numbers from the musical *The King and I*, and I fear I may have cultivated Ekarath for the wrong reasons. I've always been a sucker for royalty. He came to my fancy-dress parties in national costume, looking as you would hope a dignified young prince would look. He was quite reserved, but we got on well. And then, one term, he did not come back to school. We were told there had been a coup in Laos and, along with the rest of his family, the poor boy had been beheaded.

I was friendly with two other boys in my year, and I am wondering now if I cultivated them for the wrong reasons, too. They were both the sons of actors. William Valk's papa, so William told me, was a Czech actor born in Hamburg of Portuguese-Jewish descent. His name was Frederick Valk and, according to William, he was the greatest Shylock and Othello of his time. Just before the war, he had escaped to London and in 1956, when William and I were both eight, he died suddenly, aged sixty-one, during the West End run of Peter Ustinov's play *Romanoff and Juliet*. Perhaps William warmed to me because I was the only other boy in the class who understood the significance of his pa having been the greatest Othello of his generation. Later, I discovered he truly was: theatre historians agree, among the great Othellos, only Paul Robeson rivalled him.

Ironically, having fled Nazi Germany, Valk spent the war years in England playing German Kommandants in British war movies. Now, if he is remembered at all, it's for his role as the cynical analyst of the schizophrenic ventriloquist played by Michael Redgrave in the 1945 thriller *Dead of Night*. I met Mr Valk when I went to William's house and he shook my hand. I don't think he said more to me than hello. Perhaps that was deliberate. I saw him quoted quite recently in a book: 'It is said that those who talk so much on the stage shouldn't talk too much in private. No artist should talk at all, he should let his work speak for him.'

My best friend at the Lycée was a round-faced fair-haired English boy called Nicholas Goodliffe. We visited the museums a lot together and spent a good deal of time travelling to different tube stations on the Piccadilly Line to find the posters of the films his father was in. Memory is a strange thing, isn't it? I cannot remember what I watched on TV last night, but in my mind's eye I can see quite clearly each of the posters for the four films Michael Goodliffe appeared in during the course of just one year, in 1958: *A Night to Remember*, *Carve Her Name with Pride*, *The Camp on Blood Island* and *Up the Creek*. The last was the only one I was allowed to see at the time, in which Mr Goodliffe played Nelson on top of his column. At the end of the picture, he turned towards the camera and winked at us.

Nicholas and I were close at school, but the moment I left I forgot all about him. Perhaps all young children are like that with their friends: easy come, easy go. In recent years, since I turned sixty-five in fact, I have found more and more of my contemporaries, in retirement, with time on their hands, 'reaching out' to reconnect. No, thank you. My heart sinks at the prospect of seeing someone I've not seen for sixty years. If I had wanted to keep in touch, I would have done. I would make an exception for Nicholas Goodliffe. I do sometimes wonder what happened to him. I do know that his father, like William Valk's, died aged only sixty-one. Rehearsing for a revival of *Equus* in 1976, Michael Goodliffe had a breakdown. A few days later, he killed himself by jumping off a fire escape at the Atkinson Morley Hospital in Wimbledon.

The last time I saw Nicholas was by chance, in the Stalls of the Old Vic theatre, in September 1961. We had both gone to see a matinée performance of *Doctor Faustus*. Mr Goodliffe was playing Mephistopheles. He was wonderful.

I began going to the Old Vic in the late 1950s, sometimes with my parents, increasingly on my own. In those days, before either the National Theatre or the Royal Shakespeare Company were born, the Old Vic on the Waterloo Road was the London home of Shakespeare. My favourite play was *A Midsummer Night's Dream*. The first time I saw it, in 1957, Frankie Howerd was giving us his Bottom. (Judi Dench was one of the fairies, but I don't remember her.) I liked Frankie Howerd. I thought he was amusing. (I saw his Buttons in *Cinderella* at the Streatham Hill Theatre, too.) When I saw *A Midsummer Night's Dream* next, in 1960, Judi Dench was Hermia and Tom Courtenay was Puck. (By then I had decided that Puck was my part.) That same season, in the Stalls (for eight shillings, in Row K), I sat alone and watched the most wonderful production of any play that I had ever seen: *Romeo and Juliet*, directed by Franco Zeffirelli, with John Stride and Judi Dench as the star-crossed lovers and Alec McCowen as Mercutio. It was so thrilling and so real, I was overwhelmed. The play simply got to me. And Judi Dench got to me, too. I was twelve and she was twenty-five, but I knew from the moment I saw her that, one day – someday soon – we would act together.

John Stride was good as Romeo – but not as good as I would have been.

Alec McCowen was very good as Mercutio – as good as I hoped to be.

By the time I was eleven I already knew my childhood was coming to an end. Life at home was changing. My eldest sister, Jennifer, was at London University studying modern languages and about to get her own flat; Virginia was twenty and qualifying as a nurse at the Middlesex Hospital, mostly living in the nurses' quarters in Marylebone; Hester was coming up for eighteen, working with horses, but in and out of hospital, still struggling with bouts of mental illness that nobody seemed to know what to do about.

Pa was busy. He was legal adviser to the AA (the automobile people, not the alcoholics) and his office was a light and airy corner room on the third floor at Fanum House, the AA's headquarters overlooking Leicester Square. I used to visit him there quite often, timing my arrival to coincide with the appearance of the tea lady who toured the building floor by floor, bringing coffee in the morning ('One lump or two?') and tea in the afternoon ('Two lumps or three?'), with extra biscuits ('Custard creams or Nice?') just for me. I can see Pa sitting at his desk correcting his correspondence, leaning on his elbow, his right hand holding his forehead. Since his right hand was also always holding a cigarette, there was a yellow streak of nicotine running through his grey hair. He had grey hair from about the time he was thirty – 'useful for a lawyer', he used to say, but annoying in other ways. When we were out together he was always taken for my grandfather. I didn't mind, but I think he did.

He was always correcting his correspondence because his good-hearted secretary, Miss Webb, a homely spinster of indeterminate age, was not the world's best typist.

'She's the worst, my boy, the worst!' Pa would exclaim – showing me all the corrections and deletions required to the document in hand.

'It doesn't look too bad to me,' I'd say.

'It's terrible,' he'd protest. 'And I have to correct the carbon copies, as well as the originals, because we have to keep them on file. She's worse than useless.'

But she stayed with him for thirty years, until they both retired.

I remember visiting the office in the week she got engaged. 'Look at the ring! Look at the ring!' Pa calloohed, marching me through the glass-fronted door that led to her room and pulling her hand off her typewriter keyboard to show it to me. 'Miss Webb is engaged! There's hope for us all.' His joshing was tinged with cruelty, but I don't believe he meant it to be. 'It'll never materialise, the marriage,' he said, chuckling a little too loudly, as he closed the door on his secretary's room.

He was right. It didn't.

He was a good lawyer: the undoubted authority on all aspects of motoring law. Whenever anyone of any note was caught for speeding, or parking where they shouldn't, Pa looked after them – and invariably got them off. When he went to see the Duke of Edinburgh about some minor infringement of the Road Traffic Act, he took me with him. I can remember the scrunch of the gravel as we walked across the Buckingham Palace courtyard, then later sitting on a red velvet stool in a small anteroom while Pa was ushered into the royal presence.

'Will you be able to get him off?' I asked when Pa emerged.

'It won't even come to court,' said Pa knowingly, tapping the side of his nose.

His favourite famous client was the actress and model Katie Boyle, celebrated in those days for her appearances on *What's My Line?* and later famous as one of the hosts of the Eurovision Song Contest. Katie was very beautiful, and very funny, and she told Pa she kept on driving too fast and parking in the wrong places *entirely* because she wanted to go on meeting him. (She died, aged ninety-two, in 2018, after enduring ten years of dementia. I went to her funeral in Hampstead, feeling that Pa would have wanted to be represented. The church was packed. The left-hand side was filled with dozens of Filipino ladies – Katie's carers through her final years. The right-hand side was filled with scores of elderly gentlemen – the last of her many admirers.)

From the late 1950s, Pa was a regular on a BBC radio programme called *Motoring and the Motorist* and sometimes took me to sit in on the recordings at Broadcasting House. All the other contributors read their contributions – everything was scripted in those days – but Pa was allowed to improvise his. He knew his stuff and he was amusing. He was a natural performer. He took part in amateur dramatics. I remember him taking the lead in a play called *Miranda*. It's about a man who falls in love with a mermaid he finds washed up on the banks of the Thames. Glynis Johns, aged twenty-four, played the title role in the movie version in 1948 and again in a sequel, in 1954. I remember seeing a photograph of her in a magazine being put into her mermaid's tail and thinking to myself that this particular mermaid must join Joan of Arc, along with Juliet Mills as Alice, in my own personal Wonderland. This may seem bizarre, but it's one of the most vivid recollections of my childhood.

In the 1950s, Pa was still in his forties. He had energy and ambition. He wanted to go into politics. He was a keen Liberal and managed to get himself on to the Liberal Party's list of candidates, but he didn't pursue it because he couldn't afford to. Up until 1957, MPs were paid £1,000 a year, plus a daily allowance of £2 to cover expenses. Even when the salary was upped to £1,750 (taxable and inclusive of all expenses), that was nowhere near the amount Pa needed to survive.

Was he happy? I did not give it a thought then. I was only a little boy. Now, I think the answer must have been both yes and no. He looks very happy in all the family photographs, but I have one of his scrapbooks sitting open on the table in front of me. In it he has pasted a full-page newspaper article from 1954: 'Mr Middle Class is broke . . . on £2,000 a year'.

A page or two later, from 1956, he has cut out and pasted in a leader from *The Times*: 'The middle classes are depressed that they are being destroyed by taxation . . .'

On the next page: 'Divorce in 1957 – an *Evening Standard* investigation. Why do 26,000 marriages a year end in court?'

One of the answers to the question was: 'Financial stress and strain'.

People sometimes seem amazed that I go on working in my seventies, seven days a week, year in, year out, spending the day at my desk and going out most evenings to do a show or host an awards ceremony or give an after-dinner speech. I say it's because I agree with Noël Coward: on the whole, work is more fun than fun. Michèle says it's because I only think I have any worth if I am working. She reckons I have spent a lifetime relying on what the psychiatrists call 'performance-related self-esteem'. There is something in that (she is always right), but there is more to it, too. At home, on the kitchen wall, while I don't have those framed prints of 'Balance on the right side – happiness' and 'Balance on the wrong side – misery' (my sister Hester's daughter has them at her home in Australia), I do have, in a similar oak frame, in large lettering, a verse from the Book of Proverbs: 'A little sleep, a little slumber, a little folding of the hands to rest, and poverty will come upon you like a vagabond and want like an armed man.'

Pa was worried about money from the moment he got married until the moment he died. In 1959, when I turned eleven and the Prime Minister Harold Macmillan was telling us we'd 'never had it so good', the Brandreths were on the move again. The lease on 42 Kensington Mansions was up. Pa found us another flat, no more expensive and even closer to the centre of town: 5H Portman Mansions, in Chiltern Street, right by Baker Street tube station – Sherlock Holmes country. I liked the idea of that. I was just beginning to discover Sherlock Holmes. Although 5H wasn't quite as spacious as No. 42 had been, it was a better address: Kensington Mansions was in SW5 but Portman Mansions was in W1. And Portman Mansions had a lift.

By 1959, we needed a lift. Ma was stouter than she used to be, and she had a recurring bad back. (The sight of visiting osteopaths putting up their portable treatment tables in the sitting room is one of the recurring images of my childhood.) And there was a pram in the hallway now, and hiking a pram up and down eighty-four steps is no laughing matter.

Was Ma happy? I hope so. She had been given what she most wanted – another baby. Ma was wonderful with babies and with small children (especially boys) up to the age of nine or ten. Then her interest in them waned. Once my adopted brother Ben arrived, I was no longer the focus of Ma's attention.

I did not mind. I was changing, too.

At the age of eleven, I was quite ready to leave home. Don't get me wrong: I loved my home, I loved my parents, I was happy to be with them, to watch TV with them, to go to the theatre with them, to eat our Indian and our Chinese meals out together, to go on holiday with them . . . but I was equally happy not to. From the age of seven I had been on one or often two holidays a year abroad, in France or Switzerland, staying with families of strangers, going out and coming back on my own; I went to the theatre alone; I went to church alone; I visited the museums alone; I pushed Ben around the streets in his pram for what seemed like hours on my own. Aged eleven, I was quite ready to take on the world single-handed.

I look at my grandchildren today at around the same age and wonder if they feel now as I did then?

One of them does, I suspect. My daughter Saethryd's elder son, Rory, made his first appearance on the professional stage, in the Christmas show at the Rose Theatre in Kingston, when he was thirteen. He is looking for an agent now.

According to a certificate from the Broadstairs and St Peter's Urban District Council Entertainments Department, 'Gyles Brandreth, aged 10, was placed first in the Children's Talent Competition held at the Broadstairs Bandstand on 18 July 1958.'

On our annual summer trips to Broadstairs, I took part in every fancy-dress parade and talent contest going. I always came away with a prize, but I can't think why. Beyond vitality, there was no discernible talent on display. When asked by the compère what I was going to do, I said 'acrobatic dancing'. My routine featured neither proper acrobatics nor anything that resembled real dancing. As the band played, I simply threw myself around the stage like a whirling dervish, arms flailing, legs splaying, flinging myself into the air and on to my knees with complete abandon. I had no sense of rhythm and no sense of style, but clearly I was giving it a go and not holding back on the energy front – and in a children's talent competition (and in life, it seems) that can get you quite a long way.

In recent years, I have been asked to take part in the television show *Strictly Come Dancing*. I wouldn't do it, because I don't want the humiliation of being kicked out at the first opportunity. The older contestants who thrive on the show tend to be the rounder ones – John Sergeant, Ann Widdecombe, Russell Grant, Ed Balls – and people with at least a feel for music. I have none. When I was in pantomime, Bonnie Langford (a dazzling dancer) tried to teach me the simplest routine. Even when we had done it a hundred times, I couldn't keep in step. At the end of it, she would be facing out front, arms extended, and I'd have my back to the audience and my head in my hands.

At the end of my routine in Broadstairs, I leapt wildly into the air and crash-landed on my knees. It was a spectacular finish in its way – and disastrous, too, the first time I did it at the old Bohemia Theatre. The stage there had a stone floor. I can feel a faint flicker of remembered pain in my knees even as I write this.

My favourite Broadstairs venue was the Pavilion on the Sands, above Viking Bay, at the foot of Harbour Street, where every afternoon, in the gardens, 'Cecil Barker and his Trio' entertained, and where, every evening in the auditorium, 'Cecil Barker and his Orchestra' performed a live show. I appeared there three times a week: on Novelty Night, on Carnival Night, on Children's Night. To vary the fare, in addition to my acrobatic dancing, I sometimes 'played the drums', carrying my small drum kit on to the stage and bashing away at it much in the way the Swedish chef used to bang his utensils on *The Muppet Show*. I wasn't as entertaining as that (obviously), but I was a little boy with an impish grin and a touching enthusiasm, and the audience always applauded.

I have just googled Cecil Barker and he's there online: 'a violinist who, with his orchestra, played in Broadstairs throughout the 1950s and 1960s'. And there's a picture of me with him onstage: he is grinning broadly, leaning into the microphone to introduce me, and I am looking up at him with shining eyes. I am relieved to see I look a little apprehensive. (Given I had no idea what I was about to do, I should have looked *terrified*.) You can tell from the photograph that Cecil Barker was a kind man. I learnt two things watching him from the side of the stage at the Pavilion on the Sands: you can always recognise a violinist because he wears his buttonhole on his right lapel; and if you want the audience to like you, be likeable.

I was very happy onstage at the Pavilion on the Sands, perhaps happier there than anywhere else. I must have been, because a couple of years ago I found the theatre was up for sale and I wanted to buy it. I would have done – we had the money – but my wife said, 'No, Gyles, really *no*. You've got to start leaving your childhood behind.'

Ma loved the Pavilion on the Sands, too. She came with me to every show. I think she saw me as a song-and-dance man: Al Jolson meets Danny Kaye, with a touch of Maurice Chevalier and Fred Astaire. She never really left her childhood, either.

In fact, my happy years with Cecil Barker notwithstanding, I had no plans to be a hoofer. I was going to be an actor. Somehow, by the time I was ten, my parents had found me an agent – and a good agent, too. He was based in a block of flats on the corner of Oxford Street and Wardour Street, at the north end of Soho. His name was Landor. I don't remember much about him, except that he made it clear he was either going to 'make' me or drop me. He would give it a year. I would visit him once a week – on a Thursday afternoon after school. I'd take the tube to Piccadilly Circus and then cut through to Wardour Street.

I enjoyed walking along Wardour Street. The film companies had their offices there and, as I passed the windows, I looked out for the posters advertising the forthcoming pictures – films that might star Nicholas Goodliffe's dad, or Michael Redgrave (Ma and I had spotted one of his daughters at the dentist's) or John Mills, the father of Juliet Mills, my Alice in Wonderland. Walking through Soho, I knew that the women I passed on the way, standing in groups of two or three, in doorways or at the street corners, always smoking, often laughing, were 'prostitutes', but I had no idea what that meant. Because I was on my way to my agent and because of where they were and how they were displaying themselves, I sensed that they, too, were part of the entertainment industry. I liked that.

Mr Landor told me I needed two audition pieces. I suggested a bit of Puck from *A Midsummer Night's Dream*.

'Good idea,' he said. 'And for your modern piece, how about the schoolboy Taplow from Terence Rattigan's play *The Browning Version*? Did you see the film with Michael Redgrave?'

I hadn't, but I visited French's Theatre Bookshop and found the play and learnt the scene he wanted.

Week after week, I made my way down Wardour Street to meet Mr Landor, to run through my audition pieces for him – my Puck amused him, my Taplow he found 'effective' – and to hear that, 'Nothing has come up yet – but it will.' And one week it did. 'An English picture,' said Mr Landor, smiling.

'Good director. He did *Ice Cold in Alex* with John Mills. This is another film with Mills, but set in South Wales. It's about a young boy who witnesses a murder. Quite dark. Lovely script. You'll be the boy. John Mills is the detective. They've seen your photograph, Gyles. They like the look of you.'

I went to the audition and I gave it my all, but I didn't get the part.

For the first time in my life, I was conscious of failure.

I lost the part, I lost the agent, and I left home, all within the space of a few weeks.

PART TWO
Leaving Home

Behind the complicated details of the world stand the
simplicities: God is good, the grown-up man or
woman knows the answer to every question, there is
such a thing as truth, and justice is as measured and
faultless as a clock. Our heroes are simple: they are
brave, they tell the truth, they are good swordsmen
and they are never in the long run really defeated.
That is why no later books satisfy us like those which
were read to us in childhood – for those promised a
world of great simplicity of which we knew the rules,
but the later books are complicated and
contradictory with experience; they are formed
out of our own disappointing memories.

Graham Greene, *The Ministry of Fear*

12. Sex

I realise now that I must have been a ghastly child. Those bullies in my class at the Lycée had every reason to ambush me for my sweet money. I was insufferable: precocious, pretentious, conceited, egotistical. My friend Piotr was right to do what he did that afternoon at the ABC tea room. He put mustard in my mouth to shut me up.

I have just this minute, for the first time, opened a box of bits and pieces that belonged to my mother. In it I have found a stash of school reports and letters from teachers at the Lycée. They do not make happy reading. I had rather assumed I was the darling of the *dixième*. Not so. My energy and enthusiasm were welcomed, but my concentration was poor, my application a bit hit and miss, and my relentless, frenetic 'showing-off' detrimental to both my popularity and to my potential. I was the 'class clown' who never stopped talking. It was a serious issue that I needed to address. The teachers at the Lycée, the headmaster reported to my parents, had a nickname for me: '*le bavard*'.

My parents did not share any of this with me at the time, or if they did I don't remember it. I am quite distressed to discover it now. Of course, I knew that I was spoilt and there are moments of bad behaviour from my childhood that have haunted me ever since. For example, to this day I cannot take the Victoria Street exit from Victoria tube station in London without reliving (and regretting) the afternoon in the summer of 1955 when we went on a family outing to see a new film called *A Kid for Two Farthings*. I did not know much about the film, except that it starred Celia Johnson (one of Ma's favourites) and was about animals (so my sisters were keen). As we came up from the Circle Line and out of the underground station on to Victoria Street, we saw two cinemas facing us across the road: on the right, the cinema that was showing *A Kid for Two Farthings*; on the left, another cinema that was showing Laurence Olivier's new film of Shakespeare's *Richard III*.

'That's the film I want to see,' I announced.

'We're going to *A Kid for Two Farthings* – that's what we've come to see.'

'I want to see *Richard III*.'

'You can see *Richard III* tomorrow.'

'I want to see it now.'

'But *A Kid for Two Farthings* is only on today – that's why we've come. *Richard III* is on all next week.'

'I want to see *Richard III*.'

I was seven years old. I don't know if I threw a tantrum or just burst into tears. Either way, I got my way. We all went to see *Richard III*.

It's a shaming story. I know I felt the shame at the time. I think I asked for forgiveness that night when I said my prayers.

Why did I behave like this? Because I was pampered and indulged and accustomed to getting my own way. Anything I wanted, I was given. In one of the family albums there is a photograph of me in my playroom taken on Christmas Day, 1959. Beneath it my father has written: 'A few of my presents'. There are at least fifty presents on display.

That same Christmas we went to see *Ben-Hur*, the big film of 1959 and, at the time, the most expensive film ever made. It won eleven Oscars, one of which went to its star, Charlton Heston, then the highest-paid, most sought-after movie actor in the world. Some years later, in the 1980s, I met Mr Heston on the sofa at TV-am. We were about to go on air and I sat down next to him and put my cup of coffee on the table in front of me. As I put it down, Mr Heston picked it up and began to drink from it. He meant no harm. He simply assumed that everything that came within his orbit was for him.

That's how I was as a little boy. I hadn't played Moses like Charlton Heston, but my parents had brought me up as one of God's great gifts to the world – and I behaved accordingly.

They treated me as 'the special one' and, in consequence, my sense of entitlement knew no bounds.

I have learnt since that a boundless sense of entitlement can be a dangerous thing. When I was in my first year at Oxford University, aged nineteen, I took a fancy to a girl aged twenty-two and pursued her night and day – despite the fact that she was married to a friend of mine. I wanted her, so I felt I should have her – and she seemed quite keen at the time. Her husband, understandably, was not amused. At a party late one night (at a funfair at the home of the publisher Robert Maxwell, of all places), he told me exactly what he thought of me, punched me in the face and knocked me to the ground.

And yet, a boundless sense of entitlement can be advantageous, too. It means you aim for things you might not otherwise aim for, believing that everything you want will simply fall into your grasp. In fact, I rather think that anything I have really wanted, I have had.

I don't believe I ever really wanted to become prime minister. If I had, I would have stayed in politics longer.

I don't believe that, even as a child, I really wanted to be a film star. When, aged ten, I did not get the part in the film with John Mills, I was surprised – and disappointed – but not unduly dismayed. Anyway, what initial hurt there had been in my rejection was quickly assuaged. Mr Landor, my erstwhile agent, called to report that the part of the child who witnesses the murder in the film was now to be played by a girl rather than a boy – and that the girl getting the role was John Mills' younger daughter, Hayley.

I saw Hayley Mills in *Tiger Bay* in 1959. She was completely wonderful. In 1955, when I was seven and had seen her sister, Juliet, in *Alice Through the Looking-Glass*, I had fallen in love with her as Alice, but it was the fictional Alice that I loved. In 1959, when I was eleven and saw Hayley Mills in *Tiger Bay* – and later, when I saw her in *Pollyanna* and *The Parent Trap* and *Whistle Down the Wind* and all her other films – it was Hayley that I loved. Her eyes, her hair, her nose, her smile, her voice: I was mesmerised. Of course, I wasn't alone. For a few years she was the most famous child star in the world. At fourteen, she was voted Britain's most popular actress and won an Oscar. Anyone who is called Hayley today, whether they realise it or not, is named after her. Hayley was one of her mother's family names: no one was called Hayley until Hayley Mills came along – just as no one was called Wendy until the arrival of *Peter Pan*.

I saw *Tiger Bay* and was quite ready to accept that Hayley Mills had got my part. When my parents told me that I was leaving the Lycée to go away to boarding school, I was equally ready to accept my lot. I had been happy at the Lycée. I had hated eating the Algerian dates on Wednesdays, but I loved being able to speak French so well that French children thought I was one of them. I was surprised to be leaving the Lycée in the middle of the academic year, but I didn't complain. I left without saying goodbye to anyone, but it didn't bother me.

'Where am I going?' I asked.

'A prep school in Kent,' said Pa. 'Near Broadstairs.'

'Oh, good.'

'You'll like it,' said Pa. 'It's not like St Lawrence. They don't believe in beatings. They don't even use the slipper. No beatings. No fagging.'

'They do lots of drama,' said Ma. 'They're doing *Tom Sawyer* as the school play this term. They want you to play Tom. We've told them all about you.'

I suppose, as a child, you just accept what happens to you. My parents told me I was leaving the Lycée because, while the Lycée did the Eleven Plus (which I had taken and passed), they didn't do the Common Entrance exam, which I would need to get into an English public school. They had me down for either

Eton or Winchester – 'only the best for our boy' – but I would have to work hard to get in. I was fine with all that.

I was eleven. I did not stop to think how Pa could cope with the school fees. I did not stop to notice how Ma, with baby Ben to care for, was finding looking after me as well 'simply too much to manage'. I was just thinking about me – and possibly my place in history.

1959 was the year I left home and the year I began keeping a diary. I got the idea from Samuel Pepys. I had read in Pa's copy of *The Times* that exactly three hundred years before, in 1659, Pepys had decided to start keeping his diary – much of it in code. I thought I might do something similar. I did. I have kept a journal ever since.

Tuesday, 28 April 1959

I have arrived at my new school. It is called Betteshanger School, near Deal, Kent (telephone: Eastry 215). There is a long drive and the school is in a big, old building owned by Lord Northbourne. The uniform is grey shorts with blue shirts for everyday and white shirts for Sunday. Maroon tie. Grey socks and brown sandals. All my clothes are marked with Cash's name tapes with my name in brown: Gyles Daubeney Brandreth. There are eighty boys and ten teachers at the school. The two headmasters are called Mr Stocks, who is very old, and Mr Burton, who came with us on the school train. The train left Charing Cross Station at 4.10 p.m. Ma and Pa came to see me off. Ma cried, but I didn't, of course.

Wednesday, 29 April 1959

My bath nights are MWF. MWF = Mondays, Wednesdays, Fridays. Next term they will be TTS. TTS = Tuesdays, Thursdays, Saturdays. One of the matrons is called Angela Corfield. Before bed we have to line up and show her our teeth, our hands and the bottoms of our feet. My dormitory is called

Brackenbury. The bathroom I use is called Ganges. I am writing this in bed. I am at the bottom of the bed using my torch with the three colours to see with. I have got it on green because when it is on white the light shows through the blanket. The tuck shop is open on Wednesdays and Saturdays. I went and bought Rolos. They don't have Aeros or Spangles, but can order them if enough people want them.

Sunday, 3 May 1959
After church, letter-writing. We all sit in the Maths Room at our desks and write home. I sent Ma and Pa my news. The school play is *Tom Sawyer* but I am not going to be Tom Sawyer, after all. It is a musical play and Mr Burton says that my singing is not strong enough because we are going to do the play out of doors, either in the Dutch Garden, down by the church, or on a special stage on the path outside the Maths Room. I don't mind. (I do mind.) Everything else is quite toodly-pip. On Sundays we get pats of butter at breakfast instead of margarine. My teachers are:

Mr Glading – English and music
Miss Loewen – Art and geography
Major Douch – Latin and history
Colonel Thomas – Mathematics
Mr Gargiulo – French

Mr Gargiulo is quite strange. Jenkins is going to be Tom Sawyer. He is 13 and taller than me and he is in the choir.

Sunday, 24 May 1959
Today is Empire Day, but from this year it is going to be called Commonwealth Day. We had a special service at church. It is now letter-writing. Colonel Thomas is in charge so we have to be very quiet. I have written to Ma and Pa and Auntie Edith and Grandpa. Later I am going to be writing my play. It is called *Just His Luck*, a play in three acts for

thirteen artists. It is set in the offices of the late Lord Arthur Grimsby's lawyers. As the curtain rises all Lord Grimsby's relations are seen seated round the room chatting. It is a comedy with a twist in the tail. At lunch yesterday I sat on top table next to Mrs Stocks. Her name is Olive and she always wears olive-coloured hats. No one has EVER seen her when she wasn't wearing one of her olive hats with a pheasant's feather in it. She is nice but quite grand. After tea we had a whole school detention given by Mr Gargiulo. Three boys flicked butter pats up at the paintings in the dining room, trying to see who could score a direct hit on the faces, but didn't own up. We all stood in the gym in our house lines. We had to stand completely still for ten minutes, but every time anybody moved Mr Gargiulo started the ten minutes all over again. We were standing in the gym for a very, very, VERY long time!

Sunday, 7 June 1959
I have bought an Airfix model from the tuck shop for half a crown. It is a German fighter, a Messerschmitt Me-109. I am going to build it after letter-writing in the sunshine outside the Maths Room window. That's where we do all the model-making on Sundays. If the sun is bright enough, Jenkins can make balsa wood burn using his magnifying glass. Later we have *Tom Sawyer* rehearsals. I am in the chorus with Babington-Smith, Barda, Browne, Cumming-Bruce, Demery, Wainwright and Rule. Last night I told Cumming-Bruce my S.

Wednesday, 17 June 1959
In chapel I am now helping Mr Glading with the organ. I work the bellows at the side of the organ while he plays. I have shown him my new play which he likes very much. It is called *One Step Up*. It is in two acts and has a small cast: Sir Felix Thistlethwaite, Gustave (his butler), Slippery Sam (a thief), the Inspector and two policemen. It is a lot funnier than *Dixon of*

Dock Green! I had tea with Mr Glading in his room. We had lemonade and soft white rolls, with real butter and tinned crab. Delicious!

Sunday, 21 June 1959
Tom Sawyer was a Huge Success. Most of the parts were played by boys, but Mr Burton was the Reverend Minister, Mr Gargiulo was Old Catfish, the schoolmaster (very funny), and Miss Corfield was Aunt Polly (S). The weather was good and the audience clapped loudly. Ma and Pa came and thought that I did the scene when we painted the fence particularly well!

Sunday, 27 September 1959
Important News. There is going to be a general election on Thursday 8 October. We are going to have a mock election at school and I am going to be the Liberal candidate. Mr Glading is going to help me with the campaign. Our leader is Mr Jo Grimond. Our colour is yellow. Our message is 'People Count'. We are going to win!

Friday, 9 October 1959
We lost the election quite badly!! The Conservatives won, Labour came second, we came third. Mr Harold Macmillan (Supermac!) is back as Prime Minister. I think we fought the best campaign, but the people were not listening to us. And tomorrow we have a wet run. This has not been my lucky week!

Thursday, 21 January 1960
Played my first game of rugger. It was quite fun but rather cold. Read *Miranda* in the Art Room. It is a play about a man who meets a mermaid on the Thames Embankment and falls in love with her. Very good. Had first music practice in Mr Glading's room. X.

Saturday, 30 January 1960

Had first 'cello lesson with Mr Reid. Not very good. He is old and serious. He wears a wig. You can see that it's a wig because of the very clear parting right down the middle. It looks as if it is going to fall off. Watched men hunting in the grounds in the afternoon. It was quite good fun. They only caught one pheasant while we were there. News. I am now doing Skylarks and Nightingales. Four boys sing a hymn or psalm together on the main landing early in the morning before we get up (Skylarks) and last thing at night before lights out (Nightingales). Mr Glading conducts. He has a little tuning fork so that we get the first note right. After Nightingales, X.

Tuesday, 1 March 1960
Shrove Tuesday

Haven't thought of anything to give up during Lent yet. On Sunday saw a film, *The Titfield Thunderbolt.* Quite good.

Saturday, 5 March 1960

News. Elvis Presley has gone back to America after two years in Germany in the army. He changed aeroplanes in Scotland! At 5.00 p.m. we had the Institution and Induction of the new rector of St Mary the Virgin, Betteshanger. The service was conducted by The Most Reverend and Right Honourable the Lord Archbishop of Canterbury. Mr Glading asked him to sign my Form of Service for me and he signed it 'Geoffrey Cantuar'. X. (Mr Glading, not the Archbishop of Canterbury! Tee-hee.)

Tuesday, 8 March 1960

Happy Birthday me! I am twelve today. Ma, Pa and Ginny came on Sunday with my presents. They left a chocolate cake for me to have today. Auntie Hope sent me ten shillings. No games, good. Haircut, not good. My hair is now so short my ears really stick out. I look like a monkey. Mr Glading says he likes the way I look. X.

Saturday, 30 April 1960

Summer term. Form V. My desk is in the second row by the window. My dormitory is Northbourne. The school play is going to be *As You Like It* and Mr Burton says that I am going to be either Jacques, Touchstone or Celia. In English, Mr Glading is reading *My Family and Other Animals* by Gerald Durrell to us. He is wearing blue suede shoes. (Dark purple really.)

Friday, 6 May 1960

On Major Douch's TV we watched the wedding of Princess Margaret, the Queen's sister, to Antony Armstrong-Jones. He is a photographer and has his birthday on the day before mine!* Mr Burton has decided that I am going to play Celia in *As You Like It* and I have started to learn my lines.

Wednesday, 18 May 1960

Guess where I am? In Canterbury Hospital, gazing at a tank full of goldfish! On Monday I woke up with a horrible stomach ache. The doctor came and I was brought here in an ambulance with appendicitis. Yesterday I woke up with a bandage around my stomach feeling rather poorly. Pa came from London to see me and Miss Woodhouse [the school matron] has been to visit me too, bringing grapes. Pa brought me *The Beano*, *The Dandy*, *The Topper*, *The Beezer* and *The Stage*. Ma and Pa will take me back to school on Saturday. At least, there'll be no more games for a while!

Sunday, 5 June 1960

Whit Sunday. V nice service, no anthems, but good hymns. Ten days to the dress rehearsal and Mr Burton has just told me that I should swap my part with Bremner. Bremner is going to play Celia and I am going to play Rosalind! I am going to get a lot of lessons off so that I can learn the part

* Tony Armstrong-Jones, 1st Earl of Snowdon, was born on 7 March 1930.

and have extra rehearsals with Bremner, Demery (Touch-stone) and Strecker (Orlando).

Sunday, 12 June 1960
Stormy weather. Thunder. I hope it clears up because we are doing the play out of doors in the Dutch Garden. I know all my lines and the two costumes I have for Rosalind are very good indeed.

Saturday, 18 June 1960
Anniversary of the Battle of Waterloo, 1815
The Day, 1960. Met Ma and Pa after rehearsal and went out to lunch and came back for the performance at 2.45 p.m. The weather was perfect. It went extremely well.

> [Cutting from the *Betteshanger Chronicle* pasted into the diary]
> Brandreth's Rosalind was a delightful creation, appeal-ing to the eye whether as young woman or young man, gay yet poised, fluent in speech as in action, managing everybody in the play and cheerfully sensing the possibil-ity of managing the audience too! One knew that here was an enthusiastic natural actor delighting in his first big part. As Celia, Bremner made an excellent foil to Rosalind, easily acceptable as a girl when dressed in that most becoming costume and head-dress. He benefited very much from his rehearsing with Brandreth and their scenes together were among the best in the play.

There you are!

Sunday, 3 July 1960
V good service, with christening during it. Good week with v good music lesson with Mr Reid. Best thing was my stall at yesterday's fête. I ran it with Webb. My idea was a game called 'Highwaymen'. We started work at 2.30 p.m. and got a nice

lot of money in: £3 4s 5d!!! Bought books for Pa's birthday on the 11th. Must get him a card.

Wednesday, 13 July 1960
Did sports practice. Hurdles and racing starts. My present reached Pa safely. Letter arrived from him today:

> Dearest Gyles,
> Just to thank you for your delightful card and very well chosen books. Nothing could have pleased me more. I gave Uncle Wilfrid lunch at the Garrick today. Among others, we saw the Leader of the Opposition, Mr Hugh Gaitskell. I am just about to meet Mummy for a meal before going to the new Royalty Theatre where Mummy has bought us Stalls for the play there. It has been a lovely birthday. I'm afraid that for the next five years or so you'll always be at school on July 11th – but afterwards *wherever you may be* you must promise to come to London to have lunch with your old Pa – at the Garrick, of course. God bless you and thank you again for your gifts, card and splendid newsy letter.

Friday, 23 September 1960
Tonight I passed my Royal School of Church Music Blue Badge test. I will get my chorister's badge with three other boys at matins on Sunday 2 October. Mr Glading is very pleased. X. This term I am going to start writing my new book, *The Life of William Shakespeare*. First few days of term have been fine, except that there is a boy in my dorm called Bowden who is only six and cries himself to sleep every night. I am trying to cheer him up.

Sunday, 4 December 1960
Today the weather is ghastly. We plodded down to church in pouring rain. After v good service, Mr Glading and I brought 28 big hymn books back up to school in a howling

gale. We both got soaked. (The smudge on the top of the page is a drop of water from my hair!!) Just as we reached the building, Mr Glading slipped with twenty hymn books and I fell backwards down the steps nearly turning the umbrella I was holding inside out and dropped all my books. CALAMITY!!

Last night when I went upstairs two boys in my dorm were crying (Bowden and Lewington) so we chatted quite a while, till everybody was laughing, and then they were soon all off to sleep.

Sunday, 1 January 1961
Happy New Year!
Important Events of 1960:

1. John Fitzgerald Kennedy is elected 35th President of the United States of America – the first Roman Catholic President.
2. Adolf Eichmann, the German Gestapo Chief, is captured in Argentina. He will be put on trial in Israel.
3. *Sputnik V*, the Russian spaceship, orbits the earth seventeen times with two live dogs on board.

Important Events of 1961:

1. The farthing is no longer legal tender – as of today. (I am keeping one as a lucky souvenir.)
2. I am taking my Common Entrance exam.
3. I am being confirmed – on 19th February by the Bishop of Dover. (Why not by the Archbishop of Canterbury? That's what we want to know!)

Sunday, 19 February 1961
Today I was confirmed by the Lord Bishop of Dover in St Augustine's Church, Northbourne, Kent. It was a good service and felt as special as I hoped it would. As he confirmed me,

the Bishop rested his hand on my head. It was quite a heavy hand! Afterwards, he gave me 'A Book of Prayers for Men and Boys' which he signed for me: 'Lewis Dover'. Tonight I shall use it for my evening prayers – page 15: 'Forgive, I pray, whatever has been wrong this day.'

When you have got into bed, say:
Into thy hands, O Lord, I commend my spirit,
and go to sleep.

Monday, 20 February 1961
For my confirmation Grandpa and Auntie Edith sent me *Great Souls at Prayer*. I think it will be my best confirmation present. It has prayers by all sorts of people from St Augustine to Robert Louis Stevenson. So far I think the prayers by Christina Rossetti are best. Mr Burton has given me *A Diary of Private Prayer* which is really good too. It is like a diary and there is room on every left-hand page for you to write your own special prayers. I shall do so. I have already written something wise in the book: 'He who prays belongs to two worlds. He who prays not belongs to one.'

I am keeping my new prayer books with my Bible and torch, etc. in my bedside locker, along with the four books that I have been given by the old man in the boiler room. He used to work at Betteshanger Colliery and the books are National Coal Board notebooks, Ruled Feint, 400 pages in all. In each book in blue ink he has written out wise and interesting things – e.g. Sentiments of de la Bruyère, Thoughts of Marcus Aurelius Antoninus, Juvenal's Tenth Satire, Geological Tables, poems by Thomas Hood, the History of Canterbury Cathedral, etc. I am learning some of the Maxims of de la Rochefoucauld by heart – e.g. 'He who lives without folly is not as wise as he imagines.' 'We easily excuse in our friends those faults that do not affect us.' 'The pleasure of loving is to love and we are much happier in the passion we feel than in that we excite.' These four books are the boiler man's most treasured possessions. He has spent YEARS writing them and now he has given them to ME! I will treasure them all my life.*

Sunday, 26 February 1961
Last week we had to prepare a speech for Mr Burton on a famous person. As I wanted to be rather different from the other boys I decided to make my speech on Adam and Eve and also to make it rhyme – which I did. It was 4 minutes 45 seconds long. I got a star for it. My star total at the moment is 13. We had a history test on Friday on the Boer War, First World and Second World Wars and I got 25 out of 30. In art I have painted three pictures: 1. A television studio. 2. Inside a country house. 3. For a competition organised by Brooke Bond Tea something that could be called 'The Arrival'. I have painted a pianist on the concert platform arriving at his grand piano. There is at the moment going round the school *chicken pox* and two boys, Lewington and Boult, from my dorm have got it. Several others in the school have it and only 17 more will be able to get it as the rest of us (such as poor me!) have had it before. This afternoon we had a film, *Where No Vultures Fly*. TTS bath night (Ganges) then Nightingales with Mr Glading. XX. (He always smells of cigarette smoke and Old Spice and I smell of it now. I am writing this at the bottom of my bed with my torch on. I am going to say my prayers now. Goodnight.)

I think the diary – written in school notebooks, with assorted cryptic Xs and Ss in the margins, and with cuttings and postcards and letters, programmes and tickets pasted in – fairly reflects my happy seven terms at Betteshanger School. My preoccupations of the period are all there: plays, politics, prayer,

---

* I have. They are on my bedside table still.

praise (and my need for it). Reading the full diary (there are reams of it), I am surprised to find there was so much music in my life then. My recollection is that I loathed practising the piano and that, while I quite liked Mr Reid (the elderly 'cello teacher with the absurd toupée), and I admired the elegance of my own wrist action with the bow (and enjoyed the smell of the rosin I used on the bow), the sound I made when playing the instrument was simply ghastly. And I am sorry to report that my biography of William Shakespeare, now I've read it, is really quite disappointing. Full marks for ambition; nil for follow-through. The story peters out even before our hero has left Stratford-upon-Avon.

Some of the teachers undoubtedly left their mark on me – principally, I'd say, Mr Stocks, the senior headmaster. He was in his eighties and myopic, with soft white hair and thick bottle glasses, but when you went into his study it felt like entering a magician's lair. The first thing I remember him saying to me was, 'Busy people are happy people. Hard work is the secret of a happy life.' I have remembered that all my life. His last words to me – sent on a postcard just after I had left the school – were: 'Keep that Latin accurate.' That's it. Just those four words, followed by his signature: 'C. L. Stocks'. I have forgotten all my Latin now, but daily I say to myself – because of Mr Stocks – 'Whatever you're doing, get it right.'

The junior headmaster, Mr Burton, was in his fifties, I suppose. He had a gammy leg – the result of a wound he'd picked up when serving in the war in Burma – and I have a feeling he wore a wig, too. I pleased him because I delivered for him in the school plays, but I disappointed him because I was not interested in sport. He felt I had potential as a runner – 'A runner bean perhaps, sir', 'Very funny, Brandreth' – and believed he had found for me the running coach I needed.

'There is a young man teaching at Dover College, just down the road,' he announced one day. 'He's helping out before he goes up to Oxford. He's a runner and a wonderful coach. I've seen him in action. In thirty years of teaching, I don't think I've come across anyone more remarkable. He's coming over to Betteshanger to help coach you boys.'

The young man was Jeffrey Archer. Yes, that Jeffrey Archer. And he *was* remarkable – and, curiously, sixty years on, apart from my two sisters and Julian Fellowes, he's the friend I have known longer than any other.

Mr Gargiulo was the star of the staffroom. He was tall, dark, wiry, and charismatic in a slightly demonic way. I was suspicious of him. (Perhaps I was jealous of his popularity?) He went away for a year – to teach in a school in Nigeria, I think – and was replaced, first, by a properly sinister French master who had a sadistic manner and a fierce five o'clock shadow that led us to call him Bluebeard (he pushed his face right into yours to either snarl or leer at you) and, next (because Bluebeard only lasted a term), by a fair-haired, pink-cheeked young man who was a keen cricketer and could chuck both a piece of chalk and the wooden-backed board duster across the classroom at your head in quick succession with unnerving accuracy. Mr Gargiulo's return to the school – he entered the dining room in Nigerian national dress – was greeted with cheers and table thumping. Even I joined in.

I loved Miss Loewen, the art mistress who looked like Mrs Tiggy-Winkle. I respected Colonel Thomas, who was tall and grave, with crinkly grey hair and a very lined face. He taught us maths, which I hated, but had a natural authority, which I envied and admired. He was Badger to Major Douch's Mole. Major Douch was my favourite. Not too tall and a little bit stout, he wore a moustache and a hairstyle exactly like Hitler's – which was extraordinary, given that he was so British and so proud to be.

Major Douch's best friend from his army years was an actor: Roger Moore. Yes, that Roger Moore – the one who became 007, the film star. Moore was already famous in the late 1950s because he had starred in *Ivanhoe* on television. He was about to become even more famous starring as Simon Templar in *The Saint*. When I met him at Betteshanger, when he came to visit Major Douch, I thought he was the most handsome man I had ever seen.

Years later, when I got to know him, Roger Moore was still the most handsome man I had ever seen. He was also one of the most charming. And one of the funniest. 'Those bedroom scenes I did as Bond were fraught, you know. The girls were wearing almost nothing. I had to apologise beforehand in case I became inadvertently aroused. I also had to apologise in advance in case I didn't.' He used to marvel at his own success, saying he'd only ever been able to offer a director two looks for the camera. 'Either left eyebrow up or right eyebrow up.'

I said to him one day, 'If it's that easy, Roger, why don't you teach me?'

'Why not indeed?' he replied, and proceeded to give me a masterclass in the art of raising eyebrows.

I followed his instructions, I practised hard, I did my best, but try as I might, while I could raise my right eyebrow quite effectively, I was useless with the left one. Eventually, I said to him despairingly, 'Roger, I'm getting the right eyebrow up, but I just can't get the left eyebrow up. What's going wrong?'

'Well, Gyles,' he smiled, 'it seems you're half the actor I am.'

Samuel Pepys wrote his diary in shorthand, using – for particular passages and for sensitive material – his own private code involving words based on Spanish, French and Italian. I wrote my diary in longhand and my code was a simple one based on initial letters. S always stood for a secret. The secret I told Cumming-Bruce (a languid-looking, red-headed boy with freckles, I remember) was that my new baby brother was adopted. I am not sure why it was supposed to be a secret, but things were very different in 1960: divorce and cancer, unmarried mothers and adoption – these were topics touched on, if at all, only in hushed tones. (My children may find this hard to believe, but it's true.)

The secret about Miss Corfield was actually no more than a rumour. It was said that she didn't wear underpants at weekends. Because we were twelve years old (and ridiculous) and she was twenty-eight (and glamorous), this was something quite exciting to think about. Sex was entering our lives. An older boy occasionally claimed a younger boy, taking him to his bed for a quick cuddle after lights out. And athletic boys would climb high up into the branches of the ilex tree at the bottom of the lawn for bouts of mutual masturbation. They would go three at a time, so one could act as lookout while the other two got on with the business in hand.

I did not know much about sex. It was not something we discussed at home. Ma had left a copy of a Health Education Council booklet on the end of my bed soon after my tenth birthday and, with its helpful line drawings, that had given me all I needed to know at the time. Now I was twelve I was ready to know more and I thought a copy of *Lady Chatterley's Lover* might help me.

In 1960, Penguin Books attempted to publish an unexpurgated edition of D. H. Lawrence's 1928 novel and were prosecuted under the Obscene Publications Act, 1959. The trial at the Old Bailey made headline news and when it ended, on 2 November, with a verdict of Not Guilty from the jury of three women and nine men, I sent off a postal order for four shillings to Penguin Books for a copy of the book. On Saturday, 3 December 1960 my copy arrived – and was immediately confiscated.

Every morning when post was delivered to the school, it was all laid out on the dresser in the front hall so that people could collect what was theirs at break time. Mr Burton's study was right by the hall and he must have come along and seen the Penguin Books label on my parcel and thought, 'Aha!' I was summoned to see him. Mrs Burton was there, looking concerned but calm, and with a digestive biscuit and an orange squash to offer me. Mr Burton told me that he understood why I wanted the book because of all the fuss in the newspapers, but, he said, 'It is not a suitable book for boys to read.' I remember clearly how decent he was about it. He told me that he would not tell Mr Stocks what I had done, because he might be shocked, and he would not tell my parents either, because they might be upset. He congratulated me on my curiosity and my initiative and then gave me another package that had come in the post for me that morning. It was an advent calendar from Ma.

I never associated Mr Glading with sex, even though the X when it appears after his name in the diary means that he kissed me, and a T means that he touched me.

He took an interest in me from the day I arrived at the school to the day we both left. We were thrown together because he was the English master and English was my favourite subject: he read my plays, he recommended books to me, he improved my poetry – and made sure my poems appeared in the school magazine. He was also the senior music master, the school choirmaster, the local church organist, and the teacher in charge of organising all the music for the school plays. He had every opportunity – and excuse – to be with me every day.

I think I thought of him as someone in his late thirties, but looking at the photographs of him now, I imagine he was younger – thirty-two or thirty-three. A little less than average height, quite slim, he was good-looking in a young Dirk Bogarde-ish sort of way, with brown hair (thinning a bit), brown eyes and a friendly, knowing smile. He was always smartly turned out, with neat, well-scrubbed hands and immaculately manicured fingernails. I hadn't heard the word 'cuticles' until he showed me how he pushed his back with a special instrument he kept for the purpose in a little leather bag.

I think he first put his hand on my knee during a piano lesson when we were sitting side by side. He said, 'Do you mind?' I said, 'No.' I didn't. It didn't bother me. He first kissed me one evening after Nightingales, when we had finished singing our psalm and he had sent the other boys back to their dormitories. He tilted my head upwards and kissed me on the mouth. He said, 'I love you.' I said nothing.

I got used to his attentions and, curiously, they never bothered me. He smoked all the time and I didn't like the smell of cigarettes. By nightfall, when Nightingales happened just after lights out, his stubble was quite rough and I didn't like the feel of it. What amazed me were the risks he took. Nightingales took place on the main landing, just outside the three largest dormitories and no more than six feet from the door that led to Mr and Mrs Burton's bedroom. We would stand there together, nose to nose, for minutes on end, night after night. Perhaps the danger was part of the excitement?

I liked Mr Glading, I suppose I was flattered by the attention (he kept taking photographs of me and telling me how wonderful I was), and I enjoyed the perks: he gave me presents (books mainly – I remember liking *Little Boy Lost* by Marghanita Laski, and the murder mysteries by Ngaio Marsh: 'so much better than Agatha Christie', he said); he gave me treats (picnics in his room when we would sit on his bed and his hand would creep up my shorts); he took me on outings to Dover and Deal. He had a friend called Rex who had a small open-topped tourer and sometimes came down at weekends. I remember them taking me and another boy on an outing to Folkestone. Sitting in the front of the car, Rex and Brian (out of school he encouraged me to call him Brian, though I don't think I ever did) looked very much like Kenneth More and John Gregson setting off for Brighton in the film *Genevieve*. It was a fun day out.

I knew Mr Glading had other favourites (the boy who came with us to Folkestone – much more obviously handsome than me, with brown wavy hair and long eyelashes – was one of them), but I knew, too, that I was the special one.

This went on for more than two years. I marvel now that nobody seemed to know. During the holidays, Mr Glading wrote to me regularly – innocuous letters: 'Hello old chap, how are you doing?' – and turned up to take me out to tea and a concert at the Festival Hall. If my parents suspected anything, they never mentioned it. One of my contemporaries emailed me out of the blue the other day and mentioned Mr Glading. 'He always struck me as a mild and entirely harmless chap,' he said. But his brother remembered 'his tendency to put his hand on his knee during piano lessons and that sort of thing'.

Eventually, somebody must have noticed something, and something was done. He would be arrested nowadays, of course, and quite right, too. In those days, he was asked to move on – and he did, to an all-girls school in Suffolk. I saw him a couple of times, but we had nothing much to say to each other. I kept his letters, but I have not reread them. It seems, from trawling Google briefly, that he died a few years ago, aged seventy-eight, remembered chiefly, according to the *East Anglian Times*, for his arrangement of the Christmas carol 'One Little Angel'.

Sunday, 30 April 1961
This is my last term at Betteshanger! A new system has been devised for the servers and leaders, starting this term. There are only going to be three boys who have any authority in the school and they are Webster, Wallace and myself. We are in charge downstairs, in the corridors, in the changing rooms, etc. We are the only boys who can use the head boy's stairs, leading straight from the dorms down to outside Mr Stocks' study, and we are to be given a special tie – maroon with a silver stripe. (They haven't been bought yet.) A few boys object a little to me being made 2nd head boy as they were

much senior last term and I wasn't even a probationer server then, but all is well. I am allowed now to go to bed at last bed-bell which is at 8.30 p.m. (In the summer all bells are twenty minutes later than in winter.) My dorm is Brackenbury, where I was my first term, and there are ten boys: Bornoff (naughty), Tuckett ii (naughty), Burns (good), Anderson (naughty), Demery (good), Yeats ii (fair), Read (fair), Donald (fair) and Coackley (naughty) – and me. At first they were dreadful, but now they are behaving much better. The school play is going to be *Twelfth Night* and I am to be Feste the jester. Mr Glading is pleased because I shall have two songs ('O mistress mine, where are you roaming?' and 'When that I was and a little tiny boy') and he will be accompanying me!

Saturday, 27 May 1961
President Kennedy has announced that the Americans are going to land a man on the moon before the end of the decade – and I am not doing any art until I have done my CEE [Common Entrance exam]. I am doing extra Latin instead! I have learnt my lines for Feste and rehearsals are going well, but I have a lot of CEE work to do – history, science, geography, scripture, French, arithmetic, algebra, geometry, etc.! I am using the turquoise ink that Mr Glading has given me. I like it. And I am practising my signature. I can't decide between 'G. D. Brandreth' and 'Gyles Brandreth'. (Should my stage name be 'Gyles Daubeney'?) I had tea with Mr Glading in his room. I sat on the bed. T.

Sunday, 18 June 1961
Twelfth Night has been and gone and I survived! I thought I wasn't going to. My voice was half-gone. I was croaking badly, but the show must go on – and it did. Everyone seemed pleased and liked my black-and-white jester's costume with cap and bells. Common Entrance is tomorrow!!! There has been a bad train accident in France with 24 people killed.

Friday, 30 June 1961

Two important things to report. 1. My Common Entrance done and dusted, I am now definitely going to go to Bedales, which is what I hoped. This is good news. 2. Not such good news. Mr Warren [the games master] walked me round the gravel path this afternoon and asked me about Mr Glading. He asked lots of questions. Lots. I said nothing. I said there was nothing to say. I think he believed me. (TTIHLM. IDM. INTBL.*)

Saturday, 15 July 1961

On Thursday we had the choir outing to Folkestone and, as on all my previous choir outings, it rained! We ate our packed lunches in the bus and then groups of boys set off, each with 8/6d in his pocket to find some form of entertainment. A lot went to see a film, *Sink the Bismarck!*, which is showing with *When Comedy Was King* (with Charlie Chaplin & Co.) which Pa and I saw together and enjoyed. Others saw *VIP* with James Robertson Justice, which is also meant to be extremely good and very funny. I, however, confined myself to looking around the shops and spent nothing! I shall go home with 30/- savings at the end of term.

Yesterday, *le quatorze juillet*, in the dining room on the French table at lunch we had a really gay meal, with, besides our school fish, tomato salad, cheese, fruit and WINE. The wine was Spanish! *Vive la France!* (On the French table everyone has to speak French.)

Mr Glading is leaving at the end of term.

Monday, 24 July 1961

My last Sports Day. I ran – as fast as I could. (Not fast enough!) I did the relay – and didn't drop the baton. It was a sunny day.

---

* Code for 'The truth is he loves me. I don't mind. It's nice to be loved.'

Ma and Pa came with all the other parents. Mr Burton asked Ma to present the prizes, which was an honour. Tonight I am going home. Goodbye Betteshanger. I will not miss Mr Warren, the gym, the changing rooms (they smell!), PT, cricket, etc. but I will miss Mr and Mrs Stocks, Mr and Mrs Burton, Major and Mrs Douch, Colonel Thomas, Miss Loewen, Willy Wardale [who ran the school tuck shop and general stores], the Art Room, the chapel, the boiler room, the Dutch Garden, the church. Lots in fact. This is the end of an era! 'Come, come! No time for lamentation now, / Nor much more cause . . . Tomorrow to fresh woods, and pastures new!'

13. Oscar Wilde and friends

My next school wasn't Eton (founded 1440) or Winchester (1382), it was a place called Bedales, not as old or as eminent, though just as expensive (poor Pa), and very different – it had girls.

Bedales was founded in 1893 and became famous – notorious, even – as Britain's first independent co-educational boarding school. 'They eat their meals side by side' marvelled the headline in one of the early articles about the school, whose aim was to be everything the English public school wasn't (no beatings, no fagging, no bullying, no buggery), and whose ethos had a distinct egalitarian, Arts and Crafts, till-the-soil flavour to it. 'Work of each for the weal of all' was the school's motto. Oscar Wilde sent his eldest son to Bedales.

The school's founder, John Badley, was a disciple of William Morris, a Christian Socialist, with a first-class degree from Cambridge, married to a committed suffragette (who was a cousin of both Millicent Fawcett and Elizabeth Garrett Anderson), a man of ambition and progressive principles, abstemious (he neither drank nor smoked), tall, bearded, quietly spoken, but a natural leader. Even when he was young, around the school he was known as 'the Chief'.

Mr Badley was born in 1865 and died, aged one hundred and one, in 1967. I knew him quite well. It's because I knew him that I can say I have shaken the hand that shook the hand that wrote *The Importance of Being Earnest*. It's one of my proudest boasts. And I shook Mr Badley's hand almost on my first day at Bedales, in September 1961. One of the school's traditions is that, after evening assembly, all the staff line up and as the children file out (there were 240 of us in my day), each pupil shakes hands with every teacher and says goodnight to them by name. The Chief was in the line-up because, though now in his mid-nineties and long-retired as headmaster, after his wife's death, he had come to live in a bungalow attached to the sanatorium in the school grounds.

I got to know him because I played the board game Scrabble. Invented in America in 1948, Scrabble came to Britain in 1953, and was an instant Brandreth family favourite. As a child, I played *thousands* of games of Scrabble with my mother and my sister Ginny. In 1971, I founded the National Scrabble Championships. Later, I became a director of J. W. Spear & Sons, the company that made Scrabble. Later still, I was involved in selling the Scrabble brand to the global games giant Mattel. (That's how I came to meet Barbie, by the way – yes, the original Barbie, daughter of Ruth Handler who created the Barbie doll and sold her to Mattel. I met the real Ken, too – in real life, Barbie's brother, and . . . okay, another time. The point is: I have shaken hands with the guys who gave their names to the best-selling dolls of all time.) To this day, I am the proud president of the Association of British Scrabble Players.

Because I played Scrabble and talked about it at school (I was still talking too much), on alternate Wednesday afternoons during term-time I was sent to play Scrabble with the Chief. (Every other Wednesday, a more studious boy called Adam played chess with him. Adam, a nice guy who wore horn-rimmed glasses and was a bit of a loner, also played the double bass and, famously, was once caught in a sexual frenzy humping his double bass case in one of the school's music practice rooms – but that's another story . . .) I enjoyed these Wednesday Scrabble afternoons with the Chief (they continued for five years), even though I'm quite competitive and he won almost every game. His housekeeper, Anne, sat with us and kept the score. I think she cooked the books, but since she also cooked the scones, I didn't argue.

I did sometimes protest. 'You can't play that, Chief.'

'Why not? "Yex" is a perfectly good word. It means a small

belch or a hiccup. And I've got the X on a triple-letter score, do you see?'

'I do see – and I don't like it. You've played it before, Chief.'

'It's one of my favourite words.'

'I know it is, Chief. I've looked it up.'

'It's in the dictionary, isn't it?'

'It is, Chief – but the dictionary says it's obsolete.'

'It was current when I learnt it, Gyles.'

I loved taking tea with a man whose vocabulary was formed in the 1860s, in the heyday of Disraeli and Gladstone, when Alfred, Lord Tennyson, was Poet Laureate. I loved knowing a real Victorian who had been a friend of Oscar Wilde. We talked about Wilde a lot. I remember particularly a teatime not long after Winston Churchill had died, in January 1965. We had lemon sponge cake with butter icing and the Chief said that Churchill was the greatest Englishman of our time: 'He possessed the cardinal virtue, courage.' According to Mr Badley, Churchill's speeches during the Second World War were more than brilliant pieces of well-crafted oratory: 'They were expressions of courage that got into the national bloodstream and gave us courage, too.'

I asked him who were the greatest speakers he had heard in his long lifetime – he had been born a decade before Churchill. He said Sir Winston, David Lloyd George, and his personal friend, the Indian poet, Nobel laureate and philosopher Rabindranath Tagore. The Chief liked to quote Tagore: 'You cannot cross the sea merely by standing and staring at the water.'

He liked to quote Bernard Shaw as well (he had known him, too): 'Do not try to live forever. You will not succeed.'

I told the Chief my favourite Wilde witticism: 'After a good meal one can forgive anyone – even family.'

He told me his: 'Murder is always a mistake. A gentleman should never do anything he cannot talk about at dinner.'

I said that I had read somewhere that Bernard Shaw described Oscar Wilde as 'the greatest talker of his time – perhaps of all time'.

The Chief said that Shaw was right – but that Wilde was a conversationalist, not an orator. He also told me that much of Oscar's famous 'wit' wasn't spontaneous. It was worked on, rehearsed and studied. He recalled staying at a house party in Cambridge with Oscar and travelling back with him to London by train. Assorted fellow guests came to the station to see them on their way. At the moment the train was due to pull out, Wilde, standing at the carriage window, delivered a wonderful farewell quip, then the guard blew the whistle and waved his green flag, the admirers on the platform cheered, Oscar sank back into his seat and the train moved off. Unfortunately, it only moved a yard or two before juddering to a halt. The group on the platform gathered again outside the compartment occupied by Oscar and Mr Badley.

Oscar hid behind his newspaper and hissed at the Chief, 'You talk to them now. They've had my parting shot. I only prepared one.'

The Chief told me that the reason why Oscar was such a wonderful conversationalist was that 'he could listen as well as talk'. The Chief said, 'Wilde always put himself out to be entertaining. He was a delightful person, charming and brilliant, with the most perfect manners of any man I ever met. Because of his imprisonment and disgrace he is seen nowadays as a tragic figure. That should not be his lasting memorial.'

But, of course, it is. It is impossible to view Oscar now except through the prism of his downfall. In 1895, when he was forty, at the height of his fame and fortune, and madly in love with Lord Alfred Douglas, 'beautiful Bosie', then twenty-four, Lord Alfred's father, the Marquess of Queensberry, left a card at Oscar's club accusing him of 'posing somdomite'.* Urged on by Bosie, Wilde sued the Marquess for criminal

* The message on the card is usually reported as reading 'For Oscar Wilde posing as a somdomite' – but the handwriting is unclear: it could be 'Posing somdomite' or 'Posing as somdomite'.

libel, but it all went horribly wrong. Queensberry had a raft of rent boys waiting in the wings, ready to spill the beans about their wild nights with Oscar – some of them as young as sixteen. Wilde's libel action collapsed. He could have fled the country, but for some reason – madness, or arrogance, or because his mother said she would never speak to him again if he did? – he stayed to face the music. He was arrested, charged and, at his second trial, found guilty, and then, on 25 May 1895, sentenced to the severest sentence the law allowed: two years' imprisonment with hard labour.

In 1962, I read all about this for the first time in Pa's copy of *Famous Trials: Oscar Wilde*. I relished the courtroom exchanges between Wilde and Queensberry's counsel, Edward Carson QC.

Mr Carson: Do you drink champagne yourself?
Oscar Wilde: Yes. Iced champagne is a favourite drink of mine – strongly against my doctor's orders.
Mr Carson: Never mind your doctor's orders, sir.
Oscar Wilde: I never do.

It was gripping stuff. And heartbreaking, too. Overnight Oscar lost everything: his home, his children, his income, his reputation. For my fourteenth birthday, on 8 March 1962, I asked for a copy of *The Complete Works of Oscar Wilde* and when the book arrived I set out to read it from cover to cover – yes, all 1,118 pages. I can't have understood much, but I loved the language and learnt by heart his Phrases and Philosophies for the Use of the Young, including: 'Wickedness is a myth invented by good people to account for the curious attractiveness of others.' Inside the book to this day is the faded green carnation I pressed between its pages on my birthday all those years ago.

This was the beginning of my lifelong fascination with Oscar Wilde. In the early 1970s, when I started producing plays professionally, one of the first I put on was a stage adaptation of *The Trials of Oscar Wilde*. Tom Baker played Wilde. This was after he had played Rasputin in the film *Nicholas and Alexandra*, and before his success as Doctor Who. I thought Tom was quite mad: he turned up for a month-long season in Oxford without any luggage, except for a toothbrush, and he looked like Harpo Marx, but he had a wonderful voice and a commanding presence, and the play worked, sort of. Later I did an audio version of *The Trials* with my friend Martin Jarvis, the best voice actor in the world, playing Wilde – and everybody else. Later still, I did a two-man version of *The Trials* in which I played Wilde and my son, Benet, then a young barrister himself, played Carson and the other lawyers. I introduced the performance, telling the audience my story of meeting Mr Badley at Bedales, explaining that I'd shaken the hand that shook the hand of Oscar Wilde.

From behind me, Benet piped up: 'Can I say something, Dad?'

'Yes.'

'I had a tutor at Cambridge who, when he was very young, had had an affair with Lord Alfred Douglas, so I can say I've shaken the hand that shook the hand that shook . . .'

The rest of his line was lost in laughter and applause.

I have known and become friends with most of the noted actors who have played Wilde in our time: Robert Morley, Donald Sinden, Vincent Price, Stephen Fry, Rupert Everett, Corin Redgrave, Nickolas Grace, Simon Callow, Gerard Logan. I remember interviewing Sir Michael Gambon once.

'I shouldn't do interviews,' he growled at me from the corner of his dressing room, 'because I don't believe in them and I can't be trusted.'

'Really?'

'Really. Years ago, when I did Oscar Wilde on the telly, a lad from the *Birmingham Post* asked me if I found it difficult playing the part of a homosexual. "No," I said, "it comes to me quite easily. I used to be one." The boy said, "Oh, really?" And I said, "Yes, but I was forced to give it up." He didn't look at me. He just scribbled away. Eventually, he said, "May I ask why?" And I replied, "It made my eyes water." He didn't get the joke. He didn't know it was a joke.'

Of all the Wildes I have known, Micheál Mac Liammóir was the most hypnotic. Mac Liammóir was a phenomenon. Born Alfred Willmore in Kensal Rise in London in 1899, he reinvented himself as an Irishman and moved to Dublin where he founded the Gate Theatre with his partner, Hilton Edwards. In 1973, five years before he died, I asked him to come over to Oxford to take part in a gala fund-raiser that I put on at the Oxford Playhouse. I went to collect him from his room at the hotel and, though we had never met before, he treated me as if I'd been working for him all my life. 'Ah, dear boy, there you are. Now . . .' I helped him to tighten his truss. He could not have done it unaided. He looked like an ageing Pierrot on steroids. In broad daylight he was wearing full stage make-up: powdered face, mascara, lipstick – and an improbable wig that was too small for his domed head. For his fifteen-minute scene, he had insisted on bringing his own carpet with him from Dublin – he needed it, he said, so that he could find his way around the stage. He did a sequence from his one-man show, *The Importance of Being Oscar*, and his evocation of Wilde was a wonder to behold. There really was a strange magic in the air. Afterwards, in the wings, he held on to me, shaking with nervous energy, sweating profusely, but so happy – '*So happy, dear boy!*' – that it had gone so well.

Over the years, I have edited collections of Wilde's essays and fairy tales, and several compilations of his wit – some of which was studied (as Mr Badley showed me), but much of which was spontaneous. In court, under duress, he was questioned about a male brothel he had visited in Little College Street, in Westminster. Asked if he regarded Little College Street as 'a respectable address', he replied at once, 'Perhaps not. It is very near the Houses of Parliament.' In the 1990s, when I was an MP, my favourite place to be in the Palace of Westminster was the House of Commons Library – three long, high-ceilinged, book-lined rooms overlooking the River Thames. In those days we still had occasional all-night sittings in the Commons, and I would pass the time between votes in the library's third room, the Quiet Room, where the non-political books were kept and where, usually, the only other occupants were the lean and hungry Peter Mandelson MP, New Labour's Nosferatu, and a sozzled and shambling Old Labour lag who appeared to have no home to go to and spent his nights asleep (and snoring) on one of the Quiet Room's green leather sofas. (When I became a government whip in the mid-1990s, I discovered there were two or three MPs with money, drink and marital problems who regularly managed to find nooks and crannies within the Palace of Westminster to doss down for the night.)

On one of these nights, at around two in the morning, I was up a tall ladder in the Quiet Room, scanning the shelves, looking for something to read. I pulled out a copy of the autobiography of Sir Arthur Conan Doyle – first edition, 1924 – and began leafing through its pages. I saw the word 'murder' and glanced down at Peter Mandelson. At that stage in the game, John Major's government only had a majority of one. If Mandelson managed to murder me, the government would fall. He could do it now, in the dead of night, in the library with the paper knife. If he pulled the ladder sharply away from the shelves, I'd fall twelve feet, concussed. He could then move in for the kill – before slipping away through the Quiet Room's side door, leaving the sozzled Old Labour lag to take the blame . . .

My reverie came to an abrupt halt as I turned a page and suddenly found Conan Doyle writing about Oscar Wilde – and in glowing terms. I had no idea they had ever met, let alone got on famously, but here they were together, having dinner with an American publisher at London's Langham Hotel on the evening of 30 August 1889. This was in the aftermath of the notorious Jack the Ripper killings in Whitechapel, and the American publisher was in search of up-and-coming authors ready to write murder mysteries for him. At thirty and thirty-five, Conan Doyle and Oscar Wilde, two remarkably contrasting figures, were happy to oblige in their different ways. The outcome of the dinner was *The Sign of Four*, Conan Doyle's second Sherlock Holmes story, and *The Picture of Dorian Gray*, Wilde's extraordinary novel about the man who stays young and beautiful while his portrait grows old and grotesque. A further, incidental, outcome of the dinner was that I decided there and then, perched on top of that library ladder in the middle of the night, that I would write a novel, too – a murder mystery of my own – featuring Oscar Wilde as my Sherlock Holmes and his real-life friend and admirer, Arthur Conan Doyle, as his Dr Watson.

In several ways, that night in the Quiet Room changed my life. In due course, I unveiled a plaque outside the Langham Hotel commemorating the 1889 dinner, and wrote eight murder mysteries – seven novels and a short story: almost a million words, all told – with Wilde as my improbable detective hero and an assortment of his real-life associates – Conan Doyle, Bram Stoker and my kinsman George R. Sims among them – as the supporting cast. The books amounted to a serial biography of Wilde: everything I wrote about him was accurate – I simply added the murders and occasional quips that were my own words rather than his. (One of these I have been proud to see since in a dictionary of quotations, attributed to Wilde himself: 'There is nothing quite like an unexpected death for lifting the spirits.' Oscar would not have minded. He wasn't averse to borrowing and adapting other people's lines himself.)

My books were sold in twenty-one countries around the world and became best-sellers in several of them. 'They really seem to love you in countries where they don't know who you are,' said Michèle. At my signing session in a bookshop in Moscow, my readers did me proud, arriving wearing deerstalkers and green carnations. In Hanoi, I was mobbed. (I was excited until I realised when posing for a selfie that the crowd had gathered under the misapprehension I was Tom Hanks.) In France there was talk of a TV series with Gérard Depardieu playing Wilde at the end of his life, heavy with drink and dissipation, looking back on his glory days when he'd been on the scent with his '*meilleur ami, le docteur Doyle*'.

I have earned good money writing about the life and times of Oscar Wilde and he has taken me to some fascinating places, both promoting the books and, more importantly, researching them. I have walked the streets of Dublin, London, New York, Paris, Genoa, Sicily, Capri and Rome in the great man's footsteps. (Oscar met Pope Pius IX at the Vatican in 1877. In 2010, a well-spent *dono* of €800 secured me a discreet tour of the Pope's private quarters. It's amazing where money can get you.) When it was still a prison, I went to visit Reading Gaol where Wilde spent most of his two-year sentence. The young offender living in Oscar's old cell had never heard of him or of *The Ballad of Reading Gaol*, but because he watched *Countdown* most days he knew exactly who I was.

My Wilde obsession has brought me only good things, the best of them being one of the special friendships of my life – with Merlin Holland, Oscar's only grandchild, who, when he wants to, can look uncannily like the great man.

Oscar and Constance Wilde had two sons. The elder, Cyril, was ten and at Bedales at the time of his father's arrest. Mr Badley wrote to Constance offering to help find a good school for both the boys somewhere on the Continent. The scandal surrounding Wilde was so great the family had no choice but to flee abroad and change their name. In due course, Cyril Holland joined the army to prove to himself (and perhaps to others) that he was a real man. Captain Holland was killed in action in France on 9 May 1915, aged twenty-nine. Happily, his younger brother, Vyvyan, lived to the age of eighty. Vyvyan, barrister, soldier, translator, author, diarist, oenophile, married an Australian, Thelma Besant (make-up artist to Her Majesty on coronation day, you'll remember), and Merlin is their son. I think we get on well, both because of a shared interest in Oscar (Merlin is the world authority on the subject of his grandfather) and because there were similarities in the lives, hopes and disappointments of our two fathers.

Oscar Wilde died at about 1.45 p.m. on 30 November 1900 in a small, dingy first-floor room at L'Hôtel d'Alsace, 13 rue des Beaux-Arts, Paris. He was just forty-six. Exactly one hundred years later, in the same hotel, in the same bedroom (now expensively refurbished), a band of devotees – twenty or so of us: English, Irish, French, American – gathered to honour the man whose greatest play, according to Frank Harris, was his own life: 'A five-act tragedy with Greek implications, and he was its most ardent spectator.'

At precisely 1.45 p.m. on 30 November 2000 an Anglo-Catholic clergyman – a Canon of Christ Church, Oxford (he was tall and blond, called Beau and came from Cincinnati: Oscar would have approved) – lit a candle and led us in prayer. There was a minute's silence, and some tears, and then we toasted the shade of our fallen hero in champagne. (It had to be champagne: absinthe, Oscar's other favourite tipple, is now outlawed in France.) As together we raised our glasses and chorused 'To Oscar!' a corncrake cry came from the corner of the room.

'And Bosie!'

We looked round to see which wicked fairy godmother had come to spoil the feast . . . to find Lord Alfred Douglas's last housekeeper perched on the edge of the bed. She had come with Sir Donald Sinden.

'And Bosie!' she repeated, almost threateningly.

Some of us there were appalled to hear Bosie's name

mentioned at this special moment, because Bosie was undeniably Oscar's nemesis.

Sir Donald sought to mollify us. 'Bosie died in 1945, aged seventy-five,' he said, soothingly, producing Bosie's pocket watch from his waistcoat. 'Bosie gave it to me,' he explained. 'I was in my twenties when I knew him. He liked the fact that I had learnt some of his poems by heart. If you want to ingratiate yourself with a fellow, learn one of his poems by heart! He wasn't always easy, but he was kind to me, and I rather feel he has been maligned. He is blamed for ruining Oscar, but the truth is Oscar brought the crisis upon himself, and, in terms of the relationship, the responsibility lay with Oscar. Bosie was only twenty when they met. Oscar was thirty-six. He was very much the older man.'

Wilde was imprisoned in 1895 under legislation introduced just ten years before. Up until 1885, homosexuality had only been illegal if it involved the act of buggery, for which the punishment was penal servitude for life. This changed when Henry Labouchère MP introduced Section 11 of the 1885 Criminal Law Amendment Act, making all homosexual acts of 'gross indecency' illegal. This anti-homosexual measure – passed during a late-night debate in the House of Commons with only a few MPs present – was just a small part of Labouchère's legislation. His main thrust was to bring on to the statute book 'an Act to make further provision for the Protection of Women and Girls, the suppression of brothels, and other purposes'.

That Labouchère should want to suppress brothels rather surprised his friends, who well knew that Labby (as he was known) was a keen frequenter of brothels – and had been since his teenage years. Famously, when he was an undergraduate at Cambridge, the university proctors (the university police) had found him one Saturday night wandering along Silver Street with a young prostitute on his arm – strictly against university regulations. The proctors stopped the couple in their tracks.

'Who is this, Mr Labouchère?' demanded the senior proctor, pointing towards the young lady of the night.

'This, sir, is my sister,' said Labouchère blithely.

'That, sir,' countered the proctor, 'is one of the most notorious whores in all Cambridge.'

'I know,' said Labouchère, 'and Mother and I are so worried about her.'

The 1885 Labouchère amendment criminalised all homosexual activity and led to the prosecution of Oscar Wilde and thousands of other bisexual and gay men over the next eighty years, until the introduction of the Sexual Offences Act 1967 which legalised homosexual acts, on the condition that they were consensual, in private and between two men who had attained the age of twenty-one. (The Act applied only to England and Wales. They caught up in Scotland in 1980, and in Northern Ireland in 1982.)

The changes came about when they did because of a series of scandals in the 1950s involving high-profile figures – mostly men in the public eye caught looking for sex in public places. John Gielgud was one, arrested for importuning a plain-clothes policeman in a lavatory in Chelsea. ('You've been a silly bugger, Johnnie,' said Noël Coward. 'Only a silly gubbins,' bleated Gielgud, 'it never got that far.') The most notorious case of the time involved Lord Montagu of Beaulieu, better known later as the founder of the National Motor Museum and the first Chairman of English Heritage.

I got to know Edward Montagu in the 1970s. He was an odd cove, both extrovert and shy, approachable but difficult to know. He came to see me in my musical of musicals *Zipp!* three times. 'I adore you in your fishnet tights,' he said.

We had lunch one sunny September day by the swimming pool in the garden of Palace House at Beaulieu.

'All my life I have been an emotional man,' he told me, smiling his elfin smile, 'but all my life I have been nervous of revealing it.'

'Tell me the story,' I said. 'It was before my time.'

'You mean the story of "the Montagu case"?'

The 'Montagu case' was the cause célèbre of 1953/54 when, in two separate trials, Edward, then in his late twenties, was charged with a variety of homosexual offences and sent to prison for one year.

'Yes,' I said. 'It led directly to the Wolfenden Report, didn't it? And that led directly to the change in the law. It's important. It's your place in history, Edward.'

Suddenly, my friend pushed his plate of poached salmon to one side and began to sob uncontrollably. His shoulders heaved, his face turned bright red, from behind his dark glasses tears tumbled down his cheeks. (It's a fault in me, I know, but when grown men cry I pull away.)

'I'm sorry,' he spluttered, fumbling for his handkerchief, 'I am so sorry.'

'It doesn't matter,' I said, 'we can talk about something else.'

'No, let's go on,' he said. 'I want you to write about this. I want the truth to be known.'

Lord Montagu regained his composure. He offered me another glass of chilled Beaulieu wine. 'It's light, but it isn't bad, is it?' (He was president of the UK Vineyards Association – and I was still drinking, in those days.)

'Can we talk about the trials?' I asked.

'Yes,' he said. He adjusted his Beaulieu baseball cap: he liked the sunshine but the sun wasn't good for his skin. 'Where shall we start?'

'With the incident involving the Boy Scouts? What happened?'

'Nothing happened, nothing at all. It was the August Bank Holiday. The Scouts were camping here on the estate. It was a hot day. I suggested they might like to go for a swim. I had a friend staying and we went, too. It was totally innocent, I promise you. Later, when I discovered that a camera had gone missing, I thought it might have been stolen by one of the

Scouts, and I called the police. When they came to investigate, two of the Scouts suddenly accused us of interfering with them. The police chose to believe the Scouts, not us, and decided to press charges.'

It occurred to me that this, in itself, was unusual. (It's a painful reality that, all too often, the victims of child sexual abuse have not been believed when they've found the courage to speak out.)

'Why do you think the police believed the boys and not you?' I asked.

'The Chief Constable of Hampshire then was a man called Colonel Lemon.' Edward skewered a new potato and smiled. 'Good name, isn't it? He was an old military type and someone suggested I'd rubbed him up the wrong way because I hadn't asked him over to go shooting.'

'And there were rumours about you because of the lifestyle you led?'

'I fell in love with another boy when I was at Eton. When I joined the Grenadier Guards in 1945, I found homosexuality was a fact of life. There were a number of notoriously gay officers and I went to their all-male parties and enjoyed them. By the time I got to Oxford in '48, I'd had affairs with men and with women. I saw nothing wrong with it. It seemed to me – it seems to me – entirely natural and healthy. In London, at the beginning of the 1950s, I was having a wonderful time. One night I was dancing with debs, the next I'd be at a gay club like the Rockingham.'

'But did you realise the terrible risks you were running?'

'Oh, yes. I think it was Maurice Bowra, the Warden of Wadham, who said, "Once they make it legal, they'll spoil all the fun."'

But the charge of buggering a boy of fourteen was no 'fun' at all. If he were found guilty of the charge, which he vehemently denied, Edward knew his reputation would be utterly destroyed.

'I felt like a character in a Kafka novel. I *am* bisexual. I am *not* a paedophile. I knew I was innocent. Fortunately, as the trial proceeded the original charges were dropped and a new charge was introduced.'

'What was that?'

'Indecent assault.'

'And what happened?'

'The jury couldn't agree, and a new trial was ordered. It never took place, because almost as soon as I was released, I was rearrested on new charges. The police were out to get me, and they did.'

In the second case, Montagu and two friends – the *Daily Mail* diplomatic correspondent, Peter Wildeblood, and a West Country landowner, Michael Pitt-Rivers – were accused of conspiring to incite two young airmen to commit acts of gross indecency. Montagu pleaded Not Guilty.

'We were in the beach house. We had some drinks, we danced, we kissed, that's all. But the airmen were adults, they knew what they were doing.'

'How old were they? Twenty-one?'

'No, they were younger than that, but they were self-confessed homosexuals. We didn't corrupt them. They were experienced – Peter had picked up his companion at Piccadilly Circus. Of course, the police put all sorts of pressure on them. Their evidence was inconsistent and unconvincing, but the jury believed them, and that was that. The trial was a nightmare. My first night in prison I felt nothing but a sense of relief that it was over.'

After his year inside, what did he decide to do?

'A friend of my mother's suggested I leave the country for a time, so that when I got back people could say "I hear you've been to Africa" and not have to refer to the case at all. But I knew I had to come back to Beaulieu right away. It wasn't easy, but many people were very kind. Lord Mountbatten went out on a limb for me. He was fantastic. And to this day, whenever we are at the same function, Prince Philip always makes a point of coming to say hello.'

After lunch, Edward took me on a tour of the public parts of his house. He showed me the place at the top of the stairs where there used to be a full-sized portrait of him. 'I once saw a woman pulling her offspring away from the painting. "Nasty man," she said, "come away," as though I might step out of the canvas and molest them.'

That's how people thought – and not that long ago. In 1965, a national opinion poll found that while only 36 per cent of respondents believed homosexuality should continue to be a crime, 93 per cent agreed that homosexual men were 'in need of medical or psychiatric treatment'.

I did not feel that way. I am not sure why, as it was not an issue we ever discussed at home. It wasn't a topic that anyone talked about at school. But it was something, somehow, I cared about – because of Oscar Wilde, I suppose. In 1961, aged thirteen, I filled in the form and sent in the subscription to become the youngest member of the Homosexual Law Reform Society. And in 1967, when parliament voted to decriminalise homosexuality between consenting adults, though I was still a schoolboy, I felt I had played my part.

Nearly thirty years later, in 1994, when I was an MP, we voted to reduce the age of consent for homosexual males from twenty-one to eighteen. That night I also voted for my friend Edwina Currie's amendment to equalise the homosexual and heterosexual ages of consent, at sixteen – but we were defeated. It was a close-run thing. At the end of the evening, when I emerged from the Commons to go home, there were hundreds of gay rights activists waiting in the street. They knew which way I had voted. They cheered me to the echo. If they had had them, I believe they'd have cast rose petals in my path.

The following Sunday, however, back in my Chester constituency, I went to a fund-raising coffee morning and as I walked into the party one of my staunchest supporters – a decent, good-hearted woman in her early sixties – ran angrily across the room towards me. She was screaming and her fists were raised. When she reached me, she began to beat me about the face and chest. 'How could you?' she cried. 'How could you? You're destroying the lives of young men. It's terrible what you've done. *Terrible.*'

To me, what was terrible was that, even after the 1967 decriminalisation of homosexual acts, so many men still felt obliged to hide their sexuality.

In the early 1970s, I recall featuring in a list of 'Britain's most eligible bachelors' in *Cosmopolitan* magazine – alongside Ian McKellen, among others. We were each asked what we were looking for in a wife. Ian deftly replied that he was so demanding he wasn't sure the right girl would ever come along. Around the same time, I had my first photographs taken for the casting directory, *Spotlight*. Michèle and I became good friends with the photographer, but he never admitted to us the existence of his boyfriend. Whenever we arrived at the photographer's flat, as he let us in at the front door we would hear the door to the bedroom at the end of the corridor closing and a key turning in the lock.

Even in the 1980s, whenever I went to see Frankie Howerd, as I arrived at his house his partner disappeared into the kitchen.

'Is Dennis here?' I'd ask.

'Who?' said Frank.

'Dennis,' I said. 'I met him last time, don't you remember?'

'I don't know what you're talking about,' protested Frank.

'I can hear him in the kitchen,' I said.

'That's the cat,' said Frank.

I don't think they even had a cat.

If everyone has a secret, for more than half my life the secret that too many men felt obliged to keep was the simple fact of their homosexuality. I will never forget the day, in 1989, when the great Stanley Baxter came to see me. As an entertainer, impressionist and pantomime dame, Stanley was incomparable. As a man, he was both very sweet and a mess. He had married, knowing he wasn't really the marrying kind. He loved his wife, and looked after her, but he couldn't live with her. He wished he wasn't gay, but knew he was – 'mostly'. He came to see me when our mutual friend, Kenneth Williams, died. Ken and Stanley had been in the army together after the war and shared each other's secrets. Stanley was convinced that Kenneth's diaries when they were published would reveal to the world that Stanley was gay. I had read the diaries, and I told Stanley there was little cause for alarm. The diaries did not give much away. But Stanley would not be assuaged. He sat in my sitting room, his face white with anxiety, his hands clasped together in his lap, shaking with fear. He was sixty-three at the time.

In 2000, the age of consent for both homosexual and heterosexual behaviour was equalised, at sixteen, and in 2010, my friend David Cameron, in the face of a lot of grassroots opposition, introduced legislation giving equal marriage rights to straight and gay people.

In 2015, my friend Stewart Nicholls (who helped me create the show that eventually became *Zipp!*) and his partner Stuart were the first gay couple to be married in a church in the British Isles.

Stewart and Stuart are always guests at the Oscar Wilde birthday party I've hosted for a number of years. It's a happy event held in one of the London hotels Oscar knew in his day. We started out at the Cadogan Hotel (where Oscar was arrested in 1895), then moved to the Langham (where he met Arthur Conan Doyle in 1889), and now we have settled at Grosvenor House, an address Oscar knew because it was the London home of his friend the Duchess of Westminster. The party began as drinks for sixty or so people, but over the years it's grown because David Frost, celebrated for his parties, explained to me that you must never drop anyone from your invitation list: if you ask them once, you must ask them every year. Now several hundred come and I like to think of it as a gathering of friends of mine who in the first quarter of the twenty-first century represent the kind of people Oscar would have counted as friends of his in the last quarter of the nineteenth century.

It's the party at which I introduced Margaret Drabble and Jim Davidson to one another. It's a gathering of all sorts: writers, entertainers, artists, students, peers, politicians and ex-prisoners (sometimes they are the same people), old and young, black and white, gay and straight and trans. April Ashley is a regular. (In Morocco, in 1960, she became one of the first British people to have successful gender reassignment surgery. She is full of wonderful stories. If ever you meet her, be sure to ask her about her lunches with Albert Einstein in Greek Street.) The Duchess of Cornwall comes, not only because Oscar loved a duchess, but more specifically because her great-grandfather, Alec Shand, was secretly engaged to Constance Lloyd, who went on to marry Oscar Wilde.

There are always a lot of actors and actresses – and usually a couple of bishops. Matthew Parris turned back at the door one year because he saw a bishop in the room and his spirit rebelled, given the Church of England's attitude to gay people over the years – but I go on inviting him and the bishops, too. After all, Oscar counted clergymen among his friends and, as Rowan Williams (the Archbishop of Canterbury who looked like a Welsh druid but is one of the most remarkable people you will ever meet) reminded us when he proposed the toast to Oscar that year, the man who stood bail for Oscar – when no one else would or could – was a Church of England clergyman.

One year, I asked Cressida Dick, the head of the Metropolitan Police to propose the toast to Oscar, not knowing that Cressida and Oscar share a birthday: 16 October. Cressida came with her partner, Helen. I think they had thought of announcing their own engagement that night. They didn't, but the evening was memorable all the same. I doubt that anyone who was there will forget the impact of Cressida's speech.

'We cannot change the past,' she said, looking out over a sea of upturned faces – many belonging to men old enough to have known the time when expressing their sexuality would have made them liable to arrest and imprisonment – 'but we can look to the future and hope that it is one that is kinder, fairer, more tolerant, more loving, more humane.'

It was a strange and moving moment when the head of the very organisation responsible for Oscar's arrest smiled at us shyly and said in a quiet, firm voice, 'As the Metropolitan Police Commissioner I am proud to invite you to raise your glasses in a toast to the memory and genius of Oscar Wilde.'

Stephen Fry sent me a sweet email after the event: 'You can be very proud of what you did for Oscar tonight.'

I was.

14. School

According to Philip Larkin's celebrated poem 'Annus Mirabilis':

> Sexual intercourse began
> In nineteen sixty-three . . .
> Between the end of the 'Chatterley' ban
> And the Beatles' first LP.

I don't believe there was much of it at Bedales School in 1963. Of course, we were out in the countryside – in the sleepy village of Steep, in Hampshire, at the western end of the rolling South Downs – and there were rules. According to the boys' housemaster, there was to be 'no touching below the belt'. According to the girls' housemistress, it was 'no touching below the neck'. Holding hands was fine, and 'light kissing'.

I had been happy at the French Lycée. I had been happier still at my prep school. I was happiest of all at Bedales.

Not everyone liked it. My best friend at the school – he was my best friend from the moment I met him until the day he died in 1996, aged forty-five – hated the place. Simon Cadell became an actor, best remembered by me for his stage work, his Mercutio and his Hamlet, best remembered by most people for his brilliant comic turns on television in *Hi-de-Hi!* and *Blott on the Landscape*. Aged thirteen, he was already a fine actor when I cast him as Sherlock Holmes in my play *A Study in Sherlock*, at school. His performance as the great detective was definitive – as good as Basil Rathbone or Jeremy Brett at their best, believe me.

Simon was happy in rehearsal and onstage, or sitting with me in the corner of our dormitory listening to our LPs – *Noël Coward in Las Vegas, Marlene Dietrich in London, Flanagan & Allen:*

Underneath the Arches, emphatically not the Beatles – and, aged thirteen and fifteen, telling one another old theatre stories about actors who had died long before either of us was born.

'I love that story about Sir Herbert Beerbohm-Tree, don't you?'

'Which one?'

'Oh, you know, the night that Lady Tree came home and found Sir Herbert having a late supper with the devilishly handsome young actor –'

'Ah, yes, and as she said goodnight and closed the dining room door behind her, she murmured, "The port is on the sideboard, Herbert, and, remember, it's adultery just the same."'

Where did we get these stories from? I wonder. Simon's parents, I suppose. As I have mentioned, his father was a theatrical agent and Donald Sinden was his star client. Simon's mother was an actress: she had been appearing in the West End with Ralph Richardson in John Gielgud's production of *The Heiress* in the year Simon was conceived. I thought Simon might have been Sir Ralph's son ... with actors, you never know. In our mid-teens Simon and I both did impeccable impressions of Sir Ralph and Sir John, then in their mid-sixties, and it didn't bother us a jot that nobody else at the school seemed to have any idea who they were.

We were happy together, always, but Simon was not happy overall. He hated Bedales. He rebelled against the restrictions of school life: he wanted to drink and to smoke. He did not want to be a prisoner in a boarding school, he wanted to be a free spirit in London – or in the South of France. He ran away so often that his parents had to rent a cottage at the edge of the school grounds so he could take refuge with them at weekends. He loathed school, while I loved it.

Everything about Bedales suited me. I loved the buildings, especially the 1911 Lupton Hall, where we had assembly and did the school plays, and the 1921 Memorial Library adjacent to it: two Arts and Crafts masterpieces, the first buildings I had known, apart from St Stephen's, Gloucester Road, and the Old Vic, where just going into them lifted your spirits. I loved the heritage of the place. Never mind Oscar Wilde's son, I loved the fact that Alan Jay Lerner, who wrote both *My Fair Lady* and *Gigi*, had been to Bedales. (And later, Leslie Caron, who played Gigi, sent her children there.) Better still, George Sanders – who Ma had taken me to see in *Rebecca* and *All About Eve* – had been to Bedales. He was the sort of film star I thought I could be: debonair, bordering on the dangerous. His voice as Shere Khan in *The Jungle Book* was the voice I wanted to have.

Most of all, I loved the way that at Bedales you could do whatever you wanted. In Simon's case that meant very little. Schoolwork did not interest him: I am not sure if he took any O Levels. What was the point? He only wanted to act. I wanted to do *everything*. Except games, of course. And physics and chemistry. Maths was a bit of a pain, too. And geography was dull, dull, dull. But all the things I liked to do, I did. Bedales got me through my O Levels (even maths); Bedales got me my As at A Level (I'd been to the Lycée so, of course, the French was a doddle); Bedales got me into Oxford.

All that I have been ever since, I started being at Bedales.

My wife finds this a bit depressing. 'There's been no development in your life at all,' she says to me at breakfast most days. (She says it at breakfast because I have a Bedales mug and side plate and I like to use them in the morning.)

I am not as bad as some: the property prices in the village of Steep rival those in Holland Park because so many Old Bedalians, unable to escape the school, buy themselves country cottages near it. I very rarely go back to the school and only have a handful of friends dating from my schooldays, but the life I formed at Bedales is, in every particular, the life that I lead now.

I began my life as a journalist and interviewer at Bedales. I edited the school magazine – revamped it, redesigned it and wrote most of it (of course). My first interview was with the local vicar. ('Why do you believe in God?' 'Because he is ultimately unavoidable.') My second was with the President of Switzerland.

I began my life in politics at Bedales. In 1964 when, on the national stage, Harold Wilson defeated Sir Alec Douglas-Home to become Britain's first Labour Prime Minister since Clement Attlee, at Bedales I was the Conservative candidate in the school's mock general election. (I collected my campaign material from the home of Lady Ashcombe who lived at Hall Place at West Meon, not far from the school. That's where I first caught sight of her granddaughter Camilla Shand, aged seventeen, in her jodhpurs, hiding in the bushes, smoking a Woodbine. Fifty-five years on, the Duchess of Cornwall doesn't deny she was smoking, but she's adamant it wasn't a Woodbine.)

At Bedales I produced plays and cabarets every term and I was in the school play every year. (When I played Malvolio in *Twelfth Night*, the actor Michael Hordern's daughter, Joanna, played Olivia. Unfortunately, at the opening performance my parents were seated immediately in front of Joanna's parents and every time I came on, Sir Michael – as he became – couldn't contain himself: 'Oh God, that boy is *so* dreadful. The overacting – it's embarrassing, it's *unbearable.*' What did he know? A week later I pasted the review from the local newspaper into my scrapbook. The headline read: 'MALVOLIO STOLE THE SHOW'.)

I discovered the satisfaction of learning poetry by heart at Bedales. Rachel Field, our remarkable speech and drama teacher (in the film she'd be played by a cross between Edith Evans and Miriam Margolyes; Daniel Day-Lewis, one of her star pupils at the school, says he owes it all to her), took us up to London to take part in verse-speaking competitions. We performed poems individually and in groups, competing against other schools. Half a century later, those competitions inspired my Poetry Together project, where

GB photographed by his girlfriend Jackie, 1963

GB as Malvolio in *Twelfth Night*, Bedales, 1963

GB losing the 1964 General Election, Bedales, 1964

GB on stage at Bedales, 1965

GB at New College, Oxford, 1968

GB with Pa and brother Ben, New College, 1969

GB's 21st birthday at 5H Portman Mansions, London, 1969

[*opposite page*] Michèle Brown in the summer GB met her, 1968

The first Zuleika Dobson competition with the winner, Lady Annunziata Asquith, June 1968. Michèle Brown is sitting third from the left

Making a splash, GB's first centre spread, *Daily Mirror*, 13th June 1968

Cinderella, Oxford Playhouse, 1968, with Eliza Manningham-Buller as the Fairy Queen and Caroline Bennitt as Cinderella

Opening night: from left to right: Diana Quick, first female President of the Oxford University Dramatic Society; Sir Michael Redgrave, who performed the Prologue; Archie Harradine, who wrote the pantomime; and GB, who produced it

GB and Michèle, Christmas 1969

GB interviewing the Archbishop of Canterbury, Michael Ramsey, 1970

THIS IS GYLES BRANDRETH

He's twenty-four years old and has already made his mark as a writer and broadcaster on such vastly differing subjects as pornography and pantomime. He's got a keen eye open for all that's amusing or touching, lovable or deplorable. Modern as tomorrow, he still has a lot of time for yesterday. His ideas are wide-ranging; the words in which he expresses them are thought provoking; and we are pleased that every week he's going to be expressing them for us.

Created in Captivity: GB with his collection of prisoners' art, holding a painting by double murderer Donald Hume, 1971

Woman magazine, 1972: 'Modern as tomorrow, he still has a lot of time for yesterday . . .'

Ralph Steadman cartoon, *Nova*, 1970

Terry Pratchett cartoon, 1972

GB at a *Yorkshire Post* Literary Lunch in Leeds, 1972

GB as Snoopy, Butlin's, Minehead, 1974

groups of schoolchildren and groups of old people living in care homes learn the same poems and then meet up around National Poetry Day to recite them together and to have tea and cake afterwards. Hundreds of schools and care homes around the country take part. The Duchess of Cornwall kindly comes along to sprinkle some royal fairy dust on the proceedings. It's a wonderful thing, and it all began at Bedales in 1963. That's when I discovered, too, how easily very young people can get on with very old people. As well as having tea with Mr Badley, every week I did 'voluntary outdoor work' at the home of an elderly couple in the village. Ostensibly, I was there to do a bit of gardening. In reality, after ten minutes of light weeding, I went into their bungalow for tea. They were called Mr and Mrs Cox (their bungalow was called Merries) and they were like Mr and Mrs Jack Sprat from the nursery rhyme: he was small and timid and served the tea, while she was large, strong-willed and did most of the talking. She had been a suffragette and had marched alongside Mrs Pankhurst.

'You never do anything you didn't do at school, do you, Gyles?' is what my wife says to me.

She's right, but is it so wrong?

I began my life as a professional public speaker at Bedales. I won three guineas as first prize for making a speech on road safety in a competition organised by the local Rotary Club. That was on Tuesday, 30 November 1965. Nearly sixty years on, making speeches is how I earn the bulk of my living. Nothing has changed.

'Bless,' says Michèle. 'You'll soon be eighty and yet you're still a little boy looking for approval, coming up with your little schemes and projects, saying, "Look at me, aren't I clever?" You're still sitting in the middle of the front row with your hand up, trying to get the teacher's attention, wanting to be told you're the best boy in the class.'

Certainly at Bedales, for five years without pause, I was

busy-busy-busy, running from one project to the next. I had taken Mr Stocks' maxim to heart – 'Busy people are happy people. Hard work is the secret of a happy life' – but I had extended the philosophy with a nugget of wisdom from the poet William Blake:

> He who would do good to another must do it in Minute Particulars: general Good is the plea of the scoundrel, hypocrite, and flatterer, for Art and Science cannot exist but in minutely organised Particulars.

I had enjoyed spouting well-intentioned platitudes during the 1964 election (I thought I'd been rather good at it!) but I reckoned Blake (a natural Bedalian if ever there was one) was on to something: if you want to make a real difference, you have to do something specific. I decided to devote myself to a life of 'Minute Particulars'. I was sixteen and made up my mind (I'm not sure why) that I must improve the lot of the school's juniors, the twelve- and thirteen-year-olds. Outside of lessons, they didn't have much to do, or anywhere to do it. First, I got them their own hut in the orchard to use as a kind of junior common room – equipped with its own gramophone and toaster. Then, bizarrely, I organised cycling proficiency tests for them – bizarre because, while I had loved my tricycle aged six, I was pretty wobbly on a bike.

There was another element of my evolving philosophy – this time supplied by Lord Byron (again a Bedales natural):

> Always laugh when you can; it is cheap medicine. Merriment is a philosophy not well understood. It is the sunny side of existence.

I thought the juniors didn't have enough to do in the evening, so I organised ballroom dancing classes for them. This was a truly ludicrous idea, since I can't dance and couldn't then, but a girl in my year, Diana Ambache – a fine musician and, later, a noted champion of neglected female composers – showed me the basic steps and, somehow, with music supplied variously by Victor Silvester, Joe Loss and Lonnie Donegan, a good time was had by all.

I was beginning to think seriously about serious things. I was writing letters to the national press – prison reform was my particular passion – but I cannot pretend that my beliefs were underpinned by any proper study of the writings of the likes of Blake and Byron. My *Weltanschauung* (naturally, I did German O Level) came from the words of wisdom I collected from the Memorial Library calendar.

I loved the library. It's the only part of the school I still hanker after. I loved the wooden beams, the smell of beeswax, the complete silence . . . I liked to sit upstairs in the gallery, in the Shakespeare alcove, looking down at the ground floor below. At one end there was a giant globe, lit from within; at the other, was the Library calendar. Underneath the date, every day, there was a nugget of wisdom. One of the perks of being a school librarian was that, at the end of the day, you had first dibs at the calendar. I kept pages and pages from that calendar. I have them still. Here are just three, from November 1966, the term I left the school.

> *5 November*: 'Idleness leads to languor, and languor to disgust.'
> (Amiel's *Journal Intime*)

> *13 November*: 'If I were ambitious, I would desire no finer epitaph than that it should be said of me, "He has added a little to the sweetness of the world and a little to its light."' (Havelock Ellis)

> *21 November*: 'Perhaps the most valuable result of all education is the ability to make yourself do the thing you have to do, when it ought to be done, whether you like it or not.'
> (T. H. Huxley)

I have measured out my life in quotations. 'It saves original thinking,' as Lord Peter Wimsey liked to say. My weakness for them pre-dates Bedales, of course. It goes back to the old man in the boiler room at my prep school who gave me his precious National Coal Board notebooks filled with the wisdom of the ages, painstakingly copied out by him over months and years. And like everything else from my schooldays, it has kept me company all my life. I have published numerous books of quotations over the years and I have had number one best-sellers with two of them. I am currently the editor of the *Oxford Dictionary of Humorous Quotations*.

My fascination with famous people pre-dates Bedales, too. I have told you about T. S. Eliot. Did I mention that John Masefield worshipped at St Stephen's, Gloucester Road, as well? Masefield's successor as Poet Laureate was Cecil Day-Lewis. He sent his children to Bedales – and his wife, the actress Jill Balcon, helped me with my verse speaking. 'Clarity, simplicity, sincerity – just say the words, Gyles, as the poet has put them on the page. That's all. Anything more is too much.' Tamasin Day-Lewis was one of the juniors I tried to encourage. Tomás Graves was another. He was the son of Robert Graves. (Yes, I've shaken the hand that wrote *Goodbye to All That*.)

Sappho Durrell, daughter of Lawrence Durrell, was a couple of years older than Tomás and a couple of years younger than me. Dark-haired and wide-eyed, Sappho was breathtakingly beautiful and, even at thirteen, there was something 'different' about her. I told her she looked like Alice Liddell, the girl for whom Lewis Carroll wrote *Alice's Adventures in Wonderland* – and when I found the photograph Carroll had taken of Alice and showed it to her, she was amazed. 'You're right,' she said, 'that could be me. Perhaps I'll write *Sappho in Wonderland* one day. I'm going to be a writer, like my father.'

Her father was a lifelong obsession: she loved him and feared him. Twenty years later, in 1985, a few months after

Sappho, aged thirty-three, had hanged herself in her house in North London, extracts from her journals appeared in the magazine *Granta*. In literary circles, they fuelled speculation that sex-obsessed Durrell, who was still alive at the time, had abused his daughter when he was in his fifties and she was in her early and mid-teens. Who knows what really happened? Sappho complained about her 'wreck of a father' and his 'monstrous ego' but made no specific accusation. 'I feel very threatened by the fact that my father is sleeping with women who are my age or younger,' she wrote. 'I feel he is committing a kind of mental incest and that it is a message to me as his favourite daughter.'

Sappho told me that Bedales was the place where she was really happy. I believe it. On 6 July 1981, she added a codicil to her will: 'I should like, if possible, to be buried in Steep churchyard . . . In the event that my father should request to be buried with me – my wish is that the request be refused.'

Sappho was beautiful and she was kind. I say that, because she listened to my flirtatious chattering with great patience – and I knew, even then, I wasn't obvious Romeo material. (I had found that out the hard way: in my first term I went to audition for the Junior Play. It was a stage adaptation of *Pride and Prejudice*. Obviously, I saw myself as a natural Mr Darcy. I was cast as the ghastly Mr Collins.) One summer Sunday evening, I remember giving Sappho a yellow rose. (Where can I have got it from? Did I buy it in the village? Did I steal it from someone's garden?) Anyway, she took my gift, and smiled and thanked me for it and told me she would keep it always. At least she kept it until she disappeared behind the Lupton Hall, on the way back to the girls' house, when she may well have chucked it in the dustbin for all I know.

There was another gorgeous girl to whom I gave a rose that summer. She was a year older than me and more obviously beautiful than Sappho. 'Pooks' was her nickname, and when I presented her with my flower she simply laughed out loud and dropped it in the gutter.

There is a coda to the story. Thirty years later, I found myself booked to speak at a ladies' luncheon club in the West Midlands. When the club secretary telephoned to finalise the arrangements, she said, 'You'll meet up with an old school friend when you come. Apparently, she used to be known as Spooks or Spooky, and you were quite smitten.'

When my train arrived at Birmingham New Street, the club chairwoman was on hand to greet me and transport me to the lunch in her Volvo. The car reeked of dogs and fresh manure. She was a stout farmer's wife, with a ruddy complexion and a small but perceptible lone hair growing out of her chin. I didn't feel nostalgic enquiries about Pooks would be quite her scene, so we talked about the iniquities of the Milk Marketing Board until we reached the hotel. Over lunch we covered the price of potatoes, the state of the weather and sundry other issues that invariably crop up when you're with farming folk. Throughout my speech, I scanned the faces peering up at me in search of Pooks. I couldn't see her.

Back at New Street Station, as I clambered out of the Volvo, the stout middle-aged farmer's wife leant across the gear lever and said, 'You don't remember me, do you?'

I swear to you: there were tiny tears in the corners of Pooks' pudgy eyes.

Back at school, I had more success with Chrissie. She wasn't at Bedales when I was there, but she had been a pupil at the school. She was the elder sister of a girl in my year, and when our relationship began Chrissie was eighteen and I was four years her junior. She came back to the school to see a production of *Murder in the Cathedral* in which I played the Messenger and had a small walk-on part as one of the monks. I hadn't heard of Chrissie, and had no idea she was in the audience, until two or three days after the performance, when I received a ten-page letter from her that began, 'My dearest darling

Gyles, I saw you in the play on Friday and I have to tell you that I am now in love. Don't laugh. This is real. This is true. This is beautiful.'

This is odd, I thought, but not unpleasant. She enclosed a photograph, taken in a nightclub in Beirut (this was 1962, remember: Beirut was very different then) and an invitation to me to write back and share my hopes and dreams and 'innermost, *innermost*, INNERMOST' thoughts with her.

I wrote back. I have no idea what I said, but I have kept every one of the hundred and more increasingly intimate letters she sent to me over the next two years. Some of them included line drawings of her sitting up in bed, topless, smiling at me.

There is a coda to this story, too. One day, when I was sixteen, I was lying on my bed in my dormitory, reading a book, when a boy popped his head around the door and said, 'Your friend Chrissie is in the quad. She wants to see you.'

Chrissie and I had never met. I didn't want to meet her now. *Not* meeting her is what had made her special. I stayed where I was.

Another message came: 'Chrissie's here. She's waiting for you.'

I got up, I combed my hair, I went down to the quadrangle. I recognised her at once. She looked amazing – even sexier than her photograph.

She didn't recognise me at all. Within three minutes we had worked out that the boy she had wanted to correspond with had been another of the monks in *Murder in the Cathedral*. Chrissie's sister had identified me by mistake.

I never heard from her again.

Losing Chrissie was a relief, really. I missed her letters, but I was glad to be spared the obligation of writing back. I had so much else to do and so many other girls, nearer my own age and nearer to home, to whom I could write notes and give roses. None of them, I realise now, were girls in my year.

Sensibly, I kept my contemporaries as straightforward friends – like my dancing partner Diana Ambache (who, like me, hated chemistry and once memorably got up in the middle of class and left the room because when the Scottish teacher mentioned 'carbon dioxide' she thought he had said, 'Come on, Di – outside!') and Antonia Burrows (who sat next to me in history and endeared herself to me by doodling in biro on her thighs and showing me her handiwork). Perhaps I steered clear of making romantic overtures to my contemporaries for fear of rejection – or because I was wary of complications too close to home. Or perhaps I simply didn't fancy any of them. I did fall in love quite often, but always with girls a little older or a little younger, and it rarely got beyond the note-and-rose stage.

I remember an older girl called Ros. She was seventeen and very keen on sports and sailing. We went to the haystack beyond the orchard one afternoon and stayed so long that we almost missed evening assembly. We ran to the Lupton Hall and walked in at exactly 8.15 p.m. We were the last two people to reach our places, and there were lots of sniggers. I didn't know until afterwards that I had straw all over my back.

I remember a younger girl called Stephanie. She was fourteen and crazy. She kept sending me mad love notes across the dining room in the middle of meals. I barely knew her, but I liked her hair and her funny crooked nose. I liked her madness and devotion. I must have done. I have kept all her notes to me, every one.

I was a keen correspondent myself. Sometimes my letters were handwritten, but mostly they were tapped out with one finger on my trusty Olivetti typewriter at incredible speed. (After sixty years at the keyboard I'm still a one-finger man.) None of the recipients of my effusive outpourings appears to have kept them. This is probably a good thing if this note from Pobs (thirteen to my fifteen in 1963) in reply to one of mine is anything to go by.

I knew from the beginning it wouldn't last more than a week or so at the most . . . You say that you are too self-loving. Well, that is no complaint as I believe that everyone is, however much they pretend not to be . . . In your letter you have made everything seem far more tragic than it can be. I am sure it can't be quite so complex.

See you next term.

Love, Pobs

I kept every note every girl ever sent me. I still kept a diary, too, where, as well as recording what was going on in the real world (the assassination of President Kennedy, the Profumo scandal, Beatlemania), I was giving a day-to-day account of what was happening in my world.

Friday, 10 January 1964

Gail doesn't really love me. She says she does to be kind. I think she thinks I'm funny and a bit different from other males so she doesn't want to let go, but she doesn't LOVE me! And perhaps I love her for the wrong reasons. I love her golden hair, beautiful and long (she can sit on it!), I love her nose, I love her freckles, I love her eyelashes. (I think she's Alice in Wonderland and she thinks I'm the Mad Hatter.)

I did have two proper long-term girlfriends at Bedales: Jackie who was two years older than me, and Sally who was two years younger. Jackie and I exchanged hundreds of letters over the two or three years we were together. I have kept all of hers. She told me when I saw her recently, 'I got rid of yours a long time ago – sorry.' Jackie was the daughter of a member of staff, the matron of one of the girls' houses – and I have kept the letters *she* sent to me, too. She was anxious that I be kind to her daughter while she was taking her O Levels. I hope I was.

I had a lot of time for Jackie's mum. I spent a lot of time at her house, having cake and cocoa. I felt for her because she always seemed to be anxious about money – like Pa. Pa was forever urging my three sisters (by then in their twenties) to make profitable marriages. He really did harp on about it – it was a daily refrain. That wasn't Jackie's mother's style at all, but I am happy to report, as a coda to this story, that Jackie's elder sister, Susie, who was also at Bedales, married one of the richest men in the world and is now Lady Sainsbury of Turville CBE, still a good friend, a great patron of the arts, and someone who has succeeded in being quite unspoilt by her unimaginable wealth.

When Jackie left Bedales, we drifted apart and I transferred my attention to Sally, who helped out with the costumes on one of my plays for the juniors and then helped me out on all my schemes and projects until I left school, too. She was a good companion and a great letter writer.

Saturday, 31 July 1965
Today is Sally's 15th birthday. She is camping in a tent in France (poor girl!), but has written me a wonderful letter. She writes beautiful letters – very warm and real and full of detail. (She awoke on the day she sent her letter to find a frog in her tent – a little creature, not one of the locals.) She loves music and dress-making and sunbathing (she says she always turns puce before she goes brown). Oh yes, she also (so she says) loves me. I have just sent her an epistle running to eleven sides to thank her for doing so!

I saw Sally at school and in the holidays, too. She lived in Putney (her dad was a senior set designer at the BBC, working on *Z-Cars* at the time) and we went to lots of plays together and, occasionally, she managed to drag me to a concert. If we ate out it was either in the cafeteria at the Royal Festival Hall or the Lyons' Corner House opposite Charing Cross Station. I liked chocolate cupcakes; she liked doughnuts covered with icing sugar and hundreds and thousands.

Tea was our favourite meal by a long way, and what we could afford, but I do remember the slap-up dinner her American godmother treated us to once. It was at Simpson's in the Strand and one of the most unnerving nights of my life.

Simpson's have been serving roasts from silver-domed trolleys in oak-panelled dining rooms at 100 Strand since 1828. The basic fare has remained unchanged in two centuries: potted shrimps for starters, then saddle of mutton or pink, tender beef sliced slantingly to the bone, with real horseradish sauce, heavy Yorkshire pudding, crisp roasted potatoes, piping hot cabbage, followed by an Edwardian dessert or a savoury like Welsh rarebit or mature Stilton cheese. When we went in 1964, the ground-floor dining room was still reserved for gentlemen only, so we were upstairs and in a cosy candle-lit corner. There were just three of us at a small table: Sally, her godmother and me. When the dinner was ordered and the wine was served, we began to relax – and I stopped talking so much and started listening to Sally's godmother, who came from New England and had lots of stories to tell. We youngsters were fourteen and sixteen years old and Sally's godmother, I suppose, was in her late thirties. When she smiled, she looked alarmingly attractive. That's what I was thinking when suddenly I felt her hand on my knee.

All at once my heart stood still. I had no idea – no idea at all – what to do. I looked away. I watched the waiter carving the roast. I couldn't think what to say. I felt I could hear my heart thumping, louder and louder still. I swallowed hard and looked back at her. She smiled and turned towards Sally. As she turned, her hand travelled up my leg.

It stopped. Then it travelled further.

I had no choice. My hand went down to meet hers.

Without hesitating, she took my hand in hers and, to my bewilderment, pressed a florin – an old two-shilling coin – into my palm. She turned to look at me and narrowed her eyes, gently and slowly, in the most soul-melting way.

My head swam, my mind raced. 'What is going on? Why is she trying to pay me? This is madness!'

Then she took her hand away, leant towards me and whispered in my ear, 'You're supposed to tip the carver.'

Why hadn't my father told me that when you go to Simpson's in the Strand for dinner, the senior gentleman present always tips the carver? Pa had taught me many things – how to tie a proper bow tie without looking in the mirror was probably the most useful – but he had not taught me that.

I thought I was a sophisticated teenager. I wasn't. I did know some girls who were. They were girls I encountered through my friend Penny, a girl from another school whom I had met at the national verse-speaking competition. Through knowing Penny for a year or two I became a sort of junior debs' delight. I don't think it was my natural *métier*. I could dress the part: dinner jacket, evening shirt, cufflinks, black bow tie. I could sound the part: 'What ho! Good evening, sir! How *good* to meet you! And your lovely wife!' But I didn't feel the part. As I mentioned earlier, I was bang-in-the-middle middle class, not upper middle class at all: there's quite a distinction.

Most Bedalian girls were middle class, too: they did not 'come out for the season' as debutantes. They thought the idea was ridiculous, and so it was – though, amazingly, until 1958 debutantes were still being invited to Buckingham Palace every year to be presented at court. ('We had to put a stop to it,' Princess Margaret is reputed to have said. 'Every tart in London was getting in.' In due course, Princess Margaret sent both her children to Bedales.)

I liked Penny a lot, but to me she seemed to live in a strange world. A lot of braying went on! (And smoking. I was quite a puritan when it came to smoking.) She introduced me to her 'set' – all girls from Francis Holland School and Queen's Gate, Roedean and Benenden. They really did whinny like horses. I remember being in a hired minibus one night – it was taking our 'party' from the 'drinks' at 1 Upper Harley Street (chez

Diana Ferguson – '*Such* fun!') to Hurlingham for the Easter Egg Ball – when a big-busted girl squashed next to me said, 'Have you ever seen a match burn twice?' I said no and she proceeded to light a match and hold it up, saying, 'Look – it's burning once!' Then she took the burning match and stubbed it out on my knuckles. 'Look – it's burning *twice*!' She guffawed and guffawed and *guffawed* until I thought she was going to wet herself. The burn was very painful. (If ever we meet, I can show you the scar. It's quite small, but it's still visible.)

Penny took me to cocktail parties and balls. I took her to the theatre. I remember the night, in April 1965, when I took her to see Noël Coward's *Present Laughter* at the Queen's Theatre in Shaftesbury Avenue. She liked it. I loved it. (Nigel Patrick in the lead was so stylish. Richard Briers as the demented young playwright was hilarious. Ten years later, I was working with Nigel Patrick. Twenty years later, Richard Briers became a good friend.) The evening ended well, but it began awkwardly. I went for supper at Penny's home. I did my best to entertain her very nice parents – in my best debs' delight manner. Then I let slip that I proposed taking Penny to Shaftesbury Avenue by underground. As we set off, her father pulled me to one side in the hallway and pressed a ten-shilling note into my hand, 'A cab, I think, for Penny, don't you?' And he winked at me.

As a rule, I did quite well with my girlfriends' parents – often, in fact, I did better with the parents than the daughters. I remember that Pobs' parents were particularly charming. After one visit to her home her father gave me a lift to Hammersmith in his car – 'unheard of', according to Pobs. Normally, she said, he would hide in his study when her friends appeared. And, if my diary from the time is to be believed, 'since my departure her mother has done little but praise my "grand social manner" and ask Pobs why she doesn't bring home more boys like me!'

*

229

I'd say that anything worth seeing in British theatre in the 1960s, I saw: from Joan Littlewood's *Oh, What a Lovely War!* at the Theatre Royal, Stratford East, to Joan Plowright's *Saint Joan* in the glory days of Olivier's National Theatre Company at Chichester and the Old Vic; from Paul Scofield's mighty *King Lear* to Michael Redgrave's *Uncle Vanya* (still, for me, the most affecting performance in the most perfect production of any play I have ever seen). All my pocket money I spent on going to the theatre.

Often, when funds allowed, I took a girl with me. I remember taking Gail to see *Poor Bitos* by Jean Anouilh at the Duke of York's Theatre in St Martin's Lane (Stalls, 10s. 6d.). Donald Pleasence was mesmerising as Robespierre and it was the first time I saw Martin Jarvis onstage. (We didn't meet until the 1980s, but have been firm friends ever since. I love Martin because he is invariably positive.) Jackie had written to me saying she was free that same week – the beginning of January 1964 – 'and would like to go to anything you'd like to go to – it's up to you (like everything else) . . .' I took her to *Gentle Jack*, the new play by Robert Bolt at the Queen's Theatre, Shaftesbury Avenue (Upper Circle, 12s. 6d.). It was an odd piece, mixing fantasy and reality, but worth seeing for the stars: Dame Edith Evans, who had extraordinary presence as well as that amazing swooping voice, and Kenneth Williams, who played a kind of strange woodland sprite. He wasn't as funny as the audience hoped he would be, but he was utterly compelling: you kept watching him, wondering what was going to happen next. (Years later, when he became a good friend, 'wondering what was going to happen next' became the downside of knowing Kenneth.)

I saw lots of productions with Sally. I remember her parents kindly took us to see David Warner's celebrated 'student' *Hamlet* at Stratford. (Sally kept looking at me teasingly during the early Ophelia scenes, nudging me as though I was as difficult as the moody Dane.) I went with my own parents to see lots, too. Pa was good at getting us tickets for special occasions – like the royal film premiere of *Mary Poppins* in Leicester Square. (Dick Van Dyke's cockney accent was laughable, but we loved it all the same.) I remember Saturday, 30 July 1966. In the afternoon, with the rest of the world, I watched England beat Germany in the World Cup on TV. In the evening, I went with Ma to see Noël Coward in his two one-act plays at the Queen's Theatre. The plays weren't memorable, but he was. He was sixty-six, and looked older, but his panache was unbeatable, his speed of speech extraordinary, his style unique. It was the last night – it was Noël Coward's farewell to the stage – and I was there.

I am thinking as I am writing this what a blessed and privileged life I have had. And there's more.

On Saturday, 5 November 1966, during the half-term break, Simon Cadell and I came to London and went to the Golders Green Hippodrome to see Marlene Dietrich live onstage. She was sixty-four, a siren from the Berlin of the 1920s and the Hollywood of the 1930s, and we were in our teens, in the age of the Beatles and the Rolling Stones, but she was our heroine. We knew she would be sensational: the reality exceeded our expectations. The show was so artfully contrived: the delayed start; the sense of anticipation; the prolonged overture; the rustling of the curtains; the completely manufactured but nonetheless real anxiety ... will-she-won't-she-be-appearing ... and, suddenly, she does, in a spotlight, in *that* dress, with an outrageous floor-length fur, and *those* eyes and that teasing smile. We stood, we cheered, we *roared* – and she laughed at us and took it as her due. Every element of the evening was impeccable: her appearance, her face, her hair, her arched eyebrows, her voice, her banter, her timing, her repertoire, her arrangements. I remember thinking, 'Take a bow, Burt Bacharach – I want my *life* arranged by you!'

In the programme, there was a note about her by Ernest Hemingway: 'I think she knows more about love than anyone.

I know that every time I have seen Marlene Dietrich ever, she has done something to my heart and made me happy. If this makes her mysterious then it is a fine mystery.'

When it was over, the *moment* it was over, Simon said, 'Follow me!' We raced into the street and round to the stage door. A crowd was already gathering and a car was waiting. Simon said, 'That'll be the decoy car – let's wait at the front.'

So we did. And we were rewarded.

After about half an hour another limousine appeared and drew up in the street in front of us. A policeman arrived and then another. There was a flurry of movement around the theatre doors and suddenly she was there, before us, within touching distance. She was small and looked so gentle – and she smiled at us. As she walked towards the car, from around the building a crowd came surging – men and women, young and old – and just as I thought she was about to be trampled underfoot I realised that two men – her driver and one of the policemen – were lifting her bodily on to the roof of the limousine. They held her as she struggled to her feet (she was wearing a sort of leather miniskirt) and, on spindly high heels, she then began to teeter about the roof of the car – her arms outstretched to maintain her balance. She looked down at us, laughing, as we began to cheer. As she mouthed the words 'I love you!' her driver held up a sheaf of photographs for her – already signed – and she took them and, wobbling to and fro on the roof, began to distribute them to the adoring fans.

When the pictures were all gone, she revolved slowly, surveying the scene one final time, before lowering herself on to her bottom and edging herself towards the side of the car – and me. This was Golders Green at midnight and Marlene Dietrich was sliding off the roof of her limousine into my arms. Her legs were thrust towards me. As the policeman helped her to the ground, for a never-to-be-forgotten moment in my hands I held Marlene Dietrich's left thigh.

Marlene Dietrich was born on 27 December 1901. Maggie

Smith was born on 28 December 1934. There must be something special in the air on the night of 27/28 December. As Beatrice explains in *Much Ado About Nothing*: 'then there was a star danced, and under that was I born.' I first saw Maggie Smith onstage at the Globe Theatre in Shaftesbury Avenue, when I was thirteen, during the summer holidays in 1961. (I went with my old teacher, Mr Glading. I took him, I remember. I noted in my diary: 'Last time I'll see him I think. All over.') The play was Jean Anouilh's *The Rehearsal* (Anouilh was *huge* in the fifties and sixties) and Maggie Smith was incredibly funny. I didn't fall for her properly until a year or two later, when I saw everything she did at the new National Theatre. Most of all I loved her Beatrice in *Much Ado*. It was a dazzling enchantment, as was the production (with a Sicilian setting) by Franco Zeffirelli – the guy who had directed *Romeo and Juliet* with Judi Dench.

Years later, in the 1990s, when I was an MP, I was parliamentary private secretary to Stephen Dorrell at the time he was appointed Secretary of State for National Heritage. It was a daft appointment: he didn't rate the job, he didn't want the job. He took the job because he was offered it. (John Major said, 'I'd like you to join the Cabinet.' 'Thank you very much,' said Stephen. 'I want you to go to National Heritage,' said the Prime Minister. 'Oh,' said Stephen, his face falling, 'thank you.' And that was that.) That's the way the system works. Unless you're a big beast, you don't get to discuss these things. You just get what you're given and get on with it. Stephen, who is a good friend (I'm godfather to one of his children), had been a force to reckon with at the Treasury – and would be again later at Health – but at National Heritage he was pretty hopeless. He knew about as much about the arts as I know about nuclear fission. Anyway, one evening we were in the House of Commons waiting to vote, and having a drink, when I heard that Franco Zeffirelli was visiting the House of Lords.

'We must go and find him,' I said.

'Who?'

'Zeffirelli.'

'Who's Zeffirelli?'

'The great director,' I bleated. 'Opera, theatre, film – Zeffirelli, Stephen, *Zeffirelli!* You must go and salute him – thank him for all he's done.'

'Really? Do you think so?'

'I know so,' I insisted. 'And he's a senator in Italy now.'

'Oh, he's a politician?' said Stephen, looking marginally more intrigued. 'Okay then, if you insist.'

We went and found the great man and I introduced him to our Secretary of State for National Heritage. I also introduced myself – mentioning how I'd first fallen under his spell in the 1960s with his work at the Old Vic.

He put his hands on my shoulders and gazed intently into my eyes. 'Of course,' he cried, 'of course!' My exuberance had given him the impression that I had worked with him then, been a spear carrier or an understudy or something in those magical productions. Suddenly, he took me in his arms and held me close in his embrace.

The Secretary of State looked on, uncomprehending. I didn't care. I was being hugged by the genius who gave me two of the golden productions of my lifetime.

When I die, I'd like to be watching a play by Shakespeare at the time. He has never let me down. When I was asked to do the radio programme *Desert Island Discs*, I wanted to choose eight recordings of different actors reading different Shakespeare speeches. 'Oh God, Gyles,' Michèle sighed. I bowed to her better judgement. ('Listen to your wife' are probably the four most important words I know.) But I did choose one: Othello's great speech to the Senate (Act 1, Scene III), recorded by Laurence Olivier when he first played the part in 1964.

I saw Olivier's *Othello* in the week of 23 April 1964 – the week that marked the four hundredth anniversary of Shakespeare's birth. In the room in the basement where I keep all my memorabilia – the room that Michèle is promising to clear the moment I die: she has told me she will be calling the skip people before she calls the undertakers, and she hasn't promised that the undertakers will be Kenyon's, either – there is a whole box of souvenirs of that one week alone.

I'd been out with Jackie at the beginning of the week and her thank-you letter arrived on 23 April itself: 'You know when you kissed me goodnight it was for the first time in three and a half months – 14 weeks 1 day! I shall probably have to wait even longer for the next one. And still I love you just as much now as I did then – stupid, isn't it?' (No wonder I kept all her letters. No wonder she got rid of all of mine.)

On the Wednesday night, Pa had organised a family outing to the Mermaid Theatre, at Puddle Dock in the City, not a mile from where Shakespeare's own theatre would have been. (Pa liked the Mermaid: it wasn't as expensive as the West End.) We went to the first night of the Mermaid's quatercentenary offering, *Macbeth*. I rather enjoyed it, but the critics were scathing. They were especially unkind about Lady Macbeth, who was played by Josephine Wilson, the wife of Bernard Miles, the actor who was also the Mermaid's founder. As I recall, Miss Wilson's performance was on the screechy side, but I was sympathetic to her because I knew something that I imagined the critics did not. The sister of one of my schoolfriends, an older boy called Peter Harris, worked at the Mermaid and she had told him that Bernard Miles would often have sex with young actresses in his dressing room before and during the show. Apparently, he could be 'at it' with a girl when the stage manager called him for his next entrance and he'd just pull up his britches and walk straight out on to the stage.

That night, Pa splashed out on a celebratory supper in the Mermaid Restaurant. I have kept the menu in my archive. I had chef's *pâté* (2*s*. 6*d*.), *omelette fines herbes* (8*s*. 6*d*.) and fresh sliced pineapple (4*s*.) – Pa had it with kirsch (2*s*. 6*d*. extra).

On the Monday night I had taken Jackie to Wimpy's for a hamburger. (We liked Wimpy's – we especially liked the ketchup that came in a plastic container shaped like a giant tomato.) In her letter, Jackie said it was 'a super evening' and ended: 'I hope you enjoy *Othello* – but of course that's a foregone conclusion with his lordship in the title role!' She was right. Olivier was my hero and, on Saturday night, going to the Old Vic to see his Othello, with Maggie Smith as his Desdemona, was destined to be the climax of this unique Shakespearean week.

When I was a boy, there were five giants among the theatrical knights – all born in the first decade of the twentieth century: Donald Wolfit, 1902; Ralph Richardson, 1902; John Gielgud, 1904; Laurence Olivier, 1907; Michael Redgrave, 1908. If they were on, I was there. From roughly 1958 until each of them died, I saw whatever they did.

On 25 April 1964, I saw Laurence Olivier play Othello. Of course, you couldn't do it now because Olivier was a white man portraying a Black man, but he did it then and it was astonishing – bravura acting to catch your soul. The morning after, I described it to myself in my diary as 'the greatest performance of our age'. Perhaps it was. Who can say? Zeffirelli described it as 'an anthology of everything that has been discovered about acting in the last three centuries'.*

I was bowled over, as Jackie had predicted I would be. I loved it so much that I booked to see it again in the summer, at the Chichester Festival Theatre. I went to a midweek matinee. I went on my own. When it was something special, I think I preferred to be on my own.

After the performance, on the spur of the moment, I decided today might be the day to try to collect Olivier's

* Don't judge it by the film version. It was recorded more than a year later and much of the subtlety has gone.

autograph. As a rule, I wasn't an autograph hunter, but I did have the signature of Popov the Clown, and when Marcel Marceau, the great French mime artist, had come to London, I had been to his show and collected his autograph, too. (You know, when Marcel Marceau died, on French radio out of respect they had two minutes' noise.) 'The greatest clown, the greatest mime artist, so why not the greatest actor?' I thought. This was a good day for it, too, because they were doing a different play in the evening, so my hero wouldn't be having a rest between performances. He would be leaving the theatre to go home.

Except he didn't leave the theatre. For nearly an hour I hovered a few yards from the stage door. I watched the other actors coming out – Maggie Smith, Frank Finlay, John Stride, Derek Jacobi . . . laughing, chatting, hurrying on their way. Of course, Olivier had all that make-up to take off. I knew he'd be last . . . but still he didn't come.

Eventually, I decided I'd go in and find out if he was coming or not. I screwed up my courage and pulled open the stage door. The stage door keeper was no longer at his post. He must have gone for his tea, but he had left the inner door open and I went through it. The place was deserted and I found myself, like Alice in Wonderland, walking along a low-ceilinged, narrow, curving backstage corridor. I kept going, passing doors, passing rails of costumes, seeing no one until suddenly – there he was, coming straight towards me along the corridor. He wasn't tall. He was wearing horn-rimmed spectacles. He was dressed in a fawn-coloured raincoat, wearing a trilby hat and carrying a briefcase. He looked like a bank manager, but it was definitely him.

'Hello,' he said.

'How do you do, sir?'

He saw that I was holding a programme and a pen. 'You'd like an autograph?' he asked. He spoke softly, articulating every syllable.

'Thank you, sir.'

I held out my programme and he signed it. I was sixteen.

'Where are you at school?' he asked.

'Bedales, sir.'

'Ah, Bedales,' he said, running his tongue along his bottom teeth. 'I know Bedales. My first wife went to Bedales.'

Jill Esmond went to Bedales. Mr Badley had told me that.

'Do you want to be an ac-*tor*?' he asked, cocking his head to one side to look at me more closely.

'Yes,' I said, 'yes, I do.' Until that very moment, I hadn't been quite sure. 'I'm in the school play,' I added.

'So you are an ac-*tor* already,' he said, smiling. 'Would you like to see the stage?' he asked. 'Come,' he commanded, not waiting for my reply.

He led me back along the corridor, through one door, then another, and then, suddenly, there we were together, Laurence Olivier and I, walking side by side on to the stage of the Chichester Festival Theatre.

'When you come on,' he said, looking out over the vast auditorium, 'the first thing you must do is let them see your eyes.' He glanced towards me. 'Take your time. Make sure that you look everywhere, right to the back, right to the top – don't miss anyone.'

I watched his eyes behind his spectacles, scanning the rows.

'And when they've all seen your eyes, you can start.' He put his hand on my shoulder. 'In this play you're doing at *Bedales* –' as he said the word, he made it explode – 'for your first entrance, where do you come on?'

'From up there, sir,' I said, nodding towards the back of the stage on my left.

'And how do you come on?'

'Well, I just come on.'

'Oh, dear boy, you can't just "come on". You want to be *no*-ticed, don't you?'

'Oh yes, sir, I want to be *no*-ticed.'

'Well,' he said, swaying slightly as he spoke, and pointing to where I was to make my entrance, 'I suggest you come on *backwards*.' Again, the word exploded. 'They always notice the fellow who comes on backwards. You can be waving to someone in the wings – you see, the movement of your hand will attract the audience's attention. Come on backwards, spin round, let them see your eyes, and speak your line. You'll be noticed.'

'That's wonderful, sir,' I said. 'Thank you. Thank you! And you, sir, if you were making your first entrance, where would you come on?'

'Oh,' he laughed softly and rolled his eyes. 'I can come on *anywhere*!'

15. Holidays

While I was away at school, having a high old time with my plays and my projects, my hit-and-miss love life and my schemes for improving the world, what was happening at home?

I'm not sure I can tell you, I'm afraid. I wasn't really concentrating. Like most adolescents, I imagine, I was totally self-absorbed.

As I mentioned earlier, my move from Betteshanger to Bedales in 1961 coincided with the family's move from Kensington Mansions, off the Earl's Court Road, to Portman Mansions, off Baker Street. The new flat, in a similar Victorian red-brick block, was a little smaller than the old, a little darker, and the ceilings weren't quite so high, but it had a lift – not a wholly reliable lift (if someone on another floor failed to shut the lift gates properly the lift wouldn't move) but a lift all the same. At Kensington Mansions we had been the only flat on the top floor. At Portman Mansions, we were on the third floor, Flat 5H, on the right. On the left was Flat 5G, the home of Dr Schindler, an elderly Freudian psychoanalyst who looked exactly like one of the two old men who used to sit in the stage box in *The Muppets*. We met him occasionally on the landing and tried to make small talk, but it wasn't easy. He was Viennese and his accent was so thick it was impenetrable.

Throughout the 1960s, Pa, now in his fifties, carried on working as the AA's legal adviser from their headquarters in Leicester Square – only three stops away on the tube – and Ma, I am happy to report, began to come into her own. During the war she had taken a course on nursery education. Now she took another (based on the teachings of Maria

Montessori) and opened her own small nursery school in the front room of our flat in Portman Mansions. My brother Ben was the first pupil, but others quickly followed. Soon she had a dozen or more toddlers running all over the flat, their push-chairs cluttering up the hallway, the Montessori play equipment (the sandpit, the water feature, the climbing frame, the letter boards, the shape and number blocks, the wooden boxes in which the little ones liked to hide when they were feeling shy or sad) filling every available cupboard, shelf, nook and cranny. Ma was an outstanding teacher, and when Ben started having difficulty with reading and she discovered he was dyslexic, helping children with dyslexia became the overriding purpose and passion of her life.

At Portman Mansions Ma's schoolroom was the first room on the right – the largest and lightest room in the flat. Mine was the first on the left. At Kensington Mansions I had had a bedroom and a playroom. I did not feel I needed a playroom any more. From the age of ten, I did not feel remotely like a child. I regarded my new room not so much as my study as my office. I packed away my costumes and my puppets, and set up my office – complete with desk and swivel chair, typewriter, bookshelves and a large metal filing cabinet Pa found for me in a second-hand office furniture shop on Tottenham Court Road. When I was home, I could happily spend all day and all night in my room, making my plans, writing my plays (given our new address, I started with the Sherlock Holmes mystery in which I cast Simon Cadell at school), listening to my records (*Salad Days* was no longer running in the West End, but I was still playing the record ten times a night, if not more). I wasn't antisocial: I emerged at mealtimes or to play the occasional game of Scrabble with Ma or one of my sisters.

Immediately opposite my room was the sitting room, fur-nished quite sparsely by middle-class standards – two Ercol armchairs, a leather pouffe, a utilitarian sofa (that was also a put-you-up bed) covered in a rather grim grey fabric, two side tables, a standard lamp, a central light (a single bulb with a shade that looked like a Chinese conical hat), and over the mantelpiece a large print of one of Canaletto's famous paintings of Venice – a souvenir of the educational cruise Ma and Pa took for their silver wedding anniversary. We watched TV in the sitting room. Ma loved the *Billy Cotton Band Show*. Pa enjoyed *Panorama*. We did not have ITV: a lot of middle-class families didn't, in those days.

Down the corridor were the girls' rooms, my parents' room and, with linoleum on the floor, the kitchen and the bathroom. I see Pa most vividly in the kitchen, either sitting at the large Formica kitchen table (pale green) with his cup of tea and his cigarettes, going through the accounts, or standing by the sink, with a kitchen towel tossed over his shoulder, doing the washing-up.

Were they happy together? I always assumed so, but now, writing this, I have begun to wonder. How well do we know our parents in the end?

Pa was a successful lawyer, a well-regarded broadcaster in his field, and an equable and amusing man, but he had his money worries and his professional disappointments, and he was forever at Ma's beck and call. ('I need another cup of tea, duckie.' 'Yes, hon.') As a teacher, Ma was totally fulfilled, but she can't have been wholly happy, can she? If she had been, she wouldn't have retreated to her bed so often. And she wouldn't have struggled so much with her weight, and her headaches, and her bad back. The osteopath was always coming around, as I recall. And I have just noticed, looking through my diaries now, a couple of references to Ma's 'black bombers'. That's what Pa called them. They were large pills that Ma took from time to time. I realise now they were anti-depressants.

One of Ma's problems, as I have mentioned, is that she was insecure socially. You would not have thought so if you had met her, but she must have been. Perhaps Pa was, too. He was gregarious and outgoing to the point of eccentricity at work or when we went out for a family meal – thinking nothing of climbing up on to someone else's table in the restaurant to take a better group photograph of us sitting at ours. He would return from a visit to the Garrick Club with tales of the interesting men he had encountered – often Oxford contemporaries of his – but he never brought any of them home. Now I come to think of it (for the first time), the only outsiders I can recall ever coming to our home were either relations of my mother (chiefly my hard-drinking Canadian Uncle Jack on his annual visit, or my painfully shy Anglo-Belgian cousin, James, who could sit in silence in the corner of the sitting room for the whole of Christmas Day), schoolfriends of my mother (who had either never married or married into a lifetime of disappointment), or former colleagues of my father who had fallen on hard times. There was an elderly solicitor who had been disqualified (he looked positively Dickensian: he felt the cold and wore woollen mittens even in summer), an Anglo-Indian doctor up on a charge of buggery (I think Pa helped get him off), and my favourite, a sweet man called Michael King, of mixed-race descent, whose father had been a distinguished West Indian barrister who had befriended Pa when he was starting out at the Bar. I knew Michael for fifty years, but I never found out what he did or where he lived, so when my parents died I couldn't inform him – and when he died, I didn't know. He was a regular visitor to the flat and joined us, too, on outings to the Players' Theatre underneath the arches at Charing Cross. Whenever Ma left the room, he'd murmur, 'I've always admired a woman with a fuller figure. As far as I'm concerned, the fuller the better.' When he said it, it sounded charming not creepy.

These quaint friends – all wounded animals of sorts, I now realise – came quite often for lunch or tea. I don't recall seeing any of Pa's relations at the flat or any of his professional colleagues. I do remember the night the vicar and his wife and daughter came to dine. The ladies came in long evening dresses. The vicar wore black tie. We ate (cold meats and salad) in Ma's schoolroom, perched on tiny chairs, sitting at Montessori play tables. It was agony.

I can't remember if my sisters were there that night or not. Everyone came and went quite easily because the key to the front door hung on a piece string inside the letter box. (I marvel that we were only burgled once in ten years.) The girls were six to ten years older than me, of course, and beginning to lead their own lives. Jennifer had graduated from London University and was studying criminology at Nottingham, I think, and planning to become a probation officer. Virginia was now a qualified nurse, still at the Middlesex Hospital where, I remember, Hugh Gaitskell, the Leader of the Opposition, died in January 1962, aged fifty-six. Ginny was looking after him and admired him hugely. Hester was thinking of taking up nursing, too.

Hester still had her problems. I remember the evening during the Christmas holidays in 1961 when we found her on all fours in the sitting room, barking. Ma didn't know what to do, so retreated to the kitchen. Pa didn't know what to do, either. So with me at his side, he went next door to find Dr Schindler. 'You're the expert,' said Pa. Whatever Dr Schindler replied we did not understand, but he kindly came over and tried to talk to Hes to calm her down.

Hester would have none of it. She turned on the good doctor and tried to bite his ankle. The poor man ran back to his flat, terrified. Hester seemed a lot better after that and was quite normal by supper time.

The one thing Ma insisted on – whatever the state of the family finances – was a proper family holiday, preferably on the Continent. In the summer of 1960, for example, we drove all the way to Bavaria, to the village of Oberammergau, to witness the famous Passion Play. It lasted seven hours. The benches were hard and the dialogue was in German, but it was a collector's item and even as a child I liked collecting those. The villagers of Oberammergau have been telling the story of Christ's passion every ten years since 1634. They started doing it as part of a pact with God to protect them from the bubonic plague. It worked – until 2020, when the Covid-19 pandemic forced them to postpone it until 2022. Everyone in the village takes part in the drama, and members of the same family play the same roles, down the generations. The house we stayed in belonged to a family whose members always played the part of Judas Iscariot. 'We'd better leave our suitcases locked,' said Pa. 'You can't trust these people.'

That was a happy holiday. I remember us setting off from London at 3.30 a.m. to catch the 10.45 a.m. ferry for Dunkirk, then on Pa drove – to Bruges and Ghent and Düsseldorf – with Ma sitting next to him folding and unfolding the maps and squawking at every intersection along the way. We stopped overnight in Bruges and went for a walk through the flower market before having supper at Le Cornet d'Or. I had *sole meunière* and then chocolate mousse. I remember it still as the best meal I have ever had.

In Düsseldorf we stayed with friends of my parents who were the exceptions to the rule: they were quite normal. John Paice was my godfather and stationed in Düsseldorf with the British Army on the Rhine. My parents had got to know the Paices when they were in Germany with the Allied Control Commission around the time I was born. Their son, Peter, a little older than me, was the Guardian (or head boy) at Gordonstoun when Prince Charles arrived to spend his unhappy years there. Peter I always think of as the epitome of a thoroughly decent sort of English chap. He was tall, handsome, athletic and effortlessly well mannered, as well as a little hard of hearing. He always called his father 'sir'. I never did that, but I rather admired him for doing so.

I vividly remember the couple of nights we spent with the

Paices because in my bedroom on a bookshelf I found a copy of *Lolita* by Vladimir Nabokov and spent much of both nights reading it. As you know, the novel (reckoned by some to be the greatest of the twentieth century) tells the story of a middle-aged man who falls in love with a girl who is twelve. I was twelve. 'Lolita, light of my life, fire of my loins. My sin, my soul. Lo-lee-ta: the tip of the tongue taking a trip of three steps down the palate to tap, at three, on the teeth. Lo. Lee. Ta.' Intriguing, I thought. Is this how Mr Glading thinks about me?

Not every holiday was as rewarding. In the summer of 1964, for example, I spent all of August in France and was unhappy for most of the time. It was a bucket-and-spade holiday in Brittany and quite fun to start with, but by 13 August, according to my diary, I had had enough.

> We are in Dinard. Pa is going home tonight and I am staying here with Ma and Ben for ANOTHER TWELVE DAYS. I am staying very reluctantly and only after ghastly scenes. I want to be in London where I have WORK TO DO and PEOPLE TO SEE. I have been in France since 29 July and I am now more than ready to go home. Besides I have just endured TEN DAYS IN HELL. I have been to ten countries in ten days. It might sound like fun. It was anything but!

What happened was this: Ma, Pa and Ben stayed in Dinard, enjoying the sun and sand, while I was sent off in the family Ford Cortina to spend ten days travelling around Europe with, as my driver and sole companion, my eighteen-year-old cousin from Canada. Cousin Johnnie was the son of my mother's brother (my hard-drinking Uncle Jack) and he had come over from Toronto 'to do Europe' before going to university. He went on to have a career as a prison governor and one of the leading lights in the Canadian correctional system, but I am afraid when I was sixteen I did not take to him: 'He is a very nice chap and all that, I'm sure, but HE AND I HAVE

NOTHING IN COMMON – and he eats with his mouth open, making the most revolting noises.' As we travelled I wanted to visit theatres and cathedrals and buy books. He wanted to find 'Hitler's bunker' – truly: 'Hitler's bunker' in every one of the ten countries we visited! – and the only items he wanted to buy were picture postcards of big-busted beauties in bikinis sitting on beach balls. These cards he duly sent to his assorted girlfriends back in Canada.

The whole thing was a nightmare. On the first day we drove to Nantes and picked up a Dutch hitch-hiker called Jan who persuaded us to drive to the coast to a bar in Pornic where he said we would find Jean-Paul Sartre 'because he is always there'. He wasn't. The three of us slept sitting up in the car in a side street. After we had got shot of Jan, for the next ten nights, we spent every night sleeping in the car. I slept on the back seat, but the seat wasn't long enough – so I had to sleep with my feet sticking out of the window. Cousin Johnnie spent the nights in a sleeping bag beside the car 'looking at disgusting magazines and doing unspeakable things'. I accused him of being sex-obsessed. In Marseilles he drove us round and round the red-light district, honking the horn, trying to make the prostitutes come out of their flats to wave at him.

We sped through ten countries:

1. France
2. Spain (we fled almost as soon as we arrived, thinking we were being pursued by the police – Cousin Johnnie stole a painting from a street market in Llançà, ran down the road with it, jumped into the car and drove off)
3. Monaco
4. Italy
5. Switzerland
6. Austria
7. Germany

8. Holland
9. Belgium
10. Luxembourg.

The driving never stopped, but our conversation did. I came to hate him so much that, after a while, I couldn't bear to sit next to him in the car. I sat directly behind him instead. We played a word game for hours on end and I cheated – using a dictionary behind his back – so that I won every time. It drove him mad.

On our travels I didn't spend any of my spending money. I saved it all, so that on the final Monday, on our way back to Dinard, when we stopped in Paris, at *Magasins Réunis*, I was able to buy all the books I wanted: Baudelaire, Molière, Sartre, Cocteau – in each case, the complete works in paperback. (More than half a century later I still have them all. I have barely looked at them, of course, but I love to see them on the shelves and, now and again, I pull one out, flick through it and breathe in the smell of the pages. I still find the *Livre de Poche* smell irresistible.)

Buying the books – that was something. And in the interests of accuracy, I should mention one other good day. Towards the beginning of the trip, on Saturday 1 August, near Aix-en-Provence, I visited Paul Desorgues, a former French teacher from Bedales, on his family farm and, after lunch, tasted the sweetest, juiciest, most perfect peach you can imagine. It was the taste of a lifetime. And in the evening, in Avignon, I went to see Corneille's *Nicomède* at the Palais des Papes.

Johnnie went looking for Hitler's bunker.

From the age of seven until I formally left home when I went to university, I had at least one holiday a year in France on my own, always travelling there and back unaccompanied, sometimes staying for as long as six weeks.

When I was younger, I spent several summers with a very nice French family at their holiday home in Normandy. (I remember Odile, the tomboyish daughter of the house. I liked her, and I liked the breakfast: a *ficelle* of French bread spread with salty butter and covered with squares of black chocolate. The Ferrands were serious Catholics. We never ate before Mass, and the father of the house always made a small sign of the cross on the loaf with his knife before cutting into it.) I stayed with another nice family in Maine-et-Loire. The Rouillets were military types and a bit grander. I don't think any of the children were my age, but I remember swimming in the Loire, jumping off the riverbank into the fast-flowing water, and loving it – which is odd because, as a rule, I avoided anything that smacked of exercise. In 1960, when I was twelve, I stayed with a French couple in their apartment on Avenue Wagram, off Place de l'Étoile in Paris. They had no children, but I did not mind. I was happily self-sufficient. I visited museums and walked the streets by day, and went to the cinema and the theatre by night. Brigitte Bardot, Fernandel, and Jean-Louis Barrault were my holiday companions.

I'm not sure how Ma found the French families I stayed with. I think perhaps they advertised in the *Nursery World*.

From 1962, the pattern changed and instead of staying with families I started to stay in hostels for young people. The first was my favourite, again in Paris, a house for students run by a Madame Caumont. I was fourteen and very much the youngest resident. The others were mostly aged between sixteen and twenty, but there was one older man (in his mid- to late twenties) who clearly thought he was the bee's knees and was constantly making a play for the girls. There were plenty of girls. There was also a very pale, pasty English boy of seventeen, called Hugh, who shared my room and talked endlessly of how he was determined to save up enough money to go to a prostitute in Montmartre. I told him that I was planning to go to Montmartre, too – to the Sacré Cœur. I see now that I was a bit of a prig. I didn't smoke. (I never have.) I didn't drink. I certainly didn't take drugs, even though it was the sixties. (I wouldn't have dared: I was a coward as well as a goody-goody.) And I was glad when François, the 'older man', was asked to leave. (I don't know why he was there in the first place. We were all doing French lessons and he *was* French.) I didn't like him and he didn't like me, though I could see that he was quite amusing and clever. I liked the German and Austrian girls, Monika and Brigitta. I liked Renate, too. She gave me a lovely little wooden box on the day she left. I keep my cufflinks in it now. On the day he left, Hugh told me he had been to a prostitute near the Moulin Rouge the night before. I didn't believe him. He had no details to offer. He just tried to look pleased with himself.

It was in France in the mid-1960s that I started visiting prisons on a regular basis. Why? I don't really know. At school I ran the paperback bookshop and I had come across a book by Tony Parker called *The Unknown Citizen*, published in 1963. It was a detailed account of the life of a man who had been convicted eight times for thefts totalling £178 and had spent twenty-six years behind bars, with an average period of eleven weeks between sentences. Within a few hours of his release from seven years' preventive detention he was arrested for attempting to steal from some mailbags at King's Cross Station and sentenced to ten years' further imprisonment. I noted in my diary:

> Clearly the previous seven years had taught him nothing! . . . [It seems] our prisons are places where we hide our criminals: we do not really attempt to cure them or prepare them properly for the world they must face on release. We must change all that.

Never mind being the next Olivier: it seems I saw myself as the next Elizabeth Fry.

In Paris, where I was revising for my A Levels during the Easter holidays, I presented myself one afternoon, without appointment, at the headquarters of the French national prison service: the *Administration Pénitentiaire*, in Place Vendôme, close by the Paris Ritz. I was a teenager, obviously, but a serious-minded one, clearly, and, after a bit of hoo-hah at the front desk, I was ushered into the presence of an amiable official who listened to all I had to say and then, gratifyingly (amazingly), agreed to arrange some prison visits for me for the following week.

I went out to Fresnes, on the outskirts of Paris, to a centre where prisoners were 'sorted' before being allocated a prison, and then on by train to Caen in Normandy, to a *prison longue peine*. It was as grim as the cliché: high stone walls, clanking iron gates, rattling keys, long corridors (their walls dripping with damp), sullen prisoners in drab prison uniforms sitting on bunks made from bare boards, in small dark cells. The joshing prison warders, all smoking cigarettes, were amused to hear this bright-eyed English schoolboy asking earnest questions about the education and training facilities at the prison. '*Ce n'est pas comme ça, jeune homme.*' They made no attempt to disguise the bleakness and futility of the place. Back in Paris, my contact at the *Administration Pénitentiaire* gave me a fat book of statistics and invited me to come back in the summer to see their marvellous new prison in Corsica. I would have liked to have gone, but I was not sure I could afford it. Pa had money worries. I had money worries, too.

Thursday, 7 April 1966
14 Avenue Carnot, Cachan, Seine
Distressing financial news. I am very happy in my suburban student boarding house, but this morning I made a discreet enquiry into the cost of board and lodging: 30 fr per day – rather more than I had bargained for. I arrived on the night

of the 31st and, at present, I plan to leave on the evening of Wednesday 20th April. This will mean a twenty-day stay, costing 600 francs or £43 17s 0d!! I have £30 uncashed traveller's cheques. I also have a £5 note and £1 in French currency – but next Wednesday I go by train to Caen (to the prison there) which will eat further into my petty cash. I have no choice but to write home for more funds – £10 (or £12 if Pa wants me to get duty-free cigarettes).

My parents gave me pocket money when I was small and an allowance when I was older, but I felt bad taking it because I knew they couldn't afford it. I earned money when I could. Obviously, I had failed to become a child star when I lost that part of a lifetime to Hayley Mills, but I did my best. In 1961, for example, when I was thirteen (and Hayley was in Hollywood making *The Parent Trap*), we had an Easter holiday break at the Norfolk Lodge Hotel at Canford Cliffs near Bournemouth. It cost eight guineas per person per week, but because I volunteered to wait at table at breakfast, lunch and dinner, the cost for me was only two-thirds: £5 12s. 0d. I got tips as well, and on our last night (it was the night the Soviet cosmonaut Yuri Gagarin became the first human being in space, I remember) 'Uncle Charles', the hotel's proprietor, gave a 'Gala Dinner in honour of Master Gyles Brandreth' to thank me for my efforts. The meal included: *potage de poireau*, Dorset duckling cooked in red wine, sauce Montmorency, steamed rice, garden peas, bean sprouts, *glace Napolitaine, crème*, plus cheese board. (Tea and coffee served in the lounge 1s. extra.) I still have the menu: all the guests signed it for me.

As soon as I turned fifteen and could legally be gainfully employed, I was. In the summer of 1963, through contacts at the AA, Pa secured me a job as a clerk in the railway reservations department at the world's oldest travel agency, Thomas Cook & Son, at their headquarters in Berkeley Street, off Piccadilly. My salary was £5 plus a London Allowance of 11s. 6d.

per week. My hours were 9.00 to 12.30 and 1.30 to 5.30. It was just a holiday job, but I took it seriously and gave it my all. Indeed, within a fortnight I had improved all the systems in the department to such an extent that the whole week's work could be done in half the time – or less. I was very proud of my endeavours, and my colleagues, all very friendly older people who had been part of the Thomas Cook family for years, graciously went along with every one of my time-saving, streamlining suggestions. I enjoyed the experience so much that I went back to Berkeley Street at Christmas to see everybody. They greeted me warmly, but I was bemused to find that all my reorganisation had been undone. They had changed everything back to the way it was before.

I had happy working experiences and less happy ones. The worst was in the summer of 1966. Encouraged by Ma, a keen supporter of the Children's Country Holiday Fund (a worthy cause giving deprived children a seaside holiday), I signed up to be a kind of entertainments officer at their holiday camp at St Mary's Bay in Kent. The children were way beyond my control and the place was grim beyond words. The huts were horrible – torn lino on the floors, no curtains, cold water, disgusting lavatories – and the food inedible. The 'organisation' was hopeless and those in charge, unlike my indulgent friends in the railway reservations department of Thomas Cook, not remotely interested in the raft of 'improvements' I had in mind.

I had had a much more congenial time in Switzerland in the summer of 1965. A young, newly qualified teacher at Bedales had committed himself to a summer holiday job as an English tutor to some Swiss children and, at the last minute, found he couldn't go. He suggested I go instead. I was free, I needed work, so I went. I had no idea what to expect and no idea where I was going. I simply packed a bag, took his tickets and set off, catching the 3.05 p.m. boat train from Victoria, reaching Folkestone at 5.25 p.m. and Calais at 7.19 that evening. Then I crossed France through the night, changing trains again and again and *again*, until I reached Sion in the Valais canton of southern Switzerland at 8.34 the following morning. The teacher had told me I would be met at the station, and I was – by a huge limousine flying the Swiss flag on its bonnet, and by a pair of uniformed soldiers who snapped to attention and saluted me smartly as, dishevelled and bleary-eyed, I stumbled through the ticket barrier on to the station forecourt. It turned out I was to be English tutor and companion to the children of Brigadier Maurice Juilland, the head of the Swiss Army.

The Brigadier – strictly speaking, he was a Marshal as Switzerland's *Commissaire des Guerres en Chef*, but he preferred to be called Brigadier – was a grizzled old soldier and a tough cookie. Every morning he had the entire family up at 5.00 a.m. so that he could lead us out into the woods to gather mushrooms for breakfast. He explained that each of us had to eat the mushrooms that he or she had picked. He told me that he had found this rule very effective in ensuring that his troops learnt quickly and correctly which fungi were poisonous and which were not.

Stocky, with a weather-beaten face and steel-grey hair, he seemed to me to be quite an old man – he was probably in his early sixties – and, at seventeen, I was certainly younger than the teacher he had been expecting. But we got on well because I realised immediately that he was used to giving orders and I decided to obey every one of them to the letter. Madame Juilland was his second wife and much younger, closer to my age than to his. She obeyed him to the letter, too. So, fortunately, did his two young sons, aged six and seven. (Clearly, Brigadier Juilland was the man they would need the following summer at the Children's Country Holiday Fund camp, not me.)

I learnt a lot from the Brigadier, that summer. He showed me how to organise a picnic (he was a master of the art of the *raclette*), he taught me how to cross a glacier (slowly), he demonstrated how to take a military salute. (Years later, when I was an MP, I thought of him when I was taking the salute on the parade ground at Chester Castle. Do you or don't you salute the regimental goat? You do, because it is wearing the regimental colours, and it is the colours you are saluting not the animal. The Brigadier taught me that.) He told me he sensed he could trust me, and he needed to be able to trust me, he said, because he wanted me to accompany him and his family on his annual 'tour of inspection'. Over a week we criss-crossed Switzerland (Altdorf, Bern, Interlaken, etc.) both taking in the sights and visiting secret military installations – including a complete 'invisible town' built inside a mountain. It was as extraordinary as anything you would see in a James Bond film: the secret headquarters for the Swiss military – complete with streets, houses, hospitals, everything – ready for use in the event of invasion. He made me promise not to make a note of its location in my diary and I didn't, so I can't tell you where it is.

The high point of that summer was 13 August – Friday the thirteenth. It was a lucky one for me. A batch of post reached me from England, including a letter from the Bedales headmaster asking me to be a prefect, a letter from the Bedales drama teacher telling me that next term's play was going to be *A Passage to India* (and that she had a part in mind for me that would challenge me to play for 'truth' rather than 'effect') and, best of all, a letter from Sally telling me that she loved me very much and was missing me desperately. (I noted all this affirmation in my diary and kept the letters as well. Was I a needier child than most? And if I was, I wonder why?)

The evening of the thirteenth was memorable, too. The President of Switzerland came to dinner. Monsieur Paul Chaudet was sixty and looked like a friendly version of Adolf Hitler: he had warm eyes, but Hitler's toothbrush moustache and unfortunate hairstyle. He was the Swiss Defence Minister and one of the country's seven Federal Councillors – they take it in turns to be President. He was an old friend of the Brigadier, who made it clear to Madame (the Brigadier always referred to his wife as 'Madame') that all that was required was something quite informal – *'un repas bien simple et puis un jeu de cartes'*. Madame set about preparing the most elaborate 'simple' supper in the history of hospitality, and the Brigadier set about teaching me the President's (and his) favourite game of cards.

Even in Switzerland, even when he is an old mucker of your husband, having the head of state to dinner is an ordeal. While it taught me a few lessons, the evening was not a complete success. The culinary calamities including a soufflé that wouldn't rise and savoury jellies that wouldn't set. (Lesson No. 1: When entertaining old soldiers, 'safe and simple' is always the best bet. Besides, a simple failure is less noticeable than an elaborate one.) Happily, the wine flowed freely. (Lesson No. 2: Old soldiers never die, but they are happy to float away.) Unhappily, when one of the bottles was emptied I invited the President's wife to kiss the bottom of it, telling her that I had heard that if you did, there was an old Swiss tradition that said you would be married within the year. (Lesson No. 3: It is not the duty of the most junior guest to be the life and soul of the party.)

When dinner was over and we men settled down to cards, I happened to win the first game – and the second. (Lesson No. 4: Never play to lose, but don't always play to win. There is a difference.) We had just embarked on the third game, and this was one it looked as if the President might win, when Madame took us by surprise and suddenly announced the *son et lumière*.

'*Quoi?*' barked the Brigadier. '*Le son et lumière? Où? Quand?*'
'*Içi! Maintenant!*' cooed Madame.
'*Mais non!*' protested the Brigadier.
'*Mais oui!*' insisted Madame.

It transpired that our thoughtful hostess had arranged a command performance of the Sion *son et lumière* at 10.00 p.m. as a presidential treat. (Lesson No 5: Old soldiers don't like surprises. Not many people do. And the more elaborate and carefully prepared the surprise, the less welcome it will be.) The President and the Brigadier wanted to carry on drinking and playing cards. So did I. But Madame got her way. We all clambered into the presidential limousine and swept into town. It really was a command performance: there were just eight of us to see the show. We sat on two wooden benches for a very long hour, listening to the incredibly dreary *son* and watching the far from exciting *lumière*. It was not a jolly experience – and when it was over, though pressed to come back up to the house for a nightcap, the President and his wife decided to go home. Madame was mortified, the Brigadier was disappointed, the President was insistent – and that was that.

At ten the following morning the President's chauffeur returned. Madame answered the front door to find him standing there holding a huge bouquet of flowers and the largest, most elaborate, grandest box of chocolates you have ever seen. The moment she set eyes on them, poor Madame burst into tears. (Lesson No. 6: If you overdo the thank-you present, you give the game away.)

I kept in touch with Monsieur Chaudet and soon afterwards he kindly agreed to give me an interview for the school magazine. It was my first interview with a head of state. Over the years, I have been lucky enough to interview an assortment of presidents, princes and prime ministers, but I don't think any of them has ever given me such straightforward answers as Monsieur Chaudet did for the *Bedales Chronicle*.

In Switzerland, women did not get the vote in federal elections until 1973. This was 1966, so I asked the President why it was that women weren't yet enfranchised. 'Because men and women are not equal,' he said simply.

'Do you really mean that?' I asked.

'Yes, I do. The sexes may be complementary, but they are certainly not equal. Man is absorbed in his professional, political, social and military life, while the woman's place is in the home.'

'When there was last a national referendum on the matter and the referendum was open to all, how did your own wife vote?' I asked.

'Oh, she didn't,' he said amiably. 'She couldn't. I locked her in the bathroom for the day.'

16. 'That little extra something'

The world has certainly changed since I was a little boy. British women had the vote in the 1950s, but many did not have the luxury of a bathroom. My lovely granddaughter (born in 2007) finds this hard to believe, but it's true. When my grand-father (my mother's father) came home from India in 1947, he went to Accrington in Lancashire to live with his maiden sis-ter, my Great-Aunt Edith. He had been a colonel in the Indian Army, she was the head teacher at the local primary school, they lived in quite a smart street, Harcourt Road, but their toi-let was in a small shed, like a sentry box, at the end of the garden.

Auntie Edith was one of the best women I have ever known. Intelligent and independent-minded, kindly and unassuming, and of her time, so when she was suddenly required to keep house for her elder brother, she accepted her lot without complaint – making his cooked breakfast, prepar-ing his lunch, being home in time to cook his tea. She washed all his laundry (Monday night was wash night) and did all the shopping. There was no supermarket. When I went to stay with them, I remember queuing with her outside the butcher, then the baker, then the fishmonger, then the greengrocer . . . it was very boring. Helping with the washing was more fun: I enjoyed putting the dripping-wet sheets through the mangle.

I remember, too, walking back from the shops with her, along streets where women were on their hands and knees scrubbing their front doorsteps. (They *always* seemed to be on their knees washing their front doorsteps.) There were women, like Auntie Edith, who were teachers, and others who were nurses or shop assistants or cleaning ladies or nuns, but most women when I was growing up were housewives – and it was hard, *hard* work. People bathed just once a week because the water was heated by a coal or wood fire under a copper, and it took an age carrying the hot water in saucepans from the kitchen to the tub in the living room next door. (Grandpa and Auntie Edith also had a front room, kept immaculately and never used. I only went into it once: it was where Auntie Edith received people on the day of Grandpa's funeral.)

My only horrid recollection of post-war Accrington is of the acrid smell of chamber pots. If you needed the loo in the middle of the night, you couldn't go down to the end of the garden, so you used the potty. Up until the early 1970s, before the arrival of en-suite facilities, hotels always provided chamber pots, either kept under the bed or hidden inside a foul-smelling bedside cabinet. I remember Max Bygraves (a huge star in the 1950s and beyond) telling me how, on a family holiday once, he had given his son a beautiful white £5 note as a special present and how his son (who was exactly my age) had put it inside his bedside cabinet for safe-keeping when he went to sleep, only to discover in the morning that the precious note was floating around in a used chamber pot that the chambermaid had forgotten to empty the day before.

'That taught him an important lesson for life,' chuckled Max.

'The lesson being?' I asked.

'Never lick your fingers when you're counting your folding money.'

Unless you are approaching my age, you won't have seen one of those beautiful white £5 notes – larger than normal notes and only printed on one side. They went out of circulation in 1957 – the year the first contraceptive pills were being introduced. The pill didn't come on to the market until the 1960s – but when it did, it changed the world.

First with my friend Sheila Hancock (now in her late eighties) and then with my friend Maureen Lipman (now in her mid-seventies) I have appeared on a TV show called *Celebrity Gogglebox*. The idea is a simple one: you are filmed watching TV. The fun comes from the fact that you don't get to choose what you view: you watch what you're given, and react accordingly. It's mostly popular mainstream stuff, but some of it had our ears popping and our eyes standing out on stalks. The use of obscene language and profanity was relentless: I think it would have *killed* Auntie Edith. And it was evident from the variety of dating shows we watched that many young people nowadays don't think twice about having sex on a first date. In fact, they're expecting it. *Gogglebox* was devised by a young man who used to go out with one of my daughters. He also devised a show called *Naked Attraction*, a dating show where the contestants get to inspect each other's private parts before choosing the individual they fancy most. The close-ups leave nothing to the imagination, nor does the perky banter from the show's host: 'Now there's a lovely bit of labia . . . Sam, where are you on the cock-to-balls ratio? I think you like a big one that really fills you up.'

I can't decide if I am appalled by all this – or sorry that I missed out on it because I was born half a century too soon. How different it was, back in the day. According to the figures from the Office for National Statistics, these days only around 1,600 men and women under the age of twenty get married in Britain each year – that's a drop of 97 per cent since 1950, when more than 60,000 young people of that age tied the knot. In those days, full sex before marriage simply wasn't on: if you wanted to sleep with a girl you married her. Today the average age for marriages between opposite-sex couples has risen to nearly thirty-eight for men and thirty-five for women.

Of course, there was plenty of hanky-panky when I was young, but as a rule it stopped short (well short) of intercourse. Girls were encouraged to keep their hands on their ha'pennies. Whatever blokes did, they expected to have a virgin bride. A baby born out of wedlock was considered a matter of considerable shame well into the 1960s. Chastity was a virtue, and sex was something sacred to be enjoyed within marriage. (In the UK, the pill was available to married women from 1961, but not legally available to unmarried women until 1967 – and women in the USA had to wait even longer, until 1972.)

In 1963 (Larkin's *annus mirabilis*), the year I turned fifteen, sex was in the air almost everywhere and, suddenly, surprisingly, sex at Bedales was in the newspapers. Overnight, Judith Earnshaw, a Bedalian sixth former, aged seventeen – a girl I knew and liked and whom I was seeing on a daily basis because she had cast me as one of the leads in her school production of Maeterlinck's *Pelléas and Mélisande* (a verse drama about forbidden love) – found herself at the centre of a media storm. The cause? An article that featured in a magazine called *Sixth Form Opinion* under the headline: Is CHASTITY OUTMODED?

It appeared from the piece that some Bedalians – notably, my friend Judith – thought that it was. The story was picked up by the *Times, Herald, Sketch, Mirror*, etc., the school grounds were invaded by reporters and photographers, Judith was put into hiding, and the hapless headmaster spent forty-eight hours topping and tailing letters to parents (and prospective parents), saying he was 'extremely sorry for the distress which parents will have suffered.' I was even sorrier that our rehearsal schedule for *Pelléas and Mélisande* had been disrupted and that Judith, when she emerged from her dormitory confinement, appeared to have lost some of her creative spark.

Whenever outsiders asked about Bedales, invariably they wanted to know if we were all sleeping with one another. I used to say, 'No – it's the staff we're sleeping with!'

In our dreams, perhaps. Early in 1964, when I was still fifteen, I fell for the school nurse. I used to visit her in the sanatorium and she'd give me cocoa and biscuits. One evening, after assembly, standing together in the san's little kitchen, we kissed. According to my diary:

> We were together until midnight. We were together again yesterday and all today. I know it is wrong because she is a member of staff (and she has a fiancé!) and we can get into a lot of trouble. I know it is stupid, but it's also wonderful and I don't want to stop and nor does she. She thinks I'm amazing and I think she is rather special too! It's madness, of course, but how old was Romeo? (I know. Juliet wasn't a member of staff!!!) Help.

Happily, help was at hand. Somehow, word of the dalliance got out and I was summoned to see the housemaster. He was very friendly and said, smiling, 'A little bird tells me something that's not quite right.' He explained what he'd heard and asked me if it was true. I told him everything. He told me to go to the Library and get on with some work. He said that, if everyone was sensible, everything would be all right. I wanted to believe him, but I was terrified – more terrified, I think, than I had ever been before about anything.

The next day, I was sent to see the headmaster. I was so nervous, I was shaking. He was very friendly, too. He made me sit down in an armchair and gave me a cup of tea. He pulled his chair around from behind his desk and sat leaning towards me with his elbows on his knees. He asked me what had happened. When did it start? Who started it? How far did we 'go'? Had I written to her? Had she written to me?

When I had finished, he told me not to worry. He told me that I had done nothing wrong, but that it *was* wrong because I was only fifteen and she was a member of staff. He said that, since it hadn't 'gone too far', the best thing now was to forget all about it. I must not see her privately or ever speak to her again, or write to her. She was leaving at the end of term, anyway, to get married. He said it was much worse for her than for me. He said he didn't think he would have to tell my parents and he was sure I had learnt a lesson. By the end of it all, we were laughing. He made it very easy and I was very grateful. He said to me, finally, 'Don't talk about this to anyone, ever.' And I didn't.

In my diary, I simply wrote: 'IT'S ALL OVER.'

The lessons of this experience served me well thirty years later when, as an MP, I became a member of the Government Whips' Office. The House of Commons in my time was so like an English boarding school – the same sort of numbers, the same kind of hierarchies and cliques, even the same kind of architecture – that I understood quite quickly how life in the Westminster village worked and recognised almost immediately that the way my Chief Whip (Alastair Goodlad) and his Deputy (Greg Knight) handled wayward MPs was exactly as my headmaster and housemaster had handled me – with good humour, understanding and discretion.

The myth about the Whips' Office is that it's all threats, thumbscrews and bullying. It's a useful myth (the mystery surrounding the working of the Whips' Office adds to its potency – 'Don't talk about this to anyone, ever' is the rule), and sometimes we *were* reduced to a bit of brutality or blackmail when dealing with utterly irreconcilable headbangers who simply couldn't be persuaded to do the decent thing and vote with the government on whose ticket they had been elected.* But on the whole we found that coddling rather than confrontation achieved the best results. Every whip has a set number of MPs under his or her special charge. Mine included a gay MP who said he wasn't (even though his local paper had evidence he was picking up young men at a gay club most weekends), three alcoholics, four philanderers (there were more, of course: these were just the ones where 'revelations'

* If you want names, I refer you to my record of my time as an MP and government whip: *Breaking the Code: Westminster Diaries* (published in 1999).

about them might have rocked the government), one near-bankrupt (whose debts we helped clear: a bankrupt cannot remain an MP, so this chap represented our majority of a single vote), and several more with varying degrees of mental instability. Through the good offices of the House of Commons chaplain I found a safe place for one of these fragile souls in a suburban monastery. When we needed the MP in question to vote, the monks kindly put him in a taxi and sent him across to Westminster.

At the Lycée I first heard Aesop's fable about the competition between the North Wind and the Sun to decide which was the stronger of the two. The challenge, you will remember, was to make a passing traveller remove his cloak. The harder the North Wind blew, the tighter the traveller wrapped his cloak about himself, but when the Sun shone, warmed by it, the traveller quickly took off his cloak. At Bedales, the way in which the headmaster and the housemaster dealt with me left me beholden to them for ever. At Westminster, the same principle applied. It even worked with Ted Heath, the former Prime Minister, who, when it came to voting, could be a difficult cove. Read Ted the riot act and he'd rebel. Woo him, flatter him, go down to his house in Salisbury and tell him it was the house with the prettiest view in England (which it almost was) and he would turn up to vote when you least expected him, shoulders heaving: 'You see, I came.'

At Bedales, Mrs King (one of the teachers) had been head girl when Mr King (the deputy head) fell for her, but they did not get married until after she had left the school. As far as I know, in my time there was only one staff–pupil relationship that went too far – and I was only in part responsible. One of the girls in my year fell in love with a young French teacher – the teacher who couldn't make it to Switzerland for that summer holiday job and sent me instead. Because I liked them both, I helped them spend secret time together: acting as a decoy, being seen going over to his room arm in arm with the girl, apparently to do French revision, and then leaving her in his room alone while I sat keeping guard outside the door . . . Whatever they did, they did quite quietly, and because I wouldn't have had the courage to 'go all the way' it didn't occur to me that that's what they were up to. Anyway, she became pregnant, he got the sack, and they got married. I believe they had more children and lived happily, if not ever after at least for a while. I am still in touch with him. He kindly invites me to his local literary festival each year. Fifty-five years on, I think she now lives with another Old Bedalian.

Even if you never go back, it's a school that is difficult to escape.

I am suddenly thinking I should be writing a quality soap about Bedales in the 1960s. It's got all the storylines and some great characters. Who do I remember best? Among my contemporaries, my friend Simon Cadell, of course. And Peter Harris, who was tall, thin and gangly, clever, bespectacled and kind. We planned to publish a magazine together called *Tomorrow Today*. We saw ourselves as super-forecasters, half a century before the idea became fashionable. Peter went up to Oxford the year before I did and read Chinese. It was wonderful going to a Chinese restaurant with him: he understood what the waiters were saying to one another and wasn't frightened to chip in. I saw a lot of him, even after we left university, until one day we were out with a group of friends, and I said, simply as a joke, 'Nobody knows what Peter does, but I think he's a spy.' I never saw or heard from him again.

Peter's nickname at school was 'Fumbly'. I'm not sure why. Robert Booth was known as 'Smooth Booth' because that's exactly what he was. Consciously handsome, effortlessly elegant, he had wonderful black boots that covered his ankles and he 'treated' them with a bone before polishing them to keep them supple. He went on to King's College, Cambridge, and met E. M. Forster there ('You must call me Morgan') and then left Cambridge without taking his degree to become a male model advertising a chocolate flake bar. Extraordinary. I liked Ham Arnold, too. His father was a celebrated children's author living in the USA: Arnold Arnold. His mother was a world-famous photographer based in London: Eve Arnold. She was a small woman, who looked exactly like her son, with grey hair done up in a bun. She was very American, but I liked her because (like Simon Cadell's mother) she treated me as an equal, like a grown-up. She gave me my first Screwdriver (iced vodka and fresh orange juice) and told heartbreaking stories about Marilyn Monroe, whom she knew well and photographed many times. Ham's real name was Francis Arnold. He was nicknamed 'Ham' by fellow Bedalians because of his supposed physical resemblance to Ham the Astrochimp, the first hominid launched into outer space, in January 1961.

'Syphilis' Ehrlich was so called because the Nobel prize winner Paul Ehrlich (no relation) had pioneered research into the disease of syphilis in the late nineteenth century. Syph's real name was Michael. Bedalians weren't kind with their nicknames. There was a girl known as 'Oz' because of the size of her thighs – as in Shelley's poem 'Ozymandias': 'two vast and trunkless legs of stone . . .' There were some people at school who called me 'Supercilious Simpson'. Oddly, I didn't mind, and when abbreviated to 'Super' I quite liked it.

Was I supercilious? I don't think I was (well, no more than a bit), but I can see now that I *sounded* it. The other day on Twitter I came across a clip of me on TV in the 1960s. My fluting voice is embarrassing: a hideous conflation of Little Lord Fauntleroy, Celia Johnson in *Brief Encounter* and Leslie Howard as the Scarlet Pimpernel. And I used a hundred words when ten would do. I marvel I had any friends at all. I imagine the only reason a girl ever kissed me was to shut me up.

At least the teachers liked me. And I liked them. Who were my favourites? The headmaster, naturally. Tim Slack was only thirty-four when appointed, Tiggerish, keen and bouncy. I liked him for that, though others didn't. Being an eager-beaver wasn't the Bedales style. While the head was very young, his deputy, Cyril King, was very old. I mean *very* old: he had been teaching at the school since 1923. He was also delightfully dotty. He taught Latin and when he wanted you to start work he'd say, 'Carry on with your labours!' At first I thought he was saying, 'Carry on with your neighbours!' which led to some confusion. The housemaster, John Slater, round-faced, dapper, not very tall, a tad portly, taught history (quite brilliantly) and endeared himself to the boys by giving us cocoa and allowing us to watch *Danger Man* on his TV on a Sunday night. I assume he was gay, though that wasn't a word that existed in that sense then. Ditto George Smith who taught French and was fat, jolly and reeked of tobacco.

Christopher Cash, who taught art, was more obviously homosexual: world-weary, tall and effete, he walked like a languid Aubrey Beardsley drawing. He was an inveterate smoker, too – in class as well as out of it. He started smoking at school, he told me. He went to Stowe, 'a proper school' (as opposed to Bedales), 'where, naturally, smoking was encouraged'. He felt Bedales was full of ruffians. 'We were more mannerly at Stowe,' he liked to say. On school cabaret nights, he also liked to sing the music-hall song about the tattooed lady. He was very amusing. I visited him during the holidays at his flat in Onslow Square and he talked to me about his favourite artists: 'You know, whenever Augustus John met a child, he always patted it on the head – just in case it was one of his.'

Inevitably, the teachers I am remembering, the ones who will feature in my upmarket TV soap, are the 'characters'. The straightforward ones – like the games master – I can't bring to mind at all. I know he wore a bright purple tracksuit, but his name has escaped me . . . oh no, it hasn't. It's just come back. But let's forget it. Sport wasn't my thing.

Maths wasn't my thing, either, but I remember the maths

master vividly – Anthony Gillingham. He was a character: tall, handsome, with crinkly receding black hair, he had six children (five daughters and a son), and a pale-faced, long-suffering wife who looked like a rag doll, whom he eventually left for a younger woman. I liked Mrs Gillingham. She was an Old Bedalian herself, part of the Great Bedales Heritage. Her father had been at the school right at the beginning, back in the Oscar Wilde era in the 1890s. I liked Mr Gillingham, too. He was passionate about mathematics, sex, sailing, Gilbert and Sullivan and politics. He was a communist, I think, and an active supporter of the Campaign for Nuclear Disarmament, very much a vogue cause at Bedales at the time. He led the school contingent on the Aldermaston March every Easter, walking from the Atomic Weapons Establishment near Aldermaston in Berkshire to London's Trafalgar Square. I have always assumed that I am a Conservative (and conservative) because I was brought up like a firstborn child – and firstborns, as we know, tend to like the world as they find it and want to keep it as it is. As I write this, I am now wondering if, in fact, I am as I am because I was a teenage rebel – and what I rebelled against were the socialist values that were part and parcel of the Bedales tradition. At school, when I won the Macdonald Essay Prize I was delighted to discover it had been given by the son of Ramsay MacDonald. Naturally, Britain's first Labour Prime Minister sent his boy to Bedales.

I am telling you about these people because they loomed so large in my life – and still do. At this moment, are you thinking of the teachers who played a special part in your childhood? I hope so. There were three, in particular, who helped me along the way.

George Bird taught me German and, bless him, took an interest in my adolescent scribbling – reading the poems and plays I was writing and returning them to me with notes of advice and encouragement. He was a very tall man, and thin, and he walked with huge strides, leaning forward with a stoop.

He wore a grey moustache (as though it might have been a false one) and did not deny that before turning to teaching he had worked for MI5. He spoke Russian, among other languages, and looked like one of the cartoon spies in *Mad* magazine.

Rachel Field looked like a plump bird – lopsided (I think she had had breast cancer, not that anyone ever talked about that sort of thing), balding, beady-eyed, with the odd stray hair on her chin, she taught me whatever I know about verse-speaking and stagecraft, sent me *hundreds* of handwritten notes about my theatrical endeavours (all of which I have kept: 'it's *truth* we need, Gyles, not funny voices') and introduced me to one of my favourite authors, Elizabeth Taylor.* (Not the actress, the novelist. She was another Bedalian parent of note. At Eton, it was the boys who became famous. At Bedales, it was the parents who had been.) Rachel, I realised later, was very much like a character from a novel by Elizabeth Taylor or Barbara Pym.

Harold Gardiner (known by his initials HEG) came straight from the pages of Henry Fielding, the eighteenth-century novelist best known for *The History of Tom Jones* and *The History of the Adventures of Joseph Andrews and of his Friend Mr Abraham Adams*. HEG was very like the good-hearted Parson Adams (played by Michael Hordern – another Bedalian parent, you'll remember – in the 1977 film) though less absent-minded. HEG was a bony man with a weather-beaten knobbly face and a deep love of the English language that he passed on to me and which has been the chief delight of my life. I hope there is a heaven because, if there is, I can hear HEG reading

* As this is an autobiography, is this the point where I list my favourite novelists and you compare yours with mine? My top ten would include: Elizabeth Taylor, Anthony Trollope, W. M. Thackeray, Henry Fielding, Charles Dickens, Arnold Bennett, Anthony Powell, C. P. Snow, J. I. M. Stewart, Barbara Pym. My favourite comic writers are P. G. Wodehouse and E. F. Benson. My favourite diarist is Virginia Woolf.

Chaucer out loud again. *The Canterbury Tales* were written 630 years ago in Middle English, but the way HEG read them you understood every word. Other than my parents and my wife, this is the man who is the author of whatever it is my life has been. He educated my love of Shakespeare; he made me fall in love with Milton; he got me through my A Levels; he got me into Oxford; he started me off on the public-speaking circuit (he was the Rotarian who organised that competition I won on 30 November 1965); he encouraged me in all my little schemes and projects; he flattered me by suggesting Fielding might be my role model: 'As well as novels and plays, he was a social reformer, too.' I think about HEG and Henry Fielding most days of my life. I am writing this at my home in Barnes, a stone's throw from Henry Fielding's country house.

Because HEG was the head of English, he was the master in charge of the school magazine and indulgently blessed the various changes in its design and content that I proposed. He also suggested I might like to send the magazine to other schools and invite them to send me theirs – in case I could learn something from what others might be doing. This led to me getting school magazines of every shape and size from across the land – including one from Stowe School, where Christopher Robin Milne and Prince Rainier, as well as our art master, had been to school. The Stowe magazine came with a friendly note from its editor suggesting we might meet up in the holidays for a chat. His parents lived in a block of flats at the top end of Baker Street, by Hyde Park Corner. Mine lived at the bottom end of Baker Street by Madame Tussauds. We made a date and I went.

I liked him the moment we met. He was a year or so younger than me, taller, ganglier, with long straggly hair and ants in his pants. He did not stop moving. He swung around his bedroom and the kitchen and the hallway and the sitting room like a wild monkey jumping from branch to branch. He was a bundle of energy – and ideas.

'Tell you what, Gyles – you want to start a magazine, I want to start a magazine. Let's do it together.'

'The magazine I've got in mind is called *Tomorrow Today*,' I said. 'It's –'

'Great title,' he interrupted, 'but who's going to buy it? We should start a magazine called *Student* and every student in the country will want it.'

'There's an awful lot of students . . .'

'Exactly. Our fortune is made. When can you start?'

'Well, I've got my A Levels . . .'

'Forget your A Levels, Gyles. We're going to conquer the world together.'

'But what about university?'

'Forget university. I'm leaving school now. Who needs university? Let's get the show on the road. We can be a team, Gyles – Branson and Brandreth, yup?'

'Well, I –'

'Are you in?'

'Well, I . . .'

I did not see Richard Branson again for another thirty years. In the 1990s, when I was an MP attached to the Department of National Heritage and involved in suggesting candidates for honours, I said one day, 'How about a knighthood for Richard Branson?'

The officials pursed their lips and started to make curious sucking sounds.

'I don't think so,' sniffed one.

'He's been considered before,' said the other, 'and found wanting.'

'Really?' I persisted.

'I'm afraid so. Flies too close to the wind. How solvent is he, really? We don't want to give him a gong and then find it blows up in our faces, do we?'

'He's a risk-taker.'

'Exactly.'

'*Exactly* – and a brilliant one. He deserves a knighthood for services to entrepreneurship!'

'I'm not sure we do those.'

We did for Richard Branson. I felt I owed him one.

In 1966, at the end of the summer term, Richard left Stowe and began to build his business empire without me. I went back to Bedales, for one more term, to take my Oxford Entrance Exam. Pa had been to Oxford. If I could get in, I knew I had to go to Oxford, too.

And then what? Would I be an entrepreneur – as Richard would become and as my great-great-grandfather, the Pill Man, had been? Would I be a writer and social reformer – like Henry Fielding or my forebear, George R. Sims? Strange to say, but by then I knew I wasn't going to be an actor, after all. I remember the exact moment I became convinced of it. It was on the afternoon of 22 September 1966 and I was walking with my friend Simon through the orchard at school on our way down to town for tea and teacakes at our favourite tea shop, the Donkey Cart. Simon knew he was going to be an actor. It was his destiny. That's what he lived for. Olivier had said to me on that famous afternoon, in Chichester: 'If you want to be an actor, don't be. If you *need* to be an actor, then be one.' I had thought a lot about that. I wanted to be a whole variety of things – but being an actor, of itself, wasn't one of them. I think I had worked out, too, that I wouldn't be good enough to be a *great* actor – and if you can't be that, I thought, what's the point?

Over our tea and teacakes at the Donkey Cart, Simon and I talked about 'great acting' and 'star quality'. We talked about David Warner's Hamlet. It was all the rage – Hamlet, the contemporary student prince in his college scarf, etc. – and it was a fine performance, sure, in an interesting production (by Peter Hall), but, despite the brouhaha, did we reckon it was one of the all-time greats? No. David Warner is a fine actor, we agreed, thinking we might follow the teacake with a shared slice of Victoria sponge, but does he have that 'little extra something' – as in our favourite story of Dame Edith Evans (our favourite Dame) and the young director who had spent day after day of rehearsal telling her where to stand, when to sit, how to say this line and that . . .

Eventually, Dame Edith turned to him. 'Young man, when are you going to give me a moment to do that little extra something the audience has come for?'

'That little extra something' – that's what Simon and I wanted our lives to be about. But we knew that nothing could be guaranteed. We wrote a sketch for one of the school's cabaret nights that term. It was set in a grand hotel in the south of France, forty years into the future, by which time Simon had become a great star and I'd become an elderly down-on-his-luck waiter: I served him a drink and he didn't recognise me. Funny, we hoped – and poignant, too.

On Thursday, 16 December 1966, having survived the written papers, I travelled to Oxford for my interview at New College. There I was faced with three senior dons, led by Anthony Quinton, metaphysician and moral philosopher, in 1940 the young survivor of the sinking of the SS *City of Benares*, now the man with my destiny in his hands. The interview did not go well. Mr Quinton, well built, beaming, genial, thought to put me at my ease by starting off with some questions about my much-vaunted interest in prisons. I burbled boastfully for a minute or two, when suddenly I heard him ask me a question.

'Mr Brandreth, what is a "star" prisoner?'

I had no idea.

'It's a term quite commonly used in the English prison service,' he explained pleasantly. 'It means a first-time prisoner.'

'Oh,' I said, 'I didn't know.'

From then on in, I was all at sea.

I went back to school for the last weekend of term. I was

head boy by then. (The headmaster had asked me, 'Do you really want to be head boy?' 'Of course,' I'd said. 'I didn't think you would, you've got so much else on. You don't need it for your CV, you know,' he'd said. 'No, I'd definitely like to be head boy – thank you.') As I look back now, I think I was living out the words of Aristotle Onassis: 'I must keep aiming higher and higher, even though I know how silly it is.'

There were end-of-term duties and a long round of farewells. I saw everybody – almost. I played a last game of Scrabble with the Chief. He was a hundred and one. He won, of course.

'I'll miss our games,' I said.

'So will I,' he said. 'You don't often win, but you keep me on my toes.'

I was back home in Baker Street on Tuesday, 19 December when the telegram arrived, sent from Oxford at 3.40 p.m.

AWARDED SCHOLARSHIP NEW COLLEGE CON-GRATULATIONS = QUINTON

On Thursday the post brought this letter from HEG – Harold Gardiner, my English teacher and the best of men.

Ridge Cottage,
Steep,
Petersfield, Hants.

20 Dec. 1966

My dear Gyles,
What an extraordinary thing, that, at the last moment, neither of us felt capable of facing the other; and so the congratulations are by the more formal medium of a letter. They are none the less heartfelt, and of the warmest. You have deserved every grain of success, for the way you have done everything one could have hoped for, and then still found

the time and the drive to do more. I don't think a swelled head is a serious risk, and so I can say how much more pleased I am for your success than for any other pupil's whom I have ever taught, or whom I am ever likely to teach.

Aye,
Harold

17. Discovering America

According to the Oxford English Dictionary and my friend
Susie Dent, the lexicographer from *Countdown*'s Dictionary
Corner, the term 'gap year' has only been around since the
mid-1970s. I'm surprised. I seem to remember using it in 1967,
when I spent six months of mine in America, land of my
forefathers. I was nearly nineteen, and I loved it.

I started out in Baltimore, Maryland (birthplace of Edgar
Allan Poe), teaching French and English at the Park School,
an independent day school of 500 pupils, 95 per cent of them
Jewish and all of them wealthy: the older kids drove to school
in their own Cadillacs while the teachers arrived in Volks-
wagens. I had met some of the kids and a couple of the
teachers at an international student arts festival hosted at
Bedales the year before. That's how I got the gig. (I am now
realising how absurdly privileged my upbringing was. I took it
completely for granted at the time.)

I can't have been much of a teacher (I was making it up as I
went along) and I didn't look much like a Beatle, which was disappointing to my students, but I did at least hail from 'Swinging
London'. Every American I met claimed to 'lurve' my accent
and my 'British eccentricity'. I loved their enthusiasm, their
milkshakes, their daytime TV, their five-lane highways, their
gas-guzzling cars (some of which had their own telephones)
and the never-ending juxtaposition of the tawdry (real divorces
recreated on TV for entertainment) and the tremendous (when
I heard the novelist James Baldwin on the late-night chat shows
I thought I had never heard the English language used so well).

I spent a term at the Park and then went travelling all over:
north, south, east and west. Sometimes by Greyhound bus

(grim: I was invariably seated next to an overweight fellow traveller who did not smell quite right), mostly on Delta Airlines (student standby: half price). The Empire State Building, Niagara Falls, Disneyland, the Seattle Space Needle, the slums of Washington DC, the glories of the Mississippi – you name it, I did it. I was in New Orleans on the night Vivien Leigh died and I found the streetcar named 'Desire'. I met Julia Childs, America's Fanny Cradock, at a lunch in New England. When I toured the offices of the *New York Times*, the great Harrison E. Salisbury was there – recently returned from North Vietnam and one of the first mainstream journalists to oppose the Vietnam War.

I opposed the Vietnam War, too. One Saturday in April, I was up before dawn to catch a 7.00 a.m. bus from Baltimore to New York to join tens of thousands marching through Manhattan to the United Nations Plaza to hear Dr Martin Luther King call on the United States to 'honour its word' and 'stop the bombing of North Vietnam'. It was a memorable – and moving – experience. I saw Dr King way, way in the distance. The loudspeakers destroyed the power of his oratory, but it didn't matter. It just felt good to be part of such a huge crowd and to know that we had right on our side. (I took part in a protest march for only the second time in my life thirty-six years later, in London in 2003, when I joined upwards of three-quarters of a million people protesting against Tony Blair's Iraq War.)

Of course, in Baltimore at the Park School I was spending my time with a vocal minority – liberal, Jewish, intellectual. We all admired Dr King. Others felt differently. In the most recent presidential primary in Maryland, George Wallace, the pro-segregationist white supremacist, had secured 42 per cent of the vote. Spiro T. Agnew (Richard Nixon's future Vice-President) had just been elected Governor of Maryland. I was excited to meet him (naturally) and, sensibly resisting the temptation to tell him I'd come up with an amusing anagram of his name ('Grow A Penis' – well, I was still a teenager), I tried to talk to him about the Maryland State Penitentiary. He wasn't interested. (Perhaps the subject was too near the knuckle. In 1973 he had to resign as Vice-President when faced with allegations of criminal conspiracy, bribery, extortion and tax fraud.)

Across America, I visited prisons wherever I could. I still marvel that they let me in: I had no strings to pull, I simply wrote asking for admission and, without exception, they said yes. (In San Francisco, I even managed to spend a day up on the bench sitting alongside the judge as he dispensed justice.) The Maryland prison was one of the most disheartening. The food was good (they gave me lunch with the men), but that was all. Old lags and young offenders were thrown together in overcrowded wings, with two men in cells for one in almost every instance – except for the sex offenders and those on Death Row.

In different states I was introduced to different forms of capital punishment, including hanging, the firing squad and the electric chair. In Maryland they favoured the gas chamber.

'You want to see it?' asked the prison officer showing me around.

The execution chamber was located within a cell at the end of a long whitewashed corridor. It looked like a miniature space capsule.

'Welcome to the pressure cooker,' said my guide, with a chuckle and a wink. He pulled open the door, pointed to the metal chair inside and said, 'Come on, kid, try it for size.'

I did as I was told.

'Normally, we'd strap you in, but you don't look like the type to struggle so I'll just shut the door.'

He did exactly that and left it closed just long enough for me to become alarmed.

'Thank you,' I said as he released me.

'A pleasure,' he beamed. 'You're lucky. Most folks don't get out of here alive.'

In Maryland when they had executions, up to fifteen 'witnesses' were required to watch. Apparently, members of the public applied in droves. They carried out their last in 2005, and the state abolished the death penalty in 2013. I remember thinking, that day in 1967, that what was almost worse than the legalised slaughter was the notion of 'Death Row' itself. It was exactly that: a row of cells side by side on a corridor leading to the gas chamber.

One of the men I met had been on Death Row, alone in the same cell, and completely idle, for more than ten years.

'Hello,' I said to him, not knowing what else to say.

He looked at me, shook his head slowly and waved me away.

'He is a rapist and a murderer,' explained my guide.

And, soon after my visit, this prisoner became the 310th person to be executed in the Maryland Penitentiary.

As well as visiting prisons, I visited Old Bedalians. I had a list of the school's North American alumni and whenever I arrived in a new city I made it my business to introduce myself in the hope I might be invited round for a meal – or even a bed for the night. I hit lucky everywhere. For example, according to my diary, in Toronto, on Tuesday, 2 May 1967 (the day after Elvis Presley married Priscilla Beaulieu, incidentally):

I dined (beautifully) with Dr Edward Murphy and his wife. He is an Old Bedalian and the son of J. T. Murphy, the British Communist leader in the 1920s. Dr Murphy, who is taking me today to visit the Toronto Sick Children's Hospital where he works, showed me a photograph of himself on his father's shoulders in 1926. In the photo the little boy is holding hands with a familiar-looking figure. Yes, I can now say that I have shaken the hand that shook the hand of Joseph Stalin.

Whenever I was in Washington DC (which was quite often: I loved Georgetown), one name cropped up more than any other:

25 April 1967
I'm just in from a very plush four-hour candlelit dinner at '1786'. My hostess was Miss Emily Brown, a lovely lady, a *lonely* lady, born 1906, at Bedales in the early twenties, at the British embassy here since 1949. I was very flirtatious (Felix Krull!) – she is very lonely – and I agreed to see her again . . . She began by telling me that her years at Bedales were the worst of her life and ended by giving me £150 for the Bedales Development Campaign! (Am I feeling guilty? Just a touch.) She drank six martinis. I drank wine. Delicious wine.

At school I had read Thomas Mann's unfinished novel about the adventures of a confidence trickster, *Confessions of Felix Krull*, and in DC in 1967, aged nineteen, I realised how easy it would be to be a gigolo. You didn't have to be handsome. You just had to be young. (Once you get to a certain age, anyone under thirty is attractive.)

I visited family all over North America, too. I went up to Canada to see my mother's brother, boozy Uncle Jack, and his diminutive wife, Ede. She was a good-hearted, talkative soul, all of four foot off the ground, who favoured flaming-red hair to set off her white gangster raincoat and huge dark glasses. The pair of them drank from dawn to dusk – and then through the night. Uncle Jack would sit in front of the TV, wearing nothing but a kimono, with glass and bottle in hand, watching the hockey and occasionally shouting, 'Shut it, woman!' when Aunt Ede got too voluble in the kitchen, talking to anybody and nobody in particular.

I had gone to Toronto for my Cousin Johnnie's wedding. Uncle Jack travelled, with bottle and glass, in the bridal car. The wedding supper was dry and served at six. There was a sparkling rosé for the toasts (cries of, 'Where's the hard stuff?') but the moment the speeches were done, the dancing and the serious boozing began. The music was the Rolling Stones and the like; the bar was open and free. Still no dancer, I did my Broadstairs-style jitterbugging to 'entertain' the crowd. Each time Jack or Ede stumbled past they cried, 'Just wait till your parents hear about this, hic!' Eventually we got home and that's when the real drinking started – and it didn't stop until 5.00 a.m. Giggling, gurgling, tippling, tumbling, belching, burping, I had (and have) never seen anything like it.

And in the morning, when I emerged, they were already at it: the ladies, in curlers with cold cream covering their faces, tossing pancakes while tossing back Bloody Marys; the men in kimonos watching the hockey (there is always hockey on TV in Canada in my experience – every hour of every day), each clutching his bottle to his chest. Johnnie (much improved since our European tour) proposed that I join him for a day's hunting with ground hawks, and I was glad that I did. We escaped the House of Booze and drove into some fresh and lovely countryside and spent the whole afternoon wandering through the woods. It was quite magical – streams, glades, spring flowers, horses running free … Nothing to shoot, however. At four, Johnnie set up some old tin cans and did a bit of target practice. I took a few potshots and at least managed to hit the right hillside.

A wedding in Toronto, a funeral in New York. My Aunt Polly died, aged eighty-five, in Brooklyn. She wasn't my aunt, she was a cousin on my mother's side, and I had only met her once, but her daughter, Agnes, a good woman who had served in the US Navy, was keen for me to represent the British end of the family at the funeral, so I went – by Greyhound bus to New York and then by subway and by bus and a long, long walk along dusty side streets until eventually I reached the McManus Funeral Parlour in Brooklyn, on schedule, at 6.00 p.m. I was ushered into the Chapel of Rest and immediately startled by the number of my unexpected Black relations. The room was dimly lit, stifling hot and crowded with overweight mourners, weeping and wailing. It took me a moment to register that I had been shown into the wrong chapel. Eventually, I found the right place – but the scene that greeted me there was no less strange. The room was packed with a variety of grotesques (my relations), a number of them dressed in elaborate, flowing white robes. Cousin Agnes was a Mason and the Service of Last Rites was to be conducted by members of the Lodge of the Eastern Star.

Before the service began, I joined the line snaking past Aunt Polly's open casket. There she was, the old lady, sitting up, apparently in her wedding dress, looking better than she had done in years.

As Cousin Agnes remarked sweetly, 'Mom never wore lipstick during her life, but we think it kinda suits her in death. She'd have wanted to look her best to meet her Maker.'

The service was conducted by a garrulous Scottish clergyman and enlivened by weird chanting and ritualistic gyrations from two men and six women (Agnes among them) dressed in the druidical garb of the Order of the Eastern Star – the sort of baffling nonsense you get in weaker episodes of *Midsomer Murders*. When it was over, we all filed past Aunt Polly again and then set off for the wake, back at the McSkimming family's modest but welcoming Brooklyn home. They kept the American flag flying on their porch.

They kindly put me up for the night – in the very bed in which Aunt Polly had died just seventy-two hours before.

'We've changed the linen, of course,' said Agnes reassuringly.

I shared the room with a Canadian called Wally and his ten-year-old son. I hoped we were not related, but I fear we were.

At 9.00 the following morning, the limousines arrived to whisk us back to the funeral home. There we had a last sighting of Aunt Polly before the closing of the casket and the long drive (an hour and more) to the cemetery at Port Washington.

I was in the second limo and sat in the back row with my cousin Betty and her husband, Sloan. It was a mistake, in one way – Sloan was huge (I was squashed all the way to the grave-side) – but useful in another: they invited me down to stay on their boat in the Bahamas, whenever I wanted, and for as long as I liked. Cousin Betty had married well: her husband was Sloan Wilson, a best-selling American author whose books included *The Man in the Gray Flannel Suit* (1955) and *A Summer Place* (1958), both of which were made into major movies. I was content to be pressed up against literary greatness – and fascinated by the novelty of the limousine's electric windows.

The interment, unfortunately, was a washout. We got to the cemetery at 11.00 to find that the graves had all been flooded. After a powwow between Agnes, the Scottish cleric and the cemetery officials, it was agreed that we would 'bury' Aunt Polly temporarily in a vault. When a suitable grave dried up, she would be moved to it. No extra charge.

We were only in the cemetery for a matter of minutes before piling back into the limos for the return to Brooklyn. On the way, I caused something of a drama by needing a 'comfort break' – that's been a lifelong failing: drinking too much tea and then having an urgent, desperate need for the loo. (I am ahead of the game now: I could cross London, from Harrods in the west to St Paul's in the east, and show you all the best hotels and stores to stop off at, should the need suddenly arise.) For my convenience, the entire funeral cortège parked up outside a roadside rest room. Sloan was much amused. (And relieved. He joined me in the Gents: 'We writers must stick together.')

Back in Brooklyn, the wake resumed, with the Scottish cler-gyman leading the quaffing and sluicing. I chatted with Sloan, about women and himself (his principal preoccupations), the war in Vietnam, and the family. I asked him what lessons he had learnt in life. He said he'd think about it and send me a list. 'I like lists,' he said.

When it was time for me to go, Cousin Agnes pressed a welcome $20 bill into my hand. 'From Aunt Polly,' she said. 'She wanted you to have it. I know she did. She couldn't talk after the stroke, but if she could have done she'd have said so.'

Cousin Agnes was a good woman – like my Great-Aunt Edith from Accrington, one of the best. And I think of Aunt Polly at every funeral I attend – and that's a good number at my time of life. When my friend Richard Whiteley, the original host of *Countdown*, died in 2005, the memorial service at York Minster was a memorable affair, with two thousand in the congregation, and Barry Cryer and I among those paying tribute. I thought of Aunt Polly halfway through Barry's hilarious and touching tribute, when suddenly he halted his address, muttered, 'Excuse me,' turned on his heel, scurried down the pulpit steps and ran, hell for leather, in the direction of the Minster toilets.

Sloan Wilson and I became good friends, exchanging letters and signed copies of our books, until he died in 2003. A few days after Aunt Polly's funeral, as promised, he sent me the list of what life had taught him.

1. Liquid shoe polish doesn't work.
2. A man who wants time to read and write must let the grass grow long.
3. Beware of people who are always well dressed.
4. The hardest part of raising children is teaching them to ride bicycles. A father can run beside the bicycle or stand yelling directions while the child falls. A shaky child on a bicycle for the first time needs both support and freedom. The realisation that this is what the child will always need can hit hard.
5. Children go away and live their own lives, starting when they are about eighteen. Parents who accept this as a natural part of the order of things will see their grown children surprisingly often.

6. Friends are fun, but they are more dangerous than strangers. Strangers ask for a quarter for a cup of coffee, while friends ask for a thousand dollars, no questions asked, if you're a *real* friend. Some friends also have a roving eye for your wife and daughters.
7. Despite all the advice about how to achieve connubial bliss, a happy marriage is usually an unearned miracle. The reasons why some people get on so well together are as mysterious as the reasons why other people fight.
8. When things break around the house, call a handyman. No intelligent man is capable of fixing anything unless he has made home repair his business.

Apart from Sloan, who made a deal of money and spent even more (and drank too much along the way), my Brooklyn cousins were modest people living modest lives, decently and well.

I visited other cousins whose lives were not so ordinary. I went out to Ossining, both to visit the notorious Sing Sing penitentiary there and to call on Fox Brandreth Conner and his family, descendants of the Pill Man, who were still manufacturing the pills (largely now for 'the A-rab market') as well as producing their Allcock's Porous Plasters and their Havahart humane animal traps. Because of Dr Brandreth's huge wealth his children and grandchildren (up to my father's generation) had married well. His granddaughter Virginia, my great-aunt, had married a soldier who became one of military history's most noted strategists. General Fox Conner was a friend of George S. Patton. The general introduced him to the young Dwight D. Eisenhower who used to say that, other than his parents, Conner was the greatest influence on his life. As I type this, I am looking at a family photo of Fox and my great-aunt, on the shores of Lake Brandreth, having a picnic with Generals John J. Pershing and George C. Marshall – a few years before the advent of the Pershing Missile and the Marshall Plan. Conner had three rules of war for a democracy that he imparted to both Eisenhower and Marshall, who held to them. They were:

1. never fight unless you have to
2. never fight alone, and
3. never fight for long.

The Brandreths lived in beautiful houses in Ossining, but the family's glory days were behind them. They were comfortably off, but they were not rich. Unlike my Texas cousins.

In Houston I stayed with the wealthiest of my relations – a nice guy and a proper billionaire. My cousin H. Gardiner Symonds was an oilman, chairman and chief executive of the Tenneco Oil Company (assets in 1970: $4 billion). He kept a house in Mexico, a ranch in Texas, an apartment in New York, a place at Brandreth in the Adirondack Mountains, as well as the palatial home in Houston where I was invited to stay.

Maurice, the Symonds' houseman and chauffeur, met me at the airport – in S3, the third of the family's dozen automobiles (the numbers ran from S1 to S12). Maurice was a charming man, Black (as all the servants were), gracious and devoted to the family. He had been with them for eighteen years. In the car I sat next to him until we reached the gates of the estate, when he pulled up and suggested I might prefer to sit in one of the back seats: 'That's what Mr Symonds would expect.'

The house was a marvel and my suite not bad: a large bedroom, a larger sitting room, a boudoir and a bathroom with a vast square bath that was actually too big – sitting in the middle, you couldn't reach the taps or the sides. When I arrived I asked for a telephone (installed instantly) and a typewriter (brought out from Tenneco); my bed was made by the maid and my clothes laundered and replaced before I knew what was happening. Mrs Symonds greeted me quite formally and gave me lunch – Mexican food, hot and good, served by Maurice – and then Quita appeared. She was twenty-three (Susan was her proper name), dark-haired, brown-eyed, attractive and intelligent. I decided, there and then, that I should marry her. Yes, we were cousins, both great-great-grandchildren of the Pill Man, but that shouldn't be an impediment: the Queen and Prince Philip were cousins, too, both great-great-grandchildren of Queen Victoria, and that hadn't stood in their way.

I spent all my time in Houston with Quita, except for the day I went out to Huntsville to see what the Texas Department of Corrections was up to. I was impressed. The main jail was for repeat offenders, and there were proper education and training programmes on offer. The men weren't just cooped up in their cells all day: things were *happening*.

I was able to talk with the men quite freely – even on Death Row. One guy – he was days away from his scheduled execution – was excited to find out I was British. 'Have you met Twiggy? I *love* that Twiggy.'

Several of the men on Death Row had posters of Twiggy on their cell walls. In one, Twiggy was wearing a Union Jack minidress. This both excited and shocked the men. The idea of using the national flag as a fashion accessory they found perplexing. 'Here,' they explained, 'we have a federal law to protect the stars and stripes from insulting behaviour.'

Twiggy's most ardent admirer told me it was his dying wish that I should tell Twiggy how much he loved her.

Twenty years later, when she became a friend, I did. (I do hope there is a heaven, because then he will know.)

On my travels, I fell in love with every girl I met. Often, I'm now ashamed to say, for the wrong reasons. Quita was lovely, but I think it was the prospect of her millions (and, in fairness to me, the good I was sure I could do with them) that drew me to her. Jessie Sayre in DC was lovely, too, and nearer my age, but I have no doubt that, in my eyes, the fact that she was President Woodrow Wilson's great-granddaughter added to her allure. Jessie's father was the Dean of Washington Cathedral – she took me round it – and thirty years later, I made it the setting for a pivotal scene in my first novel, *Who Is Nick Saint?* Washington Cathedral is modelled on Canterbury Cathedral (it's *bigger* than Canterbury, of course) and they have a lovely herb garden there. I remember finding the way Jessie called it 'an urb garden' incredibly sexy. Ridiculous.

I think I *was* ridiculous. Perhaps I was a little mad? There is a strain of what we used to call manic-depression in the family. I don't remember any lows, but perhaps I was on a high much of the time without realising it: perpetually flirting, talking non-stop, ricocheting across the continent like a whirling dervish, paying for my flights by giving talks and poetry recitals, singing for my supper wherever I went. I don't remember spending one night in a hotel. If I couldn't find anyone to put me up, I went to an airport and dozed in the departure lounge.

In Southern California I hooked up with some hippies and dossed down with them on the beach. That's where I met Kim de la Rosa. She will be an old lady now. She was a teenage enchantress then. Yes, I must have been mad. I saw her as Tinker Bell to my Peter Pan.

Who were you, dear reader, when you were nineteen? Scarlett O'Hara or Marilyn Monroe? Peter Pan or Captain Hook? I think I was a touch of them all – as well as Felix Krull, of course, and Julien Sorel from *Le Rouge et le Noir* (an A Level set text). And, when I was on a rhetorical roll, making one of my speeches, Abraham Lincoln and James Baldwin. And, when I was giving one of my poetry readings, Lord Byron, Dylan Thomas, Mark Twain and Oscar Wilde, all rolled into one.

Let's agree I was ridiculous, but I was happy – and I have the lists to prove it. Inspired by Sloan Wilson, I filled my diary with lists. Here is one from Saturday, 1 July 1967.

Count your blessings, Mr Brandreth. Ten good things that have happened this week:

1. Dinner with Suzy Blaustein. (She is fourteen and very lovely. Truly beautiful. And her grandfather is the richest Jew in America. He gave $1 million to Israel this week.)

2. Dinner with Emily Brown, who is neither fourteen nor beautiful, but is rather fun and a generous hostess. We dined very grandly at the Carriage House: succulent steaks, creamed spinach, European wines. (Tomorrow we are going Chinese: Nanking on P Street.)

3. A swim in the Washington Hilton pool. (Well, it was good at the time. How was I to know I'd get a heat rash?! The itching, O Lord, the itching! The heat here is horrendous.)

4. The reception given to my talk on 'progressive education in the Summerhill tradition'! (This was for Mrs Bloom who had already given me $50 for my hour-long poetry reading to her Chi Chapter of Pi Lambda Theta group. More please.)

5. Reading *Scoop* by Evelyn Waugh.

6. Good work on the proofs of the Badley memorial magazine – corrected, cut, pasted, returned. [The founder of Bedales had died and I was editing a magazine in his honour.] Posted at 2.00 a.m. at the DC Post Office – followed by coffee at the all-night Georgetown café. (This is what I like doing best: completing a project.)

7. Arranging my meeting with James V. Bennett, long-serving director of the Federal Bureau of Prisons – the man who really knows.

8. Taking tea (and then cocktails) with Betty Ducat, vaudevillian friend of Pa's friend 'Wee' Georgie Wood. Miss Ducat has a dance school and created a dance

troupe 'The Fabulous Ducats' – four girls and boy – who were 'a complete sensation' on *The Ed Sullivan Show*.

9. Lunching with an Old Bedalian, Dr Ackerman, at the Cosmos Club at 2121 Massachusetts Avenue. It's a club for gentlemen and explorers – they don't allow black people in the place, except to wait at table. (Incredible, but true.) Dr A is so civilised: cool, calm, courteous. At the end of the meal, in his pocket diary he made a note of my interests and what I'd eaten. He does that every time he meets someone: 'Helps place them,' he explained, 'and next time we meet they're pleased with the details I appear to have remembered.'

10. Getting my hair cut in the barber's shop at the United States Senate. Oh yes. And meeting Robert Kennedy in the lift. (I didn't know it was an elevator for Senators Only. I truly didn't.)

I think this week sums up all that I like best in life – a beautiful girl, a performance that goes well, fine food, interesting people, *top people*, theatre people, prisons, politics, projects . . . and a good book. (*Scoop* is a very good book.)

And here is the last list I made that summer, flying home after six months in North America.

Monday, 14 August 1967
I am writing this on board TWA 704 from Washington DC bound for London. We left at 8.00 p.m.; we land at 8.05 a.m. Dinner has been served, the lights are being dimmed and I am reflecting on the past six months. I have travelled well over one hundred and fifty-eight thousand miles and I am returning home slightly weary, slightly tanned, slightly less stooped, slightly heavier, slightly changed.

Without consulting my notes, what are the highlights of my time in America – what are the ten moments or places that come *instantly* into my mind?

1. Last week, flying into Chicago, with eighty soldiers fresh from Vietnam – so fresh they hadn't slept since leaving Saigon. They were full of the horror of the war and the glory of it. However, they all believed in what they were doing. They talked a lot about the money they earned and how they spent it – mostly on prostitutes. 'The girls cost $20. The inflation in Vietnam is terrible.'
2. Still in Chicago: the Baha'i Temple at Wilmette.
3. In LA, sitting on top of the hill looking down over the Hollywood Bowl, watching Barbra Streisand effortlessly hold an audience of seventeen thousand in the palm of her hand.
4. Up in British Columbia, going up Howe Sound to Squamish. Normally, I'm not one for 'nature', but the beauty of this was overwhelming. (More memorable than the Niagara Falls.)
5. The Forest Lawn Memorial Cemetery – it was everything that Evelyn Waugh (in *The Loved One*) led us to expect and more. And Disneyland – it was everything Uncle Walt led us to expect and more. (I *really* liked both. They are ridiculous, but wonderful.)
6. Sitting on the hot sand drinking an iced chocolate malted on the beach at Coney Island.
7. Drinking so many martinis with James Bennett, head of the Federal Prison Service, that when I left him I could barely stand!
8. The Shakespeare Garden in the Golden Gate Park – featuring each and every flower mentioned in Shakespeare.
9. Lunch in the Senators' dining room at the US Senate. (Of course.)

10. Rescuing Kim de la Rosa from the Pacific Ocean. She had disappeared beneath the waves. It was my heroic moment, my finest hour. I dived in and brought her out in my arms! (And that I could do so is all thanks to those cold afternoons at the Fulham Baths. Thank you, Ma! And the swimming lessons were followed, I remember, by a cup of hot Bovril seated on a high stool in the Fulham Baths café. I can picture the counter I sat at and the advertisement for 7Up that was my constant reading.)

The plane landed in London on time. I took the bus to the Victoria air terminal. Ma and Pa were there, waiting for me. They looked well. We had coffee and they told me 'the news'. They hadn't felt they could share it in a letter. They wanted to tell me in person. My sister Hester had had a baby – a little girl called Polly. They didn't say who the father was or where he was. There was no question of Hes marrying him. Hester was gay: we all accepted that, though we never talked about it.

Hes had thought about having an abortion, but she didn't want that – and anyway, abortions weren't legalised in England until July 1967, three months after her baby was born. She had thought about adoption, but she didn't want that either. She was twenty-five and she wanted to keep her baby. With Ma and Pa's help, she did.

When Polly was born in the Middlesex Hospital, Hester was the only unmarried mother there. There was some hostility from the nurses, and other mothers kept asking where her husband was, but, 'She's coping well,' said Pa proudly. I could see how well Ma and Pa were coping, too. They seemed very happy to be grandparents, more united than I had ever known them. They kept saying, 'Polly is a lovely baby.'

And she was. And in time she became a lovely girl: blonde, bright-eyed and beautiful – the apple of her grandparents' eye. And now she's a wonderful woman, living in Australia with her husband and three beautiful daughters of her own.

Polly was the ultimate triumph of Hester's life. Actually, I think of her whole life as a series of triumphs. If, as you read this, you – or someone you love – are facing what appears to be insurmountable adversity, take heart from my sister's story. As a child and teenager Hester struggled with mental illness. It manifested itself in depression and hysteria, but exactly what it was, or what caused it, I don't think anyone really knew. The Tavistock Clinic said one thing; consultants at the Maudsley said another. In those days, there were still huge institutions across the country, former Victorian lunatic asylums, that housed every kind of patient, by the hundred, from teenagers to geriatric residents. Hester spent time in three such institutions – sometimes under restraint, sometimes getting electroconvulsive therapy, sometimes dosed up to the eyeballs on assorted drugs, and sometimes simply being 'observed'. As a boy, I recall visiting these institutions with Pa and being impressed by the spacious gardens, as big as municipal parks, where the patients wandered about like sheep on a hillside. I was also struck by the variety of people living there – from noisy children with learning difficulties to old men and women shuffling along the paths in their slippers and dressing gowns. The point is: after ten years or so, Hester came through it. Once considered mad, she was now demonstrably sane.

Her experience convinced her to train as a mental nurse herself – and she ended up working in a hospital (the Springfield, in Tooting) where once she had been a patient. I remember visiting her there on the famous day she dropped the dentures. The old boys in her ward had their teeth taken out at night and kept in individual glasses on a draining board near the sluice. Returning them in the morning, Hes managed to drop the tooth tray, and the dentures flew higgledy-piggledy all over the ward floor. It took her the rest of the morning firstly to retrieve the dentures and then to work out which set belonged to which old gentleman – and I seem to remember when she had tried out every set in every mouth, she still had one pair left over.

It was at Tooting, too, that one of Hester's nurse friends managed to set fire to a wing of the hospital. Burnt it right down, though happily without loss of life. The nurses did a lot of smoking in the laundry cupboard. Hester herself was a keen smoker. She used to keep her contact lenses in a match-box, I remember, and was always losing them because she lit her first fag of the day in bed, in the dark, the moment she woke up.

Hes smoked as much as Pa did, perhaps more so. She looked a bit like him, too. In her late teens she took against the shape of her own nose (which was prominent, like Pa's) and 'for psychiatric reasons' was given a nose job (a good one) on the NHS. That said, before it or after it, she had no trouble finding girlfriends. She was always funny and attractive.

She was comfortable being gay – you can spot her as one of the extras in the lesbian club scene in the 1968 film *The Killing of Sister George* – but in her twenties she did give men a go, briefly and without much pleasure or success. She joined a dating agency and when she was asked out by a bloke she'd put on a frock and make-up, to show willing. I vividly recall the New Year's Eve when she went out for the second time with a middle-aged Indian doctor who behaved like a perfect gentleman until they got to Trafalgar Square, when he tried to kiss her. Hes called in alarm from a phone box at Charing Cross, and Pa and I got into the car and went to rescue her.

Pa may have been at the root of some of Hes's problems, but he was also her guardian angel. I remember another night racing in the car with him to her flat in Tooting. She had been admitted to hospital with some sort of drug overdose. At the flat, Pa expertly checked out the bedside tables, kitchen cab-inet and bathroom cupboards, quickly flushing the drugs he found down the loo.

In her twenties, Hes took drugs and drank alcohol. Eventually, she discovered Alcoholics Anonymous, and it transformed her. Her AA meetings became her life. She became their most ardent and effective ambassador, and over the next twenty years helped to save and transform the lives of dozens of alcoholics – friends and strangers. 'He who would do good to another must do it in Minute Particulars.' Hes did exactly that. She ended up on the Isle of Wight, running a lesbian B&B and doing drug rehabilitation work at Parkhurst Prison.

She was a remarkable individual, noted for her energy and strength of character. Cancer overwhelmed her when she was just sixty. I was with her in the hospice when she died. Apparently unconscious, she hung on until Polly had flown in to hold her hand at the last. What struck me at the moment of her passing was how instantly she disappeared. The very second the heavy breathing juddered to a final stop, she vanished. Death had come and Hester was gone. There was just a lifeless body on the bed.

I am still wondering where all that energy went.

18. Dream and remember

'I wonder anybody does anything at Oxford but dream and remember,' said W. B. Yeats, 'the place is so beautiful. One almost expects the people to sing instead of speaking. It is all like an opera.' In my case, like a comic opera: with a few moments of high drama, a touch of pantomime, and an extraordinary cast. I met everybody at Oxford. *Everybody.*

For a start, I first met the Queen at Oxford. She came to the Oxford Union – the university debating society – and an assortment of us undergraduates were lined up to be presented to her. She was much smaller than I expected. With Harold Macmillan, the University Chancellor, twinkling at her side, like Gandalf, she walked into the debating chamber to wild applause and happy cheering. But the moment the cheering stopped, a sudden chill filled the air. There was an eerie silence, and a palpable awkwardness in the hall. There were eight hundred of us there, but because of the presence of Her Majesty none of us could be 'normal'. The debate itself was dismal: restrained and artificial, with everyone on their best behaviour. I discovered, that day, what all my subsequent royal encounters reinforced: no one is ever completely natural with the Queen.

It's illogical, but meeting royalty is oddly nerve-wracking and meeting the Queen totally discombobulating. Some years later, when my wife was first presented to Her Majesty, Michèle forgot to curtsey – and then remembered forty seconds into the small talk. Without warning, she bobbed right down and semi-toppled into the royal bosom. My performance on that occasion was hardly more impressive. It was a private drinks party, hosted by the Queen's racing manager, the Earl of

Carnarvon. I arrived at the last minute: I had been rehearsing for the pantomime in Wimbledon all day, and I was starving. As the canapés were being handed around, I found myself stranded in a corner of the room with Her Majesty, frantic for food, but obliged to refuse every tasty morsel that came past because the Queen wasn't partaking. I did my best, but small talk with the sovereign isn't always easy.

GB: Had a busy day, Ma'am?
HM: Yes. Very.
GB: At the Palace?
HM: Yes.
GB: A lot of visitors?
HM: Yes.
(Pause)
GB: The Prime Minister?
HM: Yes.
(Pause)
GB: He's very nice.
HM: Yes. Very.
GB: The recession's bad.
HM (*looking grave*): Yes.
GB: Set to get worse, apparently.
HM (*slight sigh*): Yes.
GB (*trying to jolly it along*): I think this must be my third. Recession, that is.
HM: Yes. We do seem to get them every few years – (*tinkly laugh*) – and none of my governments seem to know what to do about them!
GB (*uproarious laughter*): Yes. Absolutely. Very good.
(Long pause. Trays of canapés come and go)
GB: I've been to Wimbledon today.
HM (*brightening*): Oh, yes?
GB (*brightening too*): Yes.
HM (*We're both trying hard now*): I've been to Wimbledon, too.

GB (exhilarated): Today?

HM: No.

GB (Well, we tried): No, of course not. *(Pause)* I wasn't at the tennis.

HM: No?

GB: No. I was at the theatre. *(Long pause)* Have you been to the theatre in Wimbledon?

(Pause)

HM: I imagine so.

(Interminable pause)

GB: You know, Ma'am, my wife's a vegetarian.

HM: That must be very dull.

GB: And my daughter's a vegetarian too.

HM: Oh dear.

Well, I had had a long day, and she has had a long reign.

She is extraordinary. Sustained by faith and driven by duty, she is the longest-serving and most successful monarch in our history. In the run-up to her Golden Jubilee in 2002, because I knew the Duke of Edinburgh, I was given privileged access and, over a period of six months, allowed to spend time with her as she went about her official duties, walking with her, talking with her. I marvelled at how completely consistent and totally unaffected she is. If she has nothing to say, she lets silence fall. If she needs to touch up her lipstick, she does it there and then.

People ask, 'What's she really like?' I can tell you exactly. She has the interests, attributes, tastes and manner of an English (or Scottish) countrywoman of her class and generation. That's really all you need to know. Dogs and horses, courtesy, kindliness and community service count with her. She may be formally apolitical, but she is definitely not politically correct. If she chooses, she will wear fur, she won't wear a seat belt, she will go out riding without a hard hat. Essentially conservative (with radical flourishes), intelligent (not intellectual), pragmatic (not introspective), 'immensely tolerant' (Prince Philip's phrase), she does not pretend for a moment to be what she is not.

I went on several walkabouts with her. In Chippenham High Street, of all places, I remember there were *thousands* in the crowd. The Queen moved along the street at her steady pace (it never varies), nodding, smiling, shaking hands, accepting bouquets by the score. Having been in similar circumstances, on different occasions, with Princess Diana, with David Beckham, with the Beatles in their prime, I observed a distinct difference between all of them and the Queen: the Queen does not play the crowd – at all. She does not take the adulation personally – not for a moment. She is on show (her clothes are designed to make her stand out in the crowd), but she is not 'performing' in any way, shape or form. She is what she is. And what she is, is the Queen.

The fun of spending time with her was finding out unexpected things about her. She really did love all the early James Bond films – 'before they got so loud'. She really can sing 'When I'm Cleaning Windows' and the other songs George Formby sang to his ukulele when she was growing up during the war – and with Formby's authentic Lancashire accent, too. (She is the Duke of Lancaster, after all.) On the day she came to Oxford, after she'd gone I reprimanded William Waldegrave (the Union President) for not carrying Her Majesty's umbrella for her as he escorted her across the courtyard. He told me, 'The Queen insists on holding her own umbrella – always. If someone else holds it, the rain trickles down her neck.'

I first met the Queen at Oxford. I first met Bill Clinton at Oxford, too. He was a Rhodes Scholar, doing PPE (philosophy, politics and economics) like me. I don't remember him, but he claims to remember me. I do remember that when I next saw him he was President of the United States and possibly the most personally charming man I have ever encountered. And I've met a few: among them, the actors Vincent Price and Peter Cushing, and the Secretary of State for War who lied to parliament, John Profumo. (Some good actors – Ian McKellen, Ben Miles – have played Profumo on screen: they've caught his look, but not his charm. The charm explained everything.) With Clinton, his ability to focus on you to the apparent exclusion of everything else in the world made him irresistible.

I met my wife-to-be at Oxford, too. My three years there defined my life.

I went to New College, so called because that's what it was when it was founded back in 1379 – at the time when Chaucer was writing *The Canterbury Tales* and Richard II was king. I arrived in October 1967 – when the Beatles were topping the charts with *Sgt. Pepper's Lonely Hearts Club Band* and Harold Wilson was Prime Minister – but I arrived with a mindset (and an agenda) dating from the late 1920s, when my father was at Oxford, Ramsay MacDonald was Prime Minister and Noël Coward and Beverley Nichols were the bright young men about town.

You have probably never heard of Beverley Nichols, but he was once so famous you wouldn't believe it. He was a wunder-kind of the Roaring Twenties – a journalist, a novelist, a playwright, he wrote his first autobiography when he was twenty-five. (It was called *Twenty-Five* and was among the first ten paperback books published by Penguin, alongside *A Fare-well to Arms* by Ernest Hemingway and Agatha Christie's *The Mysterious Affair at Styles*. He was that famous.) When he was at Oxford he was President of the Union, editor of *Isis* (the student magazine) and performed with the OUDS (the university dramatic society.) I suspect you won't have heard of Gyles Isham, either. He was President of the Union, too, and editor of *Isis*, and his Hamlet for the OUDS led to him playing Romeo at the Old Vic and starring opposite Greta Garbo in

Anna Karenina. He is quite forgotten now, but my father remembered him and, when I was growing up, Gyles Isham was the only other living Gyles-with-a-y I had heard of.

Just as Ma never left India, so Pa never left Oxford, and I arrived there, aged nineteen in 1967, determined to deliver an Oxford career my parents could be proud of. My contemporaries were dancing to the beat of Fleetwood Mac and the Rolling Stones. I was humming the Charleston and setting my sights on achieving the glittering prizes that had meant so much to my father's generation – becoming editor of *Isis*, directing the OUDS, being elected President of the Oxford Union.

'Have a plan,' said my Great-Uncle Fox Conner's friend General Patton, 'execute it violently, do it today.' Within forty-eight hours of my arrival in Oxford, I had joined the Union, joined the OUDS, and managed to meet the editor of *Isis*. How I got hold of his name and address I don't know, but I did. He was called Peter Adamson. He was older than me, in his third year (or maybe his fourth), fair-haired, blue-eyed, quite tall, a bit rough-looking but immediately friendly. He ran the magazine from his flat in Walton Street. How on earth did I find Walton Street? I'd only ever been to Oxford once before – and that was for my interview. My father talked about Oxford all the time, but we never went there. (Pa also talked about golf all the time, but he never played. His partners gave him a set of clubs to mark his retirement. He never used them.)

I remember now: I bought a street map. I've got it still, somewhere. (I've got everything still, somewhere.) In my duffel coat, holding my briefcase, wearing my horn-rimmed specs, I walked from New College up Broad Street, past Blackwell's (the bookshop), past Univ (the university's oldest college), past Balliol, then I turned right into St Giles (a good name for a street, I thought) and then left, past the Randolph Hotel in Beaumont Street (Oxford's grand hotel in those days), past the Playhouse (the university theatre – I thought I should put a play on there), and then right again at Worcester College into Beaumont Street. Eventually I found the house, quite a way down the street on the right-hand side. I knocked on the door and Peter answered.

'Hello,' he said. 'Who are you?'

'I'm Gyles,' I said. 'I've come to talk about *Isis.*'

He laughed. 'You're keen.'

'Yes, I suppose I am.'

'Well, you'd better come in.'

He gave me a mug of tea and offered me a chocolate digestive. The flat was littered with half-full mugs of tea and half-finished packets of biscuits – and half-opened boxes of magazines and bits of artwork and long rolls of printers' proofs. It was everything I hoped it would be – and more, because there was a beautiful girl there, too.

'This is Lesley,' said Peter. 'She's my wife.'

I didn't think students had wives, but Peter did. She was twenty-one and a teacher. She had shining eyes and a happy face, and with my second mug of tea she produced a slice of cake.

'Now there's an idea for a piece,' I said. 'Oxford's best cakes! Which college is most like which cake? Balliol's a Battenberg, Magdalen's a meringue . . .' For two hours I sat there pitching ideas like billy-o.

I didn't realise it at the time, but it was the start of a lifetime of pitching. Apart from those six weeks in the railway reservations department of Thomas Cook & Son, and my five years as an MP, I have never had a job. I have spent my entire life as a freelancer, selling ideas, touting for trade. I remember walking into Broadcasting House with Nicholas Parsons when he was ninety-four and we were trying (and failing) to get a new radio series off the ground. He said, 'I've been doing this for seventy years. The pitching never stops.' Yes, life's a pitch and then you die.

The pitching in Walton Street that October afternoon went well. Peter asked me to write a piece – and then another. And soon he asked me to write a column, and by my second term I was writing for *Isis* every week. I repaid his kindness by trying to cop off with his wife – which is why, eventually (and understandably), he took a fist to me in Robert Maxwell's garden.

Was I a little mad during my time at Oxford? Perhaps I was. I certainly lived life at a crazy pace. In my first forty-eight hours at the university, as well as meeting the Adamsons, my diary records encounters with more than thirty named individuals – the first being possibly the most significant: Jack, my 'scout'. I am ashamed to say that I don't know his surname. I never thought to ask. Nor did I think to question the fact that, at the age of nineteen, I was being supplied with a manservant, there to make my bed for me, do the washing-up, organise my laundry . . . extraordinary when I think about it now.

Jack was in his sixties, I suppose, friendly but formal. He looked after me and the other nine men on our staircase. He supplied me with my scholar's gown (longer and fuller than the regular undergraduate gowns) to be worn without fail for lectures, tutorials and in hall. He gave me the rundown on the local rules and regulations. The college gates were shut at 11.00 p.m.: he advised me which wall was the easiest to climb over in the event that I was out after that. He showed me how my room had one doorway, but two doors. If I left the outer door open, it meant I was happy to receive visitors. If I closed the outer door – known as 'sporting your oak' – it meant I didn't want to be disturbed.

Who else did I meet during that first forty-eight hours? The college chaplain, Gary Bennett – he was my immediate next-door neighbour. He nodded as we passed on the stairs, but did not look me in the eye. (I got to know him in time. He had a shy manner, but a sharp wit. A conservative Anglican, in 1987 he published an anonymous critique of the Church of England establishment, and when he was 'outed' as its author, he killed himself.)

The Home Secretary's son was on our staircase, too. Charles Jenkins, son of Roy, was even more shy than the chaplain. He didn't even nod as we passed on the stair. Head bent, he just hurried by. I liked Xan Smiley: he was an amusing, fair-haired Old Etonian who looked you straight in the eye and whose father seemed to be a sort of latter-day Lawrence of Arabia. I liked Julian Radcliffe, another OE, who thought he *was* Lawrence of Arabia. I liked Victor Bulmer-Thomas: his father was an MP and Church Commissioner. I got on at once with Anthony Palliser: his father was at the Foreign Office (and became the head of it) and his grandfather (Paul-Henri Charles Spaak) had been Prime Minister of Belgium and was one of the founders of the European Union. Anthony, now one of my closest friends, was already an artist. So was Antony Dufort: he later sculpted the statue of Margaret Thatcher that stands in the House of Commons and the head of Britannia that features on the £2 coin. I liked Peter Torry, who became an ambassador. I liked David Graham, who became a merchant banker and my partner in several (not always successful) business ventures. I liked Rick Stein who became Rick Stein.

I wonder if any of us had any idea of how privileged we were? On our second night, in hall (high-ceilinged, oak-panelled, adorned with oil paintings of former New College luminaries, including Warden Spooner who gave us the spoonerism and saluted Queen Victoria's Diamond Jubilee with the cry, 'Three cheers for our queer old dean!'), the present Warden (Sir William Hayter, formerly ambassador to Moscow) did his best to remind us. 'Look up while you are here,' he said, sonorously, 'look around at the buildings. Unless you choose to live in Venice, you are unlikely to live in such a beautiful city again.'

*

305

I loved the buildings (the Bodleian Library was my favourite), but I loved the people more. Outside of New College, the group I spent most time with in the early days was the *Isis* crowd. It wasn't just my ambition and Lesley that drew me to them. They were interesting people. The editorial team included Anthony Holden (a good friend who made me editor of *Isis* when he was editor-in-chief), Denis Matyjaszek (who changed his name to Denis MacShane, became a Labour MP and ended up in prison for fiddling his expenses), and Philip Maxwell (whose dad, publisher Robert Maxwell MC, MP, could probably have taught Denis a thing or two about fiddling his expenses).

This was four years before a Department of Trade inquiry reported, 'with regret', that Robert Maxwell 'is not in our opinion a person who can be relied on to exercise proper stewardship of a publicly quoted company' – and seventeen years before he acquired Mirror Group Newspapers and proceeded to fraudulently misappropriate the company's pension fund. Intriguingly, even as teenagers we knew there was something dodgy about Robert Maxwell, the original 'bouncing Czech'. That said, I liked Philip (who was at Balliol, and an odd mix: shy and bombastic at the same time), I liked his sister Anne (who was at St Hugh's), and we were grateful to 'Captain Bob', as he was known, because he both subsidised our magazine and invited us to parties at his house, Headington Hill Hall – a huge Victorian pile on the edge of Oxford, pillared, palatial, and a touch gaudy in the decoration.

The first time I met Robert Maxwell he put his arm around my shoulder in a jovial and slightly menacing way. He had the build of a bull and the face of a toad. I told him that I was honoured to be visiting Headington Hill Hall – especially because Oscar Wilde had come to a ball at the house when he was at Oxford. Oscar came dressed as Prince Rupert of the Rhine. 'And who have you come dressed as, young man?' he growled.

The Maxwells hosted a ball every June – 9.00 p.m. to 3.00 a.m. and beautifully done, with drinks in the house, dinner in the marquee, dancing and breakfast on the lawn. It nearly went awry early in the evening in the drawing room when I was 'entertaining' the crowd with my 'impression' of our host, hunched forward, gurning and grunting, when, suddenly, I felt a heavy hand on my shoulder. I turned around – and there he was, gazing at me steadily. He held the moment, and then, slowly, he began to chuckle.

I had never been to a party like it. We all had formal dance cards (with little pencils attached to them with red string), telling us to choose five different partners for five special dances. There was a band, a pop group, a discotheque – and steaks and ribs served at the barbecue between dinner and breakfast. And I had never met a man like Maxwell before. (And I have only met one or two like him since.) He was clearly a rogue – and not a lovable one – but, somehow, we all went along with it.

Twenty years later, because by then I was doing bits and pieces of work for different companies he owned, I was still going to the Headington Hill Hall parties, still mocking him behind his back, but still accepting his hospitality. The later parties were less convivial because the Maxwell children I was friends with – Philip, his second son, and Anne, his oldest daughter, two totally decent people – had fled the family scene and Captain Bob had become a caricature of himself. He was personally amplified, and with the turn of a dial in his pocket he could increase the volume of his voice, so that at one moment he could be whispering in your ear and at the next he could be addressing every room in the house at full volume.

I met Ian and Kevin in the 1980s and thought they were ridiculous, 'acting' like tycoons, while Philip and Anne always seemed to be real people. When Maxwell Senior fell off his boat, the *Lady Ghislaine*, in 1991, Kevin became the biggest personal bankrupt in UK history, with debts of £406.5

million. Ghislaine I never knew (I hasten to add), but all I can tell you is her father was a rum one.

Through *Isis* I met a number of interesting characters. I leafed through the pages of *Who's Who* and simply wrote to them, asking if I could interview them for the university magazine. Yehudi Menuhin, the great virtuoso violinist, said no, but nicely, and encouraged me to improve my life by changing my diet. The great wartime general Field Marshal Montgomery of Alamein said no, too, but in his reply shared with me what he believed were the qualities a young person needed to succeed in life.

1. Moral courage – always do what you believe to be right.
2. Complete integrity – no lies, no deceptions – honesty and transparency.
3. Ceaseless hard work.

But usually they said yes. I went to the House of Commons for the first time to interview Sir Gerald Nabarro, the Conservative MP for South Worcestershire. He was fifty-five, 5 foot 5 inches tall, and was then appearing on television more than any other MP. With his mutton-chop whiskers, and his five cars numbered NAB1 to NAB5, he was a self-created Commons 'character' with truly appalling views. On *Any Questions?* he had asked, 'How would you feel if your daughter wanted to marry a big buck n– with the prospect of coffee-coloured grandchildren?' He said to me, 'I am not willing to be told by law that I must love my coloured neighbour or otherwise I shall be fined or sent to prison.' He couldn't abide 'revolting students' – especially those then on strike at the LSE. 'I expect undergraduates to behave like gentlemen, not undisciplined hooligans.' It was all down to 'a decline in moral standards' and there were only three remedies: bring back the noose, the lash and national service.

I went to the BBC Television Centre at White City for the

first time to interview the grand inquisitor himself, Robin Day. Young as I was, I realised that Day, famous as he was, was essentially disappointed with his life. Beetle-browed, sporting his trademark spotted bow tie, he was cross-questioning polit-icians when really he would have liked to be one. I got to know him better in the 1980s when, although he was twenty-five years older than me, we had children of the same age at the same nursery school. He regretted a lifetime spent simply making a noise, when the best of his contemporaries had been 'taking decisions and making a difference'.

I went backstage at the New Theatre in Oxford to meet Bruce Forsyth, famous then as a song-and-dance man and the former host of *Sunday Night at the London Palladium*. He was appearing in *Babes in the Wood*.

'I don't really like pantomime,' he said, but he was grateful for the money – and he liked being famous. 'Going on holiday abroad can be a bit of a shock: nobody knows who you are.' He gave me some advice I have not forgotten. 'Remember, only half the people will ever like you. Don't let the other half get you down – the bastards!'

He was quite funny, in a mirthless sort of way, and he was a trouper. On a cold Saturday afternoon in a far-from-full barn of a theatre in a really tatty hand-me-down panto, he gave his all. He came on to that stage like a whirlwind and for three hours he did not let go. I learnt a lot from watching him do that.

My first foreign assignment as an *Isis* interviewer was in Paris in May 1968 – when many thought France was on the brink of civil war or revolution.

Students and workers were on strike, occupying universities and factories, protesting so effectively that for a while the economy ground to a halt, the national government ceased to function and, secretly, President Charles de Gaulle fled to Germany. '*Les événements de mai '68*' encouraged protests around the world. (And graffiti: 'Be realistic: demand the impossible' was my favourite.) I was excited to be at the heart of the action as it all kicked off – though, needless to say, my mission was not to interview any of the revolutionary leaders. I was going to interview one of the richest men in the world: the Aga Khan. I had read in *Paris Match* that he never gave interviews, so I found his address in *Who's Who*, wrote to him, and he agreed to give his first-ever interview to me.

My time in Paris was memorable. I was first off the plane at Le Bourget and gratified to find a crowd of well-wishers corralled on the other side of the tarmac waving and cheering. Whistles blew, flash bulbs popped . . . and then they saw me and the noise subsided. It turned out they were not waiting for me on my way to interview the Aga Khan, but for Ho Chi Minh, due to arrive from North Vietnam at any moment for the Paris peace talks.

In the centre of town there were armed police on every corner. North of the Seine it was relatively calm, but go south of the river and you were in a city in the middle of a revolution: burnt-out cars, pulled-up paving stones, streets closed off. Around the Sorbonne, there were barricades and tanks and armoured vehicles everywhere you turned. At the start of the week there had been full-scale rioting. I saw no fighting, but – being a coward – I took a taxi, just in case. Crossing the Boulevard Saint-Germain, we had to negotiate our way through a throng of protesting students on the march. The taxi proceeded quite slowly and, at first, all was well – then, suddenly, our car seemed to catch the attention of a group of the protesters. They turned on our vehicle and, chanting and jeering, began to rock it to and fro. I looked out of the window, desperately trying to show them that I was a student too. The driver pressed on, honking his horn, and eventually the students let us pass. It was an alarming few minutes.

The Aga Khan lived on the Île de la Cité – which was completely deserted. At 6.20 p.m., as instructed by Miss Bishop,

Secretary to HH Shah Karim, Aga Khan IV, I made my way down a squalid backstreet to 10 rue Chanoinesse. I rang a bell, climbed to the third floor and was admitted to a plush suite of offices, where I waited.

Miss Bishop appeared. 'You haven't brought a tape recorder, have you?'

'No,' I said.

She looked relieved. 'His Highness won't want you to have a tape recorder.' She smiled. 'You will only ask the questions we agreed?'

'Of course,' I said.

She took me down into the street and showed me a little alleyway leading to rue des Ursins.

'When I get there, do I ring the doorbell?' I asked.

'There's no need,' she said. 'Good luck.'

When I reached the house I couldn't see a doorbell or a knocker. The front door was wooden, covered with heavy metal studs. As I climbed the steps, it swung slowly open. A servant in a white jacket stood within.

'*Monsieur Brandreth? Son Altesse vous attends.*'

The house was entirely lit by candlelight – a blaze of candlelight.

I followed the servant along a corridor, up a winding staircase, along another corridor, to a double door.

Without knocking, the flunkey pushed open the doors and bowed low, murmuring as he did so, '*Altesse! Monsieur Brandreth, Altesse!*'

The Aga Khan was thirty-one, slim, lithe, handsome, though the hairline was receding. He was sitting on a chaise longue facing the door. He got to his feet at once and bounded towards me, smiling, hand outstretched. 'Gyles, welcome! Come in. So good to meet you.'

He is a direct descendant of Mohammed the Prophet – through Mohammed's daughter, Fatima. I was very pleased to shake his hand. I was very pleased to meet him.

At once he said, 'What would you like to drink?'

I couldn't think what to say. My mind went blank. Then I blurted out, 'An orange juice.'

He didn't respond. I thought I had said the wrong thing – until, five minutes later, from behind a tapestry in the far corner of the room, another white-jacketed servant emerged carrying a silver salver with, on it, a huge glass of freshly squeezed blood-red orange juice. (The Aga Khan definitely did not order the drink: the man must have been hovering behind the arras listening.)

His Highness showed me round the room. We looked at family photographs. We stopped by a huge globe and I asked him to show me some of the countries where his people live. He is the leader of fifteen million Ismaili Muslims around the world. I suggested that in the West, fewer are committing themselves to religion. He said the reverse was true in the Muslim world. 'There is now more attendance at mosque and equal devotion.' He was softly spoken, very gentle. He struck me as earnest and sincere. He was frequently self-deprecating – he talked several times about his 'lack of self-assurance'.

Knowing that this was his first-ever interview, I asked him why he had agreed to see me.

'Because you are a student,' he said, 'and you wrote a very persuasive letter.'

I stayed with him until gone eight o'clock. I left feeling that I had been in the presence of a special human being. Well, we know I am a sucker for royalty.

'K', as his friends call him, wasn't married when I met him. He has since been married (and divorced) twice, put on a bit of weight and had fun with his £10 billion fortune (he has spent a lot on horses and yachts, private jets, his own island in the Bahamas – the usual nonsense), but he has done good works, too.

Everyone's human. Only our Queen is flawless. And, of

course, she and the Aga Khan are racing friends. (She has given him a knighthood, too.) Her Majesty has also been a racing friend of another mighty Muslim leader, Sheikh Mohammed Bin Rashid Al-Maktoum, the ruler of Dubai – not, I think, that Her Majesty will be seeing much of him in the future. He turns out to be more flawed than most. We knew that he had had at least six wives (and an awful lot of children) but we did not realise he was a cruel and controlling husband and father until one of his former wives, Princess Haya Bint Al-Hussain, accused him of abduction, false imprisonment, torture and intimidation. Her allegations, 'on the balance of probabilities', were accepted as fact by the High Court in London.

Sheikh Mohammed also gave me his first personal interview – on Wednesday, 8 March 2000, Ash Wednesday and my fifty-second birthday. It was an unnerving experience. It began with coffee at the Sheikh's palace in Dubai. I sat on a sofa at the end of a drawing room the size of a tennis court. I began with small talk, telling His Highness how wonderful Dubai appeared to be. He said nothing. I told him how wonderful he appeared to be. (He was in traditional robes, saturnine and stern.) Still he said nothing. We sat there in silence until a servant shuffled forward to collect our coffee cups.

The Sheikh smiled darkly. 'We Arabs do not talk until we have finished our coffee.'

Throughout our meeting, which lasted two hours, courtiers came and went, messengers approached and retreated: sometimes he received them, heard what they had to say (they spoke directly into his ear), sometimes he raised a hand and silently they backed away. I felt I was in a scene from one of Shakespeare's history plays. ('My liege, I bring news from France!')

He charmed me and disarmed me. 'I am running my country myself, with my people. I do not have advisers. I think they are a waste of time.'

'Will you ever give your people the vote?' I asked.

'What is democracy for? To make people happy and safe. My people are happy and they are safe.'

As I left he gave me a birthday present — beautifully wrapped. 'I think your wife will enjoy these,' he murmured.

At once I pictured diamonds — or perhaps pearls. Or even the keys to the white Rolls-Royce he had kindly put at my disposal during my stay. It turned out that His Highness was giving me a collection of his own love poems — translated into not very good English.

He walked me to the palace steps where peacocks had gathered to form an impromptu guard of honour. Did he have a message for me to take away from my visit?

'For you?' He pondered for a moment and then looked me directly in the eye. 'Every morning in Africa a gazelle wakes up. It knows it must outrun the fastest lion or it will be killed. Every morning in Africa a lion wakes up. It knows it must run faster than the slowest gazelle or it will starve. It doesn't matter whether you're a gazelle or a lion, Mr Brandreth. When the sun comes up, you'd better be running.'

19. Cinderella – and Michèle

My life of interviewing royalty began at Oxford. So did my life of putting on plays. I was writing weekly pieces for *Isis* – and soon after for *Cherwell,* the student newspaper, as well – and I was appearing in assorted college drama productions. I particularly remember the horror of *Bert Lives!* – an evening of alienating moments drawn from the works of Berthold Brecht and directed by the BBC's future Wales correspondent, Tim Maby. Bizarrely, we performed the show in Oxford Prison and the inmates really enjoyed it. I remember, too, appearing in a Molière play at the Playhouse, in French, playing a fey aristocrat with, attached to my pinkies, long fingernails made (by me) out of paper straws; and in a Pinter one-act play (*A Night Out*) in which I played a pompous middle-class businessman . . . I don't think either role took me very far out of my comfort zone.

My real ambition was to direct the OUDS, and to that end I sent a note to the girl who held the key that could unlock the gateway to my dream. (There was a wonderful messenger service connecting all the colleges, so you could send a note to someone on the other side of Oxford at breakfast and get a reply before lunch.) She sent back a note suggesting we meet for a drink, so we did.

Diana Quick was twenty-one, dark, beautiful, pouting, and the first female President in the history of the Oxford University Dramatic Society. When I met her for that first drink in the bar at The White Horse pub in Broad Street she was wearing a leather miniskirt. I'd never seen anything quite like it – or met anyone quite like her. She crackled with energy and intelligence: she was both exciting to be with and a bit alarming. I sensed she could eat a minnow like me for breakfast. (Later, as well as finding fame playing Julia Flyte in the TV version of *Brideshead Revisited*, she married Kenneth Cranham and her long-term lovers included Albert Finney and Bill Nighy. Yes, she was in that sort of league. Still is.) To my surprise, she did not dismiss me out of hand. She seemed amused by my idea. With student revolution running rife across the world, I thought it might be fun to do something counter-intuitive, like an old-fashioned family pantomime. She said, 'And why not?' but explained I would need to audition for the job. I would need to rehearse a scene from Shakespeare in front of the OUDS committee. A few days later, I did just that – and Diana played Juliet for me. I think it was asking her to suggest desire by putting her top teeth gently over her lower lip that clinched it. I got the gig – and that's how I came to direct *Cinderella* for the OUDS at the Oxford Playhouse and to meet my wife.

I wanted to do a Victorian version of *Cinderella*, like the ones I'd seen at the Players' Theatre under the arches at Charing Cross with Pa and Ma when I was a boy. I travelled to London, went to the Players', met their archivist (a twinkle-eyed Pickwickian figure called Archie Harradine – a Victorian himself) and settled on Byron's rendering of the fairy tale. No, not Lord Byron, the poet, but his cousin, H. J. Byron, the playwright who invented the character of Buttons for his *Cinderella* and created Widow Twankey for *Aladdin*. Diana told me I'd need a choreographer and found one for me: a sprite-like boy from Worcester College called Michael Coveney. (He became a theatre critic and a good friend, though, as a rule, when it comes to critics I'm with P. G. Wodehouse: 'Has anybody seen a dramatic critic in the daytime? Of course not. They come out after dark, up to no good.')

I secured the *Cinderella* gig in the summer term at the end of my first year. The production wasn't due to open until late autumn, but I started casting right away. I put up notices in colleges across Oxford advertising the auditions. This was the chance of a lifetime, I explained. I was looking for the girl of my dreams to be the star of my show: 'If you have what it takes to be a fairy-tale princess, please come to the Music Room in New College Cloisters . . .' And they did – in droves, each one, it seemed, lovelier than the last. And to one of them, mid-afternoon, on the fourth day of the auditions, instead of saying when she'd done her stuff, 'We'll let you know,' I heard myself saying, 'Would you mind waiting outside for half an hour or so until we've finished? There's something I want to say to you.'

There was a history lecture she didn't mind missing, so she waited. And fifty-three years on, she's still here. (She is as surprised about that as you are.)

Michèle Brown was twenty-one when I met her, dark haired, bright-eyed and, as you can tell from the photographs, absurdly beautiful. She was in her second year, reading history at St Anne's, a grammar school girl, born in Swansea, brought up in Ashford, in Kent. When I had rattled through the rest of that afternoon's auditions and I found her sitting on a wall in the cloisters waiting for me, I may have said 'I love you' right away. I certainly asked her out for dinner. I was completely bowled over. It can happen. Thirty-five years after I met Michèle, our younger daughter, Aphra, and I took our cat Bruno to the local vet. We hadn't met the vet before. When we stepped into his surgery he was looking at his computer screen. As we arrived, he turned around and saw Aphra – and in his eyes, instantly, I saw a look I recognised. They moved in together not long after, then they got married, and now they have three children. Sometimes, it seems, love at first sight works out.

Before meeting Michèle, I had only had two proper girl-friends: Jackie, who when she left school ended up in America and found a husband there; and Sally, who died of cancer aged only thirty-four. When I went to Oxford, Sally was still at school and we both knew that it was over. To mark the end of our friendship, as a souvenir and by way of saying goodbye, Sally sent me a lock of her hair. It arrived at New College on Thursday, 6 June 1968 – the day that I met Michèle.

Michèle was no pushover. She played hard to get. She was wary of men in general, I think, and me in particular – with my fluting voice and fruity manner, my non-stop talking and my immediate over-the-top declarations of love. I presented her with a book of love poems on our first date and I didn't simply use the inter-college messenger service to send her several notes a day, I also used the GPO to send her telegrams full of drama and romance. That's the way it worked in the days before texting. I can't say she responded in kind. She spent a lot of time looking at me with a gently raised left eyebrow. But I didn't mind: at least she was looking at me.

She accepted my immediate invitation to dinner since she happened to be free. We went for a Chinese: special fried rice, 3s. 6d. each, with banana fritters to follow, 9d. She listened to my endless stories with a good grace. She laughed at my jokes. She thought my wanting a blonde to play Cinderella 'a bit predictable', declined my offer of a part in the chorus, and told me she thought, anyway, she wouldn't be free because someone else wanted her to play Viola in his production of *Twelfth Night* and she felt playing the lead in a Shakespeare play would be rather more satisfying than prancing about in the chorus in panto.

I found a blonde to play Cinderella and, though not quite as beautiful as Michèle, she was excellent. Her name was Caroline Bennitt and, of course, because life really is like Anthony Powell depicts it in *A Dance to the Music of Time*, after Oxford I didn't see her for twenty-four years, until I was an MP, and she turned out to be living in a fascinating house on the edge of my constituency. We became friends again. Her husband Scirard Lancelyn Green's family had lived on the same plot of land since 1064. When they generously hosted a fund-raising event for me at the house, some of my more straitlaced party workers were a bit thrown by the eccentricity of the place (and the mice that scuttled between the kitchen and the drawing room), but I loved it. Poulton Hall is a monument to seventeen generations of delightfully dotty Lancelyns. I remember Scirard's father's desk was kept as he left it on the day he died – the post still unopened, the copy of *Punch* in just the same position on the floor. When I went to pick up the magazine, Caroline squawked, 'Don't! For God's sake, don't!'

Scirard's brother, Richard, whom I also knew, had converted his part of the house into a precise replica of Sherlock Holmes' rooms at 221B Baker Street. Some years later, Richard was found, dressed as Holmes, face down on his bed, garrotted with a shoelace that had been tightened with the handle of a wooden spoon. Murder was suspected, but the coroner returned an open verdict. Some thought the death was an elaborate suicide, intended to seem like murder, to cast suspicion on someone else – replicating the plot of one of the last Sherlock Holmes mysteries, in which a wife commits suicide in a manner designed to implicate the woman with whom her husband had been flirting. Richard was delightful, and the acknowledged world authority on the works of Conan Doyle.

I was happy with all my cast and, most especially, with my Fairy Queen. I had met Eliza Manningham-Buller in the Pinter play. She was a jolly girl, in the St Trinian's tradition, the daughter of a former Lord Chancellor, who came trailing Benenden and breeding while laughing a lot and not taking herself too seriously. I liked her, but, again, after Oxford I didn't see her until I was an MP and she sidled up to me at a Foreign Office party. She was still laughing. She had joined MI5 in 1974 and was on her way to becoming its Director-General.

Today Eliza is a Dame, a Baroness and a Lady of the Garter. Back in 1968 she was my Fairy Queen – and a good sport, helping out with assorted newspaper photo shoots I set up to promote my pantomime. In those days, Fleet Street (and all the nationals really did have their offices in Fleet Street then) reported regularly on 'goings-on' at Oxford. I made friends with the *Daily Mail* picture desk and discovered from a fellow undergraduate (Geoff Lean, who went on to be the leading environmental reporter of his day) that *The Times* Diary would pay £5 for a story. (That was a lot of money in the days when a slap-up Chinese for two cost around ten shillings.) *Cinderella* was just a student show, of course, but I wanted it to have 'that little extra something'.

With that in mind, I wrote to John Betjeman asking if he would be good enough to pen me a prologue. The future Poet Laureate replied from 43 Cloth Fair, London EC1. He had been away in the Isle of Wight making a film about Tennyson. He couldn't help me. ('I find writing to order in verse a most awful sweat.') He suggested I approach Nevill Coghill – the man who had directed my father in *Samson Agonistes*, way back in 1929. ('He knows the Playhouse, he knows the undergraduates, and he has the sparkle and fun, which years of self-pity have washed off, yours sincerely, John Betjeman.')

Coghill's prologue was perfect – and it arrived with a lovely letter which I shared with Pa: 'How well I remember your father's *admirable* performance in my first-production-ever! He was most moving. I hope his genius has descended on you in full measure.' The prologue was delightful, witty and apt, and on the first night I am proud to say it was performed by Sir Michael Redgrave.

How did I manage that? I found his address in *Who's Who* and I wrote to him. I wrote to him at length, telling him that his Uncle Vanya was, for me, the performance of my lifetime. Forty-eight hours later, I received a telegram.

WHAT FUN. ACCEPT WITH GREAT PLEASURE. REDGRAVE.

Our run was due to begin in the second week in November 1968. In the United States, Richard Nixon had just beaten Hubert Humphrey in the presidential election – and my old friend (well, I had met him once briefly in Baltimore) Spiro T. Agnew became his Vice-President. In the United Kingdom, there was a nice picture of my Cinders and her Fairy Queen in the *Daily Mail*. In Oxford, I was pretty low. The show had sold out before it opened, but I wondered: was it going to be any good? The dress rehearsal was as slow as it was unfunny. At gone 2.00 a.m. I clambered over the wall back into New College and found a note waiting for me under my door. It was from Xan Smiley.

The very best of luck.
You always have it, because you deserve it.

I have kept the note – of course. Whenever I think of it, I am reminded of Henry James' famous observation: 'Three things in human life are important. The first is to be kind. The second is to be kind. And the third is to be kind.'

It was Michael Redgrave who introduced me to the quotation. Henry James was his favourite writer. Redgrave was sixty when I met him – Pa's age, forty years my senior – and I couldn't really believe his kindness, or my luck that he was coming to Oxford, at his own expense, to help me out with my show. I went to the station to meet him. His train was late and crowded. The passengers poured out of the carriages and surged past the ticket barrier. There was no sign of the great man. The Playhouse curtain was due to go up within the hour, but where was my star? I peered down the platform and there I saw him, in the far distance, a huge frame in a dishevelled raincoat, carrying a little battered suitcase and looking about him with a puzzled, vacant air. I ran towards him.

He shuffled towards me.

'Sir Michael?'

'Yes?'

'Sir Michael!'

'Yes. Are you, er . . . ?'

'Yes.'

'Oh good,' and his large, old face broke into a sweet smile. He had a wonderful smile.

'How are you, Sir Michael?'

'Not at all well.'

Slowly, painfully slowly, we made our way to the waiting taxi.

Sir Michael explained that he felt unsteady, 'strange', and that his voice had gone, 'completely gone'. At the stage door, he murmured, 'A little port might help.'

Michèle, bless her, was on hand and ran into The Glouces-ter Arms pub next door and bought a bottle.

He wouldn't use a dressing room. He preferred to stand in the wings. He took a glass of port, gargled with it and swal-lowed it down. He took another. And another. And one more.

'How are you feeling now, Sir Michael?' I asked.

'A great deal worse,' he replied.

The orchestra had finished the overture. An expectant hush had fallen over the auditorium.

'You're on now, Sir Michael,' I whispered.

'I don't think I can do it,' he said.

'You're on!' Firmly, almost roughly, I pushed him from the darkened wings on to the stage.

As the stooped, shambling figure stepped into the spotlight he was *transformed*. Suddenly tall, erect, formidable, smiling. 'Ladies and gentlemen, good evening!' the mellow voice boomed.

The audience cheered, the magic happened.

That night, he found the energy – and the courage. Over the next fifteen years – as Parkinson's disease took a firmer grip of him, and I came to know him better – finding either became increasingly difficult. At first, no one realised what was wrong. One day (a year or so later), Michèle and I were having lunch with him in London, at the old Empress Restaurant in Grosvenor Square, when his head simply fell forward on to the table. He seemed drunk, but he wasn't. He invited us to Sunday lunch at his new house in Lower Belgrave Street soon after, and showing us round, then flopped down on to the stairs, bewildered. 'What is happening?'

He had long suffered from a dread of first nights. In 1971, at the Mermaid Theatre, we witnessed the worst of them. It was a play by William Trevor, *The Old Boys*, with Michael in the lead, and because, by the dress rehearsal, he still didn't have a grasp of his lines, for the first night the management equipped him with a hearing aid through which he could be prompted. Unhappily, in the audience we could hear the prompter better than Michael could. We reckoned we could also hear the local minicab service until the apparatus fell from Michael's ear and disintegrated, scattering in pieces on the floor around him.

It wasn't the end, rather the beginning of the end, but at least it got him to the Hospital for Nervous Diseases and a correct diagnosis. At last, he knew what was wrong – even if he didn't like it. He described this period of his life as 'a grey expanse, with intermittent shafts of light'. When we met – in Oxford, in London, off and on, over about ten years – his mind would come and go. He would talk of the early days, of his time as a schoolmaster, of how he abandoned respectability 'to fulfil my destiny' and joined the Liverpool Playhouse where, in the summer of 1935, he met and married Rachel Kempson ('Dear Rachel, she puts up with such a lot, you know'), of his daughter Vanessa and her politics ('It gives strength to her acting, it doesn't detract'), of Edith Evans.

He always came back to Edith Evans. 'If you are going to play Orlando, you must *love* your Rosalind! You know, I made love to Edith on the night Vanessa was born . . . [Acting with Edith] was like being in your mother's arms, like knowing how to swim, like riding a bicycle. You're safe . . . For the first time in my acting life, I felt completely unselfconscious. Acting with her made me feel, oh, it's so easy. You don't start acting, she told me, until you stop trying to act. It doesn't leave the ground until you don't have to think about it . . . For the first time, onstage or off, I felt completely free.'

Michael was also what my friend Barbara Windsor used to call 'Tommy Two-Ways'. All his adult life he had affairs, occasionally with women, principally with men. As a husband and father, he was flawed, sometimes cruel, often self-indulgent, but he was also extraordinary – honest, intelligent, fastidious, delightful – both as an actor and as a person. At twenty, I was thrilled beyond measure to find he was my friend. He showed me many kindnesses and, once or twice, I was able to help him, too.

I have the sound recording of his celebrated Uncle Vanya, four LPs, and I defy you to listen to them without laughing, crying and cheering out loud. Michael gave me several records. He was especially fond of his own readings of the stories of Hans Andersen, translated by his old school housemaster. I have just been listening again to his Macbeth (recorded in the late 1950s) and in my head I can still hear his Hamlet. Once, in the deserted debating chamber of the Oxford Union (of all places), he recited 'To be or not to be' just for me. It was our fifth or sixth meeting. I didn't think about it then, but perhaps it was flirtation-by-Shakespeare-soliloquy. If so, there are worse kinds.

In the fullness of time two of my other childhood heroes got their kit off and propositioned me. Frankie Howerd took me to his agent's office, locked the door behind us, pocketed the key, produced some ointment from a drawer, dropped his trousers and invited me to apply the ointment to his hopeful manhood.

'Treat it like a muscle!' he cried.

'I must get home to read my children their bedtime story,' I responded lamely.

'Please yourself,' he muttered, pulling up his pants grumpily.

Jimmy Edwards, my *Whack-O!* hero, gave me a wonderfully liquid lunch (vodka, champagne, claret, brandy) at his country cottage before stripping off in the kitchen and inviting me to join him in his Swedish sauna. That was not Sir Michael Redgrave's style. Nor James Robertson Justice's, though he was stark naked when I first met him.

Robertson Justice was the second star I persuaded to travel to Oxford to perform the *Cinderella* prologue. I asked him because I loved the character of the overbearing surgeon he had played in *Doctor in the House* and its five sequels. He came all the way down from Spinningdale, in Sutherland, for the occasion. I went to find him in his room at the Randolph Hotel.

When I knocked on the door, he simply said, 'Come!' He was lying sprawled out, stark naked on the bed, like a beached whale, a silver hip flask nestling in the undergrowth of his hairy chest.

I helped him to dress, realising as I did so that he was probably the first grown man I had seen naked. He was wholly engaging – he told me he spoke twenty languages, but it didn't seem like boasting – and, of course, my *Cinderella* audience loved him. He knew all they wanted was Sir Lancelot Spratt come to life, and he was happy to oblige.

For the Saturday matinée, I performed the prologue because Pa had brought a coachload from the office to see the show. I was exhausted (with a pain right across my chest), but I wanted him to see me speaking his old mentor's lines forty years on and to feel proud.

For the last night, inevitably, I returned to my childhood once more. Frank Muir – whom I had first met when I was eight at the Scouts' Summer Fair at Holy Trinity, Brompton – came to perform the prologue and was a complete delight. He twinkled: the audience *loved* him. Afterwards we had dinner at the Sorbonne – the French restaurant in the High Street. (Incidentally, it's where I first met Alain Descenclos and Raymond

Blanc who went on to run Le Manoir Aux Quat'Saisons: I really did meet *everybody* at Oxford.) It was a very happy evening. We talked about *Whack-O!* and Jimmy Edwards – and *Take It From Here*.

I told Frank how, as a little boy living in Earl's Court, I used to listen to *Take It From Here* in bed, under the blankets, on my tiny crystal set. With Polly (his wife) shaking her head (but smiling), Frank straightened his bow tie and kindly acted out some of my favourite moments from 'The Glums'.

'Oh, Ron beloved . . .'
'Yes, Eth . . .'
'Have you got anything on your mind?'
'No, Eth . . .'

20. Illyria

I was now seriously smitten with Michèle and pursuing her dementedly. While I was directing *Cinderella*, she was rehearsing Viola in somebody else's production of *Twelfth Night*. I got hold of him (an amiable guy reading law at Queen's College) and persuaded him (quite how I don't know) to find me a part in the play.

'Would you have time? You are rather busy, aren't you?' he said to me sensibly. (He was the sensible sort. He became a judge in Wales in the fullness of time.*)

'I've played Feste and Malvolio before,' I said helpfully. 'I know the lines already.'

'They're taken,' he said. 'How about the sea captain? It's a smallish part, but –'

'He has a scene with Viola, doesn't he?'

'He does.'

'Done,' I said.

Act One, Scene Two
[Enter Viola, a Captain and Sailors]
Viola: What country, friends, is this?
Captain: This is Illyria, lady.

I added the *Twelfth Night* rehearsals to my long list of other commitments. I was overdoing it – writing, speaking, directing,

---

* Patrick Curran QC (1948–2021). By uncanny coincidence, on the day I happened to be proofreading this page, a mutual friend sent me word of Pat's unexpected death, with a copy of his obituary from the *South Wales Argus*. It was evident his nice nature had not changed: 'He was always very encouraging of the junior Bar, especially in Chambers, and offered guidance and advice in his gentle and kindly way, without affectation and with unfailing generosity of spirit.'

wooing – and paying the price, with chest pains, night sweats and a bad back that had me permanently doubled over. I couldn't even stand up to see my love-struck face in the mirror above my washbasin.

On the opening night of *Twelfth Night*, Michèle played Viola to perfection. I am sorry to report that the same cannot be said of the sea captain. I was bent in two. ('What country, friends, is this?' 'France, lady, and here is Quasimodo to show you around the Cathedral of Notre Dame!') At the dress rehearsal I had at least remembered all the lines, but to make assurance doubly sure for the opening performance I had them written out on the sleeve of my sea captain's shirt – hidden from the audience but within my eyeline. In the event, my sea captain's cloak (made of rough brown blankets that took me back to my nursery school) obscured them, with the result that I left out half my main speech and made a non-sense of the scene.

Michèle was not amused, but she coped. Just. She coped less well with the fact that on the Thursday night of the run I did not appear onstage at all. This was my fourth term at the university and, by now, on top of the OUDS and *Isis* and *Cherwell* and the rest, I was already Secretary of the Oxford Union and running to be President. I couldn't be in two places at the same time: in my white tie and tails in the Union debating chamber on Thursday night at 8.15 p.m. and also in my sea captain's rig-out in Illyria. The amiable director stepped in to play the sea captain for me that night.

Needless to say, he wasn't bent double and he was word perfect.

Conquering the Union was my number one priority because I knew that was what counted most with Pa. Founded in 1823, the Oxford Union is one of the oldest university debating societies in the world, celebrated in my father's day because his heroes – giants like Gladstone, Lord Curzon and

F. E. Smith – had once been Union officers, and still famous in my time because more recent politicians – from Harold Macmillan and Ted Heath on the right to Tony Benn and Michael Foot on left, with the likes of Roy Jenkins and Jeremy Thorpe in between – had all first made their mark at the Union. They came back, too: to speak, to have dinner with us beforehand, and drinks in the Union bar afterwards.

I met them all and was often surprised that I was charmed most by the ones I expected to like least. Tony Benn, for example, became a friend and a mentor. His politics weren't mine, but I was captivated by his decency and humanity. And energy. As Union Secretary, one of my duties was to collect guests from Oxford Station. Mr Wedgwood Benn (in the late sixties we were a generation away from 'Call me Tony') was Minister for Technology and spent our taxi ride talking at breakneck speed about the aerospace industry. I didn't understand any of it, but I was bowled over by his enthusiasm. Years later, when I had become an MP and we were near neighbours in Notting Hill Gate, I would visit Tony for mugs of tea and we would sit in his chaotic basement surrounded by a lifetime's worth of diaries and correspondence. He developed a mania for recording everything. At our last few encounters, it was just the pair of us gossiping (he was telling me, for example, how he had been outwitted by the Queen when, as Postmaster General, he had tried to cajole her into accepting a set of stamps that didn't feature her silhouette), but he insisted I sit close enough to him so that his pocket recorder could pick up everything we said.

'Oh yes, Gyles,' he insisted, 'our chit-chat is the first draft of history.'

I introduced him to the producer who put him onstage around the country. He became a kind of thinking man's Ken Dodd, playing to audiences of two thousand plus. Middle Britain, terrified of what he stood for in the 1960s, flocked to see and applaud him half a century on.

Jeremy Thorpe, on the other hand . . . When we first met, in the Union debating chamber, he leapt over one bench, and then another, as he bounded towards me. He greeted me as though I was the most important and exciting person he had ever set eyes on. But he had a foxy look and a glint in his eye. This was ten years before his fall from grace and his trial at the Old Bailey on charges of conspiracy and incitement to murder. At the end of the evening, although flattered by his attention, I noted in my diary: 'I didn't entirely trust him; and he didn't entirely trust me.'

My immediate contemporaries at the Union included four future ministers (Robert Jackson, William Waldegrave, Ann Widdecombe and Edwina Currie) as well as Stephen Milligan, who expected to be Foreign Secretary by around 2010, when I expected to be Home Secretary. (It might have happened – if Stephen hadn't got carried away in his fishnet stockings, and if I had accepted the offer to stand in the safe seat I was invited to try for in a by-election in November 1997. In 1992, as new MPs, Stephen and I went to Brussels together to explore the mysteries of the EU institutions and were entertained by the UK ambassador to the EU. Charmingly, Sir John Kerr introduced us everywhere as the two future leaders of our party. Nobody laughed. At least, not out loud.)

Ann Widdecombe was a tad unusual, even at twenty. She had a boyfriend called Colin and they walked about together like Tweedledum and Tweedledee, rather stiffly holding hands. Her faith was always important to her. As an MP, when she travelled around the country giving speeches she took with her copies of a book, *On Christian Principles*, to distribute after the meeting. Once, she left the books in the boot of her car and shortly before the meeting was seen running frantically through the streets of Maidenhead calling out to bewildered passers-by, 'I've lost my *Christian Principles*!'

I recall getting on to a train with her at Euston when we were in government together.

As I made to move into the First Class carriage, she barked, 'Where are you going, Brandreth? We're the servants of the people, not the masters. Our tickets are paid for by the tax-payer. You'll sit in Standard Class with me.'

I did as I was told.

When she was Prisons Minister she visited every prison in the country. Willie Whitelaw told me that when he was Home Secretary he had wanted to visit every prison, but there were too many and he found it very exhausting. As he told me this, over dinner, he appeared to be crying. I don't think he was. He just drank a lot and his oyster eyes were always watery. He recalled the unfortunate day when, on a prison visit, he was meeting assorted inmates taking part in an arts and crafts class.

He chatted to one prisoner after another, asking the same question every time, 'Hello, what are you doing?'

'Pottery, sir,' answered one.

'Basket weaving, sir,' said another.

'Well done, carry on,' he replied to them, in turn. He reached the last man in the room. 'Hello, what are you doing?'

'Twenty-five years for murdering my wife.'

'Well done,' said Willie, 'carry on.'

Edwina Cohen was a fun girl to know at Oxford – and later, too, of course. I liked her when we first met in the 1960s, and I like her still, but we did have a bit of a falling out when she revealed her affair with John Major. The affair began in 1984, when she was thirty-seven and a new MP and he was forty-one and a junior whip. They had fun ('I like sex, Gyles,' she told me later, with eyes as moist as Willie Whitelaw's, 'I like it. I like it!'), and these things happen ('An affair's not a marriage, Gyles. And it's not a substitute for marriage either. It's some-thing else. It's something extra'), but to spill the beans was an unkindness to Norma Major (a good person) and to John Major (to whom Edwina used to say, 'I love you'). She did not do it for money (her publishers had no idea her book would feature the revelation when they bought it), nor for revenge (she could have brought down the Major government with the story if she had chosen to); she did it to have her place in history. She may only be a footnote, but she will definitely be there.

In my estimation, John Major was a good Prime Minister (and a nice guy) who played a pretty difficult hand pretty well, but, by chance recently, I happened to get sight of one of the obituaries that will feature in a national newspaper when he dies. It gave almost as much space to his dalliance with Edwina as it did to his contribution towards achieving peace in Northern Ireland.

While I was rootling through the obits, I came across my own. I was interested to read that when I was at Oxford I took to sweeping around the 'City of Dreaming Spires' wearing a cloak. I never did, but in an essay somewhere, my contemporary, the great Christopher Hitchens, polemicist and public intellectual, claimed that I did, so that's how history will have it. (Wikipedia, too.) I don't mind. It will look more stylish in the movie.

Chris (whom I always picture in a combat jacket with a hard drinker's bloodshot eyes) was a Union friend who took his politics seriously. So was Tariq Ali, who was a bit older than us and was viewed as a proper revolutionary. I remember Tariq and I had tea together at the Union shortly after he had joined the International Marxist Group, in 1968, and I thought, 'He can't be that bad – he's ordered tea and anchovy toast.'

How I loved tea and anchovy toast as they served it in the Oxford Union! I loved the Union's High Victorian buildings, the oak panelling, the leather sofas, the high-ceilinged rooms, especially the galleried library, with its murals by Rossetti, William Morris and Edward Burne-Jones.

One night when I was Secretary, I was charged with looking after one of the Union's more challenging guests: Dominic Behan, Irish songwriter and Republican, younger brother of the more famous Brendan, and son (so he told me) of one of the leading IRA men responsible for killing any number of British soldiers during the Irish 'war of independence'. When I met Dominic, he was already wild with drink and impossible to control. He ranted, he rambled, he lurched around the President's office, alternately breaking into song and demanding more drink. He asked me to show him where the lavatories were. I said I'd take him down to them.

He stumbled down the stairs and – on the landing – proceeded to undo his flies and produce his member for me to admire. 'I'm bursting!' he declared and then, turning towards the wall, he walked quite sedately down the corridor, peeing profusely against the wall as he went.

'Don't!' I bleated. 'That's William Morris wallpaper! It's original!'

'Fuck William Morris!' he cried, warming to his task and spraying the precious wall with ever greater gusto.

'He was a socialist, like you!' I called out desperately.

'Fuck socialism!' he declared, turning to me triumphantly and shaking the final drips in my direction.

It was another Irishman of note who gave me my 'break-out' moment at the Union: the Reverend Dr Ian Paisley, Protestant firebrand and founding member of the Free Presbyterian Church of Ulster. In my first term, I was invited to give the last speech of the night, 'telling for the Noes', in a debate on the motion 'that the Roman Catholic Church has no place in the twentieth century' – with Paisley proposing and the Catholic Conservative MP Norman St John-Stevas leading for the opposition. Normally, nobody would stay to hear the Tellers' speeches, but this debate was being broadcast on BBC2 'live and in colour' from 9.05 p.m. to its close.

I had a captive audience, and they stayed. And I had the last word – and it worked.

My speech went well. (Come on: it went *wonderfully* well.)

Being last up helped. Having the hall full to bursting helped. The lights, the cameras, the sense of occasion – they all helped.

Paisley's performance was extraordinary. He produced a communion wafer from his pocket and snapped it in two, saying, 'They dare to call this busket the body of Christ – this *busket!*' His manner was alarming, but his presence undeniable.

St John-Stevas, by contrast, was silky, smooth, amusing. When he was hissed, he immediately responded, 'Do I hear the sound of the rains of heaven landing on the fires of hell?'

Both these unlikely men were kind to me in the years that followed. I debated with Ian again soon after this – in Belfast, in a BBC television programme sensitively entitled *Flashpoint* – and discovered that the fire-and-brimstone delivery was there for show: beneath the demagoguery was a surprisingly affable and entertaining man.

I felt I had the measure of Norman right away. He was thirty-nine and I was nineteen, roughly the same difference in ages as there had been between Oscar Wilde and Bosie, as he pointed out to me. Over dinner that night (lobster mornay, roast pheasant, *marrons glacés* – the Union did us proud), he played the fruity old darling to the hilt, widening his goggle eyes as he invited me to visit him sometime to see his 'treasures' (among them Queen Victoria's bloomers) and hear him play the harp that he kept in his bathroom by the loo.

Two years later, when I was President, the BBC broadcast *Any Questions?* 'live' from the Union. (I asked them to come. They said yes. If you don't ask, you don't get. I learnt that at Oxford.) Norman was on the panel and said several nice things about me on air.

Afterwards, in his cups, he took me to one side and murmured, 'Gyles, you are far too amusing for your own good. Take care.' He said, 'I know how serious you really are, I know all about your work for prison reform, and the poor in Biafra and the rest of it, but out there they'll only remember the *clowning*.' He put his forefinger on my chin and looked into my eyes. 'You should use me as a dreadful warning. Because I try to be amusing, I'm dismissed as a dilettante and a lightweight. Ultimately, funny people fail. I'd like to drop Bagehot on their toes.' (At the time, he was editing a fifteen-volume edition of the works of Walter Bagehot, the Victorian constitutional lawyer.)

Later, he was in Mrs Thatcher's first Cabinet – but not for long. He couldn't resist calling her 'The Blessed Margaret' and, though she had a good number of gay men working within her inner circle and found Norman's campery 'quite amusing', when the time came for her to squeeze out the 'wets' he was one of the first to go.

By the time I reached the Commons, Norman was in the Lords. On my first day in parliament (it was the day Frankie Howerd died, I remember – aged seventy-five, which surprised me, as he had always seemed younger) I found three letters waiting for me in my cubbyhole in the Members' Lobby: one was from the Prime Minister (John Major), one was from Michael Portillo (whom I had never met) and one, written in purple ink with a florid hand, was from Norman: 'My dear Gyles, You will be a wonderful MP but practise a little economy of personality in the Commons. They don't deserve to have too much too soon.'

At the Union I tried to have too much too soon. I stood to be President at the end of my first year – just as Boris Johnson would do a generation later. And just as Boris did, first time round I came a cropper – despite the endorsement of *Isis*. 'Brandreth,' declared the editor in a half-page leader, 'not so much a pansy, more a self-raising flower, is far and away the most exciting candidate.' (Very generous, I thought, given my cack-handed attempt to seduce his wife.)

In the event, I lost – by four votes. I was disappointed, naturally, but not as much as others seemed to be. Ma and Pa had come down for the count, bringing a bottle of champagne with them. When I didn't win, they took the champagne home – unopened. And Pa sent me a copy of Kipling's poem 'If'.

Michèle was shocked by this: she felt they should have cracked open the champagne all the same.

I didn't. Either you win or you lose.

If you win, you celebrate; if you lose, you move on.

I moved on quite happily. There were more televised Union debates, more opportunities for clowning (I would regularly stand on my head on the despatch box), more serious moments too (I found myself appearing on *Late Night Line-Up* on BBC2 talking about the therapeutic value of art in prisons), and at the end of my second year I stood for the presidency again – and won, handsomely, just as Boris did in his day.

On the night before my election, I had dinner at All Souls, the Oxford college founded by Henry VI in 1438. All Souls has no undergraduate members, but each year recent graduate and postgraduate students can apply for a small number of fellowships through a competitive examination, often described as 'the hardest exam in the world'. My friend Robert Jackson (who had been Union President and very kind to me when I arrived at Oxford) had just become a Fellow and took me as his guest. It was an invitation he repeated quite often. I enjoyed dining at All Souls because it was one of those places where I listened more and talked less.

I remember saying to Robert, 'I like the company of clever people. In fact, I only want the company of people who are clever, funny or beautiful!'

'Well,' said Robert, 'we should manage two out of three here.'

That was the night I met the celebrated All Souls' Warden, John Sparrow. He was gently waspish, but very charming.

Robert explained, 'He likes young men – and old wine.'

Sparrow was happy to talk about his famous rivalry with A. L. Rowse, the Cornish historian and Shakespeare scholar, and acknowledged the authenticity of the fabled exchange between them. One evening at high table Rowse reprimanded Sparrow for his disdain of Rowse's work: 'You never read any of my books, Warden. Do you know *Tudor Cornwall*?' Without pause, indicating the fellow academic sitting opposite Rowse, Sparrow replied: 'Do you know Stuart Hampshire?'

The night after my election, I was back at All Souls. Warden Sparrow was again on song, repeating, at my invitation, some of his celebrated 'terse verse'. My favourite was a poem he called 'Growing Old'.

> I'm accustomed to my deafness,
> To my dentures I'm resigned,
> I can cope with my bifocals,
> But – oh dear! – I miss my mind.

'You know, Wystan writes these sorts of poems as well,' he said.

'I'm sure they're not as good as yours, sir,' I piped up instantly.

'They aren't.' He smiled. 'Of course, Wystan isn't well, poor man.' (Auden had been Professor of Poetry at Oxford in the late 1950s.) 'We're the same age exactly, but he looks so much older – with all those terrible lines criss-crossing his face. Do you know what Noël Coward said? "Picture Auden's face – now imagine his scrotum!"'

I laughed.

The Warden looked at me steadily. 'Will you be joining us here one day?' he asked.

'I don't think I'm quite up to it, sir,' I said truthfully.

Over the port and dessert he showed me the memoirs of Charles Oman, who became a Fellow in the 1880s and left a memorable account of the fellowship examination. In the history paper, Osman was able to 'ramble around all manner of topics' – the Greek conception of the state, the social conditions of medieval Scotland, the claim of Napoléon to be the successor of Charlemagne, the history of the Crusades and so forth. The account concluded: 'There remained the paper of translation from five languages, ancient and modern, where I found four of them easy enough.'

As I said goodnight, Sparrow held my hand for a moment. 'Never mind being a Fellow, I think you should dine here every night. You are very amusing.'

He had talked all evening. I had barely said a word.

I would like to tell you more about John Sparrow – and about A. L. Rowse, whom I got to know quite well, and about Maurice Bowra, the Warden of Wadham College (who famously said, 'Buggery was invented to fill that awkward hour between evensong and cocktails'). But it may be that, by now, you've heard enough about me and the fruity old queens I've known.

I was talking to Graham Norton the other day and he said, 'Gyles, are you turning into Ned Sherrin?'

Ned – writer, broadcaster, director, producer, and the creator in the 1960s of *That Was the Week That Was* – did a one-man show (rather as I do) featuring his favourite name-dropping stories. It was called *Ned Sherrin in His Anecdotage*.

Graham told me how, when he had been to see it, during the interval he had overheard a couple discussing the show.

The wife said, 'Apparently, the second half is completely different – *completely* different.'

'Really?' said the husband. 'He'll be talking about living straight people, will he?'

I suppose I have known a lot of dead old darlings. Ned was one. We wrote a sitcom pilot together in the 1980s. It was at the beginning of the AIDS epidemic and Ned alarmed (and shocked) me by telling me how he liked to go out cruising in search of unprotected sex. 'It is like feasting with panthers,' he said, quoting Wilde and echoing Edward Montagu. 'The danger is half the excitement.'

I learnt a lot from Ned. For example, he advised me, if I had a funny line I was trying out but wasn't quite sure about, to preface it by attributing it to a known wit – Dr Johnson,

Oscar Wilde, Woody Allen, Barry Cryer . . . Expecting to find the line funny because of its provenance, whatever the line is like, the audience will give it the benefit of the doubt. He also taught me the importance of good manners. Anyone who was ever a guest on his radio show *Loose Ends* always received a personally written thank-you postcard from Ned after the show. No contemporary broadcaster or BBC producer does that. It doesn't even cross their mind.

Anyway, bearing Graham's admonition in mind, I am going to try to go easy now on what my friend Simon Cadell would have called 'ageing woofter' stories. That said, I can't avoid mentioning Beverley Nichols again. I simply can't. He was *so* famous – once upon a time . . .

21. So famous – once upon a time

Beverley Nichols was President of the Oxford Union in 1919, fifty years to the term before I was. I invited him back to speak in a special debate to mark the anniversary. In the run-up to the event, he invited me to lunch. He was seventy, a little stooped, but vigorous and full of charm. He met me at the railway station and drove me to his house – a beautiful eighteenth-century cottage overlooking Ham Common, near Richmond in Surrey. He and his 'friend', Cyril Butcher, had prepared lunch themselves and it was delicious – quite perfect in fact: prawn mousse, cheese soufflé, cucumber salad, chilled Sancerre. Cyril fussed and served and cleared, but did very little of the talking. Beverley chattered non-stop. He had known everyone, from Churchill and Edward VIII to Dame Nellie Melba and Noël Coward. He had extraordinary stories to tell of Somerset Maugham's cruelty to his wife, Syrie. 'He should never have married. His marriage brought out the viciousness that lurks just beneath the surface in so many men.'

When Pa was at Oxford, Beverley was one of the most famous young men in the land. Fifty years on, he was best known for his sentimental newspaper columns, his love of cats and his skill as a gardener. He showed me his latest *Cat Calendar* and his new book on flower arranging (it included a striking arrangement featuring a whole red cabbage as the centrepiece). After lunch, he took me on a tour of the garden – his pride and joy. Occasionally he would allow groups of gardening ladies to come on a visit – and set them a challenge. After the tour, he offered them tea. After tea, if they asked to powder their noses, he directed them to the loo, where they would find that he had placed an exquisite arrangement of miniature roses inside the lavatory bowl . . .

My gala night at the Union in his honour went well.

He said to me afterwards, 'I had forgotten what it was like to play the Union. It is a subtler instrument than you might imagine.' He played it with extraordinary delicacy: he was nostalgic and reflective and yet he held them completely. He disarmed them with understated charm. (I noted in my diary that night: 'There is a lesson here!') And for those requiring something more robust, at Beverley's suggestion, we had his friend and contemporary Lord Boothby, former MP and media darling.

Bob Boothby did not disappoint – either in the debate (when he growled and gurgled and the crowd cheered) or before and afterwards when he staggered about, wheezing, drinking, smoking, like an ancient debauchee enjoying one last night out on the town. He arrived with his young Sardinian bride on his arm and I was grateful for her presence: she was thirty-three years his junior, and he needed looking after. I felt he might well die during the course of the evening. Beverley had told me such stories about him – scandals involving gangsters, mistresses in high places, love children, blackmail and worse – but said, 'Don't believe a word of it, Bob's a dear, an absolute dear.' In truth, Boothby was bisexual, twice married, for many years the lover of Harold Macmillan's wife, Dorothy, the lover of the gangster Ronald Kray and the father of several illegitimate children. But he was amusing. Queen Elizabeth the Queen Mother described him as 'a bounder but not a cad'.

Michèle looked at my list of Union debates and guests and said, not unkindly, 'It's all politics, prisons and people from the past, Gyles. What about something a bit more modern?'

I wasn't interested in anything 'a bit more modern', but instinctively I knew she was right. (Amazingly, she has been right about everything for more than fifty years. I said to her the other day, 'You know, you're always right.' 'I do know,' she said. 'To be honest, it's quite exhausting.')

My 'modern' debate was one of the best. The motion: 'That pop and culture will never meet.' The line-up included Edward Lucie-Smith, poet and critic; Tony Palmer, film director and pop columnist; Emperor Rosko, disc jockey (Michèle's choice); and Sandy Wilson, creator of *The Boy Friend* (my choice). Jimmy Young (later Sir Jimmy – and Margaret Thatcher's favourite interviewer – then a pop star and the most famous Radio 1 DJ in the land) failed to show, but my surprise substitute proved to be the star of the evening – 'It's Si-i-i-i-i-imon Dee!' That's how he was introduced at the top of his Saturday-night chat show, *Dee Time*. You've not heard of him, probably, but in 1969 he was the Graham Norton/James Corden of his day, with a weekly audience of eighteen million plus.

Simon was tall and skinny, with blond floppy hair. He arrived in an E-type Jaguar (of course) and when I went to collect him from his room at the Randolph, I found him drinking champagne with a beautiful actress/model, Joanna Lumley. They were both delightful, full of fun, crazy but intelligent. I took them on the tour of the Union: they were very taken with the Pre-Raphaelite murals and chased one another around the gallery of the Library.

They weren't together long, but Michèle and I stayed friends with both. Simon was thirty-four then and had everything: talent, looks, flair, charm, a quick way with words and women, but somehow it went wrong, and at spectacular speed. His fame went to his head. I remember being in the Barracuda Restaurant in Baker Street with him when he suddenly got to his feet and told everybody in the room that they were his guests. He picked up the tab for seventy strangers. He fell out with Bill Cotton, head of entertainment at the BBC, and switched to London Weekend Television where, in a different slot, his ratings collapsed. Every time we saw him he had become a little crazier. He lost his E-type, his Rolls, his Aston Martin, and his wife, as well as his show, and then, after a spell on the dole, became a bus driver. In 1974, he served twenty-eight days in

Pentonville Prison for non-payment of rates. Every time he left his cell the other prisoners on the wing shouted, 'It's Si-i-i-i-i mon Dee!' Later he was jailed for vandalising a lavatory seat that had Petula Clark's face painted on it. He thought it was disrespectful to her. The magistrate who sentenced him was Bill Cotton. (I knew Bill Cotton, too. Like many a TV executive, he took himself quite seriously.)

Simon died of bone cancer in 2009, but I see him daily hanging in my wardrobe. He gave me a double-sided coat hanger featuring his head and shoulders, life size, and signed Simon Dee on one side and Nicholas Henty-Dodd (his real name) on the other.

I see Joanna (and her husband, the conductor and composer Stephen Barlow) as often as I can. They are certainly my favourite kind of people: clever, funny and beautiful. Joanna exemplifies the truth of Christian Dior's observation that zest is the secret of all beauty: 'There is no beauty that is attractive without zest.' With Joanna it's her energy, enthusiasm and intelligence that make her glow. Watch her in performance and a lot happens. But is that a universal truth? I wonder.

When I came face to face with Raquel Welch for the first time, I was blown away by her beauty, but I am not sure she would pass the Dior zest test. It was her stillness that struck me – and her perfect skin.

Jane Asher had a stillness about her, too. And the most wonderful freckles. Jane – another child star, another Alice in Wonderland – was famous in the 1960s, partly because she had starred with Michael Caine in the hit film *Alfie*, but mainly because she was the girlfriend and then fiancée of the Beatle Paul McCartney – and the Beatles in the sixties were truly, as John Lennon said, 'more famous than Jesus'. I met Jane in the summer of 1968 because Michèle was a friend of another New College scholar, Christopher Hampton, who two years before, aged twenty, had become the youngest playwright in the history of the West End. I admired Christopher because he was serious about his writing without being pompous about it. I liked Christopher because he was simultaneously genuine *and* amusing. I liked him even more when he turned up at my room in New College asking if I could find a way to get two tickets for the College Ball for Jane and her Beatle fiancé. I found a way, though on the night Jane turned up not with Paul but with a 25-year-old theatre director, Bob Kidd, in whose production she was appearing at the Oxford Playhouse. They arrived around 11.00 p.m. Jane was exhausted so we left her to sleep in my room. Bob said, 'Now you can say, "Jane Asher slept in my bed."' I did just that, of course, and repeatedly – though always adding, I promise, 'Maddeningly, I was elsewhere at the time.'

I saw quite a bit of Jane and Bob that summer. I met Paul when her play opened in London: he was nice (smaller than I'd expected), but she was breaking up with him, not only because she'd come home one night to find another girl in her bed (and maddeningly, Paul was with her at the time!) but also because there were other aspects of the Beatles' lifestyle that weren't to Jane's liking (for example, LSD). Bob was wonderfully intelligent and gently charming; I think they spent time with Michèle and me that year largely because we were so removed from anything remotely 'Beatle'. Beyond 'She Loves You' I don't think I knew any of their songs.

I lived through the Swinging Sixties – I met the icons of the era (Twiggy is still a friend) and I bought a psychedelic jacket (in Carnaby Street) – but the Swinging Sixties didn't move or excite me: I didn't inhale. I had never smoked a cigarette, let alone dabbled with any kind of narcotic. Conservative and cowardly, I didn't take any risks. I never have, which is a shame, because I've noticed over the years that almost all the real achievers are risk-takers.

In the 1980s, with help from her friend Jacqueline Bayes, Michèle organised a charity ball with a sixties theme: a thousand people at Grosvenor House, with Princess Anne as guest

GB first met ...

... Julian Fellowes in 1953 – here they are, with actor Hugh Bonneville, celebrating *Downton Abbey* at the British Film Institute sixty years later

... Jeffrey Archer in 1960 – here they are signing their books together at Hatchards in Piccadilly sixty years on

... Nicholas Parsons in 1969 – here they are after doing their last show together, the year before Nicholas died in 2020

... Donald Sinden in 1965 – here they are with actor Geoffrey Palmer in 2005

... Joanna Lumley in 1969 – here they are in 2021

Then and now

GB at the Tower of London in 1951

– and at Chester Cathedral, as Chancellor of the University of Chester, in 2018

Roger Moore and Major Douch in the army in the 1940s

Sir Roger Moore with GB in the 2010s

GB on the box: in the television department of Selfridges in 1956

– and duetting with Debbie Reynolds on BBC TV's *The One Show* in 2010

GB at his desk at New College, Oxford, in 1969 (with Noël Coward and Lenin looking on)

GB at Noël Coward's desk at Firefly in Jamaica in 2017

GB addressing the Oxford Union in 1968

– and hosting the Air Cargo Awards in 2012

HRH The Duke of Edinburgh meeting GB's children, Aphra, Benet and Saethryd, in the 1980s

HRH The Duchess of Cornwall with Saethryd's son, Rory, in 2015

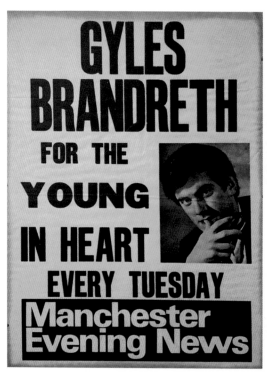

Manchester Evening News, 1971

Cinderella, Wimbledon Theatre, 1989

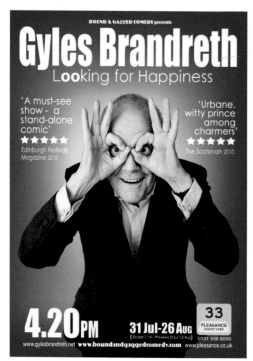

Looking for Happiness, Edinburgh, 2013

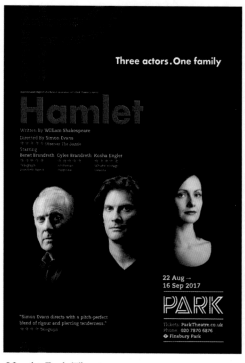

Hamlet, Park Theatre, 2017

GB in *Zipp!* 2002 (Photograph by Murdo MacLeod)

GB as Dorothy in *Zipp!* 2002

GB as Lady Bracknell in *The Importance of Being Earnest* at the Riverside Studios, 2011

GB as Widow Twankey in the *This Morning* pantomime, ITV, 2020

With Ringo Starr and Harold Wilson, 1985

With Christopher Robin Milne, 1986

With Merlin Holland, Oscar Wilde's grandson, 2016

With Cressida Dick and Stephen Fry at GB's annual Oscar Wilde Party, 2017

With Dame Sheila Hancock at the Theatre Royal, Stratford East, where GB first saw her on stage in 1958

With Dame June Whitfield on the day her DBE was announced in 2017, sixty-four years after GB first heard her on the radio in 1953

Elbow to elbow with Dame Maureen Lipman

Side by side with Dame Judi Dench

GB and Michèle on their wedding day, 8 June 1973

GB and Michèle at another family wedding, forty-five years later, 2018

2017 family photograph: children, grandchildren and partners. Bottom row left to right: Kiyo, Cassian, GB, Isolde, Michèle, Atticus, Cornelius, Rory. Top row left to right: Ian, Aphra, Benet, Kosha, Saethryd, Mark, Kitt, Jason

of honour. Michèle chose the acts: Ricky Valance, The Swinging Blue Jeans, Billy J. Kramer and The Dakotas. I invited assorted sixties luminaries to help out. Harold Wilson (1960s prime minister) proposed the Loyal Toast and David Frost (1960s star of *That Was the Week That Was*) was MC. Michael Caine (star of classic sixties movies *Zulu*, *Alfie* and *The Italian Job*) and Bobby Moore (1966 World Cup Final captain) did their stuff. Ringo Starr coped well with Princess Anne's firm belief that he, too, was a footballer.

'Do you still play?' she asked.

'Yes, Ma'am,' said Ringo.

'What do you do to keep in training?'

'Being a Beatle helps.'

(More recently, the princess met my friend Jon Culshaw who told her he was an impressionist. She asked if he preferred water colour to oils.)

Princess Anne is a good egg, and the royal with the busiest schedule. Every working day is a long one. On the night of our sixties charity ball she came to us from a lunch with the police and was off at the crack of dawn the next day for her first taste of flat racing, as a jockey. I liked her. In fact, I spent dinner rubbing knees with her, but only because the top table was tightly packed and her chair was immediately in front of the table leg so she had no choice but to sit with one knee on one side and one knee on the other. (Michèle and I had spent hours in the afternoon checking and rechecking the top table. We just never lifted the tablecloth.) When I said to the princess what fun it was to be sitting thigh to thigh with her, she arched her eyebrows, sipped her Coca-Cola and enquired about the challenges currently facing the charity. In fairness, she has to put up with a lot.

When I was last with her at Grosvenor House, only a couple of years ago, at a Save the Children fund-raising dinner, the young comedian hosting the event didn't quite catch the mood of the room. As his third gag failed to hit the mark, he gazed down from the stage at the Princess Royal, who was staring up at him bleakly, and remarked, 'You're looking at me like my dog looks at me when he catches me wanking.'

'Oh dear,' Her Royal Highness's lady-in-waiting murmured in my ear, 'I don't think the boss will be enjoying this.'

In 1968, turning twenty but still a student, I was becoming sort of famous myself. I was being asked to appear on radio and TV as 'the voice of youth' (when I really so wasn't) and I discovered that, if you wanted, you could pop up quite easily in a newspaper diary column (invent any old nonsense and phone it in) or, better still, feature in a nice photograph on page three of the *Daily Mail*. I had made friends with one of the *Mail* photographers and together we set up a raft of fun picture stories, including me standing on my head in the Union and me hiring an aeroplane to take Michèle on a date. (The *Daily Mail* hired the aeroplane and we sat in it, but it never left the ground.)

I learnt quite young how the media works.

One day in the summer of '68, sitting in my room at New College, there was a knock on my door. When I opened it I found a small, bouncy, eager young woman who had travelled all the way from London to see me. Gillian Cooke was the editor of *Honey* magazine. It spoke for 'the girls of today – young, gay and get-ahead' and, according to Gillian, they were listening.

'We sell 250,000 copies a month,' she said. 'We want you to be Luke Jarvis.'

'Who?' I asked.

'Luke Jarvis. He's young, sexy, with-it. He's *you*. He lives in Chelsea, he drives an E-type, he's got all these dolly bird girlfriends . . . I want you to write his diary – you can mention breasts but not nipples, drink but not drugs, lots of fun, you know the sort of thing. What do you think?'

'Good grief!' is what I thought. But yes is what I said, and that's how I became 'Luke Jarvis' and got my first column in a national magazine. I couldn't drive, I didn't live in Chelsea, and I hadn't the first idea what 'the girls of today' were thinking or doing – but I reckoned Michèle could point me in the right direction, and she did. I have had a variety of columns in every kind of magazine and newspaper ever since (including twenty years with *Dogs Today*), but in many ways I still regard my time as Luke Jarvis as my finest hour.

Now I write a column for *The Oldie*.

'That's the column you should have been writing fifty years ago,' says Michèle.

When I was still nineteen, at the beginning of 1968, the *Sun* newspaper came to Oxford and ran a feature on 'The Tomorrow People'. Michael Rosen, twenty-one, playwright and poet, and Diana Quick, twenty-one, 'generally talked about as the best actress at Oxford for years', got a fair look-in, but mine was the top photograph, and there was a quote from me as the main headline: 'I'D LIKE TO BE A SORT OF DANNY KAYE AND THEN HOME SECRETARY.'

Understandably, some of my contemporaries thought I needed taking down a peg. I became the victim of a number of practical jokes. After I had been elected President of the Union, an invitation to a drinks party was sent out in my name to all the heads of colleges in the university. The first I knew about it was when Lady Hayter, wife of the Warden of New College, sent me a note to say she couldn't come.

I raced round to the Warden's lodgings to see her. 'Come to what?' I asked.

'Your party,' she said. 'It sounds such fun.'

'I'm not giving a party,' I squealed. 'I couldn't afford a party,' I said, 'and please know that I wouldn't have presumed to ask you and the Warden, even if I could.'

She took pity on me and got the Warden's secretary to telephone round the other college heads to see if they had been invited to the Brandreth fantasy drinks. They all had been – and the Lord Mayor of Oxford, the High Sherriff and the Lord Lieutenant had been invited, too. Gratifyingly, Warden Sparrow of All Souls said he was sorry to hear the invitation was a spoof. He had been looking forward to it.

Another New College man, Kevin Pakenham, the eighth child and fourth son of the 7th Earl of Longford, who had cast Michèle in his college production of *Alice in Wonderland*, masterminded another practical joke. He got an accomplice to visit me in my room to tell me he was a scout working for a TV company that wanted to give me my own show. I swallowed the bait, bought the suit, had the haircut and took a train to London to meet a man who wasn't there at an address that didn't exist.

It was only after I'd been wandering up and down the Tottenham Court Road for nearly an hour that the penny dropped. I was humiliated – but flattered, too – that anyone should bother to think up such a scam. It had a lifelong effect on me. Whenever I get what seems like a nice invitation or an interesting opportunity, I always stop and think: 'Is this for real?'

When I found a note waiting for me in my cubbyhole at the porters' lodge saying 'Kenneth Tynan is coming to see you at 12' I knew it was a joke. And when there was a knock on my door at noon, I didn't answer it. I said, 'Fuck off!' When the knocking continued, I flung open the door, ready to say it again – and there he was: Kenneth Peacock Tynan, famously the first man to say 'fuck' on British television.

'Are you trying to be funny?' he asked.

'N-n-no,' I stammered. 'Come in.'

Tynan was one of my boyhood heroes. He was the pre-eminent theatre critic of his day. I loved his writing. I kept the hardback copy of *Curtains*, his collection of reviews from the 1950s, on my bedside table. I envied his life. He had joined Laurence Olivier at the Old Vic at the start of the 1960s, as the National Theatre's first Literary Manager. I knew of his legend. At Oxford in the 1940s, he had been what Beverley

Nichols had been at Oxford in the 1920s: the most outrageous, the most brilliant, the most famous undergraduate of his generation.

'Apparently, you're the new me,' he said, drawing slowly on his cigarette and inspecting me with a cold eye.

'Yes,' said his companion, a taller, broader, friendlier man, who beamed at me from behind large black-rimmed glasses and explained that he was a TV producer making a programme about Tynan's time at Oxford and that everyone said I was Ken's latter-day equivalent, which was why they had beaten a path to my door. 'I hope you can help?'

'Of course,' I said, 'of course.' I looked at Tynan again.

It was definitely him. This was no spoof.

The film they were making was called *One Pair of Eyes*. The idea was to take Tynan back to the scene of his Oxford triumphs, twenty years on.

'All we want is you being you,' said the producer, 'doing whatever you do.'

The producer was called Fred Burnley. He was thirty-five, handsome, happy, easy to be with. I liked him from the moment we met that day in the summer of 1968 until the day, just seven years later, when he died, aged forty-two, of lung complications arising from exposure to bat guano while filming a documentary for David Attenborough's series *The Explorers*.

Tynan was forty-one when I met him, but he looked older. He had a cadaverous, emaciated appearance, lank hair, a grey face, watery eyes, and slightly protruding purple lips. He held his ever-present cigarette affectedly between his ring and middle fingers. I wanted to like him, but I didn't. He didn't think much of me, either. I wanted to talk about Olivier and Marlene Dietrich (whom I knew he knew), but he only wanted to talk about sex. 'Your generation – who are you fucking and how?' I didn't know then what I know now – that he had a secret life as a sadomasochist and hired prostitutes to help

349

him act out some of his more lurid and elaborate fantasies – but I might have guessed. One of the sequences we filmed was a party scene on a boat. I spent much of the evening dancing with Ken's young wife, Kathleen. (She was lovely.) Ken spent most of the evening looking bored and now and then trying to liven things up by offering a fiver to any of the girl students who would take her top off for him. 'It's Saturday night, I want to see some tits,' he bleated, 'firm young tits.' None of the girls obliged. 'So much for the Swinging Sixties,' he said sourly. Eventually, to give them something vaguely party-like to film, I agreed to jump off the boat and into the river, fully clothed, shouting '*Whoopee!*'

Altogether I spent quite a lot of time in the River Isis for Ken and Fred that summer. Another sequence in the documentary centred on my apparent search for the most beautiful girl in Oxford – my 'Zuleika Dobson'. Max Beerbohm (1872–1956), friend of Oscar Wilde, dandy, critic, caricaturist (another of Pa's heroes and, consequently, one of mine) wrote one novel, *Zuleika Dobson, or, an Oxford love story*, a satire of undergraduate life. In the story (which includes the devastating line 'Death cancels all engagements') Zuleika is so overpoweringly attractive that young men drown themselves for love of her.

Assisted by my friend David Graham, I scoured Oxford to find the university's most powerfully attractive girls. ('There's a corker in the Science Library – third bay in.' 'In the Science Library, really?') Amazingly, the first eight we approached all agreed to take part and, on the given day, turned up at New College in their ball gowns at 10.00 a.m., as requested. We set off together in a procession of vintage cars (supplied by the BBC), led by a horse (ridden by my friend Julian Radcliffe), and made our way to a sunlit dell by the river. There we filmed a fantasy lunch and I made a short speech before choosing Lady Annunziata Asquith as the Zuleika Dobson of 1968 and giving her the crown. (Annunziata, great-granddaughter of the Prime Minister, the first Earl of Oxford and Asquith, and later partner of the photographer Patrick, 5th Earl of Lichfield, was Fred's choice. I wanted to pick Michèle, but Fred was adamant. So was Ken. Clearly Annunziata – and a title – did something for the older man.) The crowning over, the girls left and I walked into the river.

There was plenty of coverage of the event in the next day's papers, including a centre spread in the *Daily Mirror* under the headline: 'AFTER PICKING THE BEAUTY CONTEST WINNER, THE JUDGE WALKED OFF IN A SORT OF DAZE.' There were six pictures: one of me and Annunziata, the rest of me in my dinner jacket walking straight into the river, submerging, disappearing . . .

> Young Brandreth looked into her eyes and, smitten, turned away in a daze. Seeing no more the wondrous woodland, smelling no more the scent of summer, he walked plumb into the river and vanished. Dashed pity, really. Such a promising lad.

At the end of term, Michèle and I went up to London to BBC Television Centre, where Fred met us and gave us lunch. He said he'd just seen the head of London Weekend Television, who wanted to give me my own show. (I wrote in my diary: 'This is not a hoax! And, if it happens, it will change everything.') He showed us the rushes of the Tynan film.

'You look good,' he said, 'but you're far too mannered and not at all modern.' He asked me what was top of the pops that week.

The answer was 'Jumpin' Jack Flash' from the Rolling Stones, but, of course, I had no idea.

He suggested I start reading *New Musical Express*.

I did try the *NME* for a couple of weeks. It was of no interest to me.

Michèle did her best to make me 'trendy', getting me to give up my favourite Rex Harrison cardigan for the sort of chamois-leather jacket Cliff Richard was wearing. She made me take my trousers to the tailor for tapering and my hair to Crimpers in Baker Street for styling. The makeover cost a small fortune, and it was pointless.

I looked a bit different, but I felt just the same.

In 1969, I returned to Television Centre, this time to see Paul Fox, Controller of BBC1. He was forty-five and a power in the land. I was twenty-one and wet behind the ears. (And they were ears that stuck out, too. Not as badly as Prince Charles's, but noticeably – according to Michèle. That's why I needed my hair cut and shaped to cover them.) Mr Fox was a large man, with a large office, and a large retinue of secretaries and assistants. He was treated like a god (as controllers of television channels still are) and had a touch of the Buddha about his appearance. Fred had told him he should see me, so there we were.

I tried not to burble too much, but I don't think I succeeded.

He said I should go to see Aubrey Singer, Head of Features, Television, and Christopher Brasher, Head of General Features, Television.

I asked him what was the difference between Features and General Features?

He laughed. 'I'm not sure. This is the BBC!' (Nothing has changed.) He gave me a drink and looked at me as if I was a slightly exotic creature somewhat alien to his world. He said, more than once, 'You are a very strong taste, you know – a very strong taste.'

Nevertheless, I got my own show: Saturday night, prime time, on ITV.

Frank Muir had gone to London Weekend as head of entertainment. He made it happen. The show was called *A Child of the Sixties* and featured me on a stool looking back at the 1960s as they came to an end and quizzing the great and the good of the day – including Iain Macleod, soon to be Chancellor of the Exchequer, Michael Foot, soon to be leader of the Labour Party, and Elizabeth Longford, historian and mother of Kevin Pakenham, the boy who had set me up on the wild goose chase to meet the TV producer who never was. (Revenge is a dish best served hot in front of an audience of ten million. 'You can write your own ticket in TV now, Gyles,' one paper declared on the morning after transmission. Another announced, 'Suddenly, a new Frost is born.')

The producer for my show, Peter Morley, was the real deal – which is why it worked. He came to me fresh from his BAFTA award-winning triumph with *The Life and Times of Lord Mountbatten*. He was serious and made me be serious, too. He treated me like a pro, so I behaved like one. He also treated me to lunch at L'Escargot in Greek Street and I loved that: a cold vichyssoise followed by roast duck and all the trimmings (£2).

Those were the days when media folk had long and liquid lunches in Soho – lighting up between courses and often smoking right through them. I became quite a regular at L'Escargot. I used to go there with my literary agent.

Oh, yes, while still a student at Oxford, I already had a literary agent in London – quite a distinguished one, too. Her name was Irene Josephy and her clients included the novelist Angela Carter, the poet Adrian Mitchell, the journalist Paul Foot, the stammering humourist Patrick Campbell – and me. She wrote to me out of the blue, having read about me in *The Times*. She was quite eccentric. She had steel-grey hair which she claimed never to wash: its natural oils kept it clean, she said. She wanted to represent me because I was a fellow Piscean and she sensed that, though I would have problems with my feet all my life, I had high prospects. She lived in Richmond with her husband, Eric, during the week. At the weekend she went to Brighton on her own. Her office consisted of a single upstairs room in Craven Street, by Charing Cross Station. It was a large room, with bare walls and bare floorboards. Irene sat at a small table in a corner by the window, reading manuscripts, making phone calls and sipping all day from a glass of gin and tap water.

Over the many years I was with Irene Josephy she gave me many lunches (she always paid) and showed me great kindness. (When Michèle and I bought our first flat, she advanced us £2,000 for the deposit – big bucks in those days.) On the day we first met, she entertained me at another of her Greek Street haunts, The Gay Hussar. It was the favourite haunt, too, of the left-wing establishment. While we were there Michael Foot and Tom Driberg walked through the restaurant on their way to one of the private dining rooms upstairs. We sat at a tiny table on creaking, rather uncomfortable old red velvet-covered chairs. The restaurant's owner, Victor, was Hungarian and told us what to eat: cold cherry soup, roast duck and stuffed cabbage – it was delicious. Whenever I had lunch with Irene I felt (as I often did in those days) that I was no longer me, but a character in somebody else's film.

After lunch, Irene would take me to the Colony Room, a private members' drinking club in Dean Street, nearby. It was an unappetising place: a small upstairs room (reached via a filthy staircase), with green walls and faded furniture, presided over by its founder, Irene's friend Muriel Belcher, who took to me because I was twenty. Her regulars – artists (Lucian Freud), writers (Dan Farson), professional Soho bohemians (Jeffrey Bernard) – took to me for the same reason, I suppose.

I remember Dan Farson (once a pretty boy, now bloated with drink) inviting me to lunch at Le Caprice to discuss our forebears: his great-uncle Bram Stoker had been a friend of my grandmother's cousin George R. Sims. Dan fell asleep over the starter. He stayed asleep throughout the meal. Eventually, I paid the bill and left.

I remember Francis Bacon, the artist, sitting at the bar at Muriel's, simply staring at me. Whenever anyone spoke to him, he'd say, 'Piss off, you cunt – I'm looking at the boy.'

I remember George Melly, the jazz singer, being very jolly and comparatively normal.

Through Irene I met an interestingly louche crowd. She had her favourites. I was one. Molly Parkin was another. Molly, when I met her for the first time, told me that she had just 'pleasured an entire Welsh rugby team', but added, with a theatrical wink from her over-mascaraed eyelashes, that she was 'always ready for more'.

Irene's set were hard drinkers – which I wasn't. And they had lived – which I hadn't. I realised that when Irene introduced me to the publisher Anthony Blond, who offered to pay me £5 a week to write a novel for him. I didn't think I had a story to tell.

But I did have a book I wanted to write – about prisons and prison reform. After one of the televised Union debates, out of the blue I got a telegram from a publisher – Robin Denniston of Hodder & Stoughton – offering me an advance of £500 to write the book of my choice. I called the book *Created in Captivity*. Whether it was a book anyone would want to read, I didn't stop to think. I was twenty-one and playing my life by the Beverley Nichols rule book. He had been President of the Union, editor of *Isis*, darling of the OUDS, and an author with a contract at twenty-one. So was I. And, like Beverley, I had magazine and newspaper columns, too – in *Honey*, in the *Daily Mirror*, in the *Manchester Evening News* ('Gyles Brandreth – has heart – will write – every Tuesday'). And I did better than Beverley because he turned twenty-one in 1919, before the advent of radio or television. At twenty-one I had my own TV show and I was popping up on the radio all the time.

I made my professional debut as a radio broadcaster on 12 May 1969, giving an Oxford undergraduate's take on women's rights in a short talk for *Woman's Hour*. It was an afternoon programme in those days, but I was bidden to arrive at Broadcasting House at 11.30 a.m., which I did. It then took thirty minutes to reach the studio. I had to be 'escorted' and my escort was an elderly commissionaire with the face of Charles Laughton and the gait of Richard III. The old boy moved incredibly slowly, dragging his lame foot behind him, sighing with every step, and losing his way at every turn – though he claimed to have been working at the BBC since before the war. When, eventually, I reached the *Woman's Hour* suite, half a dozen female heads turned in my direction accusingly. 'We were expecting you at eleven thirty,' said the producer tartly.

After the rehearsal – though the broadcast was live, every-thing was scripted, including the interviews – we adjourned to an adjacent room for a formal lunch, with waitress service and a strict seating plan. It was like eating at high table in a women's college, with Marjorie Anderson, the programme's presenter, presiding as the Warden. She was simultaneously gracious and terrifying. I was paid a fee of £10 plus £3 travel-ling expenses.

I did quite a few talks for *Woman's Hour*, where we took our-selves seriously. It was a tad jollier over at the *Today* programme where I was befriended by its original star presenter, Jack de Manio, who had won an MC and bar during the war and sur-vived a court martial, and consequently did not take anything too seriously. Fruity-voiced and jocular, de Manio was notori-ous for his inability to tell the time correctly. He was also a committed drinker. When I first appeared on the programme, we left Broadcasting House together at 9.00 a.m. and he took me around the corner to a pub off Great Portland Street that was officially closed but opened its doors just for him. He was coming up for sixty, though he seemed much older. He was great fun, did all the talking, and introduced me to the delights of the 9.00 a.m. champagne cocktail.

I was earning money and I needed it. I wasn't interested in it (I never have been), but I knew it was important. In the autumn of 1969, when I was President of the Oxford Union,

I went over to speak at the Cambridge Union, where the President was a lovely man called Hugh Anderson. I remember the night so vividly a) because Hugh was so nice, and b) because it was there that I met Neil Shand, scriptwriter to David Frost and Spike Milligan, among others. After the debate, in the bar, Shand took me by the shoulders and told me he needed to give me some career advice.

He said, 'You've got to decide, Gyles – are you going to be a £5,000-a-year man or a £10,000-a-year man. You can get to £5,000 a year and have a good life. Aim for £10,000 and it will kill you.'

Pa was then earning around £5,000 a year as a successful London solicitor. It was a lot, but it wasn't quite enough. He was behind with the rent, behind with my brother Ben's school fees, behind with my college fees, behind with . . . well, everything.

In late October 1969, Pa came to watch me doing my thing as President of the Union. He wrote to me afterwards, full of Pa-like congratulations: 'The way you handled the entire proceedings was perfect – all the right mixture of authority and tolerance, with shafts of wit and good humour. (And your tails looked fine too.)' But the real reason for his writing was this: 'Your wretched fees. The bank will not play, but since the fees are *in advance* it is possible the Bursar will allow deferred payment. I have had to do this in the past with school fees.' Poor Pa. He had more than £500 in outstanding bills and didn't know which way to turn: 'I am so sorry to involve you in what for me has been a lifetime of money anxieties.'

I will sort it, I thought to myself. I wrote in my diary:

I will go to see the Bursar. I have money coming in from *Honey* (£47 5s. 0d. for each Luke Jarvis), £100 for the piece I have done for Michael Wynn-Jones at the *Mirror* magazine and between now and Christmas I should get a total of £875 from London Weekend TV for *A Child of the Sixties*. It will be fine.

It wasn't. On Thursday 20 November 1969, I reported to my diary:

I went to see the Bursar this morning and explained the desperate position to him. He was sympathetic, but said there was really no question of us phasing payment over a period of time. I have written to Pa. What I save from my London Weekend fee, I will use for my day-to-day expenses between now and June – food, fares, clothes, etc. I am not going to be able to earn much from January because I will be studying for Finals. If Pa can find a way of raising a loan to cover the fees, I should at least be able to pay the interest for him. I will also make what other gestures I can – e.g. paying the next quarter's phone bill. I wish I could wave a magic wand and solve it, but I can't.

That's what I learnt while I was at Oxford. There is no magic wand in this life. Survival in this world depends entirely on hard graft, good housekeeping – and luck.

Back home that Christmas, we went on a family outing to the cinema to see the latest film adaptation of *David Copperfield*. I wanted to see it because my hero and new friend Michael Redgrave was playing Mr Peggotty. Pa wanted to see it because Sir Ralph Richardson was portraying Mr Micawber – and Micawber was, without doubt, Pa's favourite Dickens character. Micawber has the famous line, which Pa knew by heart and often repeated because it summed up the story of his life:

Annual income twenty pounds, annual expenditure nineteen six, result happiness. Annual income twenty pounds, annual expenditure twenty pound ought and six, result misery.

22. 'The television star'

I didn't just work while I was at Oxford. I played, too. I went to Pimm's parties and college balls. I took Michèle punting on the River Isis – and fell in. I bought her books, I sent her telegrams, I took her out for meals. We had a favourite place: Tackley's on the High Street, where everything – from the veal cutlets to the banana fritters – was cooked at the table. I can still smell the oil from the little stove that was trundled over to our table on a rickety trolley covered with a pale pink table cloth. The two waiters (Hungarians, I think) took a shine to us and made us feel very special. I think they liked us because we came so often and were young and obviously in love. At least, I was obviously in love. Michèle was still biding her time.

Once, I took her to the most expensive restaurant in Oxford (the Elizabeth) and couldn't believe it when the waiter showing us to our table laid a napkin across my lap and slowly squeezed my genitals as he did so. Even more incredible was the bill: it came to just over £5. I had never paid so much for a meal. We had the *carré d'agneau dauphinoise* for two – thirty shillings! The occasion was our six-month anniversary, and the evening was a total disaster. It started at the cinema. We went to see the latest Hammer horror: *Dracula Has Risen from the Grave*. I thought it might have Michèle jumping into my arms. Instead, it had her hiding under her seat. (To this day, she doesn't do menace. Watching *Midsomer Murders*, the moment the cellos start to play, she's covering her face with a tea towel.)

I had gone to Oxford to study PPE. The politics I could manage; the philosophy was incomprehensible; the economics way beyond me. After two terms, they let me switch to history and modern languages – softer stuff and more my style. There were lots of lectures on offer, but I don't remember going to many of those. Tutorials, however, were mandatory – and amazing. Beyond belief, really.

Oxford's core system of teaching was – and is – based around weekly hour-long conversations between two or three students and their subject tutor. That's it. At the beginning of term, you'd go to the tutor's room, you'd sit in an armchair, you'd have a glass of sherry, and you'd discuss the subject in hand. The tutor would give you an essay to go away and write, and a week later you'd come back and read it out loud to him. Or explain that you hadn't quite had the time to finish it properly because you were appearing in a play, or editing the student newspaper, or wooing a girl who was playing hard to get – in which case, in my case, he'd suggest some poems by Baudelaire that might offer consolation or inspiration or both.

With each of your tutors you would spend a total of seven to eight hours a term. In my experience, they were all dazzlingly brilliant eccentrics, none more so than Theodore Zeldin, who looked like a cartoon of a crazed Russian conductor and whose way with words was breathtaking. He told me, 'I value conversations which are meetings on the borderline of what I understand and what I don't, with people who are different from myself.' I was certainly nothing like him. He got his first degree from London University, aged seventeen; at Oxford, soon after, he secured a double first; he was reckoned by many to be the cleverest man in Europe – 'a modern Balzac', 'the new de La Bruyère', 'unquestionably a genius'. I never got close to the border of understanding what he was saying, but I relished simply being in his presence. It was like having a weekly audience with a slightly unhinged wizard.

My history tutorials with Zeldin were one to one. I shared my French tutorials with another student, my friend Anthony Palliser. This was challenging because Anthony spoke perfect French and I didn't (his grandfather had been Prime Minister of Belgium, remember), but it was life-enhancing, too, because our tutor, Alex de Jonge, though only ten years older than us, seemed to know everything that could be known about life, love and French literature, and he shared it with us *con brio*, while pacing around his study with a riding crop in one hand and a glass of white wine in the other. (He knew everything about Russian literature, too, and later wrote the definitive biography of Rasputin.) Alex had the look of Lord Byron and the swashbuckling style of the Count of Monte Cristo. I recall coming out of hall with him one night after dinner when he was in his cups. Elegantly, effortlessly, he tumbled from the top of the flight of stone steps leading to the quadrangle thirty feet below, rolling head over heels all the way down, and picking himself up at the bottom quite unharmed, carrying on his conversation all the while.

In my final year, my history tutor was the great Richard Cobb, Fellow of Balliol, later Professor of Modern History at Oxford, and the *world* authority on the French Revolution. Cobb's claim to fame was looking at history from the people's perspective – not viewing it from the top down (from state papers) but from the bottom up (the testimony of peasants). Having been told how fortunate I was to have him as my tutor – and for one-to-one sessions, too – I turned up for my first tutorial in good time, and slightly apprehensive.

I found his staircase. I climbed the stairs. I stood on the landing outside his room and checked my watch. Just as the Balliol clock struck the half-hour I raised my hand to knock on the door – and then I heard him, inside the room.

He was bellowing at the top of his voice. 'What the bloody hell have you done with it? Damn and blast your eyes! Where the hell is it?'

I stepped back, not sure what to do.

The shouting got fiercer. 'You are so bloody, *bloody* stupid!' His rage was mounting. 'For Christ's sake, where have you put it? God, how I despise you!' He paused. 'And where the hell's my pupil?'

I knocked on the door. Suddenly, I heard a crash. It sounded as though he had heaved a great pile of books on to the floor.

Then the voice rose to a great crescendo of fury. 'Where the fuck is he?'

I knocked again.

'Come!' he called.

I turned the handle, pushed open the door and found him standing in the middle of his study, pale-faced, wild-eyed, hair all dishevelled, books and papers scattered pell-mell on the floor around him. He appeared to be alone. There was a door beyond him that led, presumably, to his bedroom. Had the other pupil taken refuge in there?

'Ah, yes, good . . .' he mumbled, beckoning me into the room. 'You must be, er . . .'

'Brandreth, yes. Am I disturbing you?'

'No, no. Find a seat. Move those books. I was expecting you. You're late.'

'I'm sorry,' I faltered. 'I thought you had someone with you.'

'No, no. I was talking to myself. I couldn't find a document I needed. Now what did you say your name was?'

'Brandreth.'

'Oh, yes,' he smiled. He had a small, round face, the colour of rust-red Tudor brick, and small, round spectacles like Billy Bunter. 'The "television star",' he chuckled. 'Shall we have a glass of wine?'

He drank copiously – at ten thirty in the morning. We got on at once and became firm friends. I had assumed he was mocking me when he called me the 'television star'. Not so. He was teasing, certainly, but he was not scornful. In fact, he took a keen interest in my burgeoning television career and when he found I had to go to London quite regularly for meetings, he volunteered to join me and give me my French Revolution tutorials on the train. We did our work in the buffet car so that he could have a beaker (or two) of wine while he ran me through the fiscal disorders of the *Ancien Régime*. If we had to change trains at Reading, we'd look in at the platform buffet to find another beaker (or two) of wine there.

Despite doing alarmingly little work, thanks to the guidance of Cobb, de Jonge and Zeldin, I secured a respectable degree: 'a good second'.

Pa had got a third, so that was all right.

My final examinations finished on the day before the 1970 General Election. On election day itself, Thursday 18 June, I took the train up to London, first thing, to vote – and to get my hair cut and styled at Crimpers – and then came straight back to Oxford to make a brief television appearance outside the Oxford Union before returning to London to be interviewed by Robin Day in the BBC Election Studio at White City for a proper fee: £35 plus £6 expenses. Jack Straw (then twenty-three and President of the National Union of Students) and I were the chosen representatives of British youth. (I remember wondering at the time which of us would become Home Secretary first.)

Backstage at Television Centre, I marvelled at the chaotic comings and goings and the sense of bewilderment mixed with hysteria in every corner that the election result was not what they had expected or planned for. They were all set for another Labour victory for Harold Wilson and, suddenly, had to change tack. The final result: Conservatives, 330 seats; Labour, 288; Liberals, 6; Others, 6. My friend Iain Macleod (well, he had appeared on my TV show that Christmas) was set to become Chancellor of the Exchequer. My hero Ted Heath was the new Prime Minister.

I had already met Ted, briefly and memorably, in Oxford the year before. He came to a sherry party at New College to which I was invited. I wasn't feeling too well and shouldn't have gone, but I did. I arrived at the last minute and joined the end of the presentation line just as the great man was being brought down it. As he shook my hand and heaved his shoulders, I heaved mine and threw up all over his brown suede shoes.

Years later, we became friends – not that anyone, I think, got very close to Ted. I went to see him in Salisbury quite often. Michèle sometimes came, too. She liked him. He liked her. With one notable exception, he seemed to enjoy the company of intelligent, slightly combative women. (He never *ever* mentioned Margaret Thatcher by name, but I never saw him without him making an oblique, disparaging reference to her. She was an obsession with him.) He was a generous host and told good stories. Churchill, de Gaulle, Adenauer, Khrushchev, Kennedy – he'd known them all.

He seemed to have a particular soft spot for dictators. He spoke of Chairman Mao almost as a hero and he counted Fidel Castro as a personal friend. 'Do you like my orchids?' he'd ask. 'Fidel gave me those. Would you like a Cuban cigar? Fidel always sends a box at Christmas.'

Ted died in 2005, old, overweight, a tad curmudgeonly to the last, but content that his place in history was assured. He was the man who took us into Europe. He signed the Treaty of Accession in Brussels, on 22 January 1972. 'It was the proudest moment of my life,' he said. 'There's no turning back,' he told me. He was wrong.

On 23 June 2016, his life's work was undone when Britain voted to leave the European Union and, around the same time, unforgivably, his personal reputation was all but ruined when police gave credence to unsubstantiated accusations of child abuse and satanic ritual murder made against him. On his one hundredth birthday, 9 July 2016, because no one else seemed available, I went down to his house in Salisbury to cut the birthday cake and propose a toast to his memory.

Everything that my life has been about began at Oxford: politics, theatre, public speaking, publishing, journalism, radio, TV, Michèle.

'You haven't really evolved very much in fifty years, have you, Gyles?' says Michèle.

I suppose not. What I'm doing now is exactly what I was doing then. Oxford is where my life's course was set. It's where I met my heroes and my role models.

I met David Frost at the Union, when I was twenty and he was twenty-nine. Later, off and on, for over forty years, I worked with him – at TV-am, at the BBC, at Al Jazeera – until he died. At that first encounter, what struck me was his pasty face and poor complexion. As I got to know him, I came to admire his energy, his chutzpah, his capacity for work, and his easy good humour, all sustained by quantities of white wine. When he had TV shows in the USA and the UK simultaneously, he got into the habit of keeping himself going in different time zones with pills to pep him up and calm him down. I remember the morning he arrived at TV-am in his Bentley, comatose, with no more than five minutes before he was due on air. His alarm had woken him, but instead of taking his two wake-up pills he had inadvertently given himself two sleeping tablets. We carted him to make-up, covered his head with cold wet towels and forced black coffee down his throat. I steered him unsteadily into the studio and lowered him on to the sofa.

The floor manager called, 'Cue titles, cue music . . .'

David sat back abruptly and opened his bloodshot eyes. 'A *joy*, Gyles,' he cried, 'an absolute *joy!*'

The floor manager began the countdown. 'Ten, nine, eight . . .'

David leant over to me and squeezed my knee. 'Isn't this wonderful?' he exclaimed. 'Aren't we blessed?'

'Five, four, three, two . . .'

'I'm on!' he cried, exultant, and turned to the camera exactly on cue. 'Hello, good morning, and welcome . . .'

I tried to learn from his example: he was nice to everyone he met, and he had the gift of being able to make disappointment and failure disappear simply by ignoring them. He was such a success because he was wholly hands-on. If he wanted you to be a guest on his show, he didn't get a researcher or producer to ask you: he called you himself.

Another workaholic hero I first met at the Union was Peter Hall, the original director of *Waiting for Godot*, the founder of the Royal Shakespeare Company and the man who took over from Laurence Olivier at the National Theatre. I last saw him when we had lunch together at a fish restaurant by the Old Vic. It was a good lunch: *moules* with salmon and Pernod for starters; then Dover sole, with a rocket and parmesan cheese salad on the side; plus a glass or two of Chablis. (Peter was a greedy eater. So was David Frost. According to Michèle, so am I.)

Peter was seventy but working as hard as ever. 'Is it bad to be a workaholic?' he asked as the waitress mopped up the Pernod sauce that was cascading down his beard and jacket. 'Is it wrong? Isn't it a great blessing to know what you want to do and to have the passion that makes you do it? I don't want to pause. I want to keep moving. I have always striven to be booked up so I can go briskly from one job to the next. I am a director: each day I want to direct; not wait for the phone to ring, or meditate on my failings.'

Peter went on working, too, because he needed the money. He had four wives, five children and a lot of school fees to pay. (He sent most of his offspring to Bedales.)

'The other day,' he said, 'my youngest daughter, Emma – she's seven – asked me, "Papa, why do you split up with all your wives?" I said, "Darling, for me, if it isn't all right, somehow it is all wrong."'

'I know what my wife would say, Peter,' I told him, 'because she says it about me. You're a narcissist. It's all about *you*, about what *you* want. Your work, your ambition have always come first. Your wives have had to accept that.'

'Yes,' he said, with a wan smile. 'In the beginning they always say they understand, they won't mind, they can manage. But in the end . . .'

Fanny Cradock told me if you want to make your marriage work, share your work with your marriage partner whenever you can. Over the years, on the whole, Michèle and I have been lucky enough to do that – in the theatre, in publishing, in TV, even in politics.

I met Fanny Cradock at Oxford, too, of course. Do you remember her? For twenty years, from 1955 to 1975, she was the nation's most celebrated (and parodied) television chef. She usually appeared in a ball gown (in the kitchen!) and always accompanied by her monocled and apparently henpecked husband, Johnnie – the man best remembered for turning to the camera at the end of one of their programmes to say, 'I hope all your doughnuts turn out like Fanny's.'

For my final debate as President of the Oxford Union, I wanted guest speakers who were larger than life – and I got them. When Fanny arrived and stepped out of her huge Rolls-Royce, I was startled to find she had no eyebrows. They had been burnt off, she told me, in a freak fire. She had drawn-on eyebrows, absurdly arched, orange lipstick *around* her lips, and a voice like a foghorn – but I loved her, and so did the Union. Johnnie was with her, naturally – and wearing his monocle. He didn't say much, but I noticed how he kept an eye on her at all times. She was quite nervous before she spoke, but once she stood up and heard the crowd roar she was away – and brilliant.

Only an old pro like Robert Morley (one of my favourite actors and one of the best Oscar Wildes) could have followed her – and he did, with considerable style. Over dinner he told me, 'It is a great help for a man to be in love with himself – for an actor it is absolutely essential.' In the debate he warmed to his theme. 'To fall in love with yourself is the first secret of happiness,' he explained. 'Then if you're not a good mixer you can always fall back on your own company.' It was a very funny, very happy evening. (Even my speech went well!) And it led to many more funny, happy evenings.

The Cradocks were good company and generous hosts. They lived in some style in a Grade II listed house in Hertfordshire, with nine ovens in the kitchen and a galaxy of star vintages in the cellar. I remember going for what Fanny called a 'light supper' with them one evening. As we arrived, our hostess was waiting for us with huge dishes of strawberries and thick yellow cream in the drawing room as Johnnie emerged from the cellar bearing a cobweb-covered magnum of 1949 champagne. We moved to the dining room to eat: caviar in sour cream, quails' eggs, lamb sweetbreads in cream with raw broad beans, followed by the richest chocolate cake in the history of the world – all washed down with a '52 red Burgundy and a white wine whose origin I didn't catch. Johnnie explained that, with a good wine, however much you drink, you don't get a hangover.

That night the other guests were an Admiral Ross and a Lady Calley. Fanny announced that we were her 'four closest friends', though I don't think any of us had met her more than half a dozen times. Johnnie beamed benevolently as Fanny prattled on: tales of her three husbands ('*Husbands*, mark you – I marry my men!'), her first child ('I was just fifteen, my dear – that's all. I knew *nothing* of the world!'), her second husband ('A disciple of the Marquis de Sade! And we all know what that involves – don't we, Admiral?'). She was outrageous ('A woman had a child at seventy-two – it is a *fact*, medical history says so') but completely endearing. Fanny's father – a gambler and a bankrupt, according to Fanny – was a prolific novelist, under a variety of pseudonyms. In the 1970s, Fanny wrote a series of historical romances herself, *The Lormes of Castle Rising*, and named her hero Gyles, after me.

If everyone has a secret, Fanny had many. She had four husbands, not three, and wasn't married to Johnnie until 1977, though she claimed to have married him in 1942. At least one of her marriages was bigamous, and when she and Johnnie did eventually wed, she gave her age on the marriage certificate as fifty-five, though her eldest son was almost fifty at the time. She had two sons and fell out with both of them. Eventually – because she took uppers and downers to cope with her mood swings and became increasingly impossible when she was on a high – she went too far on TV, casting sarcastic aspersions on the culinary efforts of a hapless member of the public. The work went, the fame faded, the money ran out, and Johnnie died. By the time Fanny died, in 1994, the only friends she could rely on were two kindly boys from a local restaurant.

It was at Fanny Cradock's Christmas party in 1969, when I was twenty-one and still at Oxford, that I first met Nicholas Parsons. We were friends for fifty years. With his affability, versatility, consummate professionalism and lifelong appetite for work, he was certainly a role model. To get him to go to a surprise ninetieth birthday party at the BBC, I had to pretend I was taking him to meet the Controller of Radio 4, to pitch an idea for a new series. He was happy to be given the surprise party, but quite annoyed that he couldn't pitch the new idea. In his nineties, we filmed *Celebrity Antiques Road Trip* together and he insisted on doing all the driving. In his ninety-sixth year he was still hosting *Just a Minute* and, to the very last, at the top of his game.

I reckon I must have appeared on almost every TV or radio panel game ever invented, from *Call My Bluff* to *Michael McIntyre's The Wheel*, from *Celebrity Squares* to *Pointless Celebrities*, from *Blankety Blank* to *QI*. I am not sure that's been a good use of my life, but I am sure that *Just a Minute* is my favourite. Why? Because the show is spontaneous and the only one recorded in real time. When you take part in *Have I Got News For You*, for example, they record for two and a half hours and edit it down to twenty-eight minutes. With *Just a Minute* it's 'as live'. There may be a nip or tuck to the links between the rounds, but the games themselves are broadcast as they happened, against the clock. That unforgiving minute is timed to the second. That's what provides the players with the adrenalin rush and gives the show its energy.

When *Just a Minute* was first broadcast in 1967, Clement Freud was on the original panel. I met him first at Oxford as well. He was famous in those days as a television chef, with a lugubrious manner, best known for appearing in commercials promoting dog food and for saying, 'If you give up smoking, drinking and sex, you don't actually live longer, it just seems longer.' When he came to the Union, we thought he was the funniest man we had ever heard. He had a unique style of delivery, dry and beautifully controlled, and a witty, acerbic turn of phrase. I remember him saying, 'Breakfast is a notoriously difficult meal to serve with a flourish.' When he was older he had another favourite line, 'I used to ask women to come upstairs and have sex, but now it has to be one or the other.' That joke does not seem so amusing today. In 2016, seven years after his death, three women accused him of child sexual abuse and rape, accusations which led to a police investigation and a public apology from his widow.

I knew nothing of the allegations made against him, but I knew him, off and on, for over forty years. Certainly, he made you laugh, but he also, always, made you feel a bit uneasy – and seemed to relish doing so. When I was an aspiring Conservative MP and he was an established Liberal one, he invited me to lunch a few times. We went to a smart out-of-the-way restaurant of his choice. I paid for the taxi. His conversation was interesting, gossipy and informed, but now and then he would throw in a line deliberately designed to disconcert me. He would watch me struggle for a moment, amused. And, at the end of the meal, when the bill arrived, although he was nominally the host, he would suggest a little gambling game. It involved making a calculated guess relating to the bill. Whoever lost the gamble would pick up the tab. I wish I could remember how it worked, because, needless to say, I always fell for it – and Clement always won.

He needed to win. He played to win. And never more so than when taking part in *Just a Minute*. Over the years, playing the game, Kenneth Williams completed more uninterrupted minutes than Freud – speaking non-stop for sixty seconds, without repetition, hesitation or deviation – but Freud was the most frequent winner by a margin. His principal tactic was to carefully watch the clock and then interrupt when there was only a second or so to go, and thus claim the prize at the finishing line.

Some of his other tactics were less subtle. I joined the programme as an occasional panellist in the early 1980s and sat next to Clement at the recordings. He would attempt to throw me off my stride by whispering friendly advice just as he sensed I was about to press my buzzer. And once, when I was about to move ahead of him in the game, he deliberately knocked my glass of water into my lap. I am reasonably competitive myself, but I was certainly outclassed.

Nicholas and Clement had been contemporaries at St Paul's School, in London, in the 1930s. For some reason (some mishap during a school athletics race, I seem to recall), Clement considered Nicholas beyond the pale and, audibly, said so, week in, week out, in the margins of the show. 'The man's a cunt – you must agree?'

We didn't. We just moved away.

Nicholas endured it with good grace, simply saying, 'It's just Clement.' It was, indeed, just Clement.

He never mentioned either of his brothers and only rarely (and reluctantly) referred to his grandfather, Sigmund Freud. Once or twice, I tried to get him to talk about his family background. He cut me off instantly. When it came to conversation – and everything else, I now see – he had to be the one in control. He had a pathological hatred of smoking and would not allow himself anywhere near a smoker of any kind.

As the years went by, I continued to see him, sometimes

around Westminster, more regularly recording episodes of *Just a Minute*. In front of the microphone, his wit appeared undimmed, but, before and after the show, in the green room, or at the hotel, I noticed he kept less company with the rest of us. He often ate alone. We were uncomfortable with him and he was uncomfortable with us. I always thought he was an odd one. I believe we all did. It seems it was darker than we realised.

Happily, more than fifty years after first meeting Nicholas and Clement, I am still taking part in *Just a Minute*, as a regular guest and occasional host. Both my radio and my TV career, such as they've been, began at Oxford – and the sort of programmes I'm doing now are exactly the sort of programmes I was doing then.

The first documentary film I fronted was in 1970 and marked the eight hundredth anniversary of the murder of Thomas Becket in Canterbury Cathedral, on 29 December 1170. It was *exactly* like an extended version of the kind of film report I make for the BBC's *The One Show*, half a century on. The highlights of our film were my interview with the then Archbishop of Canterbury, the bushy-eyebrowed Michael Ramsey, and the virtuoso violinist Yehudi Menuhin, playing unaccompanied Bach on the very spot in the cathedral where it is believed Becket died.

The filming was memorable for one reason only: it was the only time in my life that I have held a Stradivarius violin. It belonged to Yehudi Menuhin. When he arrived, the Archbishop and I were waiting for him at the top of the steps leading to the cathedral crypt. He was carrying the violin in a case handcuffed to his wrist.

'The insurance people insist,' he explained. 'It is a very rare Stradivarius.'

'Oh, how exciting,' I exclaimed as the maestro unlocked the handcuff, opened the case and, with appropriate veneration and care, took out his violin.

'It – is – *beautiful*,' I gushed.

'And it has a beautiful tone,' said Menuhin. 'I love it very much.'

'May I hold it a moment?' I asked.

'By all means,' said Menuhin. He had a quiet, gentle manner that was infinitely courteous. 'But be careful,' he added, as he handed me the precious instrument.

I took it with both hands. 'My, my,' I murmured appreciatively. 'Have you seen this, Your Grace?' I said to the Archbishop, who was standing a few steps away. 'To think I'm holding Yehudi Menuhin's Stradivarius!'

I must have turned to face Dr Ramsey with a touch too much youthful exuberance, because, as I turned, the instrument flew swiftly and easily out of my hands. I made to catch it and, as I did so, tilted the edge and sent it spinning gracefully towards the crypt. It bounced its way elegantly – and audibly – down the ancient stone stairway and landed, with a crash, at the foot of the steps, not more than a yard from the very spot where Becket had been murdered.

Menuhin's many years of meditation had been but a preparation for this moment in his life. He did not offer a word of reproach. He closed his eyes for a second and took a deep and deliberate breath. Then, quite calmly, he walked down the stone steps to retrieve his broken violin.

Carefully, he inspected the instrument. 'I think I'll have to use the other one,' he said quietly.

'You have another violin with you then?' asked the Archbishop, perhaps suddenly sensing that the age of miracles had not passed.

'Yes,' said Menuhin, 'it's in the car.'

'Let me get it for you,' I volunteered.

Briefly, his face did seem to twitch. 'Er, no, I'll fetch it myself. Thank you, all the same.' As he turned to walk back towards his car, he smiled at me. 'Don't worry,' he said. 'These things happen.'

Yehudi Menuhin was a good man. And generous. He left much of his musical archive to the Royal Academy of Music, and if you visit their museum in London's Marylebone Road you will find the Stradivarius I dropped now on display there. It has been well repaired: the damage barely shows.

The truth is I'm cack-handed and not to be trusted with anything precious. Filming at the British Museum once, I was allowed to inspect the original manuscript of *De Profundis*, the letter that Oscar Wilde wrote from the depths of his despair during his imprisonment in Reading Gaol. In another moment of excessive exuberance, I managed to spill a drop of coffee on to the priceless manuscript.

'Oh dear,' said the curator, with immense forbearance. 'We'll just have to pretend it's one of Oscar's tears.'

23. I said yes

When I left school and university, all the things I had been doing in those little worlds I simply went on doing in a slightly larger one. It never occurred to me to get a job. Apart from my five years as a member of parliament in my forties and my ten weeks in the railway reservations department of Thomas Cook & Son, aged fifteen, I have always been self-employed. Yes, I am doing now what I have always done, though possibly to less effect.

My first TV show in 1969 was at prime time on Saturday night. I have not known that since. My first book signing, soon after, was at Selfridges and the line of shoppers stretched from the table where I was sitting in the book department, through the food department, out into Baker Street and around the corner into Oxford Street. There was a reason for that. I was sharing the table with another first-time author: the actress Sophia Loren. She sold more than a thousand copies of her autobiography that day. I sold eleven copies of my book about prisons: four to my mother, four to my father, two to the deputy manager of the Selfridges book department for customers who, apparently, had especially asked him to put them by; and, yes, one to Sophia Loren.

When I left Oxford in 1970, I didn't go home to live because I no longer had a home to go to. My parents had to leave their flat off Baker Street. The lease had expired and the landlords weren't inclined to extend it. Ma's Montessori nursery school was doing well, but the arrival and departure of a dozen and more lively toddlers every morning and afternoon, with push-chairs cluttering up the hallway and nannies and parents failing to shut the lift gates properly, was annoying the neighbours. It was time to move on. Pa was strapped for cash, of course, so while he looked for another flat they could afford, he and Ma and my brother Ben moved into that single room in the faded Bayswater hotel, while Michèle and I began our life together, renting a one-bedroomed flat in a 1930s block in Muswell Hill.

I'd always assumed I'd start out in an apartment in Piccadilly, if not a mansion flat in Baker Street, but Michèle explained – with a patience that has been sorely tested but has never faltered in fifty years – that that would be madness. 'We'll rent cheaply now,' she said firmly, 'save up and buy a flat when we can.' And so it was.

Our little place in Muswell Hill cost £9 a week, all in. I don't think we've ever been happier. We had furniture from my parents' flat, including the upright piano that neither of us could play and their sitting-room sofa that opened up into a not-very-comfortable bed. We shared our bedroom with a little mouse who turned up on our third night and whom I managed to trap in an upturned colander at 3.00 a.m. We had a galley kitchen, with a tiny fridge where we kept our half-bottles of Barsac. (We didn't know that Barsac is a pudding wine: we loved it with our fish fingers and baked beans on toast – then, and still, my signature dish.) For some reason, inexplicable now, we painted two of the walls of the sitting room bright purple.

We were very happy and very busy. The various TV people we had met at Oxford all liked Michèle and all offered her work. (It's not surprising really: she was young, brilliant and beautiful.) For several years through her early twenties she worked in television – as a presenter with a BBC children's science series in Bristol, as an interviewer on daytime chat shows (they were a novelty then) in London and Birmingham, as a reporter for *This Week in Britain* travelling all over the country, as a continuity announcer with the BBC in Manchester. She didn't stop, but I don't think she found much of it much fun.

I was making programmes for the BBC in Manchester, too, and would sometimes sit on the floor in the corner of the tiny, self-operating studio watching in awe as Michèle closed down BBC1 in the North-West for the night. At least she could say she was the first woman to read the news on BBC TV.

Of course, it was only the local news. As the news editor explained to her: 'We can't have a woman reading the proper news. People wouldn't take it seriously. People wouldn't believe it.'

A few years later, in 1974, Angela Rippon became the BBC's first national female newsreader.

In June 1973, three years out of Oxford, five years to the week after we met, Michèle and I got married. We did not tell anyone. That was our secret.

We tied the knot at 11.45 on a sunny Friday morning at St Marylebone Register Office in the Marylebone Road, where Paul McCartney had married Linda, in 1969, and my parents were married, back in 1937. Unlike Ma and Pa, we knew we had to take witnesses. Ours were my friend Simon, and Michèle's friend Veronica. It was, if I may say so, a perfect wedding.

We kept it quite secret. I didn't even make a note of it in my diary. I simply circled the date. A month before, I gave the required 'notice' and made a down payment on the marriage licence of £1. We paid the balance of £2 on the day. At the beginning of the week we realised we needed a ring. We went to Hampstead to get one because it was a part of town where we knew no one, and then were completely thrown on entering the jeweller's shop to find we were being served by Donald Sinden's son Marc. We did not tell him what the ring was for – and he didn't ask.

On the great day I wore my light grey suit with the dark grey stripe. (It's in the wardrobe still, next to the Simon Dee hanger.) Michèle wore a black cotton outfit with little pink flowers on it. Veronica wore a hat. (Well, it was a wedding – someone had to.) I dropped the ring. We were all nervous. After the ceremony, Simon drove us to our favourite posh restaurant, The Empress in Berkeley Square. (In those days you could park freely in the Marylebone Road and Berkeley Square.) We sat right in the centre of the dining room and had champagne cocktails, salmon roulade, beef Wellington, and strawberries and cream. (One of our favourite actors, John Le Mesurier, happened to be at the adjoining table. We liked that.) After lunch, Simon drove us out to Heathrow and saw us on to the 17.35 flight to Rome for our two-night honeymoon in the splendour of the Hotel Napoleon, Piazza Vittorio Emanuele. On the Sunday morning, before flying home, we walked to the Vatican where we saw the Pope in St Peter's Square. He was very small and up on his balcony, but he was there and waving. We felt our marriage had been blessed.

We were going to telephone our parents from Rome to tell them our news, but, in the end, we didn't. We were too tired. We decided we would let them know in due course – which we did, two years later, in 1975, when our son, Benet, was born. We didn't want them to think he was a bastard.

In my parents' day if you wanted to sleep together you got married first. And my parents got married in secret because they knew their parents would not have approved of their union and would have tried to stop it. Michèle and I had no such excuse. My parents liked Michèle a lot, and I think her parents quite liked me, and they knew we were living together – 'living in sin', as it was still called. So why didn't we tell them we were getting married? They would have wanted to know. They would have loved to be there. At the time, I justified our behaviour by saying to myself, 'We didn't get married for *them*, we got married for *us*.' But I feel bad about it now. It was unkind, it was thoughtless, it was selfish.

I *was* selfish. And totally self-absorbed. I can illustrate the point – quite literally. At the start of the 1970s, I knew the young Terry Pratchett (of course I did: I knew everybody) and in 1971, when we were both twenty-two, he drew a small cartoon of me. You can find it among the illustrations, and it tells its own story.

I feel bad about my blind egocentricity now – and the casual cruelty of not telling my parents about my marriage – but I feel worse about something else. Throughout my twenties I was wantonly squandering all that my parents had so lovingly poured into me.

They gave me everything they could – and more. On my twenty-first birthday they gave me £21, which they couldn't afford. Pa also bought tickets for a family outing to the Theatre Royal, Drury Lane, to see a matinée of *Mame* with Ginger Rogers. It's not a great show (only one hit song) and Miss Rogers was no longer in her prime. Looking like a mature Sugar Plum Fairy, her 'dancing' involved her standing a little unsteadily centre stage, with her right arm raised high and her left foot gently tapping the floor just about in time to the music. But she was a legend all the same and my parents knew how much I liked to collect those.

Post-*Mame* we made our way to the Singing Chef restaurant in Connaught Street where a special birthday feast with a regional French flavour was served: *Anniversaire de Gyles: Alpes Maritimes.*

I had the *pâté de foie de volaille*, then the *oeufs mimosa*, followed by the *gigot rôti à l'amiral* with *ris au saffron* and *ratatouille Niçoise*. There was salad, cheese and a *pièce montée* (meringue and cream and chocolate mousse) to accompany the ritual singing of 'Happy birthday to you'. Michèle had volunteered to do a meal at the flat, but Ma was keen to go out, so we did. I was conscious of the cost. So was Pa. As I type this, I am looking at the menu that everybody signed that night and I see that my father signed it: 'Charles (Poor Papa!)'.

Alongside that menu, I have come across something perhaps more relevant to the business in hand: from Bonn, a letter from my godfather, John Paice. I don't think I had seen him or thought about him since reading *Lolita* when we stayed with him on holiday when I was twelve. I don't remember thinking his letter anything special then, but it strikes me as quite interesting now.

> *Some vague non-conformist strain in my background urges me to take a 'high moral ground' with the young, but I know so much about your parents, your environment, your interests and the demands of the world in which you will I hope live for at least another seventy years that I can only say I wish you a sense of vocation and purpose in what you do. It is probably too much to hope for happiness – at least for long periods.*
>
> *I've experienced no little pride in being your godfather – not just because you get your name in the papers – but just because I see you as the product of so much love and sacrifice and warmth (as well as the inheritor of so many gifts) that I have every reason to know pride – in what you've already accomplished and in what lies ahead.*

So much 'love and sacrifice and warmth' over twenty-one years – and what was I doing?

Whatever came along, really – regardless.

Why?

Why not? I was too busy being busy to think about a sense of *vocation* and *purpose*.

Dear reader, have you had a sense of purpose and vocation in your life? What were you doing in your early twenties?

I was writing books. I was making TV programmes. I was hosting my first panel show on Radio 4. It was called *A Rhyme in Time* and starred Cyril Fletcher, the prince of Odd Odes, Graeme Garden from *The Goodies*, and my childhood favourite from *Take It From Here*, June Whitfield.

I was revisiting my childhood enthusiasms – *Alice in Wonderland* high among them. I invented an *Alice in Wonderland* board game; I produced an *Alice in Wonderland* diary; I wrote a play about Lewis Carroll for Cyril Fletcher to star in (it wasn't very good and he never quite learnt the lines) and scripted a version of *Through the Looking-Glass* for him to appear in on TV.

At Temple Newsam House near Leeds I produced a *son et lumière* show (like the one I'd seen in Switzerland when I was sixteen) with my friend Sir Michael Redgrave in the lead. (It didn't go too well, either. The audience sat in tiered seating under a corrugated iron roof. It was August in Yorkshire, so we had anticipated rain – but not hail. The noise of the hail-stones clattering down on to the roof made several performances completely inaudible.) The next year I put on another *son et lumière* – this time at Royal Greenwich, with Sir John Gielgud and Sir Alec Guinness in the cast. (Anticipating hail, we covered the seating with a tarpaulin roof. On the night Edward Heath came to see the show, bringing the Prime Minister of Spain with him, a gale lifted the tarpaulin from its moorings. Ropes and flailing tarpaulin sheeting landed directly on top of the prime ministers' party. The police drove them swiftly home.)

In 1971, I launched the National Scrabble Championships. In 1972, as European Monopoly Champion, I took part in the World Monopoly Championships in New York – and came third. In Trafalgar Square I organised the world's biggest Christmas-cracker-pull. On the *Today* programme I tossed the world's tiniest pancake. On the front page of *The Times* – the newspaper Pa took – I was described as 'the high priest of trivia'. I was profiled in the *New Statesman* – disobligingly. Ralph Steadman, the great caricaturist of the day, drew a cartoon of me as a slavering dog chasing its own tail. In *Private Eye* I was described as 'appalling' and 'revolting'.

I carried on regardless. In fact, I quoted the line from *Private Eye* on the cover of my next book. My first book had been about prisons (John Profumo came to the launch); my second was about party games; my third about pantomime.

You name it, I wrote about it. I wrote for the *Guardian* and the *Daily Mirror*, for the *Spectator* and *Punch*. (Craftily, I had invited the editor of *Punch* to speak at the Union. This was my reward.).

I was the youngest person (by far) on the public-speaking circuit when, in June 1971, one of the circuit's most illustrious performers dropped down dead on the tennis court. Godfrey Winn was the highest-paid journalist of his day, a one-time actor and tennis star, a household name and a national treasure (a generation before the phrase was invented) and much sought after by ladies' luncheon clubs. When the agency rang a club in Haslemere to break the sad news that Godfrey would not be appearing at their lunch on Friday because it was to be the day of his funeral, the club secretary protested, 'But he must come.'

'Sadly,' said the lady from the agency, 'he can't. We'll send you Gyles Brandreth instead. He's very good and quite a bit cheaper than Mr Winn.'

'But we booked Mr Winn,' the club secretary insisted, 'so he really has to come. He signed the contract.'

'Yes, but you don't seem to understand: the poor man's dead.'

'That's easy for you to say,' retorted the club secretary. 'What you don't seem to understand is that I've had the menus printed.'

I replaced Godfrey Winn on the speaking circuit and, better still, I was awarded his weekly column in *Woman* – in those days the highest-selling women's magazine in the world. It was a big deal ('Gyles Brandreth: he's as modern as tomorrow with a lot of time for yesterday') with big promotion – in the ads for the column they filmed me walking down London streets, a wind machine blowing a gentle breeze through my thick, lustrous head of hair – but it didn't work.

I had sat next to Godfrey at a formal lunch not long before he died and uncovered one of his secrets: he wore a toupée.

The lunch was at the Dorchester Hotel before they had air conditioning. It was a sweltering hot day and I watched in wonder and alarm as the glue keeping Mr Winn's hairpiece in place trickled down his temples and on to his cheeks. He was sixty-three and homosexual, but he spoke of not being married as though it was something that hadn't quite happened yet and was about to – the moment 'the right gal' came along. When he got up to address the room I noticed two things: how nervous he was (his hands trembled without ceasing), and how much the audience loved him.

Famously, the great newspaper baron Lord Beaverbrook said, 'Godfrey Winn shakes hands with people's hearts.' That was his other secret. He was the real deal, while I was a boy with nothing to say. I had the hair, but he had the gift.

After three months, my column was cancelled.

I barely noticed. I simply bounced on. I spent three months touring the UK dressed up as the dog Snoopy. (You can find a picture of me in the costume among the photographs. I loved that costume. I felt so safe inside it.) I found myself reading poetry in the late-night God slot on Anglia TV. By way of contrast, to exercise my comedy chops, I accepted a booking as the support act to Bernard Manning at his club in Manchester.

'You're a fucking cunt, Gyles,' he told me dolefully, 'but I like you. You make me look good.' Manning's material was as appalling as his language, but he made his audiences roar with laughter, and he taught me a lot. 'Take your time, boy. Don't start till you're ready. If they get loud, you go quiet. Don't be a smartass. They've got to like you. Keep the headstand in. That's different. They like that.'

It was a weird experience performing in a vast room, like a low-ceilinged aircraft hangar, where you couldn't see the crowd for the cigarette smoke. I shared a dressing room with the two topless go-go dancers and the stripper. She was fun. Before she went on, she made me fix the sparkles to her bottom with a Pritt stick.

I did whatever came along. At St Paul's Cathedral I spoke at the Festival of Youth – and, incredibly, halfway through reading Oscar Wilde's *Ballad of Reading Gaol*, realised I was running out of time so stopped and announced, 'At this point the author died.' What on earth was I saying?

Was I mad? Perhaps I was. I was like a spinning top.

Whenever the phone rang, I never asked who it was, I simply said yes.

One day, in May 1971, when I answered the telephone the voice said, 'Is that Gyles?'

'Yes.'

'It's Frank Longford here.'

Pull the other one, I thought. Why would the 7th Earl of Longford, Knight of the Garter, former Cabinet minister, be calling me in Muswell Hill? I assumed it was another of Lord Longford's son Kevin's little practical jokes.

But it wasn't. It was the great man himself – and he wanted my help. He had decided to set up an independent commission of inquiry to look at the whole question of pornography in our time.

'It's a high-powered group. We've got two bishops, an archbishop, a High Court judge and Malcolm Muggeridge. But we need some young blood. I thought of you and Cliff Richard. What do you say?'

I said, 'Yes.'

And in saying yes, I let myself into a world as curious as anything Alice found in Wonderland. Fifty years on, I still have vivid dreams about it. I am not complaining. It was an extraordinary, eye-opening experience – and it introduced me to some fascinating figures, including Cliff.

At the first full meeting of the Pornography Commission, Cliff and I sat side by side. He was already thirty-one, but he looked much younger, dressed in a gorgeous nut-brown chamois-leather suit, with silk shirt and scarves to match. The room (a semi-basement at the Institute of Advanced Legal Studies, somewhere in Bloomsbury) was crowded and chaotic. It was like the courtroom scene at the end of *Alice in Wonderland*: a lot of colourful old cards milling about, all talking at once – clergymen, lawyers, retired civil servants, eccentric-looking academics, one or two senior journalists (I recognised Peregrine Worsthorne from the *Telegraph* looking like a dandified version of the White Rabbit), us (the young ones – auditioning for the Knave of Hearts) and a couple of token women (a pair of late-middle-aged doctors with low-slung bosoms – they looked exactly like the Duchess and the Cook).

We sat at long tables set in a square, pencils and paper to hand, adding to the hubbub, until Lord Longford, with unexpected authority, called us to order and welcomed us to 'the crusade'. (Crusade? I thought this was supposed to be an independent open-minded inquiry. Never mind. I was in Wonderland now.) He told us how, during the war, he had worked with the late Lord Beveridge on the famous Beveridge Report that had formed the basis of the welfare state. He hoped, he prayed, that our work would prove as significant.

Lord Longford was sixty-five at the time, tall, thin, a little stooped, bald with tufts of still-black hair sprouting on either side of his crown and bits of yesterday's lunch on his lapels and tie. He was the King and the March Hare and the Mad Hatter all rolled into one. I liked him a lot. He had been a minister under Attlee and Wilson, but he started out as a Conservative. When we were chatting over the pre-meeting cup of tea, he told me about his first encounter with Stanley Baldwin. In the early thirties Frank ('You must call me Frank') was a Conservative Party researcher and found himself at a country house-party where Baldwin was guest of honour. After lunch, the Prime Minister invited young Frank to join him for a stroll. The conversation didn't exactly flow, but eventually Frank thought of something intelligent to ask the great man.

'Tell me, Prime Minister, who would you say has most influenced your political ideas?'

After an interminable pause, Baldwin replied, 'Sir Henry Maine.'

'And what did he say?'

'That whereas Rousseau argued all human progress was from contract to status, the real movement was from status to contract.' Baldwin halted in his tracks. His face darkened. 'Or was it the other way around?'

From that first meeting on, Frank took me under his wing. I remember he entertained me to lunch at the Garrick Club on the day after he had been installed as a Knight of the Garter.

He was devoted to the Queen. 'She is wonderful, beautiful and very funny. People don't realise how amusing she can be.'

I suddenly heard myself asking, 'Do you think the Queen enjoys sex?'

Frank wasn't the least bit abashed. 'Of course she does,' he enthused, raising his glass of Beaune to her. 'She's a healthy Christian woman. And she enjoys riding, as I do. People who enjoy riding always enjoy sex. It's well known. Do you ride much, Gyles?'

'No, I don't.'

'I'm sorry to hear it.' He sipped at his wine before adding earnestly, 'She isn't a puritan, you know, the Queen. And nor am I. People expect me to be teetotal, but I'm not. I love wine. And I enjoy sex greatly. After all, I've had eight children. I swim in the nude, regularly. There's nothing nicer. I doubt that the Queen swims in the nude. Prince Philip might. They've got a pool at Buckingham Palace, you know.'

As well as the meetings to discuss pornography, where we would sit around in a solemn circle flicking through filthy magazines ('Good grief, a labia sandwich – whatever next?' 'Oh look, Rabbi, one of yours, I think!'), we younger members were sent out to do fieldwork in Soho: in 'the square mile of depravity', as Lord Longford called it. I was intrigued to find on these forays that our fellow customers really were wearing shabby fawn-coloured raincoats.

At one shop we spoke to the manager. We told him we were doing research for Lord Longford.

He chuckled. 'That's what they all say nowadays.'

We asked to see the most *unusual* sample of his wares and he produced a magazine called *Amigo*, a glossy publication designed for foot fetishists. It contained thirty close-up photographs (with accompanying toe-by-toe, step-by-instep descriptions) of naked feet.

I said to Cliff, 'Shall we buy a copy for Sandie Shaw?'

I don't think he got the joke.

In the interests of gender equality, and after some adverse publicity following the launch, Frank decided to get some young women involved in our venture. He invited me to join him one evening in the Ladies' Annex of the Athenaeum Club. 'I've got a couple of girls coming, Gyles. I thought we'd have supper first and then take them to see something really dirty.'

'A strip show?'

'No, a dirty film. I've brought the tickets,' he added, positively trembling with nervous excitement.

'And I've brought the raincoats,' I said, with a wink.

He definitely didn't get the joke.

'What are we going to see?' I asked.

'*Catch-22*,' he announced. 'It's new – and, apparently, it's appalling.'

'Oh dear,' I said. I tried to explain to him that I was pretty sure *Catch-22* wasn't most people's idea of pornography.

He wouldn't be deflected. 'I've been told it's quite disgusting!'

He took his young lady (a trainee publisher) to *Catch-22* at the Odeon, Leicester Square, while I took mine (a student nurse) to a double bill at a tiny cinema at the top end of Piccadilly. We sat in the front row and saw *Anybody's Body* and

Collective Marriage. Given her line of business, my nurse had seen it all before, but (let's face it) I hadn't, and (let's confess) I quite enjoyed it.

The work of the Commission went on for months and involved a lot of legwork – and sub-committees. One that Cliff and I both served on was the TV sub-committee. For its first meeting I bought myself new flared turquoise trousers, but, inevitably, Cliff outdazzled me in a sumptuous plum-velvet outfit, complete with medallions and silver and gold chains. The meeting was chaired by Malcolm Muggeridge, then sixty-eight, broadcaster and sage, whom I had already met when I interviewed him for *Isis* at Oxford. (He invited me to lunch at his house in Sussex – his wife, a fellow Old Bedalian, cooked us nut rissoles – and on our post-prandial walk he took me to meet Leonard Woolf. Yes, I've shaken the hand that held the hand that wrote *The Waves*.) Malcolm looked exactly as you'd expect the Mock Turtle to look, though in Jonathan Miller's television version of *Alice* in the mid-1960s he had actually played the Gryphon. He pursed his lips and screwed up his eyes when he spoke and talked pretty relentlessly about the sins of the flesh and the beauty of suffering.

On the sly, Perry Worsthorne explained to me that, once upon a time, Malcolm had been a bit of a goer, a bottom-pinching red-blooded ladies' man, but now that his libido had failed him he had discovered the joys of chastity and vegetarianism.

Malcolm opened the meeting by reading out to us the BBC's original statement of intent, inscribed on the wall at the entrance to Broadcasting House.

This temple of the arts and muses is dedicated to Almighty God by the first governors in the year 1931 ... It is their prayer that good seed sown may bring forth a good harvest, that all things hostile to peace or purity may be banished from this house, and that the people, inclining their ears to whatsoever things are beautiful and honest and of good report, may tread the paths of wisdom and righteousness.

We all agreed that, sadly, things weren't what they used to be – and Cliff revealed that some of the dancing on *Top of the Pops* was definitely designed to titillate – but, hand on heart, we couldn't say there was anything approaching what you'd call pornography to be seen on British TV.

'Mark my words,' said Malcolm, narrowing his eyes and smacking his lips, 'the rot's set in. If we don't do something now, within a generation nudity and profanity on the box will be commonplace, and rampant homosexuality will be offered to us by way of entertainment.'

His timing was a bit out, but he wasn't far wrong. It took two generations before *Queer Eye* became a global sensation and three before I became hooked on *Naked Attraction*.

24. 'An excursion to Hell'

The climax of my time on Lord Longford's Pornography Commission was our research trip to Denmark. We went to Copenhagen – advertised as 'Sin City', 'the most permissive place on earth' – to reap the alien porn. Just six of us went – accompanied by a press pack of at least two dozen reporters and photographers. On the flight out, I sat next to our leader.

From take-off to landing Lord Longford read the Bible (Book of Proverbs), and didn't lift his eyes from the page. 'I am preparing myself for the ordeal we are going to have to face, Gyles.'

We arrived in early evening and, over dinner at the hotel, were briefed by a British embassy official on where to find Denmark's hottest sex clubs.

'You seem remarkably well informed,' said Frank, brow furrowed.

'We try to be of service,' said the diplomat, with a smile.

After we'd eaten, Frank gave us each £10 spending money.

'That should be more than enough,' said our man from the embassy. 'You can usually get live sex for around a fiver.'

We decided to hunt in pairs and agreed to meet back at the hotel at midnight to compare notes. I teamed up with Sue Pegden, a 21-year-old social psychologist and one of the commission's official researchers, and Lord Longford went off with Dr Christine Saville, a wise old bird and prison psychiatrist.

Chaperoned by the *Daily Mirror* and the *News of the World*, Sue and I wandered sheepishly in and out of assorted sex shops and eventually ended up at the Private Club where (for £7) we had ringside seats. Stark-naked hostesses offered us plastic beakers of beer and, frankly, anything else we wanted.

As they squeezed past us along the row, by accident or design, their pubic hair brushed our noses. I started to sneeze, while the chap from the *News of the World* couldn't resist a quick fumble, which led to one of the naked girls removing his spectacles and making them disappear about her person. When eventually his glasses were returned to him, he was too self-conscious to wear them and so missed the rest of the performance.

Sue and I missed quite a bit of it, too. The press presence was inhibiting. During the more lurid moments, we simply grinned inanely at each other or gazed steadfastly at our knees.

When we got back to the hotel, Frank was looking positively wild-eyed. 'I feel exhausted, disgusted and degraded,' he shuddered.

The first club he had been to was 'small, crowded, no more than fifty in the audience'. As he arrived, he found a stout middle-aged man onstage with his trousers round his ankles being attended to by a naked dancer equipped with a battery-operated vibrator. To put it delicately, the girl was not getting much change from the fat man. Frank gazed on the scene aghast and then the penny dropped. The fat man was not part of the act: he was a visiting tourist. This was a club where audience participation was the order of the day.

Hastily, Lord Longford got to his feet and, dragging Dr Saville with him, made for the exit as discreetly as he could.

Unfortunately, the manager caught sight of him and, taking him for a disappointed customer, chased after him, 'But, sir, don't go, you haven't seen any intercourse yet. The intercourse here is excellent. I assure you it's next on the programme.'

Frank fled into the street.

'I wanted to come straight home, but, in fairness to Christine, I felt we should give another club a chance. It was even worse than the first. We were placed in the front row and, almost as soon as we arrived, a naked girl approached me with a whip. She used the whip to caress the top of my head and then looped it round my neck. She vibrated me for seconds that seemed like minutes. The next thing I knew she was sitting on my neighbour's lap caressing him indescribably. I realised what was about to happen. I could sense whose lap she was going to be landing on next. I had to get out, and I did. Don't think me faint-hearted, Gyles. I had seen enough for science and more than enough for enjoyment.'

The next day, we had a series of meetings kindly set up for us by the Ministry of Justice, including an appointment with one Jens Theander, whom they described to us as 'the pornographer royal'. As a Knight of the Garter, Lord Longford was intrigued. Was this man pornographer by appointment to the Danish King and Queen? He wasn't. He was simply the biggest noise in the Danish porn trade, a huge teddy bear of a man, twinkly and fun, difficult to resist – until he showed us some of his merchandise. It was horrific.

'Surely, you don't use children?' asked Frank, voicing the general disgust.

His reply, intended to reassure, was scarcely less appalling. 'Of course not, Sir Longford. It is against the law. These are midgets.'

The bestiality was gross, too. We were shown photographs of women sucking the penises of pigs, dogs and bulls. When I suggested this was degrading for both the women and the animals, our host said, smiling, 'Not at all. The animals love it and the girls are all volunteers.'

Peregrine Worsthorne stood gazing up at a gigantic poster of a naked young woman standing on a stepladder in between the legs of a giraffe. '*Fellatio* with a *giraffe*? Now I've seen everything.'

On our second night, we took in a blue movie. It could not have been more explicit. In the front row Lord Longford and Peregrine Worsthorne perched on tubular chairs, eyes popping as they studied outsize genitalia thrusting to and fro, up and down, in and out, on a scratchy screen. Quite soon, and quite loudly, they began to tell one another how desperately boring it was.

'Let's go,' said Perry.

'I can't,' said Frank, 'I walked out of the live show last night, I've got to sit this one out. You go first.'

'No, you're the leader,' hissed Perry. 'You must leave first.'

In the end, a compromise was reached: we endured five minutes' more thrusting and then all left together, with Perry whispering wittily as we made for the exit, 'Just as they're coming, we're going.'

On our last day in Denmark, Lord Longford and I had lunch in the Tivoli Gardens with one of the press pack. Frank pretended to be wary of the press, but, in truth, I think he relished the publicity. The trip to Denmark had turned us all into ludicrous figures of fun, but he didn't seem to mind. He told me a taxi driver had dropped him off recently and said, 'I can never remember your other name. I know you're Lord Porn, of course, but your other name escapes me.'

He even admitted that my favourite 'Longford story' might be true. In it, Frank was walking up Piccadilly and passing Hatchard's bookshop. He looked into the window for a moment and then, suddenly, stormed inside demanding to see the manager.

'Where's my new book? It's only just out. Why isn't it on display?'

'I'm so sorry, Lord Longford,' mumbled the manager, 'I didn't know about it. What's it called?'

'*Humility*, and you should have it in the window.'

Was his eccentricity studied? I don't think so. When we got up from lunch, he inadvertently put on my jacket, so I put on his. He really didn't notice. He walked back to the hotel wearing a jacket whose sleeves only reached his elbows.

After three days in the erotic Wonderland of Copenhagen, we flew home, our cases packed with free samples. As soon as we reached the customs hall at Heathrow, Lord Longford accosted a young man in uniform and thrust a thick blue folder into his hands. 'I want you to examine these magazines.

Carefully. You may have heard of me. I am the Earl of Long-ford. I was a member of the last government. I have just returned from a fact-finding mission to Copenhagen . . .'

The young man leafed through the sordid material, nodding appreciatively. At this point, Frank realised he was not addressing a customs officer but a courier for American Express. Eventually, Heathrow's Chief Customs Officer appeared and, having secured Frank's assurance that the magazines would remain in his 'personal control', allowed us back into the country.

It was a curious few days – and the beginning of the end of my time on the Pornography Commission. Frank was disappointed that all of us hadn't been as horrified by what we had seen as he had been. He believed that sex outside marriage is sinful and that pornography is the Devil's work. It was as simple as that. 'Sex should be something beautiful. What we've seen isn't beautiful. It's revolting. It is total degradation. Every instinct in me tells me that it ought not to be allowed.'

On the flight back, I'd asked him, 'Are you sorry we came?'

'No, it has been necessary, dreadful but essential. Of course, I would rather have gone to Rome with Mary. You know Mary?'

I knew Mary Whitehouse quite well. I had taken part in debates with her. She was a nice woman, a teacher-turned-campaigner, an articulate champion of traditional Christian values; to look at, she was the spitting image of Dame Edna Everage (in fact, at a party once, across a crowded room, I confused the two), but nobody's fool. She had planned to call her campaigning organisation 'Clean Up National Television' – until she looked twice at the poster, and saw the problem.

'Mary flew to Rome yesterday,' said Frank. 'She's gone to see the Pope. I said to her, "Mary, you are off to Heaven, while I am going to Hell." That's where we've been, Gyles. You do realise that, don't you? I have taken you on an excursion to Hell. Will you ever forgive me?'

Would Frank ever forgive me? I wondered. When we got

back we found that the press coverage of our trip had got completely out of hand. 'Longford Porn Team Split' was the front-page lead in the *Daily Mirror* ('Britain's Biggest Daily Sale'). According to the *Mirror* (and most of the other papers) 'a furious row' had blown up between Lord Longford and 'the younger members of his team' – i.e. Sue Pegden and me. Sue was quoted as saying, 'Some of us feel that we can no longer accept Lord Longford's rigid attitude to pornography.' (An unfortunate turn of phrase, but there you go.) I was quoted as saying that some of what we saw was an aphrodisiac; Sue was quoted as saying that some of it was 'beautiful'.

What the pressmen really wanted, of course, was to catch me and 'pretty Sue Pegden, 21' in each other's arms. At the hotel in Copenhagen, our bedrooms were on the same floor. The newspaper photographers took it in turns to hide in the corridor through the night in the hope of catching one or other of us indulging in a bit of corridor creeping. They were to be disappointed.

But Fleet Street's finest don't give up that easily and, lo, the next morning, who did we find adorning the front page of the *Sun*?

My darling Michèle.

There was a huge picture of her (looking quite lovely) alongside the ludicrous headline: 'My Life with the Porno Rebel'. According to the article: 'Michèle Brown, girl in the life of Gyles Brandreth, rebel of Britain's "Porn Squad", talked last night of their life together.'

The night after my return from Copenhagen, I went to Bayswater to have a catch-up supper with Ma and Pa. We went to a Greek taverna near their down-at-heel hotel, and over the taramasalata and kebabs (and Othello wine) I regaled them with tales of our Danish shenanigans.

They chuckled at my stories, Pa drawing heavily on his cigarettes and ordering more wine, but they were anxious about the publicity. Was it good for me? Was it good for Michèle? I sensed they were anxious about me, too, and what I was doing with my life, ricocheting in all directions – pornography, prisons, pantomime, party games. Was I spreading myself too thin? Was I throwing it all away? Pa didn't say anything specific, but I must have noticed because, fifty years on, I can see the sadness in his eyes now.

That's my secret. Now you know. I have spent a lifetime feeling bad that my father gave me everything and that I didn't deliver for him in return. I didn't even invite him to my wedding.

When I was twenty-one, I was as happy as a sandboy. When my father was twenty-one, he wasn't. I did not know that. He didn't tell me and I never asked. I never thought to ask. I only found out, by chance, this year, while writing this. My father kept a diary (I did not know that, either) and my eldest sister, Jennifer, found it in an old box and, during lockdown, decided to type it up. She sent me the diary for 1931 – the year Pa left Oxford and started out in the world, the equivalent time in his life to the time in my life I have just been describing to you here.

My diary for 1971 is full of high jinks and adventure. My father's diary for 1931 is full of yearning and despondency.

There are happy moments in his year: a college ball, a new briar pipe, red silk pyjamas bought in the Selfridges sale (30s. reduced to 23s.), rounds of golf, tea at the Lyons' Corner House, trips to 'the flicks' and to the theatre (he goes to see Sibyl Thorndike in *Ghosts* and Sir Frank Benson in *She Stoops to Conquer*), lots of reading. He learns to type; he learns to drive; he suffers 'considerably from the cutting of a wisdom tooth' and from the disappointment that Trudl – the Austrian girl who he had thought might be the love of his life – turns out not to be so interesting on better acquaintance. He loves his parents and his sisters, but he seems almost to despise his elder brother, Benjie – a scientist who got a first at Cambridge. He writes bleakly:

My present depression is one of acute mental inferiority. I am determined to read and read – but shall I be any wiser or cleverer for it? I don't think so – but oh how damnably ignorant I do feel.

He follows politics (Ramsay MacDonald's National Government is formed that August) and has political ambitions. His immediate post-Oxford ambition is to tread the boards. He has learnt a number of dramatic monologues by heart, and performs them with gusto, but the auditions he gets don't lead anywhere and his father persuades him that if he is going to 'earn a living of any sort' he had better reconcile himself to becoming a solicitor.

8 September 1931
This evening I felt most depressed and for good reason. The life I seem destined to lead holds out no possibility of advancement as I could wish for. I have made no success of all I have put my hand to and it does not seem as though I shall ever be more fortunate. I am terrified at the thought of getting into a rut, never leaving it, and ending my life as a small solicitor who has done nothing that will make him remembered after he is gone . . .

Pa wanted to be a writer, a politician, an entertainer – all the things I have been and have almost taken for granted.

Dear reader, are you living out the life you wanted to lead? Are you fulfilling your parents' ambitions for you, or your own? Or are you simply muddling through, doing your best, taking life as it comes, day by day? Or, so far, has it been a bit of a mixture of all three?

Writing this book has been an unsettling experience for me, because as a rule I avoid introspection. The Duke of Edinburgh advised me: 'Don't talk about yourself. Nobody's interested.' On the other hand, Socrates, whom I didn't know, said: 'The unexamined life is not worth living.' So here we are: we have had 400 pages of me talking about me. Along the way, I have examined stuff I wouldn't normally think about and I have discovered things, about myself and about my family, I didn't know before.

Thank you for staying the course, thank you for sharing the journey.

Strange things have happened while I have been writing this. Odd coincidences. For example, I knew I knew Terry Pratchett, but I had forgotten that I had known him fifty years ago. I last saw him shortly before he died, in 2015. He wandered into the bar at the Langham Hotel – barefoot, wearing what looked like an old RAF overcoat and nothing at all underneath: he had a rare form of early onset Alzheimer's – and, seeing me sitting there having a cup of tea before going to appear on *The One Show*, came over to say hello. He was very sweet – and hugely gifted, which is how he came to sell 85 million copies of his books in 37 languages around the world. I had no idea he had drawn that telling cartoon of me in 1971 until his agent sent it to me out of the blue on the very day, fifty years later, that I happened to be writing about him here.

Not so sweet, but also gifted in his own way, was the journalist Paul Callan. In another curious coincidence, Callan's death was announced on the very day that I happened to be leafing through my diary recalling an article he wrote about me in the 1970s and wondering whether I should mention it here. The article is only relevant because it fed into my parents' unspoken anxiety about how I was making my way in the world, and because it gave me a lifelong mistrust of print journalists – a mistrust shared by every celebrity (minor or major) and politician I know.

Callan came to interview me and I felt we got on well. Since he looked like a comical cross between Billy Bunter and

Mr Toad – and they were two of my favourite characters – I rather warmed to him. Michèle liked him, too.

Ten days' later, his article appeared in the *Daily Mirror* – it took up a full page and it was vile: 'Paul Callan meets the wonder author, lecturer and former Monopoly champion – THE BIGGEST HEAD IN TOWN – that's Gentleman Gyles of the Smug Squad'. It was the nastiest profile of anyone I've ever read.

Mid-morning on the day the interview appeared, Callan called me. My stomach lurched as soon as I heard his voice. I stood up at my desk. (I always stand up during difficult calls.)

He was very fruity. 'Hello, old chap. Sorry about the piece. You know how it is. We have to spice these things up a bit – make them readable. Anyway, I'm calling to apologise. Keith Waterhouse [another *Mirror* columnist] is standing at my elbow. He suggested I call you because I'd told him I liked you and he said, "Well, it doesn't sound like it from the piece, so give him a call now to explain." So that's what I'm doing. No hard feelings, eh?'

I mumbled something like, 'Of course not.'

'Let's have lunch,' he said.

We didn't. I never saw him again.

If everyone has a secret, I imagine Paul Callan had quite a few. I know he pretended to have gone to Eton and maintained the pretence for many years. It did not always work to his advantage. When he was twenty-five, he applied for a post on the soon-to-launched *Sun*, when it was part of Cecil King's IPC newspaper empire. He had put Eton down on his CV, only to be told at the job interview, 'We're not actually looking for public school types.'

'Didn't Cecil King go to Winchester?' protested Callan.

'Yes,' said the interviewer, 'but he's the guv'nor . . . You're not applying for his job, are you?'

'Not at this interview, no,' said Callan.

He didn't get the job, but got plenty of others over the years as a gossip columnist and celebrity interviewer. He is credited with the shortest interview ever published. Encountering the notoriously reclusive film star Greta Garbo at the Hotel du Cap-Eden-Roc, near Cannes, he managed to say, 'I wonder –' before Garbo cut him off with, 'Why wonder?' and stalked away.

Paul Callan was eighty-one when he died – impressive, given his appetite for booze and Gauloises. On the morning after I had finished writing the earlier part of this chapter about Lord Longford, I opened the newspaper and read that Longford's son Kevin, the practical joker and my New College contemporary, had died, unexpectedly, of a heart attack. Kevin was only seventy-two. And today (the day that I am writing this) I have heard of the death of Rabbi Jonathan Sacks. We got to know one another simply because we had something in common: we were born within minutes of each other, on 8 March 1948. Jonathan, a wise and good man, said, 'To be immortal all you need to do is engrave your values on the minds of your children.'

Parents and children, fathers and sons – I hadn't expected it to be like this, but that's what this book turns out to have been about.

Just as I had finished writing about Nicholas Goodliffe, my best friend at the Lycée when we were little boys, I got an email (via my website) from his brother telling me that Nicholas had died. I had barely thought about Nicholas in sixty-five years; I had forgotten his brother entirely, but his brother remembered our childhood friendship and thought I would want to know. Nicholas, his brother told me, had suffered from schizophrenia and depressive episodes. I remembered that his father, the actor Michael Goodliffe, had taken his own life. I wondered if Nicholas felt that his father had given him permission to do the same.

People do die and, in my experience, many of the best of them die too soon. My closest friend from Bedales, Simon Cadell, died when he was only forty-five. Colin Sanders, with whom I put on those ill-starred *son et lumière* shows, died just before his fifty-first birthday. When we were in business together, Colin and I lost money. On his own, as an electronics engineer of genius, Colin made a fortune. He was killed trying to land his own helicopter, coming home in the dark from a night-flying lesson. My sister, Hester, died at the age of sixty. Simon, Colin, Hester – I spoke at each of their funerals. (I have spoken at a good number of funerals and memorial services over the years – dozens of them, in fact. I have the knack of it now. I am thinking of pre-recording a short address for my own.)

I remember the very first memorial service I attended, in 1970. It was for one of my contemporaries, a tousle-haired Christian socialist, a keen Labour Party man, and reckoned by all to be the promising undergraduate of our generation.

21 September 1970
When I was President of the Oxford Union, Hugh Anderson was President of the Cambridge Union. We were friends; we were the same age; he was a really nice person; and now he is dead. It was some form of cancer. I have just come back from his memorial service at All Souls, Langham Place. The church was packed. Harold Wilson was there. Trevor Huddleston gave the address. Canon Perfect led the prayers.

Canon Perfect is Pa's age, perhaps a little older. Pa and Canon Perfect were at school together. Pa *loathed* him at school because Perfect was exactly that: perfect. At least he was perfect as far as the masters were concerned: he bullied the other boys. All my life I have been hearing about this ghastly prig of a schoolboy and I turn up at my friend's memorial service and there he is leading the prayers! I hadn't realised that Hugh went to St Lawrence College, Ramsgate, too.

Everything comes back to Pa, it seems, one way or another. And, of course, Pa died, too, at seventy-one, as he always knew he would, exactly as the fortune teller had prophesied.

His time was up and he'd run out of funds. He had to die because he had nothing left to live on.

Despite his early misgivings, Pa had become one of the leading solicitors of his day. His speciality was motoring law, and no one knew more about it than he did. But he couldn't afford to retire at sixty-five, so he worked on until he was seventy, when his partners said, 'Time to call it a day, old boy,' gave him a set of golf clubs and a farewell dinner at the Reform Club and sent him on his way.

He never got to use the golf clubs. He had been smoking all his life, so the cancer when it took hold was quick to overwhelm him. I remember sitting with my mother and my sisters in a neon-lit room off his ward at the Middlesex Hospital.

Ma, white-faced and terrified, was leaning desperately across the consultant's desk, pleading with him. 'You can't let him die. You mustn't, you mustn't.'

'We'll do our best,' said the consultant, gently, 'I promise you that.'

But there was nothing to be done. Pa was moved from the Middlesex, to home, to one hospice, and then on to another.

Ma hated the hospices. Every day, when I took her to visit Pa, she'd complain. 'They should have signs above the door saying: "Abandon hope all ye who enter here."'

She would not accept the inevitable. Understandably. All their married life, he had done all the practical things. She had never paid a bill, or had a bank account, or driven a car, or changed a light bulb. She did not know how to switch the TV from BBC to ITV. She had never had to do it. He did everything.

As the months passed, and he grew weaker and more gaunt, we all knew what was happening, but pretended it wasn't – Pa included. When one day he opened his eyes and saw the pretty face of the Duchess of Kent smiling down at him, he must have realised the end was near.

'Her Royal Highness is our patron,' the hospice's matron explained.

'Well, if you've brought her to see me, things must be worse than I thought,' said Pa, with a wintry smile.

He remained quietly cheerful to the end. Throughout his life, whatever he may have confided to his diary, he was always publicly stoical. 'When you have made your bed,' he used to say, 'you must lie on it. That's the rule.'

I hope his faith was a comfort to him. I don't know, because we never talked about that kind of thing.

He died alone at 6.30 a.m. on a cold Wednesday morning at the end of June. I went to the hospice to collect his things. They were waiting for me in a large black bin liner. There wasn't much: a suit, a shirt, his prayer book, his glasses, his wedding ring – his teeth! I went to register his death at St Pancras Town Hall and then went on to see the undertaker. I went to Kenyon's, of course. He would have wanted me to ask for the family discount, but I didn't.

The day before the funeral, I took Ma to the Chapel of Rest to see Pa for the last time. The undertakers were very friendly, easy, not unctuous. (Kenyon's really are the best.) They took us down to the basement and let us into a small room, like a doctor's surgery. Pa's body was laid out in an open coffin. It was him and yet it wasn't. It was like a waxwork and, like a waxwork, it didn't quite ring true. We stood by the coffin for a minute or two, in silence.

Ma stroked his hair very gently and said, 'Goodbye, hon. I love you.'

On the day of the funeral, the sun shone brightly and the church was crowded. Ma and I were the last to go in. We stopped by the coffin, waiting in the church porch.

Ma patted the coffin, then rested her head against it for a moment. 'He was my everything,' she said.

Mine, too.

25. I hope there is a heaven

Dear Pa,

I hope there is a heaven because I would love you to be able to read this. I want you to know it all worked out in the end.

We held your funeral at St Marylebone Parish Church. I wish you could have been there. Well, you were there, of course, but you know what I mean. Kenyon's did you proud – and you should have seen the turnout: so many people came! People loved you, Pa. They loved your jokes; they loved your English eccentricity; they loved your sweetness. Do you remember how we children called you 'dear, sweet, lovable Pa'? That's what you were.

Soon after the funeral, we put up a plaque in your memory at the church – on the left-hand side, halfway down the nave. It's made of Welsh slate from your grandfather's mine. It's very handsome – flawless, too. I say that because mistakes can happen.

When I was an MP, I was asked to unveil a plaque at the opening of a doctor's surgery in my constituency. I pulled the string, the curtains parted, and I read the words: 'This plague was unveiled by Gyles Brandreth MP'.

Do you remember the story you used to tell about the Lancashire widow who put her husband's ashes into an egg timer, saying, 'He did nowt useful while he was alive – he can do summat useful now he's dead'? Well, your ashes, Pa, are now in an elegant urn in the columbarium in the crypt at St Marylebone, in a small niche alongside Ma's.

Ma lived to be ninety-six. Amazing when you think about her blood pressure and bad back and ankylosing spondylitis and skin cancer and hiatus hernia and diverticulitis and all those dizzy spells. Hypochondria? Yes, she had bouts of that, too. But I'm not one to talk. Every time I get a slight headache I am convinced it's a brain tumour. And the truth is: Ma did incredibly well. She didn't give in, she didn't give up. She did what widows have to do: she struggled on alone. We bought her a flat (Michèle's idea) and helped with her finances as best we could, and she went back to work, teaching.

A few years after she died in 2010, I happened to be standing on the platform at Bromsgrove Station when a middle-aged man approached me. He said, 'You won't know me, but when I was seven or eight your mother taught me. I couldn't read or write. She showed me how. She changed my life. In my head, I say thank you to her every day.'

Ma went on teaching into her nineties and any child she ever taught will tell you she was the best teacher they ever had.

She never stopped thinking about you, Pa. She said she had offers of marriage in her seventies and eighties (I believed her: she could be very charming), and while she would have liked the company, she knew you were irreplaceable. You were her life. She kept a photograph of you at her bedside always and talked to you every day. On the night she died, I leant over her hospital bed and kissed her goodbye. She was too weak to speak, but she managed a small smile. She was looking into my eyes, but she was thinking of you.

Hes died before Ma – of cancer. Ben died, too – of asbestosis, after years working as a carpenter and builder. He was only fifty-one. Happily, Jen and Gin are still here, in their eighties but going strong. Your five children have given you ten grandchildren and every one of them has done you proud.

Michèle's and my three are just amazing. Benet's a QC and part-time judge. He was in the army; he's written novels; as a student, he was public-speaking champion of the world! Saethryd's a writer, too, and I reckon, having read what she writes, perhaps the most exciting (and amusing) writer of her generation. Aphra's a politician. When she stood at the last general election (in a hopeless seat) I went to campaign for her. I knocked on a dingy door in a dismal street and a surly-looking man answered.

'What do you want?' he barked.

'I want you to vote for my daughter,' I said brightly.

He glared at me. 'What's she got to offer?'

'Integrity and intelligence,' I answered, in a flash.

The man peered at me closely and asked, 'Are you sure she's your daughter?'

Why did we give our children unusual names? Because we hoped they'd be unusual people, and they are. *Nomen est omen.* Between them, Benet, Saethryd and Aphra have achieved all that you and I could possibly have dreamt of for ourselves – and more. But, better than that, they're good people, Pa. They're the best. They have the qualities that you had, the qualities that count: courtesy, kindness and courage. Ma and I were lacking in the courage department, I'm sorry to say. When a car goes much above seventy, I squawk almost as much as Ma used to. Your grand- and great-grandchildren, I'm proud to tell you, are made of sterner stuff.

When he was one, Saethryd's youngest, a little boy called Kitt, had a childhood cancer and spent a year living in and out of Great Ormond Street Hospital. He came through the seem-ingly never-ending courses of chemotherapy with flying colours. He was a little hero and his parents saw him through his nightmare year with matchless grace and courage. They were shattered by the end of it, of course. (Nobody ever tells you how *exhausting* parenthood is, do they? And, alarmingly, the tiredness that comes with having children never goes away.)

Yes, we've had our ups and downs – who hasn't? – but it's all come right in the end. I am probably the luckiest person alive. I have everything that anyone could want – and I have Michèle, too. She's been the secret blessing of my life, keeping me on the straight and narrow, keeping us solvent, keeping the show on the road. Do you remember Godfrey Winn? I know you winced when I was touted as his 'successor', all those years ago. Famously, Godfrey said, 'No man succeeds without a good woman behind him: wife or mother. If it is both, he is twice blessed indeed.' Ma was behind me from first to last, but Michèle has always been ahead of me, leading me in the right direction, or alongside, holding my hand, a good companion and my best friend. Every night, I think of you on your knees at your bedside saying your prayers. Every night, before I go to sleep, I count my blessings. I always start with Michèle, followed by you and Ma. (Don't tell the children, but Nala, the cat, usually comes next.)

I know it worried you when I was in my twenties that I was doing anything and everything that came along. Fanny Cradock wrote to me about it at the time.

15 November, 1972

You may or may not know I am in fact a witch, hopefully a white one, but just occasionally my witchlike and 'insatiable curiosity' impels me to have a little private peek forward. This, my latest peek, tells me that for some time to come you will emulate that famous character who jumped on his horse and galloped away in all directions! Curiously enough, I did exactly the same thing and, long before anyone else, arrived at the same conclusion. I had decided that my alleged early promise was not going to justify itself. You will do the same thing at some future stage, which will be a much sillier exercise than it was for me because, if I live long enough, I know I shall say I knew you were front-line material when I heard you delivering a speech standing on your head! Try everything that opportunity puts in your way. Enjoy it to the full and you will find none of it will be wasted and they will all come together in some form of outstanding success, which I would not want to know now and should not tell you if I did, because it would damage the pattern.

Now tell me I am a silly old bag and I shall not blame you — but remember.

Fanny was both a silly old bag and a wise old bird. And the good news, Pa, is that some of the nonsense worked out quite well. For example, by founding the Scrabble championships I got to know the makers of Scrabble and eventually I ended up as a director of Spear's Games – and we sold the company to Mattel in 1994, valued at $96.72 million! And because I was 'the Scrabble king' I was given a place in Dictionary Corner on *Count-down*, the first programme on Channel 4. It's still going strong and I am happy to say I have been the show's most frequent guest in Dictionary Corner. And because of *Countdown* I met Susie Dent. She's a lexicographer (the world's best) and we do a podcast together, all about words and language. It's called *Something Rhymes with Purple* – because something does: to hirple is to walk with a limp. It's had millions of downloads and was voted Best Entertainment Podcast of 2020! (Have you any idea what I'm burbling on about? Do you even get podcasts in heaven?)

The point is, Pa, everything from *then* seems to link up with *now*. Do you remember how I loved dressing up as a little boy? Well, I am doing it still. At one of the early Scrabble championships, someone gave me a hand-knitted jumper designed like a Scrabble board. I wore it on TV and people noticed, so I got other jumpers made with other designs and it became a 'thing' – my thing. I had hundreds of jumpers, some sent in by viewers, most of them made by my friend George Hostler. He created knitwear for me, Elton John and Diana, Princess of Wales.

When I became an MP in the 1990s, I stopped wearing the jumpers, but I wasn't allowed to forget them. Speaking in a debate one day, John Prescott, from the opposition front bench, began barracking me. 'Woolly jumper!' he scoffed, 'Woolly jumper!'

He kept it up for quite a while, until I pointed out to him that, 'The joy of a woolly jumper is that you can take it off at will, whereas the blight of a woolly mind is that you're lumbered with it for life.'

There was plenty of cheering and chuckling on my side, but John Prescott got the last laugh because he ended up as Deputy Prime Minister and is now wrapped in ermine and seated in the House of Lords, while I'm simply me and just here – but I am very happy where I am, and I love my jumpers. I am wearing them still and, amazingly, in certain quarters, they're all the rage again. Do you have the internet in heaven? Do you even know what the internet is? If you do, you can check out my knitwear website: www.gylesandgeorge.com. In 2022, we're opening a 'Gyles and George' jumper boutique in New York – in Lower Manhattan, a hundred yards from the shop where Dr Brandreth sold his pills on Canal Street.

Yes, Pa: Dr Brandreth, George R. Sims, the Empress Eugénie – all the family 'greats' – they still loom large in my life. I have their portraits on the wall. George R. Sims inspired my first novel (*Who Is Nick Saint?*) and is a principal character in my last (*Jack the Ripper: Case Closed*) and I'm doing a parody of his 'Christmas Day in the Workhouse' in my current one-man show. I know it's ridiculous – I know no one has really heard of George R. Sims any more – but there it is. His poems – and the poems you learnt and performed in the 1920s – are rattling around in my head, a hundred years on. They inspired me to publish an anthology of poems to learn by heart. It's a best-seller, Pa, and it's all down to you.

Do you remember how, in the 1950s and 1960s, each year Ma got a new engagements diary from the National Playing Fields Association and all the family events were noted in it? Cubs, swimming lessons, choir practice – if it wasn't in Ma's NPFA diary, it didn't happen. Well, long story short, eventually I became chairman of the National Playing Fields Association and that's how I got to know the Duke of Edinburgh. He was the president. One day, I told him about the Empress Eugénie. He doubled up with laughter. 'So now we're related, are we?' he scoffed. I think he always had the measure of me. When I last did a charity fund-raiser with him, at Buckingham Palace, not long before his retirement aged ninety-seven, I couldn't stop him from interrupting my speech. 'Boring! Too long! Don't believe a word of it!'

Oscar Wilde, Lewis Carroll, A. A. Milne – I've not let go of any of them. Across fifty years I've written books and plays about each of them – and they all feature on the mugs in my online shop. (Yes, I have an online shop! You have no idea what that is, have you? Gosh, how the world has changed since you died.) I've not done as well as Dr Brandreth, but I love selling things. When Michèle and I had our Teddy Bear Museum in Stratford-upon-Avon, I used to commute once a week to Florida to sell our Brandreth bears on the Home Shopping Network. I met Jim Henson, the creator of the Muppets, and he gave me the original Fozzie Bear! How cool is that? Fozzie now lives with the original Sooty and Paddington and Rupert and a thousand more (including Barbara Cartland's bear, and Prince Philip's, and Tony Blair's) at Newby Hall in Yorkshire. (Newby Hall is where the royal family would have gone to live if the Nazis had landed in London during the Second World War. If it's good enough for the King and Queen, I thought, it'll be good enough for the Brandreth bears.)

Michèle says I've never escaped from the long shadow of my childhood. She's right in a way – she always is – but to me it hasn't felt like a shadow. I feel I have lived my life in a magic garden where the sun is always shining, and I have never wanted to escape it.

I've kept my childhood with me and turned my childhood heroes and heroines into friends. Jimmy Edwards, Frankie Howerd, Kenneth Williams, the actor who played Billy Bunter – I got to know them all. Do you remember when I was ten how I fell in love with Hayley Mills? Well, she's now a near neighbour and one of my dearest friends. If you could see my one-man show, hers is the voice that introduces me at the start of it.

Do you remember how I used to go to the Old Vic at the beginning of the 1960s and was bowled over by Franco Zeffirelli's production of *Romeo and Juliet* with Judi Dench? Well, I now do a stage show with Judi Dench, celebrating her extraordinary career. We even sing 'I Remember it Well' from *Gigi* together. Do you remember how obsessed I was with Laurence Olivier and those early National Theatre productions at the Old Vic, and how I kept a scrapbook of pictures of Maggie Smith – as Desdemona, as Beatrice, as Hilde Wangel in *The Master Builder*? Well, she is a good friend, too. She is coming for supper in the kitchen tonight. She is so funny.

I know you loved the theatre, Pa. The last play you went to see, the year before you died, was *The Dresser*, Ronald Harwood's evocation of the world of the old touring actor-manager, based on his own experience as dresser to the great Sir Donald Wolfit. Ronald Harwood died in 2020 and Maggie Smith and I went to his funeral, both as friends of his and officially representing the Prince of Wales and the Duchess of Cornwall. Maggie had appeared in one of Ronnie's less successful plays, *Interpreters*. One night, early in the play's short run, Harwood made the mistake of putting his head around her dressing-room door.

'Hello, Ronnie,' she enquired coldly, 'and what are you up to now?'

'Struggling with a new play, darling,' said Harwood.

'Aren't we all?' was Maggie's tart retort.

Tom Courtenay, who played the title role in *The Dresser* when you saw it, Pa, was among the mourners at Ronnie's funeral. So was the historian Lady Antonia Fraser, Lord Longford's daughter, the widow of Ronnie's fellow playwright and friend, Harold Pinter. The day after the funeral, filming the canals series I've been doing with my friend Sheila Hancock, Sheila told me about the time, years ago, when she and Peter Bull had appeared together in a Pinter play in Oldham (or was it Bolton?). Anyway, on the Saturday night, Peter Bull was frantic to catch the last train back to London, but frustrated because the train was due to leave at 9.50 p.m. and the play didn't finish until ten o'clock.

'It can't be done,' said Sheila.

'Oh, yes, it can,' said Peter Bull. 'This is Pinter. We'll just cut the pauses.'

They did – and caught the train with ease.

I am telling you this because I know you love a theatrical anecdote. It's because of you that I compiled the *Oxford Book of Theatrical Anecdotes*. It's got all your favourite Frank Benson stories in it. No one's heard of him now, either, but he was a giant in his day. I've discovered from your diary that you met him when you were twenty-one – the age I was when I was befriended by Sir Michael Redgrave. He's dead, too, of course. I know Vanessa Redgrave, his eldest daughter (she's extraordinary); I shared a birthday with his other daughter, Lynn; I knew his son, Corin. And I love Corin's daughter, Jemma Redgrave. At her father's memorial service, at the Actors' Church, St Paul's in Covent Garden, Jemma read Sonya's speech from the end of *Uncle Vanya*. As she read it, she was thinking of Corin. I was thinking of you.

What can we do? We must live out our lives. *[A pause]* Yes, we shall live, Uncle Vanya. We shall live all through the endless procession of days ahead of us, and through the long evenings. We shall bear patiently the burdens that fate imposes on us. We shall work without rest for others, both now and when we are old. And when our final hour comes, we shall meet it humbly, and there beyond the grave, we shall say that we have known suffering and tears, that our life was bitter. And God will pity us. Ah, then, dear, dear Uncle, we shall enter on a bright and beautiful life. We shall rejoice and look back upon our grief here. I have faith, Uncle, fervent, passionate faith. We shall rest. We shall rest. We shall hear the angels. We shall see heaven shining like a jewel. We shall see evil and all our pain disappear in the great pity that shall enfold the world. Our life will be as peaceful and gentle and sweet as a caress. I have faith; I have faith. *[Wiping away her tears]* My poor, poor Uncle Vanya, you are crying! *[Weeping]* You have never known what it is to be happy, but wait, Uncle Vanya, wait! We shall rest. We shall rest. We shall rest.

Corin Redgrave told me about the near-farcical family dispute over the final resting place for Sir Michael's ashes. Corin, a passionate socialist, had bought a plot for them in Highgate Cemetery (for £600). Lynn wrote to her brother: 'I quite understand that you would like to bury Dad's ashes near Karl Marx. I should have preferred St Paul's, the actors' church in Covent Garden, and so would Mum, I think. But your choice means more to you than ours would to us, so you should go ahead.'

He didn't. For almost nine years the matter lay unresolved: Sir Michael's ashes remained unclaimed at Mortlake Crematorium. Eventually, Corin collected them and, for several weeks, the ashes kept him company in the boot of his car. 'Strange as it might seem,' he told me, 'I felt comforted by them. After a while I began to wonder how I had ever managed without them. Alone in my car . . . I would play music to them, and even sing to them. Sometimes they would sing back, a distant, clear, pure, baritone – "every valley shall be exalted". Once, when Radio Three was playing Haydn's "Miracle" symphony, I could hear them laughing. It couldn't last, of course, and it didn't.'

Eventually Rachel, Michael's widow, said, 'I must take Michael's ashes to St Paul's, I've promised Lynn I would.' And that's where they now are.

Corin Redgrave was always a fine actor. Once Michael had died, I think he became a great one. Michael's death set Corin free.

Pa, you gave me freedom from the start. By loving me so

much, by telling me how wonderful I was, you made me believe in myself and freed me to do anything – anything at all.

I have been everywhere I ever wanted to go. I have met everyone I ever wanted to meet. I have done everything I ever wanted to do – except, perhaps, create a myth (like Oscar Wilde with that portrait in the attic) or a magic world (like Lewis Carroll with Wonderland). I have conducted an orchestra. I have milked a cow. I have flown Concorde. (Well, I sat in the cockpit and the pilot let me think I was landing the plane in New York.) It was days before the Concorde accident that killed 109 passengers and crew. I've had a lucky life.

Did I tell you that I became an MP? And a Lord Commissioner of the Treasury. That's a senior government whip and the fellow who signs the government cheques. Every bit of government expenditure in the UK has to be signed off by a Treasury minister. The last mandate I signed was for £136 billion. The Treasury officials explained to me that with the really large amounts there has to be a co-signatory.

'Who will that be?' I asked. 'The Prime Minister, as First Lord of the Treasury?'

'No,' they said. 'It's HM Treasury, so you'll be signing the cheques with HM – Her Majesty.'

One day, when we'd both signed one of these huge cheques, I said to the Queen, 'You know, Your Majesty, the way the government insists on both of us signing these cheques – I wonder which of the two of us it is that the government doesn't trust?'

She had no answer to that.

Being an MP was quite draining. In the constituency I only met two types of people: people with problems, and people who knew they were right. But, in a small way, I like to think I left my mark. As a Private Members' bill, I introduced the 1994 Marriage Act. Until my bill came along, if you wanted a civil wedding it had to happen in a register office – often quite a dull municipal building. Thanks to my Marriage Act, you can now get married in all sorts of fun places, from stately homes to grand hotels. It's almost my proudest achievement, though when Michèle heard me being described on the car radio once as 'the expert on the Marriage Act' she crashed the gears laughing.

My other claim to fame is one you can see in Trafalgar Square. In the 1990s, when I was a parliamentary private secretary to the Secretary of State for National Heritage, walking through Trafalgar Square one day, I noticed an empty plinth in the north-west corner of the square. When I got to work, at the morning team meeting, I asked the department's Permanent Secretary about it. He was a smooth man, wholly in the Sir Humphrey mould. He made enquiries and reported back. The plinth was originally intended to hold an equestrian statue of William IV, but had been left bare when the square was designed, due to insufficient funds.

'Let's find the funds and put something on it now,' I said.

'Excellent idea,' purred the Permanent Secretary. 'Do you have anything in mind?'

'How about Christopher Robin and Winnie-the-Pooh?' I suggested, quite seriously. 'Britain's contribution to children's literature is greater than that of any other country in the world.'

'Oh,' murmured the Permanent Secretary. 'I'm not sure about that. I think it needs to be a major historical figure.'

'Margaret Thatcher, then?'

'It's Trafalgar Square. There are Nelson and two generals there already. I think it needs to be a military figure . . .'

'Margaret Thatcher in her tank on the Falkland Islands?'

We came up with a happy compromise and invited the Royal Society for Arts, Manufactures and Commerce to explore the possibilities, which they did – and the rotating works of art that have adorned the plinth ever since are the happy result. Ken Clarke, when he was Chancellor of the

Exchequer and I was Treasury whip, was kind enough to say that I was like the character in Arnold Bennett's novel *The Card*.

'What's he done?' people asked. 'Has he ever done a day's work in his life? What great cause is he identified with?'

'He's identified,' came the answer, 'with the great cause of cheering us all up.'

I'll settle for that.

When I lost my seat in parliament I decided not to fight again. What was the point? My lot were going to be in opposition for thirteen years, and I knew by then that *government* was the thing.

That's when Michèle said to me, 'Now's the time to do whatever you've always most wanted to do.'

And that's how I ended up in the West End in *Zipp!*, in Edinburgh playing Malvolio, and at the Riverside Studios in London playing Lady Bracknell. Thanks to you, Pa, I felt I could do anything.

My ultimate ambition, of course, was to play Hamlet. I used to joke that I'd played the part when I was young and it had not been a success. The critics didn't like it; the audiences didn't like it. In fact, the audiences came prepared not to like it. They threw eggs at me. I went on as Hamlet. I came off as omelette.

In the event, I was in my seventieth year when I appeared in *Hamlet* at the Park Theatre in London. Don't worry, I didn't take on the title role – though in this age of colour-blind gender-neutral casting, would anyone have dared to object if I had? I played old King Hamlet (the Ghost), believed to be Shakespeare's part when the play was first staged.

According to the play, young Prince Hamlet is thirty. Michael Redgrave played the part at Stratford at fifty. Frank Benson was still playing it aged seventy-two. (What Basil Rathbone admired in Benson's Hamlet was the way he spoke: 'He understood that a voice at night sounds quite different. No other Hamlet caught that.') Ian McKellen has just given us his second Hamlet, aged eight-two.

Hamlet is a revenge tragedy and a family drama. Ours was a family production. I played the father, my real-life son, Benet, played the son and his real-life wife, American actress Kosha Engler (*The Wire, Victoria*, the 'voice' of Maybelline) played both Ophelia and Gertrude. She played Laertes, too. And I played Polonius and Claudius, as well as the Ghost. It was directed by David Aula (a magician as well as a director) and Simon Evans (who became famous creating *Staged* on TV during lockdown, with David Tennant and Michael Sheen) and, amazingly, it worked.

At the end of one performance, we found Sir Derek Jacobi (who has played in *Hamlet* more times than any other actor alive) standing to applaud us. It was wonderful to spend two months working with my own son on Shakespeare's greatest text. As a father, who could ask for anything more?

Hamlet is the single work of art about which more books have been written than any other. It's a play about everything: life, death, love, lust, frailty, faith, sibling affection, sibling rivalry, suicide, revenge, repentance, murder. Supremely, it is a play about parental loss. At every performance, playing the Ghost, holding my son close to me, I saw you in my mind's eye, Pa, as I spoke the line that has been reverberating in my head ever since:

Adieu, adieu, adieu. Remember me.

Michael Redgrave called his autobiography *In My Mind's Eye*. The last time I saw Sir Michael onstage was in John Mortimer's play *A Voyage Round My Father*. Olivier played the part, too, when Mortimer's play was done on TV. I know from talking to Corin that Michael Redgrave was not easy to live with: he was self-absorbed, he drank too much, he was bisexual and had his male lover living in a shed in the garden.

Richard Olivier, Sir Laurence's son, told me how for years

he had felt 'very bitter and resentful' towards his father. As a child, Richard couldn't understand why his father preferred to be onstage, rather than spending time with him. 'As a child I felt I could never quite get his attention,' he said. As a teenager (Richard went to Bedales, too), he didn't know what was wrong with him. 'I had this deep sense of loneliness and emptiness.'

We've voyaged round some rum fathers in these pages, haven't we, Pa? Oscar Wilde, Lawrence Durrell, Robert Maxwell – remarkable men, for sure, but as fathers each left much to be desired. Kenneth Tynan's wife told me that when Ken's father died, Tynan (born and brought up in Birmingham) discovered that the father he knew as 'Peter Tynan' was in fact Sir Peter Peacock, a former mayor of Warrington, who had been leading a double life for more than twenty years, keeping two complete families living eighty miles apart. Ken's mother was in on the secret. Kathleen Tynan told me that Ken trusted nobody in consequence.

Prince Charles used to complain about his father's emotional repression and lack of empathy. The Duke of Edinburgh never made any complaints, but his father, Prince Andrew of Greece, broke up the family home before Prince Philip had turned ten and disappeared to the South of France, to live on a boat with his mistress.

Lord Montagu of Beaulieu's father died when he was a small boy, but he wasn't perhaps the best of role models. He had five daughters: two by his first wife, two by his second, and one by his personal assistant. (She was the model for the Rolls-Royce mascot, Spirit of Ecstasy.) Lord Montagu told me he felt lonely and isolated as a boy.

Christopher Robin told me there were times when he wished he and his father had never been born.

Beverley Nichols told me that he had tried to murder his father. He attempted to crush him to death with a cast-iron garden roller. 'I regret to say I failed.'

Pa, you weren't like any of those. You were simply the best – loving, loyal, kind, courteous, tolerant, good-humoured, self-sacrificing, indulgent. I see now from your diary that you were profoundly unhappy at times. I never knew that. You didn't achieve all your worldly ambitions, I know, but I've managed a few of them for you, and your grandchildren are doing the rest, so as a team we've done it all. And by loving Ma, by loving us, by being there and being you, you showed me that family is the best thing in the world.

It turns out I've written this book for you.

I've got to go now. Michèle has promised me a slice of coffee and walnut cake when I've finished. Coffee and walnut's my favourite.

It's time for me to let go, Pa, time to say goodbye.

Adieu. Thank you for everything.

Ever your loving son,

Gyles

Broadstairs 1951.

Epilogue: Journey's end

Michèle will vouch for the truth of this. Moments after I'd finished typing the above, she knocked on my study door.

'Have you brought the cake?' I asked.

'No,' she said. 'I've brought this. It's just arrived.'

She handed me a small package, addressed to me, post-marked Bristol.

Intrigued, I tore it open.

Inside was my father's passport. Nothing else, no paper-work, no explanation, just a blue United Kingdom passport, Number M 466545, belonging to Charles Daubeney Bran-dreth, solicitor, born Hoylake, 11 July 1910.

I have no idea who sent it to me.

When my mother died in 2010, her flat was cleared by pro-fessional house clearers and I suppose the passport must have been left in one of her full-to-bursting cupboards or chests of drawers. Perhaps it ended up on eBay. Perhaps a collector of printed ephemera picked it up in a job lot and, deciding it was surplus to their requirements, thought it might be something to do with me, managed to find my address and sent it to me.

That's not so extraordinary, I suppose, but that it should arrive at precisely this moment ... well, coincidences do happen.

The cake, by the way, was delicious.

Acknowledgements & Permissions

Since this is an autobiography, I suppose I am indebted in varying degrees to everyone I have encountered since I was born. Most of them don't feature in the book: there simply wasn't room. As I am writing this, I am thinking of my first bank manager, Frank Burrell at the NatWest in Oxford. When I was in my twenties, I owed him a great deal, literally as well as figuratively. He is just one of many acquaintances and friends who have been important to me in my life who somehow did not make it to the page as I wrote this account of my early years. They may be relieved, of course. And some of those who do feature may not be entirely happy because I have told my story my way and 'recollections may vary', as The Queen put it after Meghan and Prince Harry had told their story to Oprah Winfrey. This is how I remember my parents and my childhood. My two sisters may remember our parents and their childhoods very differently. I did not show them the manuscript before publication, so I don't know. I hope that they – and others who feature in the book – will not find what I have written too inaccurate or too intrusive.

Having published diaries in the past, I had no plans to write an autobiography. This memoir has come about entirely at the suggestion of my publisher, Dan Bunyard. I am hugely indebted to him for his encouragement and guidance throughout the process. I am also indebted to his colleagues at Penguin Michael Joseph, including Louise Moore, Beatrix McIntyre, Nick Lowndes, Emma Henderson, Agatha Russell and Olivia Thomas. Considerable thanks are due, too, to my copy-editor, Shan Morley Jones, and indexer, Catherine Hookway, as well as the book's proofreaders, Jill Cole and Bea Quick. As ever, I am indebted, also, to my literary agent and friend, Jonathan Lloyd, and to his team at Curtis Brown.

My daughter Saethryd very kindly (and patiently) dug up and sorted all the illustrations that feature in the book. Most of them are family photographs, but thanks are due to Bill Potter, Philip Ingram, Francis Loney, Michael Gell, Sydney Harris, Geoff Wilding, Roy Granger, Murdo MacLeod, the *Daily Mirror, Woman,* and the Press Association for permission to reproduce their photographs and cartoons. Thanks are also due to Ralph Steadman for the use of his caricature and to Colin Smythe for the cartoon by Terry Pratchett. The photograph of the tomb of Sir Gyles Daubeney is courtesy of Westminster Abbey and the print of Jeremiah Brandreth is courtesy of the British Museum.

The lines from 'Lines and Squares' by A. A. Milne are reprinted by permission of Curtis Brown Ltd UK and the Estate of A. A. Milne; the lines from 'Annus Mirabilis' by Philip Larkin are reprinted by permission of the Estate of Philip Larkin and Faber & Faber Ltd and Farrar, Strauss and Giroux.

Inset 1: Image 1: © Dean and Chapter of Westminster; Image 2: Alamy Stock Photo; Image 3: © The Trustees of the British Museum; Image 5: Alamy Stock Photo

Inset 2: Image 6: With thanks to *The Strand Magazine*; Image 49: With thanks to *Woman Magazine*; Image 50: With thanks to Ralph Steadman; Image 52: With thanks to Sir Terry Pratchett and the estate

Inset 3: Image 71: With thanks to *Manchester Evening News*; Image 72: With thanks to Wimbledon Theatre; Image 73: With thanks to Park Theatre; Image 74: With thanks to Bound & Gagged Comedy

Index

428